UNDERSTANDING NONPROFIT FUNDING

Kirsten A. Grønbjerg

UNDERSTANDING NONPROFIT FUNDING

Managing Revenues in Social Services and Community Development Organizations

 Jossey-Bass Publishers
San Francisco

Substantial discounts on bulk quantities of Jossey-Bass books are available to corporations, professional associations, and other organizations. For details and discount information, contact the special sales department at Jossey-Bass Inc., Publishers. (415) 433-1740; Fax (415) 433-0499.

For sales outside the United States, contact Maxwell Macmillan International Publishing Group, 866 Third Avenue, New York, New York 10022.

Manufactured in the United States of America

The ink in this book is either soy- or vegetable-based and during the printing process emits fewer than half the volatile organic compounds (VOCs) emitted by petroleum-based ink.

Library of Congress Cataloging-in-Publication Data

Grønbjerg, Kirsten A.
    Understanding nonprofit funding : managing revenues in social services and community development organizations / Kirsten A. Grønbjerg. — 1st ed.
        p. cm. — (The Jossey-Bass nonprofit sector series) (The Jossey-Bass public administration series)
    Includes bibliographical references (p.   ) and index.
    ISBN 1-55542-538-0 (acid-free)
    1. Charities—United States—Finance. 2. Community development corporations—United States—Finance. 3. Nonprofit organizations—United States—Finance. 4. Fund raising—United States.
I. Title. II. Series. III. Series: The Jossey-Bass public administration series.
HV91.G78 1993
361.7′068′1—dc20   92-41368
                                                                 CIP

FIRST EDITION
HB Printing   10 9 8 7 6 5 4 3 2 1   *Code 9342*

A joint publication in

The Jossey-Bass
Nonprofit Sector Series

and

The Jossey-Bass
Public Administration Series

Contents

Preface

This is the story of how nonprofit social service and community development organizations manage their relationships with different funding sources. Usually quite small, these two types of organizations account for the bulk of charitable nonprofit organizations in the United States, although they are dwarfed in size and influence by their much larger cousins — hospitals, universities, and major cultural institutions. I examine how these two types of organizations experience their funding relationships — the trade-offs, advantages, disadvantages, and motivations they encounter and how they survive the challenges.

Scope and Treatment

Rather than presenting an abstract theory or a mechanical checklist on how to manage a particular funding source, *Understanding Nonprofit Funding* provides a comprehensive, fine-grained analysis of the structure and management of nonprofit funding relations. My aim is to describe the complexity of the organizational world that smaller nonprofit organizations inhabit and to reveal its underlying order. It is a world of multiple and disparate funding sources and diverse organizational environments, each favoring some types of funding relations and discouraging others. The environments reflect both the nature of services delivered and the structure of key institutions in the field — the scope and form of public and private sector activities, the number and size of other nonprofits active in the field.

By linking nonprofit resource relationships to the specific policy environments of two service fields, I provide the basis for assessing how the structure of public policies affects the operation and management of nonprofit organizations. In turn, these macro-level observations allow for a systematic interpretation of the structure of human services in the United States and a comprehensive understanding of the nonprofit sector, its internal composition, and its role in U.S. public policy.

My basic approach is to examine how nonprofit organizations manage the challenges presented by diverse funding sources, complex organizational environments, and the interaction of the two. I present data from in-depth case studies of thirteen nonprofit organizations in social services and community development. The case studies illustrate the environmental constraints and management contingencies that particular funding sources present for nonprofits in the two fields. I also draw on several surveys of nonprofit organizations, including two statewide surveys I conducted in 1991, and on detailed analysis of public spending patterns.

The bulk of this book is devoted to a detailed documentation of nonprofit fiscal patterns, the underlying structure of nonprofit funding sources, and the range and nature of management tasks and contingencies associated with the major types of funding. I pay special attention to restricted grants and contracts and provide systematic documentation of the management tasks that funding sources, especially public ones, impose on nonprofit organizations. I also show how tasks and contingencies associated with managing funding relationships in turn have implications for a range of other organizational resources, performance measures, and general strategic management.

Much of the methodology used to obtain systematic data on funding relationships is new. It can be applied to other types of organizations than those described in this book. It can also be useful in analyzing the relative influence of organizational type, environment, and size on management strategies and organizational performances.

Audience

The question of how nonprofits cope with funding relations has direct and obvious relevance for nonprofit managers. It is also important to their funders, both public and private. All parties must understand how resource relationships operate if they are to implement their own goals and collaborate constructively. The material presented in this book will be equally useful to professionals involved in organizational and management studies. It addresses such key theoretical questions as how organizational environments and resource relationships condition organizational behavior at the microlevel of individual organizations. Problems of resource relationships and management contingencies associated with them are central for understanding nonprofit organizations. Some problems are particular to nonprofits, but many apply to other types of organizations as well. While the book focuses on nonprofit organizations, many of the findings will also apply to organizations that operate under different legal auspices, such as public agencies or private businesses.

Overview of the Contents

This book is divided into four sections. Part One gives a conceptual overview of the nonprofit sector and of theory and research on the management of nonprofit funding. Chapter One reviews the scope of the nonprofit sector and its economic, social, political, and community functions. I outline basic organizational imperatives that affect all organizations, such as the volume and nature of market demands, professional and institutional models of action, resource structures, interorganizational relationships, charter and purpose, and internal organizational structures. Finally, I discuss contingencies of special interest to nonprofit organizations, such as location in the political economy and access to distinctive resource bases.

Chapter Two outlines the research framework for the remainder of the book, emphasizing how theoretical perspectives from the literature on organizational environments, resource dependency, and strategic management help explain key issues surrounding the management of nonprofit funding sources. These perspectives serve as the basis for developing thirteen organizational profiles in the detailed case studies that follow. The chapter specifies the criteria by which these organizations were identified, describes the major sources of data that I draw on for documentation, and provides a brief history and description of the participating organizations.

Part Two reviews the funding patterns for nonprofit organizations, examines major types of nonprofit funding sources, and explores key contingencies associated with each. Chapter Three establishes the relative importance of the four major forms of funding for nonprofit organizations: fees, special event revenues, donations, and public funding. Chapter Four looks at patterns of growth and stability in these types of funding for the sector as a whole and their prevalence among social service and community development organizations. The chapter also documents the diversity of funding patterns for individual organizations in the social service and community development fields, as well as the extent to which changes in overall revenue for the case-study organizations can be linked to service fields and form of program development.

Chapter Five discusses fees and sales revenues, a major, growing, and controversial source of revenues for nonprofit human service organizations. Findings from two case studies of fee-reliant nonprofit social service organizations show the strengths and weaknesses of organizational strategies in establishing and expanding fee-for-service markets. Chapter Six examines special event revenues and management strategies for generating them. I present data on three nonprofit community organizations that organize major special events; each structures its work and marketing efforts very differently.

Chapter Seven explores patterns of volatile donations for six social service agencies and five community development organizations. I analyze problems associated with generating income from donations, including gaining access to or control over donors and linking donations to agency domains. I also consider the implications of relying on donations for organizational structure and for defining the role of the board.

Chapter Eight describes the driving force of public funding in the nonprofit sector. Drawing on case studies of four nonprofit social service agencies and three community development organizations with government funding, I document differences between the two types of organizations in patterns of stability and continuity over a period of five years. I present evidence of increasing management overhead associated with public grants and contracts in recent years and argue that the complexity of these tasks (documented in Part Three) contributes to the primacy of government funding for nonprofit organizations.

Part Three examines how nonprofits manage the overall coordination of their resource relationships. I pay special attention to the work and strategies involved in managing restricted grants and contracts that come primarily, but not exclusively, from government sources. Chapter Nine describes the system of interorganizational funding paths that links governmental agencies to one another and to nonprofit and proprietary service providers. The chapter also includes a discussion of various private funding sources. I then probe the major phases of work involved in managing government funding sources and contrast them with the more flexible structure of tasks associated with direct client fees, service charges, special event revenues, individual donations, and corporate or foundation grants.

Chapter Ten explores the idiosyncratic nature of the restricted grants and contracts system and reviews the technical problems that it presents for management and strategic planning. I examine problems of overall coordination, delayed payments, cash flow, and personnel turnover.

Chapter Eleven offers strategies and patterns of adaptation that nonprofit agencies can use in their efforts to manage internal resources — for example, matching staff skills with program demands, establishing organizational leadership and structure, developing agency philosophy, and defining the role of the board. Other strategies help agencies coordinate the priorities of their funding sources with the agency mission, develop resource flexibility to cushion themselves against funding jolts, and engage in networking.

Part Four summarizes key findings and elaborates on implications of the findings. In Chapter Twelve, I assess the research approach and further explain the conceptual framework that has emerged from the study. I argue that funding sources differ in their resource characteristics along several dimensions, each with important implications for management strategies. After reviewing how and why organizational environments differ in various nonprofit service fields, I discuss the implications of the model for theory and research, and for funders and practitioners.

The Epilogue returns to some of the macro-level issues raised in Chapter Three. I discuss the ramifications of nonprofits' reliance on fees, donations, and government grants and contracts and explore the overall role of nonprofit human service organizations in U.S. social policy. The appendixes include a summary of methodological procedures, a copy of the instrument used to obtain data on restricted grants and contracts, and detailed tables on individual grants and contracts for one of the case-study organizations.

Background

I am intrigued by the historical and ideological roots of this reluctant welfare nation in which I have lived now for close to thirty years. It presents such a contrasting model to the one I came to expect when growing up in Denmark, with its highly developed, comprehensive, and widely accepted public welfare system and its strong endorsement of social rights.

My present interest in U.S. nonprofit organizations developed out of earlier work that focused on the public welfare system, especially the ways in which variations among state-operated Aid to Families with Dependent Children (AFDC) cash assistance programs reflected evolutionary models of citizenship and social rights. As I studied the complex system of intergovernmental relations affecting the AFDC program, I began to look more closely at supporting service systems and the connections between public sector activities and those of nonprofit organizations.

These interests received a major boost from my involvement in the Urban Institute's Nonprofit Sector Project (directed by Lester Salamon), for which I served as the Chicago field associate from 1982 to 1987. The Chicago portion of the project produced a detailed analysis of public spending, an assessment of historical trends in the relationships between the public and nonprofit sectors in several different service fields, and three waves of data collection from a panel of nonprofit organizations. Subsequently, in 1991, I directed two additional statewide surveys of human service organizations; these surveys examined, respectively, the service structure of the child welfare field and the structure and adequacy of nonprofit human service facilities.

The public spending analysis highlighted the importance of nonprofit organizations to certain public sector activities (social services, health) but not others (income assistance, housing, community development). The historical analysis suggested that service fields had evolved according to four different patterns of institutional relations between the sectors: cooperation, accommodation, competition, and symbiosis. The findings guided my choice to focus on the fields of social service and community organization, which represent two of the four patterns I identified. Results from the five surveys guided my design of the case-study approach and also provided baseline information and a broader context for the case studies.

Acknowledgments

The Case-Study Project itself began as a simple class project for a two-course sequence, the Chicago Area Policy Workshop, that I taught in early 1988 for the Center for Urban Research and Policy Studies at the University of Chicago. At the time, I was visiting the School of Social Service Administration (SSA) and on leave from Loyola University Chicago. I am grateful to both institutions for making the experience possible, to Larry Lynn for initiating and facilitating the visiting appointment, and to Jeanne March and faculty and students at SSA for making my stay a very productive and rewarding one.

The three Chicago Urban Scholars Fellows in the workshop — Christopher Edmonds, David Kennedy, and Donald Sheppard — and graduate students Robin Broder, Barbara Huyler, Bogdan Pukszta, Joanne Watson, and Joanne Williams helped articulate the theoretical issues and develop the research design, and they participated actively in the data collection efforts for three of the organizations.

Warren Friedman of the Chicago Alliance for Neighborhood Safety (CANS) volunteered to be our pretest for the case studies and made the key suggestion that we examine the entire funding structure of nonprofit organizations, not simply a limited number of grants and contracts as we had planned. He argued convincingly that individual grants and contracts would seem out of context unless understood as part of an organization's overall experiences and strategies. He was right.

When I returned to Loyola University in the fall of 1988, I also expanded the design to cover a total of twelve organizations (ultimately thirteen). This expansion would not have been possible without financial support from several funding sources, for which I am extremely grateful: the Joyce Foundation, the Program on Non-Profit Organizations (PONPO) at Yale University, the Chicago Community Trust, the Woods Charitable Fund, and Loyola University Chicago. Brad Gray, Bruce Newman, Trinita Logue, Jean Rudd, Tom Bennett, and my colleagues at Loyola University provided important moral support as well. Of course, neither they, their associated organizations, nor anyone else bears any responsibility for the analysis presented here.

The financial support provided me with release time from teaching, funded the production and distribution of a working paper for PONPO (Grønbjerg, 1990a), and supported several graduate students at Loyola University. I acknowledge the participation of these students, especially Susan Waldhier, Jack Harkins, Carol Dragon, Jing Zhang, Patricia Kohl, Vijay Kamath, Cynthia Weber, Christine Wiegand, Ramola Joseph, Isabel Calhoun, James Wang, and Father Anthony Abela — without their efforts, I would still be collecting data. In addition, graduate students from sociology, social work, and education gave extensive and very helpful feedback on an earlier draft of this book as part of a course on organizations and organizational change in the fall of 1991 at Loyola University. Ed Marciniak and Gary Oniki provided valuable technical expertise that facilitated my search for appropriate community development organizations. I also acknowledge the technical support provided by Loyola University's Center for Instructional Design in the production of graphs for this book.

I have benefited from presenting the findings to graduate students at the Kellogg School of Management at Northwestern University and the Business School at the University of Chicago, members of the Donor's Forum of Chicago, and participants in annual meetings for the Independent Sector Research Forum, the Association for Research on Nonprofit Organizations and Voluntary Action (ARNOVA), the American Society for Public Administration, the Midwest Sociological Society, and the Association for Public Policy and Management. Other scholars at Chapin Hall Center for Children at the University of Chicago, the University of Minnesota, and Case Western Reserve University have provided valuable feedback as well.

In addition, Carl Milofsky, Judith Saidel, Meyer Zald, Dennis Young, Joseph Galaskiewicz, Zeke Hasenfeld, Jeff Brudney, Mark Chavez, Helena Lopata, Fred Kniss, Alan Shrader, Ross Scherer, several anonymous reviewers, and the executive directors of the participating organizations read some or all of the manuscript or preliminary reports (for example, Grønbjerg, 1990a, 1991a, 1991b, 1992). They provided insightful and challenging comments that I did not always accept with as much grace as I would have liked. But I am grateful to them for their efforts and patience and have attempted to be responsive to their suggestions.

One person in particular has helped me beyond the limits of what one could reasonably expect from a colleague, friend, and spouse. Gerry provided badly needed encouragement at critical points, when things looked overwhelming and difficult. He took over many of the household responsibilities at those times, and still has more than his share. He only occasionally grumbled about a spouse who took on too many responsibilities and could not detach herself from her work. Throughout, the questions that he asked turned out to be among the most helpful I encountered. He responded to my ramblings with greater patience and insight than I can offer in return.

Finally, I express my deepest gratitude to the executive directors, staff, and board members of all the participating organizations. They not only agreed to talk to me and my students about a wide range of issues at considerable length but also in almost all cases allowed us to go through cash journals, audit reports, board minutes, and boxes of other documents that most organizations consider confidential. In spite of the demands we made, they responded with cheerful cooperation.

Their cooperation and willingness to participate in the project provided a unique opportunity to combine systematic review of some emerging theoretical issues with practical insights. As always, the encounter with reality proved to challenge many preconceptions. I have learned a great deal from coming to grips with them. I am impressed by the challenges these managers face and by their efforts in meeting them. However, a close reading of this book will reveal that my Danish roots are still showing. I am intrigued by nonprofit organizations and the critical contributions they make to U.S. society, but I am not convinced that they necessarily present the preferred mechanisms by which public mandates should be executed, at least not under the funding structures currently in place. As I show in this book, the present system not only creates very high transaction costs for all participants, including service recipients, but also makes planning, execution, and assessment of policy initiatives extraordinarily difficult.

Chicago, Illinois Kirsten A. Grønbjerg
March 1993

For Gerry

The Author

Kirsten A. Grønbjerg is professor of sociology at Loyola University Chicago and faculty associate of the Chapin Hall Center for Children at the University of Chicago. A native of Denmark, she earned her B.A. degree (1968) in sociology at Pitzer College and her M.A. (1970) and Ph.D. (1974) degrees in sociology at the University of Chicago. She has held faculty appointments at the State University of New York, Stony Brook and at Hofstra University, and a visiting professorship at the School of Social Service Administration at the University of Chicago.

Grønbjerg served as the Chicago field associate for the Urban Institute's Nonprofit Sector Project from 1982 to 1987 and was one of the principal researchers on the Hardship and Support Systems in Chicago project. She is copresident of the Association for Research on Nonprofit Organizations and Voluntary Action (ARNOVA) and a member of many local and national research committees on philanthropy, nonprofit organizations, social policy, and needs assessment. She is also active in several human service organizations and serves on the board of United Way of Chicago as coordinating chairperson for needs assessment in the areas of human capital development, family life, community development, health, and discrimination in the Chicago area.

Grønbjerg's particular interests include the structure of public and private human service systems. She is the author of several books, articles, and reports on U.S. welfare policies and the nonprofit sector—among them, *Mass Society and the Expansion of Welfare, 1960–1970* (1977) and *Poverty and Social Change*, with David Street and Gerald Suttles (1978). She has recently completed research on the facility needs of nonprofit human service organizations and on the structure of private youth service organizations in Illinois, as well as on longitudinal changes in the grants and contracts system of a large state human service agency.

UNDERSTANDING
NONPROFIT
FUNDING

PART ONE

Perspectives on Nonprofit Funding

Nonprofit organizations have attracted increasing attention since the late 1970s, when the United States (and other nations) began to curtail the growth of public spending for human services. Successive presidential administrations have looked to nonprofit organizations as one of several mechanisms for shaping public sector activities. The U.S. Small Business Administration and economists committed to market models have complained that nonprofit service providers engage in unfair competition and are inefficient. The Internal Revenue Service and public budget administrators facing growing budget deficits have sought ways to limit the volume of funds that escape taxation, including those controlled by nonprofit organizations. And moral entrepreneurs of all stripes have used the nonprofit form to promote their own particular agenda.

As these examples suggest, nonprofits play important and diverse roles. This section reviews some of the most important features of the nonprofit sector in the United States. The two chapters draw on relevant theoretical perspectives to develop a framework for the more detailed analysis that occupies the bulk of this book.

ONE

The Vital Importance of
Funding Relations:
Sectoral and Organizational Perspectives

Almost all Americans have contacts with nonprofit organizations: they work for them, sit on their boards, donate funds or time to them, interact with them as representatives of other organizations, use their services, or are affected by their advocacy efforts on a wide range of policy issues. But many people probably do not truly understand how nonprofit organizations operate, what drives their activities, or how they get the resources they need in order to survive. Managing funding relations is a difficult task for nonprofit organizations. Youth Outreach, a nonprofit organization in Chicago, is a case in point.

A Year in the Life of Youth Outreach

The fiscal year that began on July 1, 1987, was a typical one for Youth Outreach. The budget of $1,470,450 was adopted at the September board meeting, in time to meet the United Way deadline of October 1. This was an increase of 6 percent from the year before. Although the budget was not met, it was close. By June 30, 1988, Youth Outreach had received $1,411,061 in revenues but had cut operating expenses to achieve a small surplus of $3,013. During the year, Youth Outreach provided about 98,000 hours of individual and group counseling, creative arts activities, and job development services to some 8,300 youths through local outposts in seven low-income communities across Chicago. Most of the clients were African-American (66 percent) or Hispanic (26 percent).

To provide this variety and volume of services and meet the payroll of forty-six full-time staff members (not counting twenty-one student interns), Youth Outreach pursued a variety of funding sources. It was able to renew two commercial contracts to conduct personnel training for a large corporation and a large federal agency and received some interest earnings on a small endowment. However, it had to keep the endowment in low-interest–bearing liquid accounts in order to meet cash-flow problems. Other funds came from seven different special events put on by its three auxiliary boards and from a thrift shop it operated jointly with two other social service agencies.

Agency staff and board members also reviewed funding criteria of several hundred different foundations and corporations and decided to target 156 of them, including 47 that had not previously been solicited. Not all of those targeted were in fact solicited, but by the end of the fiscal year, gifts had been received from 73 foundations or corporations, another 23 requests were still pending, and 19 had been turned down. Youth Outreach also received funds from 2 to 3 churches and women's groups and sent 1,361 letters of solicitation to individual donors during its year-end appeal and another 823 letters during the spring appeal. Of the 299 donations received in response to the mailings, 205 were from active donors, 83 from new donors, and 11 from individuals who had made donations in the past but not in the preceding year.

In addition, Youth Outreach requested and received its usual allocation from the United Way and from the religious federation of which it is also a member. The agency applied for, and was awarded, a special grant from the United Way that would be rolled into its annual allocations after eighteen months. As a member of the United Way, Youth Outreach had to prepare detailed information on service statistics and financial support in two rounds—projections for the year (due eight months before the start of the fiscal year) and actual performance (due four months after the end of the fiscal year).

However, by far the greatest amount of effort went into managing the agency's public grants and contracts. Youth Outreach reviewed and decided to respond to twelve requests for proposals (RFPs) or contract specifications for fourteen different programs under the auspices of federal, state, and local governments (some of which did not issue formal grant or contract specifications). The fourteen programs included three administered by nonprofit organizations that acted as pass-through organizations for public agencies—a role that Youth Outreach itself played for two other nonprofit organizations. One of the proposals was denied, but those that were approved involved Youth Outreach in an intricate funding network, which consisted of six different federal agencies, seven state agencies, and five city agencies, in addition to the three nonprofit administrating agencies and the two nonprofit subcontractors (see Figure 1.1).

Some of the grants and contracts required both preproposals and full proposals; some did not coincide with the agency's own fiscal year period (and therefore required two rounds of efforts during the fiscal year); and some were amended during the program period. As a result, Youth Outreach had to prepare, submit, and seek approval for twenty-nine proposals or program plans. To meet reporting requirements, Youth Outreach prepared and submitted "in a timely fashion" seventy-six fiscal reports and ninety separate program reports. Some of the latter approached 200 pages in

Figure 1.1. Selected Funding Paths for Youth Outreach, Fiscal Year 1988.

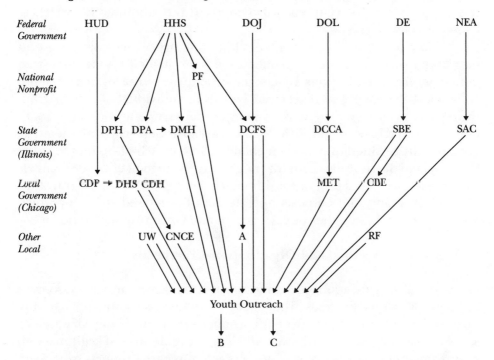

Note: Figure 1.1 excludes funding from 73 foundations/corporations, 299 individual donors, 2 churches or women's groups, 1 jointly operated thrift shop, 3 auxiliary boards, 2 commercial clients, and endowments.

Key to Abbreviations

Federal Government

HUD – Housing and Urban Development
HHS – Health and Human Services
DOJ – Department of Justice
DOL – Department of Labor
DE – Department of Education
NEA – National Endowment for the Arts

National Nonprofit

PF – Private foundation

State Government

DPH – Department of Public Health
DPA – Department of Public Aid
DMH – Department of Mental Health
DCFS – Department of Children and
    Family Services
DCCA – Department of Commerce and
    Community Affairs
SBE – State Board of Education
SAC – State Arts Council

Local Government

CDP – City Department of Planning
DHS – Department of Human Services
CDH – City Department of Health
MET – Mayor's Office of employment and
    training
CBE – City Board of Education

Other Local

UW – Local United Way
CNCE – Community network
    coordinating entity
RF – Religious federation
A, B, C – Local nonprofit service
    providers

Source: Adapted from Grønbjerg, 1991a, p. 13.

length, and some were due within two to three days after the end of the reporting period. Youth Outreach also prepared and submitted 128 vouchers or requests for payment.

Although Youth Outreach's overall funding structure is complex—and demanding on staff and board members—it is not atypical for medium-sized human service organizations. In fact, the structure could easily be even more complex if the agency also received fees from individual clients or from third-party insurance programs, as many social service agencies do. Youth Outreach could have sought such revenues, because most of its staff members are clinically certified to provide mental health counseling. Youth Outreach is also spared the complications that might arise from managing the facilities in which it operates its programs: although it rents space for the central office staff, all programs and outposts operate out of borrowed space for which Youth Outreach has neither outlays nor maintenance responsibilities.

Sectoral and Organizational Perspectives

Of course, all organizations seek to secure and manage a variety of resources to accomplish specific goals. They must obtain access to appropriate supplies, space, and expertise in order to produce a particular range of goods or services. They must also achieve sufficient recognition and legitimacy to ensure that potential clients or customers will purchase products from them rather than from their competitors. In a money economy, organizations generally must obtain exchangeable resources (revenues), to get the input they need in order to operate. Revenues are therefore critical resources that organizations must secure and manage effectively if they are to survive. Some organizations meet the challenge better than others. What accounts for the difference?

Most organizations are thought to operate under the discipline of market processes: those that can manage resources and meet demands are able to obtain the input they need at a low enough cost and sell their output at a high enough price to obtain sufficient profits to survive; those that fail to do so will cease to exist. This fundamental assumption is the basis for all market economies and guides most of economics and management science. The process is often described in terms derived from population ecology (or social Darwinism): organizations arise and decline or die selectively, depending on whether their particular characteristics and individual transformations suit the existing (but usually changing) environment. Over time, this dynamic process is thought to result in a better fit between the population of organizations and the key elements of their organizational environment, such as market structures and demands.

But what happens to organizations, such as Youth Outreach, that appear to escape the discipline of market processes? Like all public and nonprofit organizations, Youth Outreach has access to subsidies (in the form of tax appropriations or donations) that eliminate or soften the impact of traditional market tests of effectiveness and efficiency. For that reason, many analysts of the economic persuasion usually assume that public and non-profit organizations have inherent propensities for inefficiency (Bennett and DiLorenzo, 1989), perhaps to the point of becoming permanently failing organizations (Meyer and Zucker, 1989).

However, for nonprofit organizations at least, donations and government grants and contracts may be thought of as providing a similar discipline to that which the market provides for private firms. Only limited donations or public funding is available, and each nonprofit organization must obtain access to funders (customers) and convince them that it meets their needs or priorities as well as or better than other nonprofits. Very little is known about how efficiently these nonprofit funding relationships operate, what kinds of overhead costs they impose, what fit they promote between the official mission and actual practices of nonprofit organizations, or what quasi-monopolistic or manipulative practices nonprofit organizations may some-times adopt as a consequence.

These are key issues on several counts. For policy analysts, they raise critical questions about the effective and comprehensive delivery of services to meet broadly defined human service needs. For funders, they affect assessments of their own performances. For the nonprofit organization or its executives, the issues transform themselves into management problems: how to satisfy a more or less diverse set of funders and, at the same time, structure the work of the organization to maintain staff morale and accomplish spe-cific organizational tasks.

Developments in organizational and management theory also suggest that efforts to examine nonprofit organizations receive high priority. New perspectives in these fields increasingly focus on organizational environ-ments and interorganizational relationships. On these dimensions, non-profits present important comparisons to other types of organizations be-cause of their distinctive relationships with the public and for-profit sectors and their access to special resource bases. A careful analysis of nonprofit funding sources, and of the actual operation of resource relations at the organizational level, therefore addresses questions of significant theoretical and practical importance.

That is the aim of this book. It examines how two types of nonprofit organizations, social service and community development organizations, secure and manage resources. I apply theoretical perspectives on organiza-tional behavior (for example, organizational environment or resource de-pendency perspectives) to nonprofit organizations. The empirical analysis bears on a range of resource issues that nonprofits encounter in their efforts to secure different funding sources and manage the challenges that these sources present. I focus on four major types of nonprofit revenues—fees, special events, donations, and public funding (government grants and con-tracts)—and examine the administrative work and contingencies that non-profit organizations encounter in dealing with each. I discuss other revenue sources, such as income from rent or endowments, only peripherally.

The documentation comes from case studies of medium-sized non-profit social service and community development organizations with distinctive funding profiles. The detailed case-study data and contextual analysis show how resource processes operate at the organizational level. The diverse funding experiences make it possible to examine how nonprofit funding sources differ in their underlying structures, in the nature of inter-organizational funding relationships they set in motion, and in the range and nature of management tasks and contingencies they impose. These tasks and contingencies in turn have implications for how nonprofits secure other resources (such as staff and legitimacy), assess their own performance, and position themselves strategically. By linking these issues to the different policy environments in which social service and community organizations operate, I also lay the basis for a more analytical understanding of how nonprofits operate across service sectors and in different political economies.

The existing literature does not adequately address these topics. Much of the organizational and management literature pays little systematic attention to nonprofit organizations, except for the largest and most institutionalized ones. The growing body of data on nonprofit funding sources is primarily prescriptive, descriptive, or generalized to the sector as a whole (Salamon, 1987; Van Til, 1988; O'Neill, 1989; Hodgkinson, Lyman, and Associates, 1989; Hodgkinson, Weitzman, Toppe, and Noga, 1992). Other studies attempt to apply management strategies from the existing literature in public or business administration to nonprofit organizations. These latter efforts fail to recognize the structure and complexity of funding sources available to nonprofit organizations, the extent to which those organizations have built-in multiple goals (for example, separation between clients and customers, need to meet both funders' priorities and the organization's own mission), and the nature of the policy and interorganizational environments in which they operate.

Importance of the Nonprofit Sector

Before elaborating on the driving forces that influence the behavior of nonprofit organizations, I want to clarify my use of the term *nonprofit* to describe organizations and briefly portray the scope and functions of the nonprofit sector. The sector is variously characterized as *philanthropic, charitable, voluntary, independent, third,* or *nonprofit* (Young, 1988a; Van Til, 1988; O'Neill, 1989). The latter two terms come closest to capturing key characteristics. Some nonprofits are not especially philanthropic or charitable (Simon, 1987; Andersen, 1989; Herzlinger and Krasker, 1987; Grønbjerg, 1990a). Nor are they easily defined as voluntary. Many have no members or other constituencies to which they are fully accountable. As my findings show, because of funding contingencies, policy setting tends to gravitate away from the organization's board and toward executive directors.

Certainly, few if any nonprofit organizations are independent. Rather, nonprofits have extensive and complex interactions with and dependencies on a variety of other organizations. The public and for-profit sectors are driving forces that shape the organizational environments in which they operate. But nonprofits are more than the residual category implied by the "third-sector" nomenclature. Indeed, the three sectors interact quite differently in specific service fields.

The term *nonprofit* has gained increasing prominence and recognition in the field. It also captures the dilemma that many of these organizations face: how to prevent rational preoccupation with financial success from overriding efforts to pursue normative and substantive goals. The case studies show how funding relationships operate to make this dilemma a continuing challenge. For some nonprofits, the result is the type of commercial, as opposed to donative, orientation that Hansmann (1980, 1987) has discussed extensively.

Scope and Functions of the Nonprofit Sector

Whatever the difficulties of terminology, nonprofit organizations form an integral part of the organizational landscape in many societies (James, 1989; Kramer, 1981). However, a broad understanding of their importance has been hampered by the absence of a consistent terminology to describe them and by the lack of comprehensive data bases to document their scope and functions, especially over time (see Appendix A). The diversity of nonprofits' activities also complicates efforts to generalize findings from one subsector (for example, studies of foundations, hospitals, museums, universities, or social service organizations) to the rest.

Size and Economic Scope

Nevertheless, the nonprofit sector has gained prominence in recent years, as witnessed by professional developments and the growing volume of research (Independent Sector, 1989). The sector includes a large number of organizations with important economic functions in U.S. society. Nonprofits number at least one million tax-exempt organizations, including some 500,000 "charitable" nonprofits eligible to receive tax-deductible donations. Charitable nonprofits had combined expenditures of about $390 billion in 1989—about 7 percent of the gross national product—with a similar share of the civilian labor force (Hodgkinson, Weitzman, Toppe, and Noga, 1992; U.S. Bureau of the Census, 1991). They completely dominate some service fields, constitute significant portions of others (Rudney, 1987), and play a critical role in delivering public services and otherwise expanding and modifying the range of public goods because of their access to tax-deductible donations.

Social, Political, and Community Functions

Nonprofits also have important social, political, and community functions. For example, their concerns with achieving substantive goals (Kalberg, 1980) and meeting community needs have obvious affinity with professional codes of ethics that emphasize altruism and the public benefit (Pavalko, 1972; Hall, 1969; Majone, 1984). Such nonprofit organizations as churches, universities, hospitals, and social welfare agencies were among the earliest to employ professionals, thereby establishing criteria for professional employment in other types of organizations.

Professionals are still prevalent in nonprofit organizations. Professional definitions of problems may therefore guide nonprofit goals, and professional models of client relationships determine how nonprofits structure service activities. Because of their stated commitment to substantive goals, nonprofits may be less able than other types of organizations to defend themselves against these professional ideologies, limiting their ability to address the most difficult (and important) community needs (Bush, 1988; Jacobs, 1990; Cloward and Epstein, 1965; Dressel, 1984; Trolander, 1987; Grønbjerg, 1989a, 1990a).

Historically, nonprofit organizations have also provided important alternate routes of mobility for women and minorities, otherwise barred from most positions of authority. Blacks (but not Hispanics) and especially women have found the nonprofit sector accepting of their skills. Both groups are overrepresented in the sector (Preston, 1985; Trolander, 1987; Sommers, 1983; Covelli, 1985; Hodgkinson, Weitzman, Toppe, and Noga, 1992), although the glass ceiling still limits their access to top executive positions (Johnson, 1989).

Nonprofit organizations may provide greater access to skills, status, and decision-making authority for other workers as well. Nonprofit workers are less likely to consider themselves overeducated for their jobs (13 percent versus 33 to 35 percent) and are much more likely to view their jobs as challenging than workers in private business or government, even when one compares workers in jobs with similar titles (Mirvis and Hackett, 1983). However, nonprofit workers may become trapped in these organizations. Their credentials may not transfer to "central" or "important" positions in the "real" economy, because they train and practice in organizations commonly viewed as inefficient and peripheral by for-profit managers. Such a view fails to recognize the complexity of work involved in managing the diverse resource relationships that characterize most nonprofits.

Nonprofit organizations probably receive their greatest recognition for what many see as their defining characteristic: the organized expression of social cohesion. All societies engage in such efforts through a range of social institutions. However, the United States is relatively rare in its continued celebration of philanthropy, voluntarism, and altruism as reflecting core national values (Tocqueville, 1898). The number and strength of nonprofits, the size of donations, and the extent of volunteer participation (Hayghe, 1991) provide outward manifestations of these values and confirm democracy at work. The lack of complete documentation on any of them prevents explicit analysis of how they receive their actual expressions.

Philanthropy, voluntarism, and altruism are highly salient values in U.S. society because they cater to — and reinforce — other core values, such as ethnic and religious heterogeneity, a weak role of the state, and celebration of individualism (Grønbjerg, Street, and Suttles, 1978; Salamon, 1987). Historically, most nonprofit organizations emerged from and drew on established but distinctive bases for social organization (for example, religious, ethnic, and residential groupings). In the process, they may have further promoted and prolonged social cohesion fragmented along these lines.

Nonprofits also mediate social change directly. Social movement organizations exploit the nonprofit organizational form to create or promote new bases of cohesion in order to foster change in other institutions, especially public ones. Such new bases come into existence when advocacy organizations identify and mobilize special constituencies around such issues as environmental protection, racial integration, civil rights, abortion, political reform, women's rights, and gay and lesbian rights.

Social movement organizations have their own dynamic processes (McCarthy and Zald, 1977; Jenkins, 1987) but face challenges common to all nonprofits: how to pursue missions while, at the same time, managing diverse resource relationships. The case studies show that resource relationships create imperatives that nonprofit managers control only imperfectly. For social movement organizations, the search for patronage and support means that efforts to promote innovation and social change may translate into a process of cooptation (Selznick, 1949; Jenkins, 1987).

Other nonprofits may contribute less explicitly to social change, but all serve as special adaptive mechanisms (along with government and economic organizations) through which populations come to grips with their environment and technology (Hawley, 1950; Yancey and Eriksen, 1979; Fuguit and Kasarda, 1981). Thus, block clubs mediate between community residents and public policy priorities (Taub and others, 1977), while nonprofit human service organizations supplement, compete with, or operate on par with governmental agencies and private businesses (see also Ware, 1989).

Organizational Perspectives

Whatever their special functions might be, nonprofit organizations are first and foremost organizations. As such, they are subject to a series of dynamic forces that shape organizational actions and adaptations across the board. On the other hand, they also operate within political economies and resource constraints, two forces that derive from their nonprofit status and combine to create special contingencies that shape a broad spectrum of nonprofit decision making.

Organizational Imperatives

All organizations operate in response to driving forces. Many forces are external to the organization and constitute part of the environment in which organizations operate, but they also affect organizational choices. They include the volume and nature of service demands, the state of current technology or professional and institutional models of action, the structure of available resource streams, and the actions of other organizations in the same domains. Other forces reflect more internal dynamics, such as the organization's official purpose or mission and its formal organizational structure. Each has general as well as special applications to nonprofit organizations.

Meeting External Demands. The general state of the economy, the scope and structure of public sector spending and taxation, and a variety of secular trends shape the volume and nature of overall demand levels in the economy. These factors also condition demands for the types of services nonprofit organizations traditionally provide. For example, shifts in the types and locations of jobs, the recent shrinking of the middle class, continuing racial segregation, limited job advancement opportunities for women and minority groups, increasing rates of poverty among children, deteriorating public schools, diminishing access to comprehensive health care, and similar failures in private and public investments create a broad but changing range of service demands and community needs.

Because nonprofit organizations define themselves as addressing broadly defined community needs, they must respond in some manner to the changing service demands created by these developments if they are to maintain their legitimacy. However, their efforts have been hampered by low (compared with other nations) and declining levels of public spending for social welfare purposes. Although public welfare spending has increased, almost all of the growth has been for income insurance payments (for example, Social Security) and medical benefits, rather than income assistance and services for the poor.[1]

Investments by state and local governments may exacerbate or compensate for these national patterns in local communities. Compared with other large metropolitan areas, units of state and local government spend relatively little for welfare purposes in the Chicago area, even when spending from federal sources is counted. As a result, nonprofit human service organizations encounter particularly high demands for subsidized services in this region (Grønbjerg, 1986, 1989a, 1990a), making it difficult for them and their funders to judge organizational effectiveness solely (or even partly) on the basis of service demands.

All organizations must also adjust to changes in technology or professional and institutional models of actions and adopt new procedures when the new technologies or models become institutionalized and generally

accepted (DiMaggio and Powell, 1983; Zucker, 1988). Otherwise, the organization may lose its competitive edge or come to be viewed as an inappropriate
and undesirable participant in the wide range of exchange relations that
form the basis for organizational survival.

Organizations that rely on industrial technology to accomplish their
primary purpose (for example, manufacturing firms) can make their own
relatively independent decisions about which of several available technologies to use. Others are unlikely to question these decisions as long as the
technology produces desirable and measurable results in the form of profits.
The situation is more complex for organizations that seek to accomplish
substantive goals (for example, prevent drug abuse or reduce racial tension)
or provide services that are intangible and therefore difficult to evaluate and
measure (for example, counseling or community organizing). Most likely,
they will have to conform to established procedures or other rationalized
rituals (Meyer and Scott, 1983) in order to maintain their legitimacy in the
larger organizational environment.

Professional ideologies and similar paradigms endorsed by key institutions (such as public authorities or private foundations) present nonprofits
with an array of available models and procedures for how to structure
activities or manage finances. Some practices become fully institutionalized
in the form of official regulations (for example, required format for tax
returns) and licensing requirements. Adherence to these paradigms en-
hances an organization's legitimacy among other organizations, but most
models (especially service models) are complex and not sufficiently well
established to provide clear guidelines for decisions (Hasenfeld and Brock,
1991). As the case studies show, the lack of good technology probably makes it
difficult for nonprofit managers to determine whether specific practices required by funders promote or interfere with the organization's own mission.

The structure of resources affects how organizations secure the variety
of resources they need in order to maintain activities. They need to process
input in the form of raw materials or clients. They need human resources,
expertise, technology, and equipment to process the input and distribute
the output, and they need access to space (rented, owned, or donated) in
which to operate. For each type of resource, the aggregate level available to all
organizations depends in part on macro-level trends (for example, the state
of the economy or the effectiveness of the school system) or on the actions of
other organizations (for example, federal reserve bank actions for credit
availability).

In all cases, revenues play a critical role because they constitute a
convertible resource that organizations can use to obtain most other types of
resources needed to stay in operation. As the case studies show, the utility of
revenue sources depends on the amount and timing of the revenue, the
predictability of the source, and the nature of the exchange involved in

obtaining the revenue. Standard assumptions about what constitutes a product or a service unit establish parameters for how resource exchanges operate. So do institutional practices concerning payment—that is, whether customers pay up-front before services are provided (as in university tuition) or afterward (as in legal services).

The environment for any given organization also includes the actions of other organizations within its domain. This is specifically the case when consenting organizations agree to formalize their resource relationships by means of contractual agreements about the exchange of stipulated goods and services for specified payments. The actions of government or self-appointed industry regulators may have broader and less specific resource consequences, with federations, coalitions, and industry or issue associations seeking to shape these actions in a variety of ways. Organizations that participate in these types of interorganizational relationships or engage in boundary-spanning activities more generally may develop some control over their environment (Pfeffer and Salancik, 1978).

Articulating External Demands with Internal Structures. A final set of driving forces relates to internal aspects of the organization and their articulation with environmental factors. Two of these are critical: the domain in which the organization is active (its purpose or line of business) and its internal arrangements of power, authority, and differentiation. Presumably, organizations come into existence because their founders have determined that there is a need or market for particular activities and because they have obtained the necessary resources to begin operations. For nonprofit organizations, the process of establishing a charter or organizational purpose involves articulating a rationale about the nature and scope of community needs, determining how to link these needs to the (usually complex) goals of the organization, and specifying how particular activities will meet these needs.

Nonprofits may choose to focus on niches in which they can provide an already established set of activities (products) to underserved client populations (markets), or they may select the more difficult task of developing new activities for which demands are not well established. Previous analysis suggests that nonprofits tend to adopt the former strategy and that they rely heavily on prior definitions of community needs as developed by other organizations (Grønbjerg, 1986, 1989a).

Organizations are assumed to monitor environmental conditions on an ongoing basis in order to maintain as close a fit as possible between those conditions and their own activities. However, few organizations make drastic adjustments in their core activities once they have established themselves and overcome the liability of newness (Aldrich, 1979; Hannan and Freeman, 1977, 1984). That is because major changes in core activities require organizations to develop new forms of institutionalization and establish new interorganizational relationships.

Similarly, nonprofit human service organizations tend to determine community needs at the time of establishment, make only marginal adaptations subsequently, and refrain from aggressive efforts to reexamine needs or undertake major changes in approach (Grønbjerg, 1990a). As the case studies show, such inflexibility may well reflect the complex patterns of dependency on funders that nonprofits experience and the difficulties they have in managing funding relationships while also maintaining an independent orientation toward goals and services.

Finally, much of the literature on organizations has pointed to the importance of internal structural arrangements of organizations. For example, organizational size is related to the degree of differentiation (Blau and Scott, 1962; Blau, 1956). Similarly, authority structures and the distribution of power interact with informal relationships among members of the organization (MacGregor, 1960).

The early and persistent preoccupation in the literature with such organizational imperatives and other internal arrangements is understandable. Organizational structures reflect organizational choices, are subject to manipulation and change by organizational members, and directly affect organizational outcomes. Analysis of organizational structure therefore constitutes a logical first step in understanding organizational behavior. Closed systems of this type are also easier to conceptualize and analyze than the much more complex focus on how organizations interact with their environment (Scott, 1992; Aldrich, 1979; Thompson, 1967). However, the case studies show that the policy environment in which nonprofit human service organizations operate and the resource structures to which they have access have major implications for a range of internal management strategies. An adequate understanding of how nonprofits operate requires careful attention to the relationship between environmental features and internal organizational structures.

Special Nonprofit Contingencies

Other driving forces create contingencies that have special meaning for nonprofit organizations. The most important of these is the structure of the political economy in which they operate, including distinctive relationships to public and private sector organizations and the characteristics and range of resources to which they have access because of their nonprofit status. The state of the economy, investment and location decisions by business corporations, the payment levels of public assistance grants, and the quality of public schools all affect the types and magnitude of problems nonprofit organizations encounter among their clients or in their communities. The same institutional actors provide nonprofit agencies with subsidy funding in the form of donations or public grants and contracts and therefore control key aspects of the services nonprofits provide (Milofsky and Romo, 1988).

These features set parameters for the management strategies and service models available to nonprofits. They also contribute to distinctive patterns of interorganizational relationships and institutionalized myths about organizational effectiveness (Meyer and Scott, 1983; DiMaggio and Powell, 1983). The combined operation of these factors varies significantly among different service sectors. These sector differences also coincide with variations along a range of other characteristics that affect entire populations of organizations (such as degree and source of professionalization, or number and size of competing organizations).

Location in the Political Economy. The U.S. political economy reflects both the special character of the U.S. welfare state and the dominance of the market economic system. Nonprofit organizations occupy somewhat special positions in this economy because of their distinctive relationships with public and private sector organizations. They deliver significant proportions of public goods, and they compete with and benefit private sector activities. Not surprisingly, these relationships and the structure of the political economy in general dominate important features of the organizational environments in which different types of nonprofit organizations operate.

Nonprofit organizations maintain distinctive relationships with the public sector because of the peculiar nature of the American welfare state. The late development of national social welfare policies and the general reluctance to expand public mandates (for ideological and other reasons) are intricately related to the emergence of a welfare system in which nonpublic service providers, especially nonprofit organizations, play an important role in executing public mandates (Grønbjerg, Street, and Suttles, 1978; Sosin, 1990; Wilensky and Lebeaux, 1965).

However, there is considerable debate on the causal relationship among these developments. Some say the nonprofit sector served to delay the welfare state because it allowed a limited definition of public goods to persist by providing an alternative to the assumption of public sector responsibility (Douglas, 1983, 1987). In this view, the prominence of the nonprofit sector, combined with its rooting in ethnic and religious fragmentation, delayed the development of consensus about an expanded range of public goods (government failure). In a more extreme formulation, the nonprofit sector is seen as helping prolong support for a capitalist or laissez-faire ideology that favors a limited state in spite of the growing inadequacies of such a model (Grønbjerg, Street, and Suttles, 1978; Wilensky and Lebeaux, 1965; Piven and Cloward, 1971, 1982). Others argue that the nonprofit sector declined because of increasingly evident shortcomings in its own operations, thereby prompting the development of public welfare efforts to compensate for nonprofit failures (Salamon, 1989a, 1989b).

All of these perspectives provide the nonprofit sector with legitimacy and visibility because they portray it as deflecting, absorbing, or promoting specific public policy issues and shaping the debate itself (Ostrander, Langton, and Van Til, 1987). Consequently, any debate about the extent to which public sector activities can and should be privatized and the conditions under which any third-party government should operate must address the role of nonprofit organizations (Rehfuss, 1989; Salamon, 1989a, 1989b). The range of issues includes such important details as whether nonprofit organizations help maintain a safety net for the poor, whether they promote cost containment efforts in the public sector, and the extent to which they impose localized or private control over public sector activities.

Whatever the answers to these questions, their formulation highlights the diverse organizational contingencies that nonprofit organizations encounter in their relationships with public sector agencies. That is because the size and structure of public sector activities differ significantly across policy arenas. Although public welfare expenditures are significant for both cash assistance and health care programs, public agencies directly control and administer the former but rely heavily on nongovernmental organizations to deliver services in the latter. Public spending for social services is much smaller in scope than for health care ($62 per capita versus $492 per capita in 1984 for the Chicago–Cook County area), but the public sector's proportionate reliance on nonprofit infrastructures is about the same (45 percent versus 50 percent).[2] Public sector reliance on nonprofits is much smaller in housing and community development (about 5 percent of public spending) and in education (Grønbjerg, Kimmich, and Salamon, 1985).

The mechanisms by which the public-nonprofit funding relationships operate also differ greatly among service fields. In education and health, the payment structure gives extensive control to market forces and to the mutual selection process between recipients and providers. The amount of public funds received by nonprofit organizations in these fields depends on the degree to which they attract and accept clients who carry cash or credit from public sources, such as tuition grants, student loans, and eligibility for Medicare or Medicaid reimbursements.

Public-nonprofit payment structures in most other fields are organized more along the lines of formal grants and contracts that link provider agencies directly to the respective public agencies. In this case, clients have little to say about the size of the public-nonprofit exchange, and market forces are correspondingly attenuated. Such major variations in the scope and structure of public sector activities exercise considerable control over the organizational environment in which different types of nonprofit organizations operate.

Nonprofit organizations also maintain distinctive relationships with private sector organizations. The prominence of private market activities in the United States (and their protection in public policy and law) means that private sector organizations dominate economic conditions and structure the economic and social needs that nonprofits seek to address. However, the relationships are more complex than that. Nonprofits have specialized economic functions in a market economy and serve as an arena in which economic elites exercise power. Both of these features differ among service industries.

Economic theories of nonprofit organizations (Hansmann, 1980, 1987; Rose-Ackerman, 1986) usually imply that nonprofit organizations play narrow but important functions in compensating for imperfections in standard market relationships. They solve two kinds of problems: market failure and contract failure. Market failure occurs when demands for a particular product or service are so low (thin) that private firms cannot generate a sufficiently high profit margin or a large enough volume from the activities to stay in business. Because nonprofits have access to private donations and are exempt from certain taxes and fees, they can subsidize service activities or products and meet operating costs.

Over time, the availability of such services or products may help change consumer tastes and stimulate demand sufficiently to entice profit-making organizations into the market niche. Most likely, nonprofit arts and cultural organizations have helped create new market niches that now attract fully commercial enterprises as well as individual performers.

Contract failure occurs when the customer does not have sufficient information to evaluate the quality or competitive value of goods and services available in the marketplace. This is most likely to be the case if the quality of the service is difficult to determine up front (for example, counseling) or if the customer possesses limited abilities to exercise judgment (for example, because of age or impairment). In these cases, market transactions occur under conditions of asymmetric information that impede the free operation of market forces. Customers may not know what they buy, and providers can exploit this to maximize profit for their own private gain without affecting demands. Such transactions are irrational from the point of view of maximizing efficiency and effectiveness.

Nonprofit organizations avoid these difficulties because they are legally restricted from distributing any economic gains to private individuals. As a result of this nondistribution constraint, they have no incentives to exploit customer ignorance. They can therefore operate for the benefit of the customer and create an environment of trust that offsets problems otherwise associated with asymmetrical information. These information problems are severe in the field of social services and beset education and health as well. However, over time, nonprofit organizations may institutionalize customer transactions to the point that these procedures can be transferred to for-profit counterparts (for example, the adoption of appeals or case review procedures).

In both market and contract failures, nonprofits pave the way for proprietary incursions into the market niche. By creating new markets or establishing standards for organizational behavior, nonprofits attract private sector firms or allow them to overcome customers' fears of exploitation. These trends are likely to intensify as the private economy continues its restructuring and shift toward a service economy, away from manufacturing.

At the same time, nonprofits are increasingly turning to fees and service charges to supplement their revenues. These developments—the intrusions by for-profit organizations into nonprofit market niches and the cultivation by nonprofit organizations of for-profit revenue streams—suggest that the boundary between the two sectors may become increasingly blurred and contentious. So far, representatives from the for-profit sector have been most vocal in defending their territory, claiming that nonprofit organizations compete unfairly with small businesses (Bennett and DiLorenzo, 1989).

The for-profit sector is already very active in several fields of direct interest to nonprofit organizations. In health care, individual providers or group practice models traditionally have dominated the field. In recent years, for-profit hospitals and long-term care facilities have gained increased prominence. In community development and housing, private developers, real estate agents, financial institutions, construction firms, and private property owners dominate. In contrast, for-profit organizations are relatively few and unimportant in most social service activities (with the exception of day-care and homemaker services) and in education (especially higher education).

Given the dominance of private firms in the American society, and the amount of financial resources they control, it is not surprising that nonprofit organizations have sought to establish explicit linkages with them. Non-profits pursue such relations when they solicit corporate donations, and they formalize the linkages when they appoint corporate leaders to serve on their boards of directors. As a result, the nonprofit sector constitutes an arena within which economic elites exercise and consolidate power.

In part, nonprofit organizations are able to attract sizable corporate support and top corporate leadership to their boards when these linkages present status opportunities or claims to legitimacy for both parties (Galas-kiewicz, 1985, 1986); large, well-established nonprofit organizations have been quite successful in attracting corporate support and leaders (or their spouses) to board memberships (Ostrander, 1984; Odendahl, 1990; Schiller, 1989; Useem, 1984; Brilliant, 1990). Corporate participation in nonprofit boards also serves direct economic interests for both parties. Well-connected boards of directors provide nonprofits with personalized access to important resources, such as corporate or foundation grants, in-kind support for special events and marketing efforts, or financial and legal advice. For corporate leaders, financial support for nonprofit organizations and membership in nonprofit boards of directors provide indirect opportunities to promote corporate interests and extend their sphere of influence.

These opportunities develop as corporate leaders interact with one another in the neutral settings provided by nonprofit organizations and through specific actions by individual firms. The latter include efforts to create goodwill or market recognition for particular corporations (through cause-related marketing), shape policy agendas and definitions of problems, and, more generally, ensure that corporate positions or interests are known and incorporated into nonprofit activities as well as in the corporate world

(Useem, 1984; Schiller, 1989). For nonprofit organizations, the process may result in co-optation and deflection of organizational goals.

Obviously, the nonprofit organization's size and prestige and the opportunities it provides for networking or exercise of leadership will influence corporate interests in it. However, some nonprofit industries offer greater strategic advantages to private firms than others. This is obviously the case for service fields in which for-profit and nonprofit organizations compete with one another and where corporate influence on nonprofit activities may serve explicit economic interests for proprietary organizations (such as health or community development organizations). Alternatively, some nonprofit services significantly affect critical resources for corporations (for example, institutions of higher education in the form of expertise and technology) or enhance the quality of life for corporate staff and leadership (arts and cultural institutions), but do not directly compete with them.

These two driving forces in the U.S. political economy—distinctive manifestations of both the limited welfare state and of the dominant market system along the lines of service fields—create equally *distinctive patterns of institutional environments* for nonprofit organizations in the United States. A simplified model (shown in Table 1.1) suggests that nonprofit organizations may relate to the political economy in four ways. Each pattern is dominated by a particular type of nonprofit–public sector interaction, which arises out of the interplay of the two driving forces (see also Grønbjerg, 1987). In the United States, each type of interaction largely coincides with a particular service field.

The four patterns in this model provide a strategic rationale for identifying nonprofit service fields with systematic differences in organizational environments. My selection of the social service and community development fields for in-depth analysis of resource relationships follows this rationale. As Table 1.1 shows, the two fields operate in institutional environments that differ diametrically on the two key dimensions, occupying the upper left and lower right diagonal cells.

In the pattern of *cooperation* between the public and nonprofit sectors, there are insufficient incentives for the proprietary sector to enter the field

Table 1.1. Nonprofit Institutional Environments.

		Dominance of Proprietary Service Sector	
		No	*Yes*
Public Sector Dependency on Nonprofit Sector	*Yes*	Cooperation (Social Services)	Accommodation (Health)
	No	Competition (Education)	Symbiosis (Community Development)

because of market or contract failures: too few people want the service and those who do cannot afford it, or the services themselves are not easy to standardize or evaluate. In this case, the service arena has been left to the public and nonprofit sectors. Their shared commitment to substantive goals and the limited public resources devoted to the field encourage early public dependence on the more developed nonprofit sector for execution of public mandates. The result is cooperation between the two sectors, although the balance of influence may shift between them. The child welfare and broader social service fields exemplify this approach.

In the pattern of *accommodation*, the public and nonprofit sectors are also mutually dependent on one another, but the proprietary sector has clear and extensive interests in the service fields for historical reasons and because the field has a large, perhaps even universal, market—everyone wants the service. The nonprofit sector has little alternative but to attempt accommodation with both the public and proprietary sectors. This pattern is likely to characterize fields with large volumes of expenditures by both the public and proprietary sectors, such as the health service field.

An alternative pattern, that of *competition*, occurs when sizable public resources are devoted to developing a strong but highly specialized public sector that directly delivers primary services. The extensive assumption of public responsibilities means that a proprietary sector does not come into existence. The establishment of direct public services means that the public sector does not depend on the nonprofit sector to execute its mandates. As a result, the public and nonprofit sectors operate under an implicit division of labor, but one that easily deteriorates into direct competition, especially under conditions of scarcity. This pattern is exemplified by the education field.

The final pattern is called *symbiosis* to emphasize relations of coexistence to mutual advantage, sometimes to the point of mutual exploitation. This pattern occurs where the proprietary sector has strong, even primary, interest in the service fields. Public investments are also extensive. Under these conditions, the role of the nonprofit sector becomes a highly specialized one. It cannot compete with the other two in delivering direct services, but it can mediate or draw attention to the decision-making process of the two other sectors. These interactions characterize the community development field.

These patterns capture key aspects of the organizational environments in which nonprofit organizations operate in the United States. Although they vary by service fields, those differences reflect the types of underlying structural dimensions discussed previously. The number, size, and legal status of organizations (public, nonprofit, for-profit) vary systematically among these four types of environment, reflecting the amount and form of public and private sector investments. So do the structure of interorganizational relationships, pressures toward isomorphism and adoptions of particular patterns of operation (including professionalization), and the dynamics of birth, death, and transformations of organizations. The research findings presented in this book support the value of carefully specifying these distinctive organizational environments in which nonprofit organizations operate.

Distinctive Resource Base. Like all other organizations, nonprofits must secure and manage resources on an ongoing basis, but with several important variations. They have access to a greater variety of revenue sources than other organizations,[3] but are less able to control them. Most nonprofit service organizations rely on a bewildering array of funding sources, as shown by the example of Youth Outreach earlier: grants and contracts from government; donations in the form of foundation grants, corporate support, direct individual giving, United Way funds, church donations, federated funding, and bequests; earned income from dues, fees, service charges, rent, and product sales; and other income from endowments, investments, and special events.

Although not all nonprofit organizations have income from such diverse sources, most types are fairly prevalent. For example, column 1 of Table 1.2 shows that in 1982 at least three-fifths of Chicago-area nonprofit service organizations received funding from government, from a combination of fees, dues, and service charges, or from direct individual donations; two-fifths obtained foundation grants or corporate support; one-quarter had revenues from United Way, from endowments and other investments, or from fund-raising and sales of products; and one-fifth received support from religious and other federated funders.

In order to secure funding from any of these sources, nonprofit organizations must undertake the types of tasks described earlier for Youth Outreach: write grant proposals, enter contractual relationships, organize special events, solicit donations, meet United Way membership obligations, market themselves to fee-paying clients, maintain membership lists and collect dues, invest endowments, and so on. These tasks involve nonprofit organizations in specific relationships that create particular exchange expectations.

For example, both earned revenues and restricted grants and contracts (from any source) require nonprofits to provide specific services or activities in return for the revenue. However, when the funds come from government grants and contracts or donations, there is a separation of clients and customers: that is, the person or organization who receives the service (client) does not pay the cost (customer). These nonprofits lack access to simple market tests of their effectiveness, and their efforts to satisfy both customers and clients may produce multiple or conflicting goals.

Nonprofit organizations are also less able to directly control the continuation of their revenue streams than other types of organizations. Unlike government agencies, nonprofit organizations cannot point to legally mandated services over which they exercise a monopoly and for which legislators must allocate tax dollars. Consequently, they participate with less legitimacy

Table 1.2. Nonprofit Revenue Sources, Chicago Nonprofit Organizations, 1982.

Revenue Source	Percentage of Organizations with Any Support from Funding Source	Percentage of Total Nonprofit Revenue Base
Donations	80	24
gifts from individuals	62	6
foundation gifts	41	3
corporate gifts	37	3
contributions from United Way	28	7
contributions from religious groups	15	—
gifts from other federated funding sources	8	5
Fees/Dues/Service Charges	71	39
Government Funding	63	29
Endowment/Investment	30	4
Other[a]	28	4
Total	NA	100

Note: (NA) indicates not applicable. Numbers in column 1 do not add to 100 percent because organizations may receive funds from more than one source. Numbers in column 2 may not add to 100 percent because of rounding errors. The analysis is based on 309 organizations that provided information on both total revenues and their sources of revenue for 1982.

[a] Includes special events, sale of products, rent of facilities.

Source: Nonprofit Sector Project for Chicago, special analysis.

in the political process and must protect themselves from charges of lobbying in order to maintain their tax-exempt status. Unlike businesses, few nonprofit organizations have ready access to customers who are able and willing to pay the entire costs of services received. Therefore, advertisements, sales strategies, and other attempts to manipulate demand have limited impact.

Rather, the management tasks for nonprofit organizations vary from one funding source to the next. They involve individual nonprofits in a series of highly specific funding relationships that differ greatly, even among similar types of funding. Most of these relationships link the recipient organization directly or indirectly to a large and diverse number of other organizations to form complex systems of mutual dependencies. These linkages constitute funding arenas in which boundaries are difficult to identify (Milofsky, 1987). Each individual funding source presents nonprofit service organizations with an ongoing series of strategic opportunities and contingencies. Nonprofit administrators—if their organizations are to continue to operate—must manage these opportunities and contingencies with some degree of effectiveness and must understand how they combine and interact.

The literature on resource dependency suggests that such resource structures affect how organizations develop and express relationships with other organizations, the range of boundary-spanning activities in which they engage, and how central those activities are to the organization. As the case studies show, nonprofit revenue sources differ in the nature of the exchange relationships they create (customers versus clients), the degree and type of competition they involve (few versus many competitors, protected versus open competitive systems), the extent to which they provide predictable and controllable funding, and the degree of dependency they encourage (broad versus narrow). These features have important internal consequences for the organizations, particularly for the structure of power and management control, the range of strategies to manage staff, and the extent and nature of planning efforts they pursue.

Summary

Understanding how nonprofit organizations manage their funding relationships is important on both theoretical and practical grounds. Practitioners—nonprofit managers, public and private funders—have direct self-interest in these issues. Policy makers need to understand the issues in order to adequately assess the role that nonprofits play in the provision of public and private goods. Organizational theorists need to understand whether and how nonprofit organizations differ from other types of organizations, such as private firms and public agencies, if their models are to have adequate explanatory power.

On some dimensions, nonprofits resemble all other organizations. They must respond to the volume and nature of market demands, adhere to accepted professional and institutional models of actions, secure a variety of resources, establish a charter and an organizational purpose, and institute a proper organizational structure.

On other dimensions, nonprofits are subject to special contingencies that are unique to them: they have a distinctive location in the political economy and access to equally distinctive resource bases. The political economy is driven by two forces that vary across service fields: structure of the U.S. welfare state and the dominance of market organizations. These two forces combine to create four types of institutional environments for nonprofit organizations—cooperation, accommodation, competition, and symbiosis—which coincide with service fields. The social service and community development fields exemplify types that differ on both of the dimensions and provide strategic opportunities for assessing how institutional environments affect organizational behavior.

Notes

1. Per capita spending for income insurance programs and medical benefits increased almost ninefold between 1950 and 1988 in constant dollars and jointly accounted for 63 percent of all public welfare spending by

1988. In contrast, per capita spending for means-tested income assistance and other services for the poor has grown at much more modest rates, barely doubling over the 1950–1988 period (adjusted for inflation). By 1988, these programs accounted for only 9 percent of all public welfare spending.

2. An additional 25 percent of health care spending went to for-profit organizations.

3. Other types of organizations also have a great variety of resource streams. Business firms, especially large corporations, have many different product lines and investments. Governments rely on various user fees and tax bases. However, in each case, simplifying conditions reduce the complexity of managing the multiple streams. For business firms, common standards of evaluation—profit margins, asset ratios, and the like—facilitate the assessment of resource strategies. For governments, the involuntary nature of tax payments converts resource decisions into a common framework, consisting of estimating the potential units to be taxed, necessary enforcement efforts, and overall returns.

TWO

Funding and Nonprofit Management: Theories and Research

Like Youth Outreach, described in Chapter One, all organizations obtain resources from their environment. Their managers must therefore pay careful attention to how the environment is structured and how it changes. Some environmental conditions cut across all industries (for example, increasing cost of credit); others are particular to an industry (for example, public funding cuts in child welfare). Major nonprofit service industries (for example, social services, health, education, arts, and culture) differ on several dimensions to which managers must pay attention in order to recognize implications for their own organizations: the bases of knowledge or technology, the size and composition of organizations that make up the industry, the extent and nature of linkages to the public sector, and presence and strengths of for-profit competitors. These features combine to create highly specialized patterns of interorganizational relations that contribute to distinctive "normative climates" for the fields (Meyer and Scott, 1983, p. 14; Milofsky, 1987).

The specific nature of management problems depends also on the types of resources available to organizations. The case studies show that nonprofit funding sources vary in predictability, controllability, linkage to organizational activities, and range and amount of management efforts they require. These two-dimensions — characteristics of the service field and the structure of resource relations — set broad parameters for organizational strategies.

Because these features are particularly complex for nonprofit organizations, nonprofit managers must master a greater range of resource skills than administrators of other types of organizations. They not only must understand the line of business they are in (as all managers must do) but also must recognize specific contingencies presented by their diverse funding sources, in order to assess funding opportunities; translate funder priorities into service or program activities that promote agency missions; and coordinate funding relationships with other agency resources, such as staff expertise, information networks, board capacity, and agency structure.

Theoretical Approach: Three Dimensions

The framework on which the remainder of this book is based takes as its point of departure theoretical perspectives on organizational environments, resource dependency, and strategic management. These perspectives are useful starting points because they identify some of the key questions that surround the management of nonprofit funding relations. However, individually they fail to capture the full complexity of what nonprofits are up against. As I show in this book, organizational environments and funding sources interact to create complex contingencies against which management strategies must be developed and assessed.

Organizational Environments

Following the institutional model of organizational behavior (Hannan and Freeman, 1977, 1984; Aldrich, 1979; Meyer and Scott, 1983; DiMaggio and Powell, 1983; Kimberly, 1975), I argue that individual nonprofit service industries constitute unique organizational environments. I focus on two such environments, which exemplify different patterns of relations between nonprofit agencies and the public sector and where proprietary organizations also play very different roles.

The Social Service Environment. In the social service field, the pattern approximates cooperation because the public sector depends on nonprofit service providers to execute public mandates. This dependence derives from and bolsters shared goals. The absence of a strong proprietary sector supports the assumption of good faith in contractual relations. Although both public and private sectors provide subsidy funding, public funding is especially important to social service agencies. A 1982–1985 panel study (see Appendix A) found that almost all (90 percent) social service agencies included in the study had at least some government funding in 1982. It was the primary funding source for more than half (55 percent). Both the proprietary and public sectors, but especially the latter, influence the types and volume of services that nonprofit social service agencies provide (Milofsky and Romo, 1988).

The size and density of organizations in the social service field and the extent to which relationships among them are institutionalized also contribute to environmental contingencies that social service agencies encounter. In 1982, social service agencies accounted for the largest proportion of charitable nonprofit organizations in the Chicago area, except for churches.[1] Of the 3,000 organizations that were not hospitals, schools, or funding agencies, about 65 percent (2,000 agencies) provided at least some social services, and almost one-third (900 agencies) concentrated most of their activities in social services or closely related fields (Grønbjerg, Kimmich, and Salamon, 1985, p. 16).

Such a dense organizational field makes it difficult for any one organization to keep track of competitors and potential collaborators without specialized structures to do so. Larger agencies may have sufficient resources to do this on their own, but about four-fifths of social service agencies have revenues of less than $1 million. The large number of agencies and their extensive linkages to the public sector promote high levels of institutionalization. Indeed, the field has numerous, active, and occasionally powerful federations, coalitions, and other bids for coordinated action. The overall structure is complex and consists of layers of nested systems of interorganizational relations.

Federated funding organizations are especially important. They control access to sizable and highly efficient streams of donations. The funds concentrate decision making over these resources in boards of directors on which corporations and large social service agencies have influential representatives. Federated funders can (and do) use their fund allocations to control or otherwise discipline individual social service agencies, whether full members or not. As Pfeffer and Leong (1977) and Provan, Beyer, and Kruytbosch (1980) have pointed out, such consolidated resource systems create numerous opportunities for mutual dependencies and vigorous power plays. The Chicago federated funding systems are no exception.

The region contains more than ninety separate United Way organizations, most of which participate in a metropolitan-wide, coordinated fundraising effort (the Crusade of Mercy) and a highly complex but only partially coordinated fund-distribution system. For the 400 or more social service agencies that are members of suburban United Way organizations, the distribution system involves decisions about fund allocation at three separate organizational levels before the funds reach any service agency: the Crusade of Mercy, the United Way of Suburban Chicago, and then one of the almost ninety separate local United Way organizations.

The United Way of Chicago (which receives about half of the $100 million plus raised by the Crusade of Mercy each year), grants base allocations to some 140 member agencies at levels that are virtually guaranteed from year to year. There are also small programs of short- and long-term grants to agencies that meet minimal membership standards. Almost two-thirds (65 percent) of broadly defined social service agencies in the 1982 panel study received at least some funding from a United Way organization, although very few relied on it to a great extent.

The three major religious federations in Chicago (Catholic Charities, Jewish Federation, Lutheran Social Services of Illinois) conduct their own fund-raising. The panel study shows that almost one-fourth (23 percent) of Chicago-area social service agencies received some funding from religious or other federated funders in 1982. The three religious federations coordinate their strategic public policy activities with those of other large, citywide social service agencies through several coalition structures. The large agencies also exercise considerable influence over the United Way of Chicago. The five largest (revenues of $15 million or more in 1990) jointly received almost $17 million from the United Way of Chicago in 1990. That represents about 32 percent of all United Way allocations, but only 8 percent of their own combined revenues (ranging between 3 and 18 percent), suggesting that the balance of power is in their favor. Indeed, at least one of the five has threatened to bypass the United Way of Chicago and obtain funding directly from the Crusade, in effect as a competitor of the United Way.

Other signs also point to a highly institutionalized social service sector in Chicago. The 1985 panel study found that almost half (48 percent) of the social service agencies were members of at least one nonprofit coalition or federation (not counting funding federations). The great majority (86 percent) of social service agencies had close contacts with other nonprofit organizations in the form of shared resources, board members, or programs.

Most significant, however, is the complex and institutionalized relationships that nonprofit social service agencies have with public agencies. Historically, major child welfare agencies in Illinois were intimately involved in shaping fundamental social service policies in the city and state. They remain among the organizations most called on to help formulate or comment on social policies. They view themselves as indispensable partners for public agencies, providing high-quality professional social services, and therefore entitled to adequate public reimbursements. The state has accepted these claims, at least in the child welfare field, and established a formal structure for negotiating rate setting with nonprofit child welfare agencies.

Indeed, key state agencies depend on access to a reliable, cooperative infrastructure of nonprofit organizations in order to carry out their own mandates, especially in the areas of child welfare, community mental health, and substance abuse treatment and prevention. Consequently, as the case studies show, nonprofit social service agencies interact closely with public agencies, especially in the day-to-day provision of services, to the point that public agencies are an integral part of the social service funding arena. In short, the social service field is characterized by a highly complex system of cooperative, interorganizational relationships. There are corresponding pressures toward isomorphism and adoption of particular patterns of operation.

The Community Development Environment. In the community organizing and development field, the pattern of relationship to public and private sectors approximates symbiosis, because nonprofit organizations play an intervening or mediating role in the overwhelmingly political interactions of the other two. The public and proprietary sectors each attempt to enlist community organizations on their side, just as community organizations may negotiate alliances with either.

The community organizing and development field contains many fewer organizations. Only 16 percent (or about 500) of Chicago's estimated 3,000 nonprofit organizations (excluding churches, hospitals, schools, and funding organizations) provided any services in the housing and community development fields in 1982. Less than 5 percent (150) concentrated at least half of their expenditures in that area. These are much smaller proportions than for social services (65 and 33 percent, respectively).

Community development organizations also have less extensive relationships to public funding sources and less developed systems of funding federations than the social service field. The 1985 panel study found that two-thirds (67 percent) of community development organizations received at least some public funding, compared with 90 percent of social service organizations. It was the major source of funding for only one-quarter (27 percent) of community organizations, compared with more than half of social service agencies.

Only in recent years have special federated funding structures come into existence for community development organizations, but none control large amounts of funds. For example, the Local Initiative Support Corporation (LISC) for Chicago was established in the mid 1980s and provides program and some operating support to nonprofit community development organizations from a mixture of private and public funding sources. LISC has targeted annual operating support of $50,000 for four years to as many as thirty development organizations in the Chicago area, only a fraction of the funding available to social service organizations in the region from the Crusade of Mercy or through major religious federations. Only five community development organizations are members of the United Way. They receive small annual allocations (less than $64,000 per year), and their combined total of $250,000 in 1990 accounted for less than half of 1 percent of total United Way allocations.

Other differences in the degree of institutionalization of the two service fields are less striking. Indeed, community development organizations are somewhat more actively involved in coalitions than social service organizations. The 1985 panel study found that 63 percent of community organizations (compared with 48 percent of social service agencies) were members of coalitions or federations (other than funding federations). However, the two types of organizations are very similar in the extent to which they engage in collaborative efforts with other nonprofit organizations: 84 and 86 percent, respectively.

Although public funding, density of organizations, and degree of institutionalization are important, the organizational environment for nonprofit community development organizations depends much more on the nature of investment decisions in local communities and on the prominent role played by private sector organizations in shaping those decisions. That creates a highly specialized role for nonprofits in the community development field. In contrast to social services agencies, they rarely have the capacity or resources to provide relevant services themselves (for example, to repair housing or undertake community development). Only recently have new sources of public and private financial support become available to them for such purposes, but not in large amounts.

Instead, the role of community development organizations has centered on identifying needs or gaps in public services and on closely related efforts to promote or resist proposed public or private sector developments. Some engage in limited partnerships with the public or private sectors, especially in the planning phases of housing and community development projects, but also as managers or coordinators of ongoing efforts. However, brick-and-mortar activities highlight land-use and geographical considerations and therefore local politics. That makes involvement in politics a much more salient and legitimate activity for nonprofit community organizations than in other fields. Rather than direct services to a client population, they focus on community organizing, attempts to stimulate economic development, and intensive lobbying and organizing efforts aimed at local politicians, businesses, and industry — activities that have important consequences for the agendas of both public and private industry sectors. Nonprofit community development organizations therefore often find themselves mediating or directly involved as partisans in inter- or intra-community conflicts.

These types of activities have been promoted by a series of historical factors in Chicago. Prominent among these are demographic and political forces that created community problems, on the one hand, and strengthened the sense of community, on the other. Rapid population growth until the late 1940s meant that housing was of critical concern to large portions of the city's population, especially low-income residents and some racial and ethnic groups. Urban renewal, demolitions, and condominium conversions have continued the housing pressure for those groups. Changes in the city's industrial mix and its recent economic decline have also served to keep community development and environmental issues high on the agenda.

In addition, high levels of ethnic and racial residential segregation have facilitated the establishment of local organizational infrastructures, and maintained their salience. Racial and ethnic residential succession and urban renewal efforts also contributed to the development of "defended neighborhoods," which are among the most easily mobilized by existing nonprofit organizations (Suttles, 1972, 1990; Taub, Taylor, and Dunham, 1984). The political machine, with its emphasis on ward-based neighborhood services and voter mobilization, has also served as a focal point for many of the city's nonprofit community organizations. The breakdown of the machine and the ensuing council wars have intensified the political role of Chicago's nonprofit community organizations in recent years. They have come to form the basis for new political constituencies and alliances. Community-based nonprofit organizations are therefore important organizational resources for public agencies and private business and industry. Often difficult to control, they represent forces of political mobilization with which the other sectors have to contend.[2]

The different organizational environments under which nonprofit social service and community organizations operate create different parameters for the management strategies (and service models) available to organizations active in these two arenas. The different environments also contribute to distinctive patterns of interorganizational relationships and institutionalized myths about organizational effectiveness (Meyer and Scott, 1983; DiMaggio and Powell, 1983).

Resource Dependency

Following the resource dependency model of organizational behavior (Pfeffer and Salancik, 1978; Dess and Beard, 1984; Pfeffer and Leong, 1977; Provan, Beyer, and Kruytbosch, 1980), I argue that funding structures provide the critical context within which nonprofit decision making takes place. Key nonprofit funding sources (fees, donations, government grants and contracts) differ in how predictable and controllable they are and therefore in the uncertainty they introduce into organizational decision making. They differ in the range and nature of management tasks they require and therefore in the amount of effort organizations must devote to these tasks and in how routinized the tasks can be. They differ also in whether they separate clients (service recipients) and customers (sources of funds) and therefore in how sensitive they are to market forces or organizational strategies to manipulate the quality and cost of services (service domain efforts).

In general, organizations attempt to reduce their dependency on, or increase control over, specific funding sources. Such resource strategies increase the predictability and continuity in funding and improve the organization's ability to plan the allocation of resources, staff, space, and activities—all issues of concern to managers. However, the effectiveness of resource strategies depends on the environment in which the organization operates and on the institutional patterns of funding relationships in which it participates.

These institutional patterns differ for social service agencies and community organizing/development organizations, although there are also variations within the two groupings. Nevertheless, social service agencies tend to experience stable public funding, which allows them to routinize management tasks and predict available resources. They encounter much greater volatility in donations. Their donations usually do not involve ongoing and reciprocal relationships, but their government grants do. Income from special events, individual donations, and corporate and foundation grants depend largely on decision makers who are external to the agencies and who do not directly benefit from the service activities involved.

In contrast, many community organizing/development organizations view public funding as relatively uncontrollable and turbulent, even if they have an ongoing funding relationship. This is consistent with earlier analysis that shows that public agencies rely much less extensively on nonprofit organizations to deliver mandated activities in this field than in social services. Lower public reliance on nonprofit organizations means that non-profits have less leverage over public agencies in community organizing/development than they have in social services.

Many community development organizations have greater opportunities for developing ongoing and reciprocal relationships with local community donors, because local property owners and a broad range of community institutions may benefit directly from their activities. For that reason, many of them are able to generate relatively high and stable levels of local donations or membership dues. They view these revenues as documenting their legitimacy within the community; and the legitimacy, in turn, becomes a critical resource for undertaking effective community action.

Because of the different conditions under which community development organizations interact with public agencies and with donors, their funding relationships and resource strategies are more complicated and political than for social service agencies. Also in contrast to social services, the private market, rather than nonprofit or public organizations, traditionally functions as the primary service provider: banks and savings institutions provide financing, realty and construction firms supply housing, manufacturers and businesses furnish jobs and commercial services, and the public sector develops and maintains public infrastructures, such as streets, bridges, and sidewalks. The recent expansion of public mandates to include housing and more broadly defined community development also involves considerable capital investments in infrastructures and has become an important source of public funding for the finance, construction, and real estate industries.

Strategic Management

The literature on strategic management in organizations usually makes explicit references to particular environmental features or equally distinctive characteristics of resource relations (Kimberly, 1975, 1979; Rowan, 1982; Ylvisaker, 1987; Hall, 1987), suggesting that the effectiveness of specific resource strategies and management choices vary by service field and type of funding reliance. I explore whether and how nonprofit organizations engage in strategic planning, the extent to which they control or influence a range of organizational resources, and the consequences of specific organizational strategies. However, I did not have access to direct information on strategic management practices prior to selecting the organizations for the case studies. Instead, I assumed that either very stable or very turbulent funding patterns would reflect strengths and weaknesses of the strategies used by the different types of nonprofit organizations. This assumption seems to have some validity. Two organizations (one social service organization and one community development organization) that we had initially identified as having turbulent funding histories have since folded. A third organization with a turbulent funding (Christian Therapists) survived only by reorganizing and sharing the executive director with a sister organization.

Strategies or other management actions that seek to position the organization within a particular political economy or organizational environment are especially important. So are efforts to manage the organization's funding relationships in order to secure a broad range of resource opportunities and to define and pursue organizational missions in ways that are responsive to clients and community needs. None of these efforts are likely to be fully successful unless nonprofit managers coordinate them with the appropriate use of other organizational resources, such as staff expertise, information networks, board capacity, and decision-making structures. The nonprofit administrator must solve these management problems with at least some effectiveness if the organization is to survive.

Even so, the dynamic nature of these processes makes it difficult to apply any standard criteria or guidelines for assessing strategies. Rather, managers and organizational analysts need to recognize the existence of these processes. They may not make optimal decisions, because it may be impossible to fully consider all factors, but they must at the very least know the types of forces that are likely to affect their organization.

Organizational Profiles and Selection

Because of the complexity and changing nature of these processes, it is difficult to capture them adequately in cross-sectional surveys. To examine how organizational environments and resource dependency affect management strategies, I therefore rely on in-depth case studies of nonprofit organizations that differ along the three key models of organizational behavior outlined above: two types of organizational environments (social services and community development), reliance on three types of resources (commercial, donation mix, public), and two indicators of strategic management outcomes (funding stability and turbulence). As shown in Table 2.1, the combination of these criteria produces twelve organizational profiles.

In-depth case studies of a nonprofit organization from each profile demonstrates these patterns in greater detail than would be possible in a large-scale, cross-sectional survey. The use of case studies allows for careful attention to dynamic processes, and built-in comparisons among the organizations make it possible to examine how variations in resource structure (types of funding sources, funding stability) influence and reflect specific management strategies within two different types of organizational environments (social services and community development).

Considered individually, the three dimensions capture a sizable proportion of nonprofit organizations (Grønbjerg, 1986). Nevertheless, their combination into profiles or typologies and the strict criteria applied to each dimension (see Appendix A) eliminate some nonprofit organizations from inclusion. That makes it more difficult to generalize the findings to the

Table 2.1. Case-Study Profiles

Service Domain/ Funding Stability	Primary Funding Sources		
	Commercial	Donation Mix	Public
Social Services			
Stable	X	X	X
Turbulent	X	X	X
Community Development			
Stable	X	X	X
Turbulent	X	X	X

Note: (X) indicates case-study profile. The Case-Study Project included one organization from each of the twelve profiles. One other community organization was included for comparative purposes.

broader population of nonprofit social service agencies or community development organizations. However, the dimensional sampling approach (Arnold, 1970) does make it possible to address key conceptual issues and develop a set of theoretical interpretations that are grounded in empirical reality.

Selection Criteria

Most of the participating organizations were selected from an existing panel study of nonprofit human service organizations in the Chicago–Cook County area with four waves of data collection over the 1982–1986 period. As described in Appendix A, we identified candidate organizations for the twelve profiles by applying the following criteria: (1) major field of activity in social services or community development, as reflected in mission statement, proportion of service expenditures, or inclusion in published lists of community organizations (for community development organizations); (2) primary funding reliance on government, donations, or commercial income, as reflected in annual revenue data over the 1981–1985 period; and (3) major differences in funding stability as measured by average annual changes in inflation-adjusted revenues over the same period.

We also applied two other criteria: location in Chicago and medium size. The location criterion serves practical constraints but also ensures that the organizations share similar environmental conditions. The size restrictions eliminate important sources of management contingencies, especially problems associated with managing facilities, multiple sites, and complex divisions of labor. However, medium-sized organizations are more typical of the general population of nonprofit organizations (average revenues of about $1 million in 1982, median of $220,000; Grønbjerg, Kimmich, and Salamon, 1985), and they rarely have access to sizable financial reserves or powerful boards that might obscure typical contingencies associated with different funding streams.

The elimination of very large organizations excludes highly institutionalized and complex organizations, making it possible to manage the extensive data collection involved in the analysis and allowing for more direct comparison with community organizations, most of which are fairly small. For example, the panel study found that 50 percent of community development organizations had expenditures of less than $100,000 in 1982, compared with only 20 percent of the social service agencies. The exclusion of small organizations ensures that the participating ones have survived normal predicaments associated with being newly established, the so-called liability of newness crisis. Very small organizations also tend to be highly dependent on a single staff member or a key board member. They are therefore likely to experience greater instability and to experience major threats to their survival because of otherwise minor or idiosyncratic changes in staff or funding.

Data Sources

We used a great variety of methods to obtain as much relevant information as possible from each of the case-study organizations (see Appendix A for a detailed description of data sources). We analyzed a wide range of documents (especially audit statements and tax returns) for as many years as possible, but relied extensively on a special data collection instrument for analysis of restricted grants and contracts. In spite of some delays in securing the full cooperation of a few organizations, almost all provided full access to agency files.

We also interviewed the executive director, other key staff members, and occasionally board members in order to examine agency resource strategies and closely related topics, such as cooperation with other organizations, staff development, and agency structure and culture. Directors and staff members spoke frankly and knowledgeably about the difficulties they encounter in managing funding relations. For the community development organizations, we also examined 1980 census data and newspaper articles over the 1980–1990 period about the organization or the community in which it is located. Several other types of data and sources provided supplementary information.

These analytical strategies make it possible to document detailed changes in funding sources over four to twelve years (depending on the organization) and examine efforts to develop, secure, and manage fees or program-restricted grants and contracts over one fiscal year. The sample of organizations is small, but carefully selected to allow for systematic comparisons. Equally important, the process data extend for six to twelve years and include hundreds of decisions.

The Case-Study Organizations

As described in Appendix A, we were able to select most of the case-study organizations from among candidate organizations in the panel study that met our profile criteria. In a couple of cases, we had to extend our search for appropriate organizations to include recommendations from experts in the field and analysis of available (but often incomplete) financial records on public file. The organizations finally selected match the expected profiles quite well.[3] As Table 2.2 shows, the organizations pursue fairly typical missions or target populations.

The following descriptions of the case-study organizations indicate the types of organizations they are, the range of activities in which they engage,

Table 2.2. Description of Case-Study Organizations.

Agency Profile	Mission/ Target Population	1988 Revenues	Percentages from 1984–1988 Average		
			Public	Donations	Earnings
Social Service					
Alcohol Treatment: Public/Stable	Alcoholism treatment	$ 319,000	82	3	6
Hispanic Youth Services: Public/Turbulent	Hispanic youth	965,000	89	9	—
Youth Outreach: Mixed/Stable	Minority youth	1,429,000	48	44	3
Immigrant Welfare League: Mixed/Turbulent	White ethnic population	584,000	42	29	11
Minority Search: Fee/Stable	Minority search	560,000	—	25	67
Christian Therapists: Fee/Turbulent	Christian therapy	111,000[a]	1	18	77
Community Organizing/ Development					
Economic Development Commission: Public/Stable	Economic development	291,000	90	5	—
African-American Neighbors: Public/Turbulent	Black empowerment	362,000	47	39	12
Community Renewal: Donation/Stable	Community protection	320,000	—	98	—
United Residents: Mixed/Turbulent	Coalition/ development	428,000	52	41	1
Preservation Council: Events/Stable	Community preservation	296,000	—	—	91
Hispanic Neighbors: Events/Turbulent	Hispanic empowerment	256,000	3	21	70
New Town Sponsors: Events/Turbulent	Community promotion	115,000[b]	—	45[b]	53

Note: (—) indicates less than 1 percent. The percent values reported in the table do not add to 100 percent for each organization because the table excludes revenues from interest and other miscellaneous sources.

[a] Down from $265,000 in 1987.

[b] Down from $267,000 in 1987. Almost all of the revenues from donations supported special event activities.

Source: Case-Study Project.

and some of the most important events in their recent history. For the
community development organizations, the descriptions also include information about the communities in which they are located. The names are
fictitious and chosen to capture key orientations.

The order of their presentation anticipates comparisons among service fields, types of funding sources, and management strategies that form
the basis for the volume. Thus, all social service agencies[4] are grouped
together to highlight one of the major arguments of this volume: that service
fields coincide with organizational environments and impose particular
types of constraints on organizational managers. Within each of the two
major groupings—social services and community development—I focus first
on the two organizations with primary reliance on public funding, then on
the two with donations or mixed funding, and finally on the two that rely
mainly on commercial revenues. This order of presentation follows a second
major argument: that nonprofit resource streams create their own contingencies. For each of these groupings, I pair an organization with a history of
stable funding with one that has a record of major funding change, in order
to demonstrate the need to account for the differences.

Social Service Agencies

The six social service agencies illustrate the diversity that characterizes social
service agencies in general. They provide assorted services for diverse target
populations. Most serve mainly a particular geographical community, but
others have multiple sites or target the entire metropolitan area. They also
vary widely in age, with two dating back to the 1920s and one becoming
formally incorporated only in the early 1980s.

Alcohol Treatment—Public/Stable. Alcohol Treatment relies primarily
on public funding from one single state agency and has had a relatively stable
funding history. It was founded in the early 1970s, and its original mission—
to provide alcoholism treatment—grew out of needs identified by board
members of a local mental health center under public auspices. It currently
operates alcohol and drug abuse programs in a lower-income, multiracial
community. Its staff of fourteen (in 1988), including three part-time staff
members, provide most services on site, including outreach, intake, assessment, referrals, and counseling.

The agency has been licensed to provide outpatient alcohol treatment
services for adults since the mid 1970s. It obtained a drug treatment license
in 1986 and has recently sought to expand its services to youths. The new
focus on drug abuse reflected recognition by the agency's staff and board that
an increasing number of clients displayed a pattern of both alcohol and drug
abuse. The change also paralleled a similar shift in priority by the agency's
primary funder and allowed it to benefit from increased public attention to
drug abuse and avoid a funding cut that might otherwise have occurred as

public grants and contracts shifted from alcoholism to drug abuse services. The organization has had the same executive director since the late 1970s.

Hispanic Youth Services—Public/Turbulent. Hispanic Youth Services also relies primarily on public funding, but from a large number of different sources. It has grown rapidly in recent years and has also expanded its donation base. It was established in the mid 1970s as a drug abuse program for Hispanic and some African-American youths in a low-income, primarily Hispanic, neighborhood. It emerged out of a larger community organization that has since collapsed. Currently, it provides services relating to teenage pregnancy, substance abuse, gangs, literacy, job training, and community organizing. At the time of our data collection (1988), it had a full-time staff of twenty-four.

According to its director, the range of services has remained relatively unchanged since at least the early 1980s. However, some of the programs have grown and become more clearly articulated over time in response to funding opportunities. The agency provides relatively few services at its office location and relies instead on rotating and temporary space in a variety of nearby community or commercial facilities. The agency was started by its current executive director, who returned to the organization after a six-month leave of absence shortly before we started our case study.

Youth Outreach—Mixed/Stable. As the vignette at the beginning of Chapter One demonstrated, Youth Outreach relies on a mix of donations and public funding from many separate sources. Youth Outreach has had a relatively stable funding history and is an old, established youth service agency founded in the 1920s. Some years ago, its current director decided to decentralize its services. It now operates an increasing number of outposts in borrowed space that is located in low-income, minority communities across the city. Using a team approach, the agency provides a variety of counseling, advocacy, educational, and cultural services in most of the outposts to school-age youths, primarily high school students. It has recently added a vocational component to its program activities.

Youth Outreach has had the same executive director since the early 1970s and during the 1988 fiscal year had a full-time staff of forty-six, including twelve paraprofessionals and clerical staff members. In addition, the agency provided clinical and management training for twenty-one student interns from local schools of social work.

Immigrant Welfare League — Mixed / Turbulent. Immigrant Welfare League also relies on a mix of donations and public funding from different sources. Established in the 1920s, it has grown rapidly in recent years. Its name identifies its white ethnic base, which includes a substantial population of older and second-generation immigrants and a growing population of recent immigrants, including many undocumented workers. The organization has added a number of service components since the late 1970s, including employment and training; a shelter for alcoholic, homeless men; counseling for battered women; immigration services; and a senior citizens' program.

Immigrant Welfare League has also experienced a number of administrative changes. The agency had six executive directors during a period of six years immediately prior to our study, including one director who defrauded the agency and two acting or interim directors. In 1988, the organization had a full-time staff of twenty-one and two part-time positions.

Minority Search — Fee/Stable. Minority Search relies primarily on fees and has had a stable funding history. It was founded by the executive of a major corporation in the early 1970s with the goal of helping promising minority college students (with majors in business or technical fields) establish corporate careers. Since then, new affiliate agencies have expanded the program to a number of other cities. The affiliates maintain some independence, but all carry the same name, report their finances jointly, and coordinate their activities through a national office.

Minority Search develops corporate internship placements for minority college students accepted in its program from across the metropolitan area. Participating corporations pay a flat annual fee per intern, in return for which the agency trains, counsels, and monitors the student interns. In recent years, Minority Search (and most of the affiliates in other cities) has sought to work with promising high school students to expand the recruitment pool and has begun follow-up work with alumni of the program. The agency has had the same executive director since the late 1970s and has a staff of thirteen (in the 1989 fiscal year), including two support staff.

Christian Therapists — Fee/Turbulent. Christian Therapists also relies primarily on fee income but has experienced a turbulent funding history. The agency was separately incorporated as a nonprofit organization in the early 1980s but had operated as an outreach of a local nondenominational church for almost ten years prior to that and still maintains close linkages with the church. It defines itself as a Christian counseling agency and provides therapy and counseling at its office in one of the city's lakefront communities with highly diverse family income levels. Its revenues come primarily from third-party payments or sliding fees paid by individual clients.

Christian Therapists has experienced major structural, programmatic, and funding changes over its fourteen-year span, including six executive directors, five site locations, two waves of staff resignations, major growth and decline in revenues, turnovers in the board of directors, the initiation and subsequent suspension of three new programs, and the establishment and later loss of three satellite therapy centers in suburban locations. Most of these changes occurred over the 1986–1988 period. In the 1989 fiscal year, the agency had a full-time staff of two (one therapist and one office manager), a part-time executive director, and several part-time therapists.

Community Organizations

The seven community organizations also have features that are typical of community organizations in general. They are engaged in a variety of community organizing or economic development activities. They represent all regions of Chicago and diverse neighborhoods. The communities range from poor to affluent; some are predominantly white, others are racially integrated, and some are almost entirely Hispanic or African-American. Some of the organizations are relatively old, dating back to the 1940s; others were established only in the 1980s.

Economic Development Commission — Public/Stable. Economic Development Commission relies primarily on public funding from state and local sources. It was selected to represent a stable funding history. It has in fact experienced some funding turbulence but has put into place a funding structure that promises to provide it with a stable, growing source of local tax revenues. It was established in the mid 1970s with the purpose of supporting neighborhood investment decisions by an affiliated for-profit consortium of local financial institutions. Like many other Chicago communities, the area was affected by the expansion of adjacent black residential concentrations, redlining, and competition from nearby suburban shopping malls. These forces, in operation since the 1950s, had become manifest by the early 1970s and threatened the vitality of the local business district and of residential investments.

As of 1980, the local community in which the organization concentrates its efforts was overwhelmingly inhabited by an aging population of second- and third-generation ethnic whites, except for tracts bordering an area that became entirely black in the 1960s and 1970s. Almost all of the housing stock was constructed before 1940, and half is owner-occupied. The community is home to several institutions that have sizable local real estate holdings and provide a range of commercial and educational services to residents of the local community and adjacent areas. Because of their local investments and dependence on local customers and clients, these institutions have actively sought to shape the development of the area. Among other efforts, they helped establish Economic Development Commission and have provided it with leadership and ongoing support.

Since then, Economic Development Commission has become formally affiliated with a Special Service Area Taxing District that it helped create. It also maintains overlapping board memberships with other local community organizations in the area. The organization's name identifies the general geographical area in which it is active, rather than any specific neighborhood. Its executive director has been with the organization for more than ten years but currently divides his time between the organization and consultation to funders and other community organizations.

Economic Development Commission had a full-time staff of ten in 1989, in addition to a part-time executive director and a part-time volunteer. It shares some of its staff with two affiliate organizations, for which it provides management and program services in return for financial reimbursement. The sharing of staff ensures coordination of activities among the organizations and provides added flexibility in managing the impact of funding changes.

The organization identifies its major activities as support for local commercial development through a variety of activities that range from loan-packaging and promotional activities to direct involvement in commercial development projects. The latter includes efforts to change local zoning ordinances as well as active financial participation and management. The organization also provides assistance to homeowners and other residential services and participates in the development of residential projects.

African-American Neighbors — Public / Turbulent. African-American Neighbors was reputed to rely heavily on public funding and to show a turbulent funding profile. Indeed, the organization's public funding has been so turbulent that only in five of the ten years for which we have complete data did it approach 70 percent reliance on public funding. The average is closer to 50 percent.

African-American Neighbors operates in a community that once contained affluent residences but began to experience economic decline early in this century and then underwent dramatic racial transformations after 1950. Most residents are black and extremely poor, with 1980 poverty rates exceeding 60 percent in several census tracts. The area contains a number of public housing projects and many deteriorated or vacant housing units. Few shops remain in the area, many commercial buildings have vacancies and marginal uses, and the area contains large stretches of vacant land. The community is characterized by the full range of problems associated with extreme poverty and racial isolation in the inner city: gangs, drug abuse, crime, unemployment, illiteracy, welfare dependency, and inadequate housing.

The organization was founded in the 1960s by a group of ministers and social workers who worked in the area and had strong roots in the civil rights movement. They were concerned about deteriorating economic and social conditions as the community completed the process of racial transition. African-American Neighbors has maintained a strong activist orientation, has continued affiliations with the civil rights movement, and has been heavily involved in black political empowerment efforts in the city.

During the first few years of its existence, the organization was funded by church donations. It had a part-time director, and most of its programs were managed by volunteers. In the late 1960s, the organization became more institutionalized, with formal bylaws and a board of directors. New funding and technical support from a large church-affiliated community assistance organization made it possible to hire a full-time director and staff and to begin a more extensive set of program and organizing activities. The current executive director was hired as a community organizer and staff member at that time. He has served as the executive director for the last fifteen years.

During his tenure, the organization has expanded its program activities to include housing rehabilitation, employment training, economic development, anticrime efforts, and advocacy for community residents. It helped create several new organizations and at times maintained complex interorganizational relationships with them. One of these is a local development corporation, with which it shares board members, staff, space, and management functions. Another is a community health clinic, with which it has less formal ties. The organization had a staff of twenty-one in 1989, including four staff members and the executive director who split their time between the organization and the affiliated development corporation.

African-American Neighbors has experienced a number of internal conflicts and has been the subject of continued, and at times vigorous, criticism from both within and outside the community. As a result of the organization's involvement in mayoral politics during the early 1980s, it lost the substantial level of public funding it had obtained just prior to that period.

Community Renewal—Donation/Stable. Community Renewal was one of the few organizations in the original panel study that received a significant proportion of its revenues from donations but had no public funding or much income from fees or dues. We chose to include the organization because it illustrates the complex manner in which highly concentrated and tightly coupled funding relationships shape strategies and interactions with other organizations.

Community Renewal was established in the early post–World War II period with the goal of maintaining and strengthening residential, commercial, and other institutional investments in one of the many communities affected by major racial and economic changes in the city during and after World War II. Its first director served for more than twenty-five years, but two recent directors have left after four years each. At present, the local community in which the organization is located is racially mixed and has maintained its attractiveness to residents with middle and upper-middle incomes. The community is home to several well-established institutions with sizable local real estate holdings. These institutions provide a range of cultural, educational, and health-related services to community residents and the larger metropolitan region.

The largest of these institutions (hereafter referred to as the Community Institution) employs and serves a large number of local residents and has expanded its investments, including residential investments, in the local area over a period of years. Because of these investments and its broad range of involvement with community residents, the Community Institution has actively sought to shape the development of the area. Among other efforts, the Community Institution not only helped established Community Renewal but also has provided it with substantial ongoing support as well as funding for special projects. Community Renewal has received relatively stable support for its basic operating activities but also has had access to fluctuating funding for off-budget projects. It had a full-time staff of four, one part-time staff member, and a student intern in 1989.

Community Renewal identifies its major activities as crime monitoring and prevention in collaboration with the police and the Community Institution's security force. It also monitors city services, building code enforcement, general housing conditions, and planning developments that affect the area. The least formalized part of its efforts involves attempts to encourage community activities and involvement. Its close identification with the Community Institution shapes the role that it can play in relating to other community organizations and sets parameters for how actively and visibly it can pursue specific agenda items.

United Residents—Mixed/Turbulent. United Residents relies on a mix of funding sources and has experienced considerable funding turbulence. It serves as an umbrella organization for a variety of civic groups, business organizations, and block clubs in a Chicago community with very diverse ethnic and racial populations. It was established in the early 1960s at a time when the community had a stable but aging white ethnic population. Younger families were moving to suburban or outlying city neighborhoods, and the community was experiencing the onset of residential and commercial decline. Until the late 1960s, the organization appears to have directed its efforts toward general health and welfare issues in the community (including the improvement of recreational facilities and schools, the maintenance of housing stock, and the enhancement of commercial and retail areas).

In the late 1960s, United Residents assumed a more aggressive posture toward rehabilitation and revitalization of the community. This appears to have coincided with an influx of a greater variety of ethnic and racial groups, a rapid deterioration in the housing stock and commercial strips, and the hiring of the current executive director. The community has several well-established institutions and businesses that have a substantial stake in preserving the neighborhood. Representatives from these institutions have taken a major interest in the organization and provided it with volunteer leadership.

United Residents has a complex, multilayered structure with a staff of thirteen, including two executive directors. Although it operates as a traditional umbrella community association, with a membership of block clubs, civic and business groups, single-issue organizations, institutions and individuals, it also has development arms devoted to its major program focuses — housing and economic development. These development corporations share the not-for-profit status of the organization. They also share office space, fiscal administration, and, at times, staff members.

The economic development arm of the organization was formed in the late 1970s by one of the organization's constituent business groups in order to promote commercial revitalization and stem deterioration in the retail strips. The economic development organization has its own executive director but shares board members, space, staff, and financial reporting with United Residents. Subsequently, in response to federal and city funding opportunities and concerns expressed by member organizations, the organization started a housing development corporation to promote the rehabilitation and construction of affordable housing in the community. The housing development arm shares board members, space, staff, financial reporting, and executive director with United Residents.

The development of separate organizational vehicles for the development efforts and the associated dual-leadership structure extend the number and variety of high-level contacts that the organization can maintain with key funding sources, public and private sector decision makers, community leaders, and local organizations. They also allow the organization to segment key activities into specialized efforts and to use these as mechanisms for selectively communicating with external and internal audiences.

Preservation Council — Events/Stable. Preservation Council relies primarily on proceeds from a major cultural event it organizes each year and from which it has accumulated a large surplus that allows it to maintain stable operations. The organization and a closely related umbrella group were both established in the early post–World War II period with the primary purpose of maintaining and strengthening residential, commercial, and other institutional investments in the face of major racial and economic changes in the community. The two organizations were established with key support from major local institutions and are jointly credited with organizing successful urban renewal efforts in the area. The community has changed from a predominantly blue-collar, ethnic, industrial community into a white-collar, diversified, desirable residential neighborhood, although it borders on a large public housing project with a high concentration of low-income residents.

The community is home to several well-established institutions with sizable local real estate holdings and houses a number of flourishing commercial establishments. These institutions and establishments provide a range of cultural, educational, health, recreational, and entertainment-related services to community residents and the larger metropolitan area. Several of these institutions employ local residents and have expanded their investments, including residential investments, in the local area over a period of years. Because of these investments, and their broad range of involvement with community residents, the community institutions have actively sought to shape the development of the area. They were also instrumental in establishing the organization and the umbrella group and have provided them with leadership and support since then.

Preservation Council limits its attention to a small section of the community, as do the other affiliate members of the umbrella group. Like other affiliates, it focuses on arts, cultural activities, planned development, and community preservation. Its community preservation activities include tree planting, efforts to maintain the historical character of the neighborhood, and attempts to minimize congestion. The organization has a large membership list of residents and commercial establishments from its local area who pay flat, annual membership fees depending on the category of membership involved.

Preservation Council organizes a major special event, from which it derives almost all of its operating funds. With the proceeds from the event, it also provides funding for several other organizations, including relatively small amounts to the umbrella group, several local schools, and a fixed 40 percent of net proceeds to a local youth club with which it maintains close relationships and some shared board members. About a year prior to our study, it hired a full-time office manager (a former board member) to replace a previous part-time director who had worked at the organization for a number of years. It hires a number of part-time instructors to teach short courses on a variety of topics but otherwise relies on a large contingent of volunteers (more than 500) from both within and outside the community to organize the annual special event.

Hispanic Neighbors—Events/Turbulent. Hispanic Neighbors has relied primarily on proceeds from a major event in recent years but has experienced considerable turbulence in its funding history. The neighborhood in which it operates is one of the city's oldest and most stable Hispanic communities. The community ranks relatively low in family income (more than a quarter of families had income below the poverty level in 1980) and shares a range of problems arising from unemployment, crime, drug use, and related activities.

Hispanic Neighbors was established during the post–World War II period as a coalition of local institutions and organizations to undertake a range of civic activities. Currently, each of the coalition members is represented on its sixteen-member board, but none pay dues to the organization. The current director has served for several years, was a board member prior to that, and has long-standing relationships with the organization and the community in which it is located. The organization had two additional full-time staff members in 1989, including an office manager and a housing coordinator-manager, and hires several people on a temporary basis to work on the major special event.

Initially, Hispanic Neighbors sponsored clean-up campaigns and poster contests and sought to improve community-police relations. It did not undertake aggressive planning efforts until the 1960s, when it became an active participant in community action efforts associated with the War on Poverty programs. It then developed a wide range of services provided by paid staff. This shift in focus and the declining role of volunteers reportedly created conflict within the organization that almost led to its demise in the late 1960s. The organization was revitalized when several volunteer seminarians began documenting community problems, provided the manpower and inspiration to organize activities, and helped the organization present itself to philanthropic and public funders. The organization encountered another crisis in the late 1970s, however, when its funding declined dramatically again.

Since then, Hispanic Neighbors has been actively involved in fostering the community's Hispanic heritage and views its primary purpose as helping local residents gain and use community power. In addition to housing issues, it has focused on mobilizing the community around improvements in educational programs and facilities. The construction of a new high school, whose name and programs reflect the community's Hispanic heritage, was a major victory for it and its member organizations. The organization has also sought to capitalize on the Hispanic focus on family issues in its organizational efforts, and it has been a prime mover in implementing the school reform movement and mobilizing local school councils and parent efforts.

The organization resembles Alinsky-type organizations in the primacy it gives to empowerment and local organizing activities and in its consistent reference to all active community residents as leaders.[5] However, these empowerment efforts have not been without their costs, and newspaper reports suggest considerable conflict between the organization and several other organizations with which it has been closely affiliated from time to time, including two development organizations it helped establish but over which it subsequently lost control.

The organization and its director were also closely linked to a citywide effort to organize minority, especially Hispanic, communities into a more unified political force. The citywide coalition provided it with central management services and training for volunteers. The organization broke with this effort as well, but it subsequently established networking and training relationships with a competing organization to which its director is closely linked.

New Town Sponsors—Events/Turbulent. New Town Sponsors relies primarily on dues to support its normal operations, but obtained sizable donations for a major cultural event that it initiated on an annual basis in the early 1980s. It has since discontinued its involvement in the event and has experienced major funding turbulence because of these changes. It was established by a group of developers and related organizations in the early 1980s with the goal of promoting and coordinating investment in an area of the city that previously had large stretches of vacant land and abandoned industrial or commercial space. Since the mid 1970s, the community has experienced considerable investment through both new construction and loft conversions for residential and commercial developments, and it has seen a major increase in middle-income and upper-middle-income residents.

The area adjoins a large number of major commercial, financial, and related service institutions, in which many of the new residents are employed. The area is also in close proximity to several major cultural institutions and attractive recreational opportunities. New Town Sponsors emphasizes these employment and cultural amenities in its publicity and promotion efforts. However, in spite of large-scale investments, the area still has locations with broken sidewalks and unattractive or underutilized commercial space. Moreover, the area is in relatively close proximity to public housing projects and low-income minority communities, often viewed as threatening by the middle-income households that developers would like to attract to the area. The neighborhood itself includes a large and active police station (not mentioned in the organization's public relations literature) as well as a number of social service institutions catering to a persistent population of transients and homeless people. These features have contributed to a long-standing reputation of seediness for the area.

New Town Sponsors sees its major purpose as overcoming these negative images so as to attract new investments and safeguard existing ones. Consequently, it focuses its efforts on reviewing and coordinating planned development for the area and improving city services. These activities are of major interest to the developers, large financial institutions, and local commercial establishments that helped establish it and dominate its board. Recent newspaper reports suggest that the area is now sufficiently developed that plans for new construction or for rehabilitation of existing space will increasingly compete with established usage. The organization has sponsored both a residents' association and a merchants' association. However, it chose to limit its own focus to development issues and to encourage the separate establishment of these two associations. The residents' association retains one seat on the organization's board, as do two nonprofit institutions located in the area.

As part of its promotion efforts, New Town Neighbors has sought to develop and participate in several different special events since its establishment, in order to bring people to the area and familiarize them with its residential amenities and growing commercial and entertainment opportunities. However, although at least one of these involved significant amounts of revenues and expenditures, none have become a major source of revenue for the organization and most have just about broken even. Instead, the organization relies on membership dues from owners of local commercial and residential properties, who pay a fixed rate linked to the property's assessed evaluation rather than flat annual dues per property owner. New Town Neighbors has had two executive directors over its ten-year history and had a full-time staff of two in 1988, including the executive director.

Summary

The management of nonprofit funding relations requires careful attention to the environment in which the organizations operate and to the structure of resources to which they have access. The environment in which nonprofit social service agencies are active differs from that of their community development counterparts. There are many more (and somewhat larger) social service agencies than community development organizations. They are more likely to rely on public funding and to have other institutionalized relationships in place. They are of greater importance to public funding sources but have less direct utility to private firms. Because of these differences in environments, the two types of organizations encounter different expectations, opportunities, and contingencies.

Nonprofit funding sources impose their own exigencies, although modified somewhat by environmental conditions. The combination of these two factors creates a great variety of funding arenas for the two types of organizations, each characterized by a particular configuration of normative expectations between funders and the recipient nonprofits. Strategic management takes place in the context of this mosaic and must be assessed on that basis.

To do so, I undertook in-depth analysis of funding dynamics, contingencies, and management activities for twelve organizations (plus one). They differ systematically on the three dimensions derived from major conceptual models in the literature: two organizational environments (social services, community development), three major types of funding dependency (commercial, donation/mixed, public grants and contracts), and two indirect indicators of strategic management (stable funding, turbulent funding). All are of medium size and pursue fairly typical missions.

Notes

1. In 1982, the Chicago metropolitan area contained an estimated 102 nonprofit hospitals, 67 colleges and universities, 806 elementary and secondary schools, and 3,047 other nonprofit public-benefit organizations (Grønbjerg, Kimmich, and Salamon, 1985, p. 9).
2. These developments may also account for why several models of local communities and their mobilization originated in Chicago. The settlement house movement, the Chicago school of sociology, and the Industrial Areas (Alinsky) movement of the post-1930s provide perspectives on

local communities and have motivated public and nonprofit leaders to focus on their organization.

3. One additional organization is included because we had data on it and it provided an interesting contrast to others selected.

4. I refer to all organizations in the social service field as *agencies* and to all those in the community development field as *organizations*, to make it easier for the reader to note the difference between them.

5. "Alinsky-type organizations," named after Saul Alinsky, are organizations that — as Alinsky did in the 1930s — attempt to create local community cohesion and empowerment through carefully targeted confrontational strategies directed at outside institutions with vested interests in the community. The Industrial Areas Foundation, established by Alinsky, served as a training ground for community organizers, who subsequently worked in other cities and communities (Alinsky, 1946, 1971; Bailey, 1974).

PART TWO

Structure and Management of Nonprofit Funding Sources

To explore the dynamic processes of how nonprofit organizational environments modify relations to different funding sources, I deliberately set out to find and examine organizations that appeared to have responded differently to the interaction of these two sets of forces. I found them, and the wealth of data is almost overwhelming. Each of the thirteen organizations described in Chapter Two has its own tale of triumphs and frustrations in securing particular types of funding and has developed its own accommodations with specific funders. It is easy to get captured by the stories of successes and disappointments that their managers recount—indeed, this book contains some of the most interesting and telling ones that I encountered.

To make sense of these encounters, I found it necessary to go beyond the experiences of individual organizations and look to the underlying structural dimensions of the funding sources themselves. Only then was it possible to examine in greater detail whether, how, and why funding relationships take on different characteristics for social service agencies compared with community development organizations. In turn, these comparisons form the basis for identifying even broader structural features that are likely to apply to nonprofits active in other service fields and even to organizations operating under different types of legal auspices, such as public agencies and private business firms—a task I undertake in Chapter Twelve.

The next several chapters contain the results of the first phase of this analysis. Although presented here as a coherent framework, the process was an inductive one. The theoretical perspectives outlined in Chapters One and Two guided the initial formulation of issues and questions, but the fully developed analysis of exchange relations emerged only at the end. I present it here to provide the context for the case-study findings.

As is evident from the chapter titles in this section, the discussion uses funding sources as the organizing principle. In part, that reflects the empirical reality. Managers of nonprofit social service and community development organizations think in terms of specific funding sources: how much the street fair will net this year, how well the revised letter and mailing list will do in soliciting individual donors, whether the governor's deal with the state legislature will hold up across the board, or at least in the child welfare field. The focus on funding sources also makes it possible to highlight and illustrate the intricate and highly diverse nature of relationships that nonprofits develop with different funding sources.

The funding relationships are complicated by forces at the macro-level. Declining corporate profits or threats to the legitimacy of the United Way system affect how individual nonprofits interact with each type of funding source. Nonprofits differ in how vulnerable they are to macro-level developments, because service fields vary in whether and how particular types of funding relationships are prevalent and fully institutionalized. Declines in corporate profits may disproportionately affect community development organizations, and United Way losses will hit social service agencies more severely. However, these macro-level forces still leave room for considerable variation among organizations, reflecting differences in their strategic positions and past practices.

Chapter Three lays the groundwork for this broader analysis of funding relations by identifying first general criteria by which I found it useful to assess and characterize funding sources. Readers who are very familiar with major nonprofit funding sources and their characteristics may want to skip this chapter. Some readers may also be familiar with overall trends in major types of funding sources for the social service and community development fields included in Chapter Four. This chapter describes the context within which management decisions take place and shows how macro-level trends manifest themselves at the level of individual organizations. It also shows the diversity within and among the two types of organizations examined in this study.

Such diversity begs for analysis and interpretation: how does it come about, and what are the consequences? Chapters Five through Eight provide at least some answers to these questions for fees, special events, donations, and government grants and contracts. For each source, I draw on the experiences of individual organizations to illustrate how the processes of developing and maintaining these types of funding relationships operate.

THREE

The Scope and Breadth of
Nonprofit Funding Sources

The process of obtaining and managing financial resources occupies much of the time and energy of top executives, as it did for the thirteen organizations in this book. Revenues are scarce and difficult to obtain, and some involve demanding exchange relationships that restrict organizational choice. Under these circumstances, resources exercise considerable control over organizational activities—especially in nonprofit organizations, which tend to be small and cash-poor and have limited ability to resist efforts by funders to exert influence.

This chapter outlines structural characteristics of funding sources and applies them to the wide range of sources available to nonprofits. These characteristics are of considerable importance to nonprofit managers, because they shape contingencies and opportunities. Macro-level trends in the overall growth or decline of specific funding sources modify or accentuate the contingencies and opportunities, but they differ for the social service and community development fields. Therefore, managers in these two fields face disparate strategic choices about funding sources that are otherwise very similar.

Major Nonprofit Funding Sources: Importance and Characteristics

Nonprofit managers claim with some legitimacy that any source of funding is important if it provides their organization with revenue. However, there is more to it than that. Some sources are more important than others, whether in terms of the proportion of organizations that receive the funding, the amount of dollars involved, or more qualitative or structural characteristics that determine the amount and nature of work involved in managing the funding.

Defining Importance

For analytical purposes, I distinguish among three ways of assessing the importance of funding sources: the extent to which the source is commonly used by nonprofit organizations (its institutional importance), the extent to which the sector or individual organizations rely on the source (its resource dependency value), and the uncertainty and management complexity associated with the source (its investment cost). Each captures some element of the organizational environment in which organizations obtain their resources and highlights particular contingencies for managing funding sources.

Funding Prevalence. Beyond the simplistic argument that a funding source is important if an organization has access to it, a source is also important if it is shared widely among organizations. Because many organizations obtain funding from a particular source (a macro-level characteristic), the source is important even to those who do not have it (a micro-level impact).[1] Widely shared funding sources become part of the standard repertoire of options that individual organizations explore on a regular basis. Procedures for obtaining and managing them are institutionalized in the form of normative expectations about what nonprofit managers should do to ensure organizational success (Tolbert, 1985). Nonprofit managers must understand and address such expectations if they are to promote the organization and protect their own reputations. Correspondingly, unusual funding sources may increase management complexity, because the organization has to establish tasks and structures with few guidelines, although it also has greater leeway in designing procedures to meet its own specific needs.

As Table 1.2 showed, four-fifths (80 percent) of nonprofit organizations have some income from donations, and about two-thirds or more have revenues from fees, dues, or service charges (71 percent) or from government grants and contracts (63 percent). At this gross level of categorization, each of these three major funding sources is sufficiently institutionalized to be part of the standard repertoire of options nonprofit managers pursue.

However, with the possible exception of government funding, each of the three types also lumps several distinct sources together, as do most other surveys or analyses of nonprofit funding sources. Only donations from individuals (and unspecified government funding) appear to be sufficiently widely shared among nonprofit organizations to qualify as important on this criterion. Certainly, as Table 1.2 shows, nonprofit managers are more than twice as likely to have experience in—and thus encounter expectations about—securing individual donations (received by 62 percent of Chicago-area nonprofit organizations) than in obtaining and maintaining United Way membership (received by 28 percent). They are even less likely to have experience in, or face expectations about, obtaining revenues from other federated funding sources (received by only 8 percent of the organizations).

The first two columns of Table 3.1 suggest that patterns of funding prevalence differ somewhat for social service and community development organizations. Government funding, donations from individuals, endowment income, and perhaps also United Way support are significantly more

Table 3.1. Funding Prevalence and Dependence for Chicago Area Nonprofit
Social Service and Community Development Organizations, 1982.

| | Funding Prevalence | | Funding Dependence | |
| | Percentage with Any Revenue from Source | | Percentage with Half or More Revenue from Source | |
Funding Sources	Social Service	Community Development	Social Service	Community Development
Donations	90	80	28	47
gifts from individuals	70	33[a]	5	7
contributions from United Way	65	40[b]	—	—
foundation gifts	52	73	3	13
corporate gifts	45	53	—	—
gifts from other federated funding sources	23	13	—	—
contributions from religious groups	15	20	—	—
Government Funding	90	67[a]	55	27[b]
Fees/Sales/Dues	58	60	5	13
Other	60	13	3	7
endowents, investment	40	7[a]	—	—
special events, misc.	40	20	3	7

Note: (—) indicates less than 1 percent. Percentages are based on responses from forty social service organizations and fifteen community development organizations that provided complete information for all funding sources. The first two columns do not add to 100 percent because organizations may receive funding from any or all of the sources. The last two columns do not add to 100 percent because the remaining organizations have mixed funding, with no single source accounting for half or more of total revenues (9 percent of social service agencies and 6 percent of community development organizations).
[a] Difference between two types of organizations significant at .05 level.
[b] Difference between two types of organizations significant at .10 level.
Source: Special analysis of data from the Nonprofit Sector Project for Chicago.

pervasive among social service agencies than among community develop-ment organizations.

Most of these differences follow expected patterns. Government fund-ing for social services is both more extensive and more likely to be channeled through nonprofit service providers than for community development. So-cial service agencies are more likely to have endowment income, since they are larger (median expenditures of $322,000 in 1982 versus $106,000 for community organizations) and older (43 percent were established before 1960, whereas only 22 percent of community organizations were established before that date). Similarly, most United Ways define their primary purpose as supporting social service activities, and community organizations receive less than 1 percent of allocations by United Way of Chicago.

The pattern for individual donations is less obvious, although the greater prevalence among social service agencies may reflect a spillover effect from the United Way system. Individual donors may have been socialized to think in terms of supporting social service agencies, making it easier for these agencies to obtain this type of support. In general, managers of social service organizations are more likely to encounter sustained expectations about developing these types of funding sources than their counterparts in community development organizations.

Funding Dependence. Although some funding sources may be very prevalent among nonprofit organizations, they may be unimportant in their direct economic impact if the amount of money involved is small. Assessing the importance of funding sources therefore also requires attention to the amount of funding involved and patterns of funding reliance or dependence. Each source involves the recipient organization in a particular type of exchange relationship, and organizations that depend disproportionately on a particular funding source must devote relatively high proportion of their energies to managing that relationship. This definition of importance forms the basis for the resource dependency perspective and for closely related efforts to determine how different patterns of funding reliance interact with organizational behavior. It is also the basis for the approach I follow in this study.

The last two columns of Table 3.1 show the proportions of social service and community development organizations that depend on particular funding sources to a significant extent, defined here as receiving half or more of their total revenues from that source. Government funding is important to a larger percentage of social service agencies (55 percent) than community development organizations (27 percent), and the reverse may be true for donations from all sources combined. However, in spite of the wide prevalence of dues, fees, and service charges, relatively few depend on these sources for half or more of their total revenues, even when the sources are combined in a single category.[2]

High reliance on one single funding stream is likely to have fateful consequences for an organization, because it becomes dependent on a relatively narrow range of environmental factors or on idiosyncratic events associated with the stream. However, while that increases risks, it also greatly simplifies management tasks and allows the organization to specialize and fine-tune its management efforts. Spreading the risk by developing diverse funding sources increases management complexity because the recipient organization must master many different funding relationships. Obviously, complexity and dependence are closely related contingencies that organizations may trade off for one another, but cannot avoid entirely.

As in the case of funding prevalence, funding dependency may be analyzed at both the level of individual organizations (micro-level) and the level of the entire service field (macro-level). Macro-level patterns influence individual organizations. Nonprofits that operate in a service field in which government funding accounts for the bulk of overall revenues will be affected by changes in such funding, even when they do not have any themselves. That is because the number and size of other organizations with which they compete, collaborate, or otherwise interact most likely *are* influenced directly by government policies.

Uncertainty and Discretion. Funding sources also differ on a range of structural characteristics that are more difficult to quantify but nevertheless have important consequences for recipient organizations. Some funders demand complex or intensive levels of management efforts, and others do not. I have found it helpful to think of these structural characteristics as reflecting external attributes of uncertainty and internal attributes of discretion.[3]

External attributes refer to the structure of funding opportunities to which recipient organizations have access. These structures form part of the broader environment within which nonprofits operate. Most writers on organizational environments argue that both instability and complexity contribute to uncertainty (Duncan, 1972; Dess and Beard, 1984; Aldrich, 1979; Koberg and Ungson, 1987; Millikin, 1987; Emery and Trist, 1965; Jurkovich, 1974; McCann and Selsky, 1984). Just as organizational environments differ in stability (stable versus unstable) and complexity (simple versus complex) (Daft, 1989, chap. 2), so may the structure of nonprofit funding sources.

Instability creates uncertainty—and imposes high demands on management—because unexpected jolts may occur: rain may ruin the special event, a corporate sponsor may downsize or go bankrupt. In contrast, most United Way allocations are stable and very certain. Under conditions of potential instability, managers must devote considerable energy to protecting the organization against jolts, whether they take place or not. Moreover, because jolts are likely to be unanticipated both in their magnitude and form, protective efforts are apt to be insufficient or misdirected, and managers must therefore devote efforts and resources to repairing the damage after jolts have occurred (Meyer, 1982).

Organizations with unstable funding sources, then, should face greater management uncertainty. However, as I show in subsequent chapters, assessing the stability of funding sources and the corresponding management implications turns out to be quite difficult. For recipient organizations, funding stability involves continuity (the actual experience of stability), predictability (the likelihood of future stability), and controllability (the ability to enforce future stability).

These dimensions are not mutually exclusive but interact with one another, and some may be associated with greater uncertainty than others. Funding sources may be continuous in that they provide funding year after year, as most United Ways do to their members. A history of continuous funding may increase the likelihood that the funding will continue, but it does not guarantee funding predictability (since, for example, an annual campaign might be hit with a major scandal or controversy). Nor does predictability mean that funding will be continuous—agencies may know that a grant is given for only three years and cannot be renewed. On the other hand, although funding continuity and predictability do not ensure controllability, the reverse may be true. Organizations that have leverage or power over funding sources (controllability) are likely to be able to ensure the future receipt of the funding (funding predictability and continuity). Certainly, both predictability and controllability imply active management efforts to keep informed about future funding trends and to maintain and develop influence and control over funding sources.

Although funding stability simplifies planning and limits uncertainty, it may be costly in other ways. Continuity in funding allows organizations to fine-tune their management approach, but it also limits their ability to pursue new opportunities or transfer the highly specialized skills to other funding sources. Reliance on predictable sources allows organizations to reduce scanning efforts but limits their outreach and awareness of larger environmental conditions.

Organizations that rely on funding sources over which they have little control may seek to buffer themselves against the effects of funding interruptions by reducing dependence on the funding source or intensifying boundary-spanning activities to obtain advance warning about coming actions. Efforts to obtain and maintain leverage over funding sources require equally or more demanding efforts at boundary spanning than simply obtaining advance knowledge about changes.

Complex as opposed to simple organizational environments also impose management contingencies. Complexity is high when nonprofit organizations receive funding from many different types of funding sources, because each type is likely to require somewhat different skills. Obtaining revenues from many diverse funding sources therefore requires nonprofit managers to master a great range of exchange relationships. Complexity makes it difficult for managers to predict the outcomes of organizational activities, because they must make decisions on the basis of incomplete, overwhelming, or not fully understandable information.

Complexity may also be relatively high even if organizations receive funding from many streams of the same type. That is because nonprofit managers must give a minimum amount of attention to each discrete funding stream, to ensure that the exchange relationship meets the expectation of both participants. The larger the number of such relationships the organization maintains, even if the relationships are of a similar type, the less likely the organization is to know the specific interests and concerns of individual funders. Therefore, the greater is the uncertainty it encounters.

In addition to these external characteristics, funding sources also differ in features that have more explicit effects on the internal structure of the recipient organization. The amount of flexibility and required management efforts affects discretion. Funding sources may leave the recipient organization free to decide how it will use the funding, with full discretion over the internal allocation of resources. Other sources do not. Proceeds from special events tend to be entirely flexible, while government grants usually are highly restrictive and require the organization to use the funding according to predetermined line-item expense categories. However, flexible funding provides the organization with few guidelines for making complicated decisions or establishing appropriate organizational structures.

The amount and nature of work that the organization must perform to obtain the funding—the investment demands of the funding source—have obvious management implications as well. All funding sources require some efforts to obtain them; but the type of work may be quite different, it may be more or less intensive, and it may involve narrower or broader segments of the organization's staff and structure. Reliance on inflexible funding sources exposes the organization to external control over its internal management arrangements, while sources that require high investments absorb a large proportion of organizational energies. Both features limit management discretion.

Subsequent chapters show how different types of funding sources compare in prevalence, dependence, and structural features. These characteristics create intricate contingencies for organizational managers and require careful consideration of alternative strategies. However, as I show, the contingencies—and hence the strategies—are likely to differ for social service and community development organizations, even for the same types of funding sources.

Nature of Exchange Relationship

Describing funding sources in terms of their degree of uncertainty, complexity, and management discretion gives a more realistic portrayal of what nonprofit managers are up against than simply showing their prevalence or economic importance. However, to understand why these conditions characterize particular funding sources, I have found it helpful to look more closely at the nature of the exchange relationship between the source and the recipient organization. The exchange relationship is the vehicle through which funding sources achieve many of their key structural characteristics. If nonprofit managers are to alter these structural characteristics or just control them better, they must pay attention to how and why funders choose to interact with them. Only then do they have a conceptual basis for modifying their funding relations.

The nature of the relationship depends on how closely the exchange resembles traditional market transactions between supplier and customer, as in the case of earned or other self-generated income, in comparison to subsidy support. The relationship also varies according to the characteristics and institutional interests of the organization's exchange partners—for example, whether they are individuals or organizations.

Self-Generated Income: Earned Revenues. Some nonprofit funding sources involve direct market transactions: returns on investment, rental income, fees or other charges for services and products, dues, and proceeds from special events. The exchange relationships involved in securing these types of revenues have well-established counterparts in the for-profit sector, from which nonprofit organizations may adopt a variety of marketing or other strategies. In all cases, the nonprofit organization generates the income directly through its own efforts. It delivers a resource, product, or service for which there is a market demand among consumers, who in turn are willing to pay the organization to meet the demand. In most cases, the organization's clients, those who consume the service or product, are also its customers, those who pay for the service.

Nonprofits do not have owners and cannot distribute annual surplus in the form of profits or dividends. However, they may obtain investment income when they accumulate surplus over time or come to own capital in other ways, as when they receive endowments in the form of capital gifts. Nonprofit managers are expected (and at times required) to invest the capital so as to maximize interest or dividend payments.

The for-profit sector has developed a great variety of investment instruments for managing capital assets. Nonprofit managers may be more or less informed about the range of commercial strategies, but they are unlikely to look beyond them because they are familiar to their board members (who may make the investment decisions) or because well-established investment strategies carry immediate legitimacy. Nonprofits that own capital resources therefore engage in commercial transactions with institutional investors, such as banks, brokers, real estate developers, or mutual funds. Most of the case-study organizations received investment income of this kind, but not to any significant extent.

Some nonprofits may apply some substantive (value) reasoning to their investment decisions. Nonprofit hospitals may refrain from owning tobacco stock, foundations may provide low-cost loans to nonprofit organizations, and community organizations may bank with local lending institutions. However, little is known about the extent to which nonprofits make such decisions more frequently than other investors, whether they do so more extensively than previously, and what the short- and long-term financial costs — if any — may be.

Nonprofits may also own real estate property that provides them with rental income. In fact, the Illinois facilities project (see Appendix A) found that 21 percent of nonprofit social service agencies in Illinois had rental income, as did 14 percent of organizations primarily involved in community development, housing, or advocacy (Grønbjerg, Nagle, Garvin, and Wingate, 1992). Nonprofits own, purchase, or build property to house their own programs. Community development organizations create or participate in housing investment corporations that rent to local families or businesses. Nonprofits also receive real estate as gifts from individual donors or from commercial institutions. For example, savings and loans institutions have increasingly donated property to nonprofit organizations in order to write off bad loans associated with the property. In other cases, some landlords donate or sell property to nonprofit organizations in order to circumvent code violations or housing court orders.

Donated or other owned real estate property may not be suitable or needed for the activities of the organization and therefore may provide opportunities for rental income, in which case it may require specialized management skills and direct outlays for maintenance and improvements. As in the case of investment income, the for-profit sector has developed a variety of strategies for managing such income streams—for example, different lease arrangements or property management contracts. Nonprofit managers make use of such strategies, but they are not fully confident about their abilities to do so effectively. The Illinois facilities project found that 41 percent of nonprofit human service organizations thought it would be useful for them to obtain more information on owning or managing buildings (Grønbjerg, Nagle, Garvin, and Wingate, 1992).

Two of the six social service organizations included among the case-study organizations owned buildings and rented space to families or local businesses, as did several of the community development organizations. For two of the community organizations, rental income amounted to a substantial proportion of total revenues, but only for a relatively short period of time in their histories.

Like for-profit organizations, nonprofit organizations may also get income from fees, sales, and service charges when they deliver products or services that consumers pay to receive. They have access to the entire range of commercial transactions in structuring their relationships with customers and may choose to apply them fully. Or they may employ sliding fee scales that take the customer's financial resources into account. For-profit organizations engage in similar practices, but for different reasons, when they provide discounts to preferred customers. In the case of nonprofit organizations, however, the sliding fees and service charges may be insufficient to meet the full costs of providing the goods and services. Sliding fee structures also require the organization to establish procedures for discriminating among customers and may involve complex administrative structures.

As I show in Chapter Five, several aspects of transactions associated with fees and service charges have important management implications. The transaction may be directly with the customer or may involve a third party when insurance companies pay the charges. In the latter case, the third-party payer acts as a co-consumer and exerts control over the transaction, that is, establishes payment scales, accepts only certain products or services for reimbursement, and in other ways institutionalizes the relationship.

The customer may be an individual person or an organization. This distinction is important because organizations generally control more resources than do individuals. Transactions with individuals are therefore likely to involve relatively small purchases (for example, hours of counseling) or have long periods of inactivity if they involve large purchases (such as college tuition).Transactions with organizations may provide the recipient organizations with larger streams of revenues on a more continuous basis. In addition, transactions with individuals are likely to be more fragile than those with organizations, because the latter involve more contractual forms of decision making.

Finally, the transactions may involve a fixed customer base, people who purchase the services on a continuing basis for a sustained period of time and with whom the organization can develop an established and well-informed relationship, as in the case of day-care services. Or the customer base may be fluid, as in the case of appendectomies or short-term counseling. In this case, the organization must seek a constant stream of new customers to replace those that have received the service and no longer need it.

Strategies for obtaining membership dues resemble fees and service charges in many respects. These strategies involve marketing the organization and its activities to individuals or organizations by emphasizing that it provides services of sufficient value to warrant the level of payments that dues represent. However, dues have major advantages over fees and service charges because they eliminate some of the uncertainties associated with straight commercial transactions.

By definition, dues payments reflect ongoing transactions by creating a structure (membership) that ties the consumer to the organization for a period of time, usually a year (fixed customers), and are extended on a cyclical basis through the renewal of memberships. That reduces the amount of effort the organization must devote to finding new customers, allows it to obtain better information about customer interests, and increases its ability to schedule and plan work on a cyclical or regular basis. Dues usually involve flat charges, although the organization may distinguish between categories of members. Even so, dues are relatively easy to administer.

The benefits that members purchase through the payment of dues may extend beyond the narrow self-interests involved in traditional market transactions (for example, receipt of publications, discounts, access to services). Members may pay dues not simply because of direct benefits to themselves but because they believe the organization promotes important societal goals that they share. Under these circumstances, dues become the functional equivalent of donations for both the donor and the recipient organization — documenting the extent of community support that the organization enjoys. That is often the case for professional, fraternal, advocacy, and community organizations.

Those recognized as charitable organizations have official documentation of their importance: their goals have sufficient public value that they are exempt from taxes and eligible to receive tax-deductible donations. For tax purposes, dues are not donations. However, in practice, the boundary between the two appears murky. For example, several of the community organizations included in the case studies appear to shift their definition of payment streams among these categories. It is also difficult to decide what it actually costs to generate dues payments and whether they constitute net profits or losses.

Finally, proceeds from special events also involve commercial transactions in which customers pay an inflated price for services. Most special events cater to the interests of potential customers in particular types of entertainment or confirm or satisfy customers' status aspirations. Organizations that seek proceeds from special events must understand and cater to entertainment tastes or concepts of celebrity status, both of which are likely to be unstable over time and to vary from one person to the next.

As in the case of dues payments, proceeds from special events may cross the boundary to donations. Customers may attend the event not simply for the direct benefits they receive but because they support the purpose of the organization. With the possible exception of street fairs and other events that are open to the general public, most customers probably assume that the price they pay to attend special events exceeds the normal commercial charge for the event. In some cases, nonprofits specify the excess charge involved, in order to allow customers to treat it as a legitimate, tax-deductible donation to the organization. More commonly, customers and recipient organizations appear to view the entire price as just another form of donation.

Subsidy Revenue from Donors and Public Agencies. Most other types of revenues available to nonprofits involve some form of subsidy to underwrite a broad or narrow range of organizational activities. Donations from a variety of sources and grants and contracts from government agencies make it possible for the recipient organization to expand the range, quantity, or quality of services or products beyond the levels that its own market activities can support.

However, subsidy revenues separate customers from clients. The customer (donor or tax payer), who pays a nonprofit organization to deliver a product or service, does not directly consume the product or service, and rarely even knows the client who does (the drug addict, high school dropout, or refugee). This is a critical separation, because it means that efforts to satisfy client needs or demands do not necessarily satisfy customer needs or demands—and vice versa. In the case of the self-generated sources of revenues discussed above—rent, fees, sales, service charges, dues, and proceeds from special events—the customers are the clients.

Individuals make donations to nonprofit organizations for a variety of reasons, including economic incentives (lower taxes), status aspirations (search for recognition), and support for social action (expression of cohesion, promotion of social change). A nonprofit organization that seeks donations from individuals will emphasize its support for a particular social action, because that distinguishes it from other organizations that also seek donations. The opportunity to affect social action in a particular direction is a powerful incentive for some donors and may result in the organization's being co-opted by them (Odendahl, 1990; Ostrander, 1984).

The more sophisticated nonprofits pay close attention to economic and status incentives as well. The development and marketing of planned giving programs, such as trusts and bequests, emphasize tax advantages for potential donors, as does the year-end timing of solicitation appeals. The distribution of pins, emblems, mailing labels, and the like, allows donors to publicize their support and markets the organization to other donors. The publication of annual reports or lists of donors not only meets legal require-ments to identify sources of support but also serves to provide donors with name recognition (for example, "We regret that we cannot publish the names of donors who contribute less than $25").

The naming of buildings, rooms, chairs (academic or otherwise), and other property in recognition of large donations highlights efforts to provide donors with degrees of recognition (and corresponding status). The listing of donors by named categories that reflect donation amounts reveals similar attempts to differentiate the amount of rewards for donors. The number and designation of such categories are truly impressive and bewildering: there are angels, guarantors, benefactors, sponsors, patrons, friends, supporters, and donors, among others — and not necessarily in that order. At times, each of these categories may be further differentiated by the addition of such adjectives as *distinguished*, *major*, or *sustaining*. However, neither the category names nor amounts are standardized from one nonprofit organization to the next.

These practices are part of a general trend in which nonprofits in-creasingly seek to specify a particular product that a given level of donations will support (for example, a donation of "$7 will feed a homeless cat for a month" or "$129.84 will print one page of the magazine"). Indeed, some fund-raising professionals refer to the process of deciding what level of donation deserves a given tier of recognition as "selling the project." Such an approach blurs the distinction between donations and product sales by encouraging donors to shop for the best bargain. It also demonstrates the strength and intuitive appeal of commercial-like transactions. The development of cause-related marketing, in which businesses employ charitable donations to orga-nizations of the customer's choice as ways to promote their own products, further blurs the boundary between commercial and charitable transactions.

Like fee-paying clients, most donors do not know exactly how their contribution is used (unless they specify certain activities as a condition for the gift). They expect the recipient organization to use the funds responsibly and for appropriate purposes. For that reason, individual donors tend to be repeat donors: having made the assumption once, they are likely to believe that the condition of trust still holds. To increase their batting average in the solicitations game, nonprofits therefore rely heavily on exploiting any exist-ing contact with potential donors, such as prior donations, attendance at special events, membership in the personal networks of board and staff members, or affiliation with an organized constituency (for example, geo-graphical, religious, ethnic, or ideological communities). However, most individual donors have only limited opportunities to verify their assumption of trust directly or to develop informed judgments about the recipient organization, as they might if they were also clients of the organization. These features make the initiation and maintenance of donation transactions more difficult and uncertain than is the case for market transactions.

The remaining sources of donations are other organizations, such as businesses or corporations, churches, foundations, and federated funding organizations. There are some advantages to seeking donations from organizations rather than from individuals: fewer potential donors and more information about them in the public domain (for instance, in business news, publications or annual reports) simplify efforts to identify them and obtain useful information about them (such as focal interests or financial capacity). They are likely to control larger amounts of resources, thus promising greater return for the effort to seek donations. And they have staff, procedures, and complex decision-making structures, thus ensuring more systematic attention to requests for donations as well as possible access to multiple appeal routes.

On the other hand, organizational donors are more likely than individuals to require recipient organizations to exhibit specified types of organizational behavior as a condition for making the donation. Such requirements include making formal requests for donations in writing, specifying the activity for which support is being sought, preparing reports on accomplishments, designating official contact persons, and submitting financial documents for review. These traits exemplify the tendency toward isomorphism that develops when organizations interact with one another (DiMaggio and Powell, 1983).

Among organizational donors, corporations probably resemble individuals most closely in the extent to which they expect to receive financial, status, and social action benefits (Galaskiewicz, 1985, 1986; Useem, 1984). The exchange relationships with other types of organizational donors are less likely to reflect direct financial interests because these donors are nonprofit organizations themselves and therefore are not subject to tax incentives, thus removing one of the major financial inducements.

For nonprofit donors, the exchange relations are also likely to downplay status benefits and to focus primarily on social action benefits because the donors themselves are expected to pursue substantive goals. For example, some of the financial support by churches to nonprofit service organizations reflects attachments to particular organizations (such as those sharing similar religious auspices). In other cases, mainline churches have identified specific social issues for support, as have many foundations and most federated funding organizations.

However, there are major differences in the extent to which recipient organizations establish ongoing exchange relations with nonprofit donors. Foundation grants, like individual or corporate donations, tend to be time limited and involve considerable uncertainty in terms of the amount and continuity of support. In contrast, major religious federations, United Way organizations, and alternative funds (environment, civic rights) operate as membership structures. Member organizations are entitled to ongoing support from year to year in return for adherence to specified governance, fundraising, reporting, and/or program criteria. These institutionalized relationships require recipient organizations to give up varying degrees of organizational discretion in exchange for stable, predictable funding.

Government grants and contracts involve even more explicit exchange agreements. Primarily for historical reasons (Grønbjerg, 1987; Brown, 1941; Johnson, 1931), nonprofits (especially in the social service field) frequently control resources that complement or substitute for similar types of public resources and therefore are of particular interest to public agencies: they own or operate particular types of facilities (such as group homes, day-care centers, health clinics, and homeless shelters), employ staff with certain types of skills or training (for instance, therapists or community organizers), or adopt specific service models (such as drug prevention or job training) that relate closely to legislative mandates for public activities.

To access these existing resources and infrastructures, public agencies award grants and contracts to nonprofits, in return for which the latter agree to undertake specified tasks, in particular locations and/or for certain clients, using preestablished reporting formats, during a designated period of time, and subject to stipulated monitoring efforts in exchange for a given level of funding and, at times, some level of technical support. In service fields where government agencies rely extensively on nonprofits to execute public mandates, contractual relationships between nonprofits and public agencies are numerous, complex, and involve significant exchanges of funds.

As I show in subsequent chapters, these are demanding, institutionalized exchange relationships that can involve all levels of government, at times simultaneously, for a given funding stream. The relationships differ somewhat as to whether the funding consists of grants, fee-for-service agreements, or performance contracts. These payment structures are variously modeled on donations (grants) or commercial exchanges (fee-for-service and performance contracts).

In the case of grants, the recipient organization agrees to perform specified tasks (for example, engage x number of low-income pregnant teenagers in parent-education programs during the next y months) and must document that it has done so while using the funding for designated expense categories. In fee-for-service agreements, the subcontractor gets paid a fixed price per unit of service that it provides (for example, per hour of client counseling or per client day of institutional care). Usually, the payments cover only eligible clients and cannot exceed a specified maximum number of units for a given period. The organization must document that it has delivered the service units to eligible clients. In performance-based contracts, the organization gets paid according to how well it meets specified program objectives. It may receive a fixed payment per unemployed teenager who completes a training program and an additional fixed payment if the teen is subsequently employed for a minimum period of time. It receives no payments if it does not achieve any of the performance requirements, regardless of the amount of efforts it invests or the number of clients it serves.

Each of the funding sources discussed here involves a particular form of exchange and is institutionalized to some degree. Each constitutes what Milofsky (1987) and others describe as a funding arena in which exchange partners relate to one another in distinctive ways. When both parties are organizations, the partners are especially likely to follow standard, expected patterns that transcend decisions or preferences by individual organizations. Even if the funding originates with individuals, as in individual donations, client-paid fees, or attendance at special events, the relationships adhere to institutionalized procedures for securing the funding—that is, the use of recognized techniques for building donor commitments to an organization. There are equally institutionalized expectations about what the specific exchange is likely to involve, that is, status recognition and tax advantages to donors, flexible funding for recipient organizations.

Summary

Financial resources differ in how prevalent they are and therefore in how likely organizations are to have experience with them or easy access to such knowledge. They vary in how much they contribute to total revenues and therefore in how critical they are to organizational survival. They vary also in how likely organizations are to have continued access to them, how similar they are to other revenue sources to which organizations may have access, and in how much discretion they leave for internal management decisions, and therefore in how much attention organizations must devote to them.

The degree to which funding sources absorb management energy in these manners depends to a significant extent on the nature of the exchange relationship involved. Two dimensions are especially important: (1) whether the exchange approaches a market exchange for which well-established norms and procedures for commercial transactions hold, or whether it approaches a subsidy transaction in which those who pay for the service do not consume it; and (2) how similar the exchange partner is to the organization itself, whether it is an individual, private firm, government agency, or other nonprofit organization.

Notes

1. This is no different from recognizing that the gender composition of a classroom (macro-level characteristic) affects the behavior of individual students (micro-level impact) or that the racial composition of a neighborhood alters how residents conduct themselves.

2. Other types of nonprofit organizations excluded from this analysis, such as day-care centers, health-related agencies, membership associations, or arts and cultural organizations, are likely to depend much more heavily on funding from these commercial sources.
3. These structural characteristics are elaborated in greater detail in Chapter Twelve. I focus on only a few key elements here.

FOUR

Trends in
Nonprofit Funding Patterns

Resource relationships change over time as broader social and economic trends favor some funders and not others. Resource relationships also
change as new practices in fund-raising, contract writing, and similar procedures become established and widely shared among funders or fund
recipients and past practices disappear from the organizational inventory.
Changes in resource relationships over time and differences in the volume of
financial resources they produce for nonprofit organizations in turn contribute to the overall growth and development of the sector and of individual
organizations.

Growth and Stability in the Two Sectors

These overall patterns are difficult to determine because the nonprofit sector
lacks an adequate historical data base, except for fields with the largest and
most institutionalized organizations, such as hospitals and institutions of
higher education (see Appendix A). Nevertheless, some general assessments
are possible. I summarize likely patterns of growth and stability for specific
revenue streams as they relate to the two sectors included in this study. By
necessity, I focus most of my attention on the social service field because little
systematic work has been done on community organizations.

Increases in Earned Revenues

Little is known about long-term trends in earned revenues for the two sectors.
However, most available information suggests increases in both prevalence
and overall amount. As Table 3.1 shows, about three-fifths of Chicago-area
social service and community development organizations had fees and other
sources of earned revenues in 1982. By 1984, a sizable proportion of both
groups were further exploring a range of for-profit activities. For example,

while only 7 percent of the organizations had tried to establish a for-profit subsidiary during the 1982–1984 period, an additional 22 percent were planning to do so over the 1984–1986 period. Similarly, 32 percent had instituted or were planning new or increased fees and service charges and 30 percent had instituted or were planning product sales to generate revenues. Indeed, adjusted for inflation, fees and service charges increased by 38 percent and added 7 percent to the aggregate income of Chicago-area social service agencies between 1981 and 1984—their major source of growth.[1]

Other indications include the numerous manuals, guidelines, reports, and articles that encourage nonprofit organizations to explore earned revenue options (and to worry about tax problems associated with relying too much on unrelated business income). For example, in volume 1 of its bibliography on the literature of the nonprofit sector, the Foundation Center lists sixty-eight entries under nonprofit entrepreneurship (Derrickson, 1989). The second volume, published one year later, includes forty-five additional entries (Derrickson and Kurdylo, 1990).

Most of this material has appeared in the last five to ten years, suggesting that a growing number of consultants and other analysts have recognized opportunities for advising nonprofit organizations about these topics, whether because earned revenues have actually increased or because the U.S. celebration of market forces has increasingly infiltrated the nonprofit sector to legitimize its pursuit of market transactions. The well-publicized cuts (or threats thereof) in federal spending for broadly defined welfare purposes since the late 1970s have undoubtedly provided further incentives—and legitimacy—for such experiments.

These factors are likely to have increased the amount and penetration of earned revenues across the board for all nonprofit categories. However, the two sectors included in this book also have special and somewhat different interests in seeking earned income. For example, social service organizations, and professional social workers in particular, have long endorsed the requirement that clients pay a fee (even just a token amount) for services received. They have argued that the payment of fees serves important therapeutic functions because only clients who are committed to accepting the professional's services are likely to obtain full benefit from any treatment received. The payment of fees demonstrates—and requires—some minimum level of commitment.

Clients that are willing to pay fees, of course, also serve the obvious function of confirming that they find the services and the organization of value and utility. The result is likely to be a self-reinforcing process by which social workers find personal and professional rewards, and nonprofit organizations find revenues, in serving fee-paying clients (Hasenfeld, 1978). They may pursue such clients to the point of disengaging themselves from the poor (Cloward and Epstein, 1965), because low-income clients cannot pay much and have complex problems that are difficult to serve effectively (Grønbjerg, 1990b).

The pattern is more complex for community development organizations. Many community organizations have membership structures and view the pursuit of dues-paying members as a legitimate part of their purpose. Just as fee-paying clients document that clients are committed to self-improvement in the case of social service agencies, dues-paying members document community involvement and support for community action in the case of community development organizations. For both types of organizations, earned revenues are likely to have had persistent legitimacy over time.

For community development organizations, several more recent conditions are likely to have increased access to, and legitimacy of, fees and service charges. Inner-city neighborhoods have experienced major and prolonged decline as middle-class families, businesses, and manufacturing firms moved to the suburbs after World War II. The more recent economic decline of the Northeast and the Midwest has accelerated the effects for these regions. These developments have forced increasing numbers of community organizations in cities like Chicago to devote sustained attention to housing and economic development in their communities to counteract these trends.

To do so, community organizations have taken on a wide variety of new initiatives in partnerships with local businesses, real estate developers, and manufacturing firms, at times also involving governmental units as active or passive partners. In some cases, the result has been the development of formally incorporated joint ventures between for-profit establishments and nonprofit community organizations, with the latter receiving a share of the profit (that is, earned revenues). Regulatory developments at the federal level, such as community reinvestment requirements for financial institutions and efforts to eliminate redlining, have opened up additional market niches — and sources of earnings — for community organizations. Many of them have worked closely with financial institutions to help local commercial establishments negotiate the borrowing process in return for loan-packaging fees.

Local businesses, like all for-profit establishments, have obvious affinities for commercial transactions and expect to pay for services received. Community organizations that seek to support and provide services to for-profit establishments are likely to benefit from such expectations. They may encounter few if any protests by community residents, board members, or clients if they charge for their services.

Growing Prevalence of Special Events

Special events are sufficiently widespread to be among the types of activities in which nonprofit organizations normally engage. As shown in Table 3.1, about 40 percent of social service agencies and 20 percent of the community development organizations reported income from a combination of special events and other sources in 1982. Almost half (50 and 44 percent, respectively) reported in 1984 that they had tried to raise funds from special events over the previous two years (1982–1984), and an even larger proportion (69 percent) indicated that they were planning to do so during the next two years (1984–1986). A more recent survey, with explicit questions about special events revenues, shows similar levels of participation. For example, almost half (47 percent) of human service organizations in Illinois report some income from special events in 1990, although only about one-quarter received as much as 5 percent of total revenues from them (Grønbjerg, Nagle, Garvin, and Wingate, 1992).

The actual prevalence of special events is not well established, because most surveys do not include questions about the extent to which organizations engage in this type of activity or about the amount of revenues they generate. Even when such questions are asked, revenue data from surveys are difficult to use effectively because most organizations are likely to report only net revenues (in agreement with the reporting format of IRS tax forms). Gross revenues would provide a better indication of the scope of events activities in which nonprofit organizations engage. Selective accounts and newspaper reports provide anecdotal evidence of large and extremely successful events and also document that some nonprofits obtain significant proportions of their total revenues from such activities. However, there are very few data or scholarly research studies on how widespread or important special events are and even fewer on whether social service agencies differ from community development organizations on these dimensions.

Uncertain Trends in Donations

Historically, many nonprofit organizations were founded by major gifts. Most nonprofits receive donations; in fact, donations constitute a significant proportion of some nonprofits' operating revenues (Hall, 1987; McCarthy, 1982). However, in spite of the prevalence of donations, no single type of donor dominates funding to social service or community development organizations (see Table 3.1). Even when all types of donations are combined, only one-quarter (28 percent) of social service agencies receive more than half of their revenues from donations, and just 8 percent get 70 percent or more this way. Those that rely heavily on donations tend to be quite small and to have turbulent funding histories.

A higher proportion of community development organizations rely extensively on donations. Almost half (47 percent) get most of their revenues from donations, and one-third obtain more than 70 percent this way. Their greater dependence on donations most likely reflects their ready-made access to constituency groups: local businesses, schools, churches, hospitals, and community residents. As a result, they do not always distinguish between donations and dues, referring to community support as dues when highlighting their expectations of regular, ongoing support from these groups, but reporting the revenue as donations to make it tax deductible for those who pay it.

However, several studies suggest that donations to human service organizations have failed to keep up with growth in other revenue sources, especially fees and other earned revenues. Salamon, Musselwhite, Holcomb, and Grønbjerg (1987) found that the average Chicago nonprofit organization (exclusive of hospitals and educational institutions) lost 4 percent of its donation revenue between 1981 and 1983. Corresponding donation losses occurred in several of the other fifteen communities included in the Nonprofit Sector Project. Galaskiewicz and Bielefeld (1990) found similar patterns for a Minneapolis–St. Paul panel study of nonprofit organizations during the 1980–1988 period. Donations did increase, but not as much as fee income, and accounted for a smaller share of total revenues at the end of the period than at the beginning.

The Illinois Department of Children and Family Services (DCFS) provider project (see Appendix A) shows that inflation-adjusted aggregate revenues increased by 18 percent over the 1985–1990 period for 225 child welfare organizations in Illinois with complete information for both years (Grønbjerg and Stagner, 1992). However, aggregate donations for the organizations declined by 3 percent, while government funding and fee income each increased by 22 percent and special events receipts by 13 percent.

Several factors may account for the relatively slow growth in donations for these organizations.[2] Thus, national data show that the overall level of donations (adjusted for inflation and population growth) increased from 1960 until the 1970s, stabilized until the early 1980s, and then increased modestly again (Grønbjerg, 1988).[3] However, related data suggest that human service organizations lost ground in securing their share of donations, especially during the early 1970s. Social welfare organizations, primarily social service organizations, received only about 10 percent of these funds,[4] virtually unchanged since the mid 1970s but down from 14 percent in 1970.

The relatively small increases in donations to these organizations (primarily social service but also community development organizations) suggest that they have been particularly vulnerable to economic and social trends that either threaten the overall level of donations or affect donors of particular interest to them. For example, communities dominated by manufacturing industries and homogeneous populations generally have high levels of donations (Wolpert, 1989). As manufacturing industries move to rural communities or leave the country and as immigration and natural increase add disproportionately to the size of minority groups, donations may stagnate or decline. Such community transformations have been widespread in the United States and characterize Chicago as well. They also affect some donors and service fields more than others. The result is likely to be particularly intense competition for donor dollars among social service and community development organizations.

Greater Competition for Individual Donors. Most donations are made by individuals (84 percent in 1989); foundations and bequests accounted for only about 6 percent each and corporations for the remaining 4 percent.

Almost all of the change in the overall level of philanthropic donations is accounted for by changes in individual donations, especially in recent years, and by growth in donations to religious organizations.[5] The competition for individual donations is therefore likely to have become more intense for social service and community development organizations.

Community economic transformations, as well as the increasing inequality of income distribution in the United States (Michel, 1991), may account for these trends. Lower-income groups disproportionately give their donations to churches, while upper-income groups tend to favor educational and cultural institutions (Odendahl, 1989, 1990). Although lower-income groups donate a larger proportion of their income than middle-income households, their average donation is smaller and they are more likely to decrease their donations compared with previous years (Hodgkinson, Weitzman, and the Gallup Organization, 1988). The growth of lower-income families and corresponding decline of middle-income groups may therefore reduce contributions to nonprofit human service agencies (while increasing demand for their services).

The amount of donations they receive from individuals is threatened by other developments as well. A variety of groups now promote a wide variety of advocacy issues (from environmental conditions to abortion and school prayer). Almost all of them have sought support from individuals and appealed to them on the basis of ideological beliefs. The direct involvement by national political figures in many of these issues (for example, the Reagan and Bush administrations' full-scale attack on abortion rights) has given salience to these issues and visibility to the advocacy groups, and in the process has galvanized support for the groups. Human service organizations are likely to face greater difficulty in achieving similar levels of visibility and personal salience for their appeals.

Changing Composition of Churches and Sacramental Organizations. Churches receive the largest proportion of all donations (mostly from individuals). They redistribute part of their revenues (about 17 percent) to other nonprofit organizations, primarily denominational organizations, and small amounts of support directly to individuals (Hodgkinson, Weitzman, and Kirsch, 1990). The form and amount of redistribution reflect the financial health of the congregations and their preference for supporting the services of other organizations rather than undertaking the activities themselves.

The extent to which churches provide financial support of this type varies with different religious ideologies. Some accept broad stewardship for human conditions; others focus on inner-worldly religious life. The recent decline of mainline liberal denominations (Wood, 1990; Roof and McKinney, 1987) probably means that church support for human service organizations has declined correspondingly. Conservative, fundamentalist, and new religious sects are likely to fund only a narrow range of activities, most of which they control directly.

Declining Resource Base of United Way Organizations. United Way fund-ing was equivalent to about one-quarter of all philanthropic donations for welfare purposes and stood at $3.1 billion nationally in 1990. However, aggregate United Way campaigns have only in the last couple of years recovered losses during the late 1970s and early 1980s to recapture the 1970 level of $9 per capita (in constant 1981 dollars), up from $7.20 per capita in 1982. The United Way of Chicago has generally exceeded these amounts. Allocations to member agencies amounted to about $6–$8 per Chicago resident (in 1981 dollars) from the early 1930s through the mid 1950s. Allocations then increased to about $12 by the late 1960s and stayed at that level through the early 1980s. Since then, allocations reached $14 in 1987 and have stayed close to that level through 1990.

The United Way is one of the most institutionalized means of obtain-ing donations for social service agencies (Brilliant, 1990). Traditionally, local United Way organizations solicit employers to make corporate contributions to the annual campaign, encourage employees to have a portion of their paycheck withheld as a donation, and manage the collection of donations. The funds are then allocated by volunteer committees in the form of base allocations to nonprofit service agencies that meet membership criteria and agree to restrict their own fund-raising efforts. The centralized fund-raising structure, high reliance on volunteer decision making, and emphasis on membership standards are devised to collect funds efficiently and ensure their effective use. The system of base allocations aims to provide member organizations with stable, flexible funding.

In recent years, however, most United Way organizations have been under considerable pressure to match a stagnant revenue base with demands for more inclusive allocations. Few have had sufficient increases in annual campaign contributions to offset inflation, and some have had declines in annual collections. The stagnant revenue base reflects the community eco-nomic transformations described above and the changing utility of the United Way's exclusive reliance on workplace solicitation.

The economic restructuring of the corporate economy means that a larger proportion of local places of employment are owned by corporations located in other cities or nations. These firms are less likely to participate in local United Way campaigns. The decline of manufacturing firms also leaves fewer employers with a large number of well-paid, disciplined workers. The growth of service industries and of small businesses means a corresponding increase in low-paid workers and a large number of new businesses to solicit, incorporate, and socialize into the annual campaign.

The workplace solicitation system has also come under political pres-sure. The effectiveness of the system in obtaining access to donors and securing donations has meant that increasing numbers of nonprofits have sought access to the system. The dominance by business groups in local

United Way organizations and the fairly demanding membership requirements mean that newer, controversial, or activist organizations have found it
difficult to obtain funds or membership (Trolander, 1987; Brilliant, 1990).

However, under pressure from civil rights organizations and other
advocacy groups, most United Way organizations have opened up their
membership to newer groups. Yet, even when admitted to membership, they
obtain very small levels of support because only small increments of funds
are available once older members have obtained their base allocations. For
example, over the 1987–1991 period, new members in the United Way of
Chicago received average allocations of less than $50,000, while existing
members had average allocations of more than $500,000. Moreover, the
increase in member organizations places additional strain on the capacity to
increase allocations to existing members and contributes to conflict within
United Way organizations.

For the same reasons, a growing number of United Ways, under pressure from federal employees and other groups, have also had to relinquish
their monopoly on workplace solicitations. Some have abandoned the system of base allocation to member organizations in favor of competitive
awards or designations by donors for particular categories of services or
specific recipient organizations. The United Way resource base, then, appears to be declining at the same time as local United Way organizations have
become locations for turf battles among competing demands.

The United Way of Chicago exemplifies these tensions. It has adopted
an intermediary strategy of temporarily freezing base allocations while
phasing in a new priority system that distributes 10 percent of allocations in
the form of competitive, three-year grants for high-priority problems in low-
income communities. The grants are open to member organizations and
other agencies that agree to meet minimum membership standards over the
period of the grant. The priority grant system has met with considerable
opposition from agencies with long membership in the United Way and
correspondingly large base allocations. The grant system has survived so far,
but only because Chicago annual campaigns have been successful enough to
phase in the grant program while also awarding several "one-time" increases
to base allocations.

Mixed Patterns for Corporate and Foundation Donors. Per capita corporate contributions have increased from just over $3 in 1975 (in 1981 dollars)
to about $5 in 1981 and since then have fluctuated between $5 and $6.
However, corporate donations for health and human services have remained
level since 1975, while support for other beneficiaries has increased. In 1989,
38 percent of corporate philanthropy benefited educational institutions
(primarily higher education). Health and human services jointly received 26
percent, down from 41 percent in 1975.

The same factors that threaten the workplace success of United Way
campaigns also affect direct corporate donations to nonprofits. Increasing

international competition and declining productivity of American businesses suggest that nonprofit organizations are likely to encounter long-term problems in obtaining corporate donations, except perhaps as part of marketing or promotion strategies. The growth in absentee corporate owners and in small businesses may hurt social service agencies most severely, because they are likely to find it difficult to convince these owners or managers of the need to support social service activities. These same trends may be less fateful for community development organizations, because they tend to view small businesses (at least) as clients and potential dues-paying members and are likely to cater to their interests.

Foundations are closely tied to corporations. Some foundations are operating arms of major corporations, while others are established by individuals whose wealth derives from business activities. Still others are independent foundations with assets and earnings that stem from corporate investments. Most have corporate or business representatives as members of their boards of directors. Foundation support for nonprofits is therefore likely to parallel corporate donations to a significant extent. National trends suggest fairly close correspondence between the two. Private foundations awarded about one-quarter of their funding to welfare purposes (25 percent), with health accounting for an additional 17 percent in 1989. Since 1980, private foundation grants have increased from $6 per capita (in 1981 dollars) to almost $10 in 1989, with welfare sharing proportionately in the increase, although health has experienced a decline.

Other developments may also affect corporate and foundation support for social services and community development. Both types of giving programs are becoming increasingly professionalized, with corresponding emphasis on standards and criteria for recipient organizations. The emergence of funder coalitions (including local foundation councils) and attempts to establish effective giving criteria will most likely also favor organizations that demonstrate management skills and organizational capacity. Smaller human service organizations may find it difficult to meet these expectations.

These structural changes in donation sources, combined with an overall increase in the number of nonprofits, suggest that competition for donations is likely to become increasingly difficult for both social service and community development organizations. Certainly, solicitation efforts have become increasingly sophisticated, with carefully designed marketing strategies, elaborate media campaigns, and impressive campaign goals. Such efforts are likely to be beyond the scope of smaller nonprofit organizations, such as those that dominate the community organization field and are found frequently in the social service field as well.

Although they may fall even further behind as the solicitation process becomes more elaborate and institutionalized, as changing tax structures erode economic incentives to donations, and as recessions and economic restructuring diminish surplus income, it is not for lack of trying. Many have explored a wide range of fund-raising strategies. Survey data from 1984 show that the vast majority of social service and community development organizations either tried or planned to seek foundation funding (90 percent), use board members for fund-raising (87 percent), or develop long-range fund-raising plans (76 percent). About one-third either tried or planned to seek membership in the United Way (39 percent), obtain inclusion in wills (32 percent), or hire outside fund-raising experts (30 percent). Social service agencies were significantly more likely to have engaged in the latter three strategies (47–42 percent) than community development organizations (19–0 percent).

Curtailment of Previous Growth in Government Funding

Government funding has been available to nonprofit organizations in a variety of service fields for many years, although not continuously or persistently. Until the 1960s, federal policies discouraged financial transactions between nonprofit organizations and government agencies, although state and local governments frequently provided financial support to nonprofit social service agencies delivering institutional care for children, the aged, and the disabled (Grønbjerg, 1987; Coll, 1969; Werner, 1961; Johnson, 1931).

The introduction of social services for public assistance recipients (1956, 1962), the War on Poverty (1965), and the 1973 amendment to the Social Security Act (Title XX) transformed the relationship between private and public welfare. The two became directly linked when amendments to the Social Security Act mandated that public assistance recipients be entitled to appropriate services (1956) and allowed state and local governments to contract with nonprofit social service organizations (1962) to provide such services. The Community Action Programs of the War on Poverty (1965) and Title XX (1973) made additional public funding available to nonprofits by subsidizing social services, community organizing, and other benefits to people who were not welfare recipients.

Since then, the system of grants and contracts between government agencies and nonprofit human service organizations has become extensive and fully institutionalized (Grønbjerg, 1981), and public grants and contracts have come to be the single largest source of revenue for nonprofit service agencies. Excluding hospitals and educational institutions, public funding accounted for an estimated 32 percent of aggregate revenues for Chicago-area nonprofit organizations in 1981 (Grønbjerg, Kimmich, and Salamon, 1985), more than donations or fees (28 percent each).

As Table 3.1 showed, public funding is prevalent among the types of nonprofits included in this study. Fully 90 percent of Chicago-area social service agencies and 67 percent of community development organizations reported some public funding in 1982. For more than half (55 percent) of the social service agencies and more than a quarter (27 percent) of the community development organizations, public funding was the major source of funding, accounting for more than half of all revenues.

These data come from the early 1980s, when broad cuts in federal funding for a variety of social purposes had been under way for several years. The major recession during the same period strained state and local government efforts to compensate for the cuts, and they reduced their own spending as well. As a result, public funding for nonprofit organizations declined significantly during the early 1980s. This was the case for Chicago-area nonprofit organizations (Salamon, Musselwhite, Holcomb, and Grønbjerg, 1987), although the social service agencies among them held their own.

Since then, fragmentary data suggest that public funding for nonprofit human service organizations has increased. Hodgkinson and Weitzman (1989) estimate that charitable social and legal service organizations gained about 15 percent in total government support over the 1984–1987 period. By 1987, the level of public support exceeded the 1977 level by 3 percent. Similarly, public funding for civic, social, and fraternal organizations (which includes community development organizations) increased by 18 percent over the 1984–1987 period and exceeded the 1977 level by 15 percent (all adjusted for inflation). These analyses are based on estimates of changes in federal spending and may not incorporate changes in state and local government spending.

The survey of Illinois child welfare agencies discussed previously provides additional documentation (Grønbjerg and Stagner, 1992). For the 225 organizations that provided complete revenue information for both 1985 and 1990, total revenues increased from $269 million to $319 million, and growth in public funding accounted for almost all (16 out of 18 percentage points) of the increase. For the average organization, public funding increased by about 68 percent over five years previously (all in constant 1989 dollars). It is difficult to know how representative these trends are, because they reflect in part legally mandated expenditures for child abuse and neglect cases.

Comprehensive data on the extent of public funding are difficult to obtain because of the large number of governmental units involved and the lack of information about what types of organizations receive government funding. Most likely, public funding for nonprofits follows patterns of public spending for some welfare purposes and developments in relevant aspects of public administration.

Public welfare spending from all levels of government has flattened out in recent years, following a long period of significant increases. Per capita public welfare spending more than quadrupled between 1950 and 1978, up from $585 in 1950 to $2,477 in 1982, until increasing to $2,785 in 1988 (all in constant 1981 dollars). However, most of the increase has come in the areas of income insurance and medical benefits (each up ninefold to, respectively,

$1,061 and $690 per capita in 1988). Expenditures for AFDC and other means-tested income assistance did not even double during that period (up to $216 per capita in 1988).

All other welfare services targeted at low-income groups accounted for less than 2 percent of total public welfare expenditures in 1988, although that was about a tripling of real spending per capita in 1950 ($45 per capita in 1950, $126 in 1988). Nonprofit social service and community development organizations are likely to receive most of their public funding from this smallest and slowest-growing component of public welfare spending.

In spite of such real growth in public welfare spending, more detailed analysis suggests that all levels of government are giving lower priority to human service needs, pointing to future erosion of public funding for nonprofit human service organizations. Federal spending for social insurance and human services has declined from 54.3 percent of federal outlays in 1980 to 50.4 percent in 1987 and from 11.3 percent of the gross national product (GNP) to 11 percent in the same period. State and local government spending has also declined, down from 8 percent of GNP in 1975 to 7.4 percent in 1987. The proportion of total state and local spending allocated to social welfare purposes has similarly declined from 65.3 percent to 59.6 percent (U.S. Bureau of the Census, 1991). The increasing participation of powerful interest groups in the political process through political action committees and lobbying efforts—especially by such industry groups as defense, real estate, energy, banking, construction, agriculture, and transportation—probably accounts at least in part for these developments.

In local communities such as Chicago, state and local government spending may deviate from these national trends. Illinois consistently trails other industrial states in many public policy efforts, although its per capita income ranked it among the top six from 1929 through the late 1970s, when it dropped to eighth place. The city of Chicago also has not established strong commitments to human services from its own funding sources but relies extensively on state and federal grants for much of its human service efforts and keeps these funds separate from its own "corporate" spending. As a result, public spending for human services in the Chicago area from all levels of government compares poorly to other major metropolitan areas (Grønbjerg, Kimmich, and Salamon, 1985).

Current trends point to future constraints in meeting human service needs in Chicago through public efforts. Although the federal government provides most of the funding for human services in Chicago (about half), the state controls most of the spending (almost two-thirds) but has faced continuous fiscal problems since 1982. It has made few if any attempts to compensate for the reduced value of federal funding or to implement any extension of services, except in the child welfare field. In general, Chicago-area social service agencies probably have not experienced major reductions in their public funding but, rather, have experienced a lack of growth and an erosion of purchasing power.

Public spending for community development activities and support for community organizations have seen much more drastic changes. Beginning with public housing developments and urban renewal efforts in the 1950s, the Community Action Programs of the 1960s, and a variety of anticrime and employment and training programs since then, federal funding increasingly targeted inner-city communities. Nixon's Revenue-Sharing Program and Carter's Community Development Block Grants sought to provide local governments with financial resources to address key problems of housing, development, and community organizing, while reducing direct federal involvement. Some of these funds became available to community organizations and constituted a new source of funding for them.

However, almost all of these programs have been eliminated or severely curtailed, with corresponding effects on the level of public funding available to nonprofit community organizations. At best, public funding from these sources has become unpredictable, highly competitive, and increasingly embroiled in local politics. Still, a range of innovative funding sources of particular interest to community organizations has come into existence under the sponsorship of state and local governments. These sources include publicly guaranteed revenue bonds and special service area taxing districts. In the latter case, community organizations may organize and help establish the taxing district, administer the funds, and perform the required activities in return for management fees.

Diversity of Patterns for Individual Organizations

Trends in major types of revenues are also important because each type activates particular exchange relationships. Growth in earned income indicates the extent to which service fields are becoming increasingly market oriented and crossing the line to for-profit establishments. Trends in donations and public grants and contracts determine the volume of subsidized services available.[6] The combination of these developments determines the size of the respective fields and indicates how the environment in which individual nonprofit organizations operate has changed.

However, the fates of individual organizations may deviate significantly from these trends. Each organization brings its own configuration of resources, decisions, and traditions to bear on its resource relationships. This diversity among individual organizations may not show up in most cross-sectional analyses.[7]

Nor does the diversity surface in analyses of aggregate trends. When information from many different organizations is merged, data from organizations with large increases in funding are combined with data from those with large decreases during the same period, so that they may offset one another and produce a pattern of no apparent change. Aggregate trends are also driven by the experiences of large organizations because they account for most of the funds available to the entire set of organizations examined.

Aggregate funding may increase, then, if most of the largest organizations experience growth, even if the much larger number of smaller organizations have decreases in funding. Their more typical experiences are obscured.

In fact, year-by-year analyses for individual organizations reveal very high levels of funding turbulence, both in terms of total revenues and with respect to gross categories of funding sources. The panel study of social service organizations in the Chicago area shows that over the 1981–1984 period, some individual organizations lost as much as 44 percent of their total revenues, while others gained some 733 percent (adjusted for inflation).[8] One-fifth of the social service organizations (19 percent) lost at least 10 percent of their total revenues (adjusted for inflation) over the four-year period as a whole, while more than one-third (35 percent) increased their size by at least 25 percent over the period. Annual changes were less extreme, but still impressive. Each year, some organizations lost at least a quarter of their total revenues, while others more than doubled and even tripled theirs.

These patterns also hold when changes in overall funding levels are decomposed into major sources of revenues. To show how widespread these changes have been for individual organizations, I developed an index of funding turbulence based on how much changes in each of four major funding sources (earned revenues, donations, government funding, or other income) contribute to the organizations' overall growth or decline.[9] The index separates those organizations that experienced only relatively modest changes in broadly defined funding sources (amounting to no more than 5 percent of base income from any one funding source) from those that had seen extensive change (up or down) in at least one major funding source (equivalent to at least one-quarter of the agency's total revenues in the base year). I classified the remaining organizations as having an intermediate level of turbulence.

As Table 4.1 shows, for each year over the 1981–1984 period, between one-third and two-fifths of social service and community development organizations experienced such substantial changes in at least one major funding source that the source by itself changed the organization's total revenues up or down by at least 25 percent. For some organizations, the patterns are extreme. For example, each year some organizations lost government funding that amounted to 30–40 percent of their total revenues the previous year, while others saw increases that amounted to half or more of total prior year revenues. The patterns are similar for changes in donations (losses of 18–40 percent of total revenues versus gains of 30–85 percent), fees (losses of 10 percent versus gains of 20–290 percent of total revenues), and all other revenues combined (losses of 17–19 percent versus gains of 13–40 percent of total revenues).

Such extreme fluctuations highlight the need to examine resource dynamics of individual organizations as an important counterpoint to aggregate and sector-level analyses. Certainly, it is perilous to generalize from aggregate trends to the experience of individual organizations. Without

Table 4.1. Extent of Funding Turbulence Among Chicago-Area Social Service and
Community Development Organizations, 1981–82, 1982–83, 1983–84, 1981–1984.
(N = 50)

	Percentage of Organizations Experiencing Degrees of Funding Turbulence			
Year	Extensive	Medium	Minor	All
1981–82[a]	31	44	24	100
1982–83	34	57	8	100
1983–84	38	52	10	100
1981–1984	44	50	6	100

[a] Community development organizations are somewhat more likely to have extensive turbulence than social service agencies ($p < .10$).
Source: Nonprofit Sector Project for Chicago, special analysis.

explicit attention to these types of resource dynamics, it is not possible to give
full consideration to the origins, consequences, and strategies associated
with funding stability as opposed to funding turbulence. That, of course, is
the major purpose of this study.

These findings have methodological implications as well. Obviously,
studies that rely on financial data from a single year are likely to miss
important pieces of information about individual organizations, perhaps the
most critical part. Similarly, comparisons of revenues that use only end-point
data (for example, comparisons that compute changes between 1981 and
1984, but not year-by-year changes in between) may produce misleading
results. Rather, such changes should be based on average revenues from two
adjacent years, to reduce unwarranted conclusions about the magnitude and
direction of changes. Even so, it is difficult to get good, consistent information for individual nonprofit organizations, because audit categories and
accounting procedures change over time (see Appendix A). Information
(usually estimates) for current fiscal years is particularly unreliable, because
funding from any given source may change in unpredictable ways over very
short periods of time.

Funding Dynamics Among the Case-Study Organizations

These findings on funding dynamics provided one of the major incentives
for undertaking the more detailed case studies described in this book. I
hoped that the case studies also would help explain findings (Grønbjerg,
1986) which showed that changes in program specific funding, such as
earned revenues or government grants and contracts, were not tightly coupled to changes in program activities.

The findings on extensive funding turbulence among individual nonprofit organizations raise critical questions about how (and whether) the
experience of turbulence relates to or interacts with coherent program

development or planning efforts. The answers to these questions have important implications for social policy and for theories of organizational behavior.

I developed detailed data on the patterns of funding dynamics for the thirteen organizations included in the Case-Study Project (six social service organizations and seven community development organizations) using available audit reports and tax returns for as many years as possible for each organization. As described in greater detail in Appendix A, the resulting data base is neither consistent nor complete and varies considerably in level of detail. This finding alone suggests that nonprofits active in these two service fields have not yet developed a sufficiently high level of institutionalization to generate standardized and widely accepted formats for reporting relevant fiscal information (or most other types of organizational data).

The first question I sought to address was whether the organizations participating in the case study by 1988–89 (when the data collection took place) still matched the funding profiles I had selected them to represent, but which in most cases had been derived from data collected four to six years previously. A related question was how far back in time the profiles and patterns of dynamics had persisted prior to the period of the panel study itself (1982–1985).

Persistent Funding Dynamics Among Social Service Agencies

As Figures 4.1 through 4.6 show, the six social service agencies match their expected profiles quite well, both in overall funding stability and in persistent reliance on major funding sources. During the five years between 1984 and 1988 for which complete information was available for all six agencies, the three stable social service agencies (Alcohol Treatment, Youth Outreach, and Minority Search) saw annual change in total revenues that averaged 5 to 7 percent (all adjusted for inflation). In contrast, the three turbulent agencies (Hispanic Youth Services, Immigrant Welfare League, and Christian Therapists) saw annual changes (mainly growth) that averaged 27 to 40 percent. Moreover, with one exception, these patterns of change or stability persisted beyond the 1984–1988 period for which complete information was available for all six agencies. Alcohol Treatment (Figure 4.1) experienced substantial funding changes during the late 1970s, shortly after it was established, but has seen only moderate annual changes since 1980.

The six social service agencies also show persistent patterns of reliance on broad categories of funding. For four of the six, annual percentages of funding from each of the agency's major funding sources usually deviated by no more than 3 to 7 percentage points (one standard deviation) from averages computed over the full period for each organization. Almost all annual percentages were within 6 to 14 percentage points (two standard deviations) of their respective averages. For the remaining agencies (Immigrant Welfare League and Christian Therapists), one single, highly deviant

Figure 4.1. Revenues, 1976–1988 (Adjusted for Inflation), Alcohol Treatment.

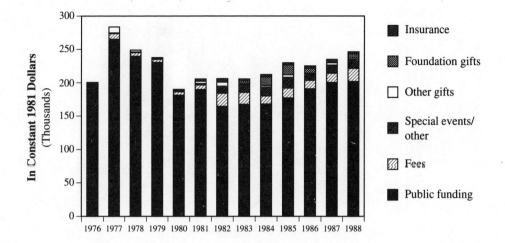

year increased the standard deviations to 16 to 20 and 12 percentage points, respectively, for their major funding sources. If these deviant years are excluded, the standard deviations decrease to 9 to 13 percentage points for Immigrant Welfare League and to only 3 percentage points for Christian Therapists.

Otherwise, as Figures 4.1 and 4.2 show, Alcohol Treatment and Hispanic Youth Services both continue to rely extensively on public funding, although the proportion has declined somewhat in each case from more than 95 percent to about 80 percent in recent years. Both agencies were

Figure 4.2. Revenues, 1983–1988 (Adjusted for Inflation), Hispanic Youth Services.

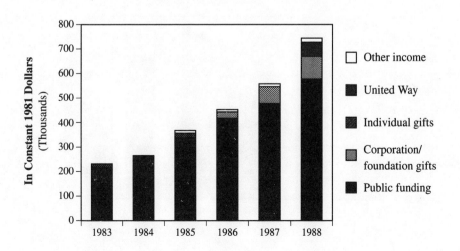

Figure 4.3. Revenues, 1982–1990 (Adjusted for Inflation), Youth Outreach.

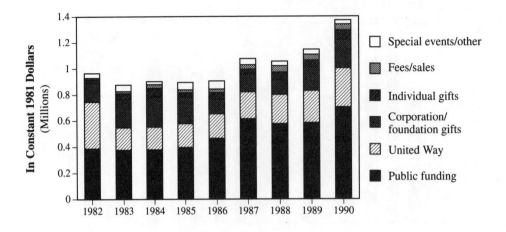

started in the mid-1970s with primary funding from public substance abuse programs.

Figures 4.3 and 4.4 show that Youth Outreach and Immigrant Welfare League both have continued to rely on a relatively even mix of donations and public funding over the period, although both have shifted toward a somewhat greater reliance on public funding in recent years. Both were established in the 1920s and relied primarily on a variety of donation sources until the 1970s, when they obtained sizable public grants and contracts. Figure 4.4 is somewhat misleading for Immigrant Welfare League, because it does not

Figure 4.4. Revenues, 1985–1989 (Adjusted for Inflation), Immigrant Welfare League.

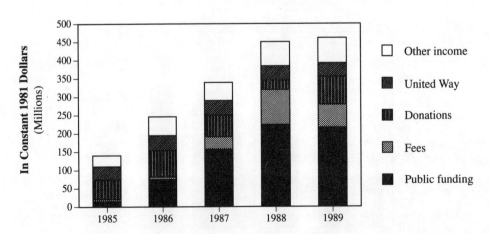

Figure 4.5. Revenues, 1979–1988 (Adjusted for Inflation), Minority Search.

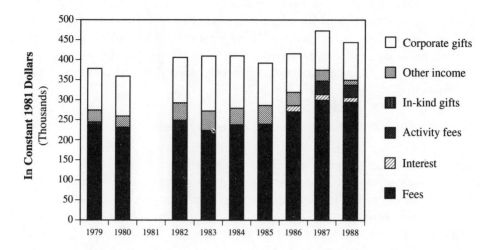

Note: Data for 1981 are missing.

include years prior to 1985, when revenues were higher. The 1985 fiscal year was a highly atypical year for the agency. Public funders temporarily suspended several grants in that year because of fiscal irregularities by its executive director. Partial information and survey data from the panel study suggest that the same patterns of mixed reliance on government and donation funding existed during the 1981–1984 period at funding levels that ranged between $140,000 and $240,000 (in constant 1981 dollars).

Similarly, Figures 4.5 and 4.6 show that Minority Search and Christian

Figure 4.6. Revenues, 1983–1988 (Adjusted for Inflation), Christian Therapists.

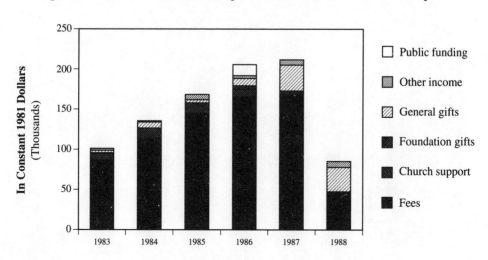

Therapists have continued to rely primarily on fees for the bulk of their revenues throughout the period. Both organizations have followed this pattern since they were established (in the late 1960s and early 1980s, respectively). However, in 1988, Christian Therapists temporarily lost both staff and client fees, so that fee income dropped to 56 percent of total revenues. Since then, fee revenues have increased again to more than 80 percent of total revenues.

Changing Funding Dynamics Among Community Development Organizations

In contrast to the patterns of persistent funding dynamics among the social service organizations, the case-study analysis suggests that the community development sector is far less predictable. For example, almost all the community development organizations experienced major changes in the overall amount of revenues they receive from year to year (see Figures 4.7 to 4.13). These patterns of growth and decline did not coincide well with initial expectations, as was the case for the social service agencies. Rather, the "stable" organizations experienced annual changes in total revenues that averaged 16 to 19 percent over the 1984–1988 period. These changes are very similar to the average annual changes of 9 to 29 percent for the "turbulent" organizations.

Also in contrast to the social service agencies, most of the community development organizations experienced major shifts in their reliance on key funding sources. For all but one of the seven organizations, annual percentages of funding from major funding sources usually deviated by 11 to 22 percentage points (one standard deviation) from averages computed over the

Figure 4.7. Revenues, 1980–1988 (Adjusted for Inflation), Economic Development Commission.

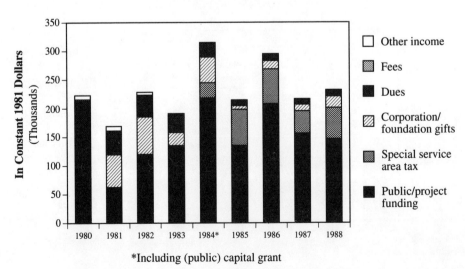

*Including (public) capital grant

Figure 4.8. Revenues, 1980–1989 (Adjusted for Inflation), African-American Neighbors.

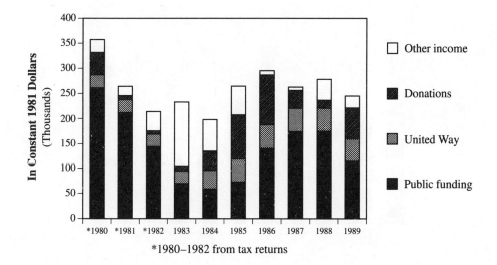

*1980–1982 from tax returns

full period for each organization. This compares with standard deviations of only 3 to 7 percentage points for most of the social service organizations. Only Community Renewal relied persistently on its major funding source (donations from the Community Institution) over the entire period, with a standard deviation of only 4 percentage points from the average of 85 percent.

Economic Development Commission and African-American Neighbors were both expected to rely extensively on public funding. As Figures 4.7 and 4.8 show, only the former did so for most of the period. It was established

Figure 4.9. Revenues, 1980–1988 (Adjusted for Inflation), Community Renewal.

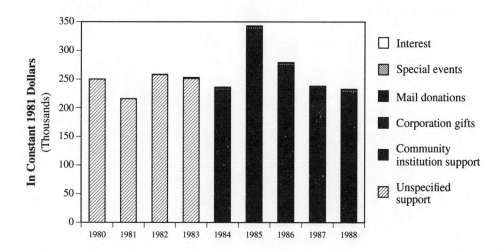

Figure 4.10. Revenues, 1981–1989 (Adjusted for Inflation), United Residents.

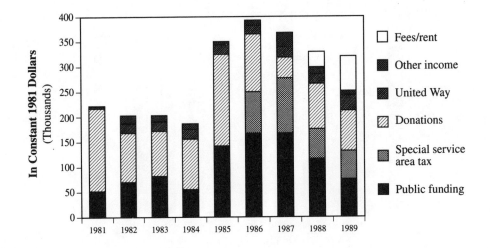

with private funding in the mid 1970s but rapidly increased its reliance on public funding after 1980. The proportion of public funding increased especially after 1984, when it began to receive tax revenues from a local Special Service Area (SSA) taxing district. African-American Neighbors is somewhat older, but otherwise followed the same path of early reliance on private donations and rapidly increasing public funding in the late 1970s. It lost almost all of these funds in a 1982 dispute with Mayor Byrne but regained most of them when a new, black mayor (Harold Washington) took office in 1984. These developments contributed only in part to major shifts in the

Figure 4.11. Revenues, 1978–1990 (Adjusted for Inflation), Preservation Council.

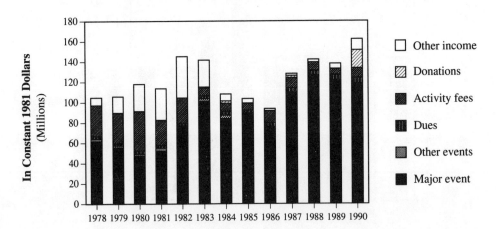

Figure 4.12. Revenues, 1969–1989 (Adjusted for Inflation), Hispanic Neighbors.

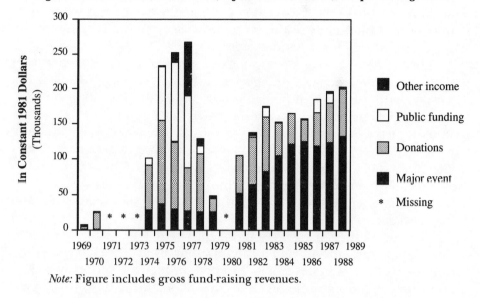

Note: Figure includes gross fund-raising revenues.

organization's reliance on other revenue sources, such as rent income and donations.

The patterns are more consistent but still diverse for United Residents and Community Renewal. United Residents (Figure 4.9) was expected to rely on a mix of public funding and donations and did so in terms of average percentages for the period (45 and 47 percent, respectively). However, individual years deviated considerably from those averages, and the organization did not receive public funding until the late 1970s. It obtained access to tax revenues from an SSA taxing district (as did the Economic Development

Figure 4.13. Revenues, 1982–1988 (Adjusted for Inflation), New Town Sponsors.

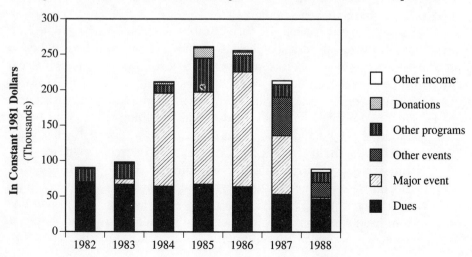

Commission), but the district was terminated after three years. Community Renewal (Figure 4.10) was expected to continue to rely primarily on donations from the Community Institution, as it has done since its establishment. It did so consistently for the entire period.

Finally, the last three organizations were expected to rely primarily on fees or other earned revenues. As Figure 4.11 shows, Preservation Council did so for the entire period, as it had done since its establishment. In contrast, Hispanic Neighbors (Figure 4.12) experienced major shifts in its funding base, from early reliance on donations, to substantial proportions of funding from public sources in the 1970s, to major reliance on special events revenues in the 1980s. Finally, New Town Sponsors (Figure 4.13) has continued to receive a stable revenue base from dues, but over a short period of time added and then subsequently discontinued large amounts of sponsorship funding for its special event.

To examine these patterns of turbulence in greater detail, I computed annual dollar shifts in individual funding sources as a percentage of the organization's total revenues from all sources in the base (prior) year. This computation employs a common standard for comparing shifts in different funding sources over time for the same organization and for comparing the experiences of different organizations. It shows the extent to which an annual change in a given revenue source contributes to the overall growth or decline of the organization. For each year for which complete data were available, I defined an organization's degree of funding turbulence as the largest contribution that any funding source made to the organization's overall growth or decline in that year.[10]

Table 4.2 summarizes the results of this analysis for all thirteen case-study organizations and shows the number of years in which they experienced a given level of funding turbulence—that is, at least one funding source changed sufficiently to increase or decrease the total size of the organization by the given percentage range. The last column shows the average turbulence scores for the organizations over the respective number of years for which data were available.

The table confirms that the three "stable" social service agencies have fairly stable funding sources. The largest dollar changes in individual funding sources averaged only 5 to 9 percent of total revenues in the prior year, and in most years the turbulence scores were less than 15 percent. In contrast, the three "turbulent" social service agencies have much higher turbulence scores. They had dollar changes in individual funding sources that on the average added or subtracted 21 to 27 percent to their total revenue base each year. In most years, the turbulence scores were at 15 percent or more.

Table 4.2 also confirms that the community development organizations consistently experience higher degrees of funding turbulence than the social service agencies. Their turbulence scores average 24 percentage points, compared with 16 points for the social service organizations. Two of the three "stable" community development organizations are somewhat more

Table 4.2. Degree and Frequency of Funding Turbulence for Thirteen Case-Study Organizations.

Type of Organization	Number of Years in Which Organizations Experienced Turbulence within a range of:						Mean Turbulence (percentage)
	+25%	20–24%	15–19%	10–14%	5–9%	0–4%	
Social Service — Stable							
Alcohol Treatment	1	1	—	1	3	6	9
Youth Outreach	—	—	2	2	1	3	9
Minority Search	—	—	—	—	4	3	5
Social Service — Turbulent							
Hispanic Youth Services	1	2	1	1	—	—	21
Immigrant Welfare League	2	1	—	—	—	—	27
Christian Therapists	2	1	—	1	1	—	25
Community Development — Stable							
Economic Development Commission	5	—	2	—	1	—	22
Community Renewal	1	1	2	2	1	1	17
Preservation Council	1	1	1	6	—	2	14
Community Development — Turbulent							
African-American Neighbors	4	3	—	2	—	—	23
United Residents	2	1	1	3	1	—	21
Hispanic Neighbors	8	1	1	4	—	—	34
New Town Sponsors	3	—	1	1	1	—	39

Note: (—) = less than 1 percent. Turbulence scores for a given year are defined as the largest dollar shift in any funding source as a percentage of the organization's total revenues in the base year.
Source: Case-Study Project.

stable than the remaining ones, but still have turbulence scores of 14 to 17 percentage points and a relatively large number of years with very high levels of turbulence.

However, a closer review shows that each of the three "stable" community development organizations has been buffeted somewhat from the impact of funding turbulence. For example, Economic Development Commission received a large federal grant ($400,000) for a capital project in 1984 that it reported as cash income in that year. I subtracted that grant from the revenues shown in Figure 4.7, but could not make similar adjustments for other smaller grants received in the same and subsequent years for the same project. The organization also uses a cash accounting system that fails to distinguish between operating and capital funds, making it appear that greater funding turbulence occurred than the organization actually experienced.

Similarly, most of the shifts in total revenues for Community Renewal (Figure 4.9) reflect its receipt of "off-budget" allocations from the Community

Institution for occasional special projects, such as legal fees in connection with lawsuits against local property owners who violate building codes. These projects were handled by legal firms, and the organization served only as a pass-through mechanism for the Community Institution. Finally, Preservation Council (Figure 4.11) maintained a substantial fund balance for the entire period, enough to cover at least one full year of operations. It could maintain its basic activities fairly easily if total revenues declined significantly. As a result, all three "stable" organizations showed more stable patterns of operating expenditures than implied by their revenues, or than was the case for the "turbulent" organizations.

Overall Assessment

The persistent patterns of funding reliance among the social service agencies and their systematic differences in funding stability are not surprising, since I had sought to select organizations with those particular funding profiles. Nevertheless, I selected these organizations on the basis of survey and interview data that covered the 1981–1984 period. The case-study analysis shows that those funding profiles persisted through at least 1988 for the social service agencies, when I terminated the data collection for them. The findings support a basic hypothesis from the resource dependency literature: that organizations institutionalize their dependencies on particular funding sources but differ in their efforts and abilities to maximize or control them.

The institutionalization is likely to occur because it is less costly for organizations to continue to manage funding relationships with which they have become familiar than to meet the overhead costs, uncertainty, and learning curves involved in exploring new funding relationships. In addition, staff and board members of the organization develop vested interests in continuing existing funding relationships. As I show in Chapters Five through Eight, accommodations as well as contacts and skills (and hence status in the organization) that are appropriate to one type of funding source may not easily translate to other sources.

The community development organizations present a different pattern. Not only did patterns of funding reliance frequently not persist over time, but each of them experienced fairly high levels of funding turbulence. These findings also confirm the difficulties I encountered in identifying stable community organizations in the initial data base. Yet the special circumstances surrounding the "stable" community development organizations (for example, mix of capital and operating funds, off-budget funding, and large fund reserves) help explain why they had a reputation for stability and why data for short periods of time might suggest such a pattern.

The shifts in funding profiles among the community development organizations reflect in part the recency and instability in public funding for community development activities discussed above. However, as I argue in Chapters Seven and Eight, the community development organizations also maintain more politicized relationships with both the private and public sectors than the social service agencies. For example, the experience of African-American Neighbors demonstrates the vulnerability of community organizations to funding decisions made within the context of local politics and highlights the nature of leverage that they may acquire or forfeit, depending on the political role they play. Under these circumstances, the type of institutionalization of funding relationships predicted by the resource dependency literature is less likely to occur.

These findings also confirm my second basic argument: that the organizational environment of social service agencies differs in systematic ways from that of community development organizations. As I show in the next several chapters, detailed analysis of four major types of nonprofit funding sources (fees, special events, donations, and government grants and contracts) corroborates this conclusion, but also reveals more complicated patterns.

Summary

Overall growth and stability in nonprofit funding sources depend on how economic and social trends affect different types of exchange relationships. Documenting these trends is difficult because adequate data are rarely available, especially for social service and community development organizations. Nevertheless, the best estimates suggest that earned revenues are likely to have increased, special events to have become more prevalent, and donations from all sources to have become more competitive and difficult to obtain for both types of organizations. Trends in government funding show more divergence for the two service fields. In spite of significant increases in total public spending for welfare purposes, social service agencies are unlikely to have experienced marked fluctuations in public funding, except for growth in a few program areas. In contrast, community development organizations have seen marked decline in their sources of public funding following a period of equally remarkable growth.

There are substantial differences in funding dynamics among individual organizations—differences that are not captured in aggregate analyses for the entire nonprofit sector or for particular service fields. Some organizations have very high rates of growth in total revenues, some have large losses, and some are quite stable over time. These revenue changes reflect the net result of experiences with the different funding sources to which organizations have access, so that major growth in one source may offset or accentuate changes in another.

These individual experiences are contingent on several factors. They depend on developments in the organization's environment that limit its options. The community development environment appears to be more turbulent than that of the social service field, making it more difficult to maintain stability in the former than in the latter. Within these types of environmental parameters, patterns of funding dynamics also reflect strategies and choices that individual organizations and their managers make, and the internal resources they have available to follow them through. Finally, there is evidence that funding dynamics are not driven mainly by particular types of funding sources. Organizations with reliance on similar funding sources vary greatly in funding turbulence, and individual funding streams have similar ranges of overall funding shifts.

Notes

1. This financial analysis is based on a relatively small sample of twenty-nine social service agencies that provided full information on all revenues sources for each of the four years. Similar information was available for only nine community organizations—too few to warrant a separate analysis.

2. Because government provides a substantial proportion of nonprofit funding in these two fields, they are thought to be vulnerable to "free-rider" problems when taxpayers decline to donate to them because government funding will ensure that they continue to provide services. However, historical trends show that growth in public spending for most social purposes has eclipsed, but not replaced, nonprofit organizations in those fields (Grønbjerg, 1981). Comparative studies of local communities also suggest that such a crowding out of private donations is at best an incomplete explanation (Wolpert, 1989).

3. In constant 1981 dollars, per capita donations grew from $151 in 1960 to about $240 in the 1970s and early 1980s before reaching $341 in 1989.

4. About half (45 percent) went to religious organizations in 1989. Almost as much (41 percent) went to nonwelfare activities (such as health and hospitals, education, arts and humanities, and civic and public affairs). Donations to social welfare organizations declined during the 1970s, from $33 per capita in 1970 (in 1981 dollars) to $21 in 1980, but then increased again to $34 in 1989.

5. As discussed in Appendix A, data on donations for different types of organizations are particularly inadequate because they come from special surveys that cover only certain types of organizations or from tax returns of nonprofits required to file returns (small organizations and churches are exempt from filing).

6. Access to subsidy revenues allows nonprofits to contribute to horizontal equity for low-income clients—depending on whether and how such clients obtain access to services.

7. Most surveys include questions about finances for only one year, usually the current or most recently completed fiscal year, because it requires more cooperation to get organizations to give information for several years.

8. The number of community organizations with complete funding information is too small to warrant separate analysis; however, the patterns appear roughly similar to the social service organizations.

9. The amount of change in any one source of revenue is computed as a percent of the organization's total income in the prior year. This is different from computing the percentage of change in the particular revenue source in which the amount of change is computed as a percentage of the income from only that revenue source in the prior year.

10. This is identical to the turbulence index discussed in Table 4.1. However, in that analysis I used a cutoff point of 25 percent or more for any one funding source to mean high turbulence and a score of no more than 5 percent in any one funding source to mean low turbulence. Here I use more detailed categories and compute the average of actual scores.

FIVE

Raising Money from Fees: Management Challenges and Marketing Strategies

As Chapter Four showed, fees are a major and increasingly important source of revenue for nonprofits in both the social service and community development fields. This persistent growth suggests that nonprofits find fees an attractive and easily managed revenue source. It is not surprising that fees should be attractive; after all, given the preponderance of for-profit organizations, that is how most organizations obtain their revenues. Indeed, the entire economy is structured so as to promote and support the generation of earnings.

However, nonprofits typically are established to pursue substantive, value-directed goals, not commercial success. Fees are therefore a useful place to start the more detailed analysis of major nonprofit revenue sources.[1] What makes fees attractive to nonprofits? What contingencies do nonprofits face when they attempt to generate fees? What strategies are available to them for managing this type of revenue? Addressing these questions provides a useful context for examining other funding sources that nonprofit managers usually portray as more demanding.

The analysis shows that fees are attractive because they maximize management discretion over the allocation of staff and other internal resources. They also solve problems of how to develop strategic responses, since marketing schemes are well developed and fully institutionalized in the commercial sector. These schemes have broad recognition and immediate appeal to both individual and institutional actors. Nonprofit managers, consultants, or board members are not immune to these forces and are likely to look to self-generated sources of revenues when other resources are unpredictable, scarce, difficult to manage, or just thought to be so.

However, nonprofits that seek fees face three broad sets of contingencies that are not well recognized and for which good strategies may not be easily available, at least for social service and community development organizations. They must decide (1) whether and how to modify predominant models for identifying clients and making client relationships more predictable, (2) how to expand their market niche without undermining their commitment to substantive goals, and (3) how to control staff and client interactions that are usually hidden from direct observation by managers.

Management Objectives, Control, and Uncertainty

For nonprofit organizations as well as for proprietary businesses, patterns of stability, growth, and decline in fee income reflect general economic conditions as well as a wide range of organizational strategies. The latter include the organization's ability to develop and manage a client market or product line, establish an appropriate and competitive pricing structure, safeguard the market against competitors, and position itself for changes in client supply and demands.

In the social service and community development fields, these decisions occur in an environment of uncertainty and lack of control over important aspects of the resource relationships. In both of these fields, markets are relatively fragmented and not highly institutionalized. Nonprofit managers can exercise a fairly high level of control over their selection and development of market niche and price structure, but they have much less control over the supply-and-demand characteristics of clients. Nonprofits tend to be small organizations without access to sophisticated market analyses; the types of services they provide for fees are not well established or recognized by potential clients; and customers tend to be individuals who are interested in relatively short-term services. Such features create considerable uncertainty about how to project changes in the numbers and purchasing power of potential clients and how to shape tastes through marketing efforts. For somewhat the same reasons, nonprofit managers have little control over, or even knowledge about, the number and capacities of their competitors.

This is in sharp contrast to other nonprofit service fields, such as health and education, where the markets are highly structured and controlled by a few large institutions (such as key government programs, major insurance companies, professional associations, and licensing organizations). Market and pricing structures are therefore more fully developed and management choices correspondingly circumscribed to fit within established parameters. The services are of interest to virtually the entire population; and the organizations themselves are large, have sophisticated marketing capacity, and are easily identified by competitors and clients alike.

For social service and community development organizations, uncertainties associated with market structures and the absence of major institutional actors to control fee structures mean that fee-dependent organizations are relatively free to control the content, structure, and timing of management tasks. This up-front flexibility serves as one of the main attractions of fee income to these organizations. As a result, fee-related management efforts in these fields are less standardized and more closely intertwined with

internal features of the organization than is the case with government funding or with managing fees in other fields, such as health and education.

Perhaps for these reasons, nonprofit managers from the social service
and community development fields appear to assess fees quite positively. Of
the sixty such managers who responded to interview questions in 1985, more
than half agreed that fees are flexible in how and when they can be used (65
percent), are easy to administer and account for (70 percent), allow the
organization to develop new programs that are really needed (52 percent), do
not force the organization into areas where it has little experience or ability
(76 percent), enable the organization to serve the clients that it would like to
serve (50 percent), and are worth pursuing (68 percent). On the other hand,
only about one-third agreed that fees are the type of funding they would
prefer to rely on (35 percent) or are easy to plan for the future with (38
percent). Managers of community development organizations were significantly more likely than their counterparts in social service agencies to agree
that fees are flexible (84 versus 56 percent) and enable them to serve the
clients they would like to serve (69 versus 42 percent).

On several of these dimensions, fees were viewed less favorably than
most types of donations. However, they rank significantly higher than United
Way support and government grants and contracts in flexibility, ease of
administration, and not forcing the organization into areas of little experience. These findings suggest that it is important to assess how fees and other
types of earned income are structured, what kinds of management efforts
they require, and how they interact with other nonprofit revenues. The
volume and types of fees that organizations receive provide some element of
direct feedback on strategies, because fee income is directly linked to productivity—the organization earns fees when its products or services are
sufficiently attractive and inexpensive to attract enough customers to offset
the costs of producing them.

Strategies for Managing Fees

Five of the six social service agencies and two of the seven community
development organizations had income from client-paid fees or service
charges. However, with the exception of two social service agencies, fees and
service charges (exclusive of special events proceeds) account for only a small
proportion of total revenues (12 percent or less) and fees remain less important than efforts to generate special events income, donation revenues, or
government grants and contracts.

My review of management contingencies and strategies associated
with fee income therefore relies on findings from Christian Therapists and
Minority Search, both of which receive more than two-thirds of their revenues from fees. I use my discussion of how these two organizations have

sought to market themselves and secure fees on a continuing basis to illus-trate more general principles that underlie organizational strategies to establish and expand fee-for-service markets.

Market Niches and Programmatic Developments

As Figures 4.5 and 4.6 showed, Christian Therapists and Minority Search dif-fer greatly in funding stability. Most of these differences can be traced to di-verse programmatic developments that reflect their particular market niches and to closely related and equally distinctive organizational strategies.

Christian Therapists—Initiating New Ventures. The official name of Christian Therapists does not identify its religious orientation, but it por-trays itself as providing individual mental health counseling in a Christian context. It derives the bulk of its revenue from sliding scale fees paid by clients directly, although some clients have access to health insurance pro-grams that cover therapeutic treatments from which Christian Therapists receives third-party payments. It also receives donations, most of them di-rectly or indirectly linked to the Christian Church, which helped establish the precursor to the agency in the late 1970s.

Christian Therapists has undertaken several new ventures since its official establishment in 1982 (it operated as an outreach program of the Christian Church for eight years prior to that). These include services directed at residents in a nearby public housing project, therapy and counsel-ing through three suburban satellite centers in local churches, and outreach to patrons in the relatively affluent neighborhoods near the agency's main office. All but the latter were suspended within two to three years. Christian Therapists also continues to serve as a training base for psychotherapists-in-training from several institutions located in the Chicago area.

As a result of these programmatic developments, Christian Therapists has also undergone major structural and funding changes. Over a fourteen-year span, the agency has had six executive directors, five site locations, two waves of staff resignations (including the executive director and eleven of twelve staff members in one six-month period of the 1987–88 fiscal year), growth and subsequent decline in revenues (by 60 percent in one year), and turnover in the board of directors (including four board presidents over a two-year span).

Most of these changes occurred during the 1986–1988 period and reflected a major staff-board conflict that emerged in 1987, when staff members proposed that the agency adopt a group practice model. Under this model, staff members would operate the agency without an executive direc-tor, be compensated in proportion to the fees they generated, and the church would convert its donations into a form of third-party payments for church parishioners whom the agency served, but who were unable to pay the full fee. When the agency's board (dominated by the church) rejected the staff proposal, eleven of twelve staff members resigned. Shortly thereafter, the executive director also resigned, but agreed to continue in a part-time position until the agency could find a new director.

At the time we conducted our research, a former board member served as a part-time director, one full-time and a couple of part-time staff members provided therapy, and the agency had just hired an office manager. Shortly thereafter, Christian Therapists hired and subsequently fired a director with impressive credentials but uncertain immigration status. Most recently, it has come to share its executive director with another organization that is also affiliated with the church.

The programmatic and structural changes have had direct and substantial impact on revenues. Fees grew at annual rates of 14 to 31 percent during the 1983–1986 period as the agency established satellite offices in suburban communities and undertook other program initiatives. Fees stabilized in 1987 and then dropped 70 percent the following year because the agency abandoned the initiatives and its resigning executive director and other staff members appropriated most of its client market and became direct competitors.

With the exception of one government grant (about 7 percent of total revenues in 1986), almost all nonfee income has come from contributions by the church and its patrons. Although donations more than tripled between 1983 and 1987, their annual changes, up or down, accounted for less than 5 percent in overall growth or decline in any given year. Only in 1988 did donations constitute a significant proportion of revenues (36 percent, up from 17 percent in 1987), reflecting both the significant loss of total revenues in 1987 as fees plummeted and successful efforts to solicit donations in order to meet the crisis. For 1988, total revenues were 15 percent lower than they had been in 1983 and about 60 percent lower than the 1986 high-budget year.

The agency's difficulties in developing and managing fee revenues reflect several structural factors: internal conflicts about how to reconcile its mission to serve as a Christian ministry with efforts to develop and expand the market for its services, the fragmented and fragile client market (therapy for individual clients) in which it operates, and difficulty in developing a loyal staff or otherwise control key organizational resources.

Minority Search—Fine-Tuning the Basic Approach. Minority Search's basic program (and those of affiliate agencies in other cities) consists of developing corporate internship placements for minority college students it has recruited. Participating corporations pay the agency a flat annual fee for interns placed with them, in return for which Minority Search provides training and supportive services for the students, to help them manage the joint obligations of college and internship placement. The agency monitors students' academic and social progress as well as their performance in the internship placement. Students receive no stipends from the agency but are paid by the corporations, and they understand that on graduation the sponsoring corporation may offer them employment.

In recent years, Minority Search and most other affiliates have begun to work with promising high school students to prepare them for participation in the basic program by offering preplacement guidance, participation in local events, and the promise of internship placements during their college careers. It has also begun to work more deliberately with the growing number of graduates of its program and has created a dues-supported Alumni Association. The latter allows Minority Search to monitor and promote the ongoing careers of its interns and provides access to role models and sponsors for its current and future interns.

Minority Search defines these new programs as supportive of and subordinate to its primary effort of serving its corporate clients. It has developed separate sources of funding for these programs, to reduce the likelihood that they will interfere with its attention to fee-paying corporations. The new programs represent a fine-tuning of the basic program rather than major new initiatives. Minority Search has undertaken no other programmatic changes but has reorganized its staff positions in order to create finer salary gradations and increase opportunities for upward mobility within the agency.

Revenues and funding composition have remained stable. During the 1979–1988 period, revenues increased by 16 percent, equivalent to an average annual growth of slightly over 1 percent, adjusted for inflation. Only during one year, 1986–87, did revenues grow significantly in inflation-adjusted dollars (by almost 15 percent), but they declined almost 6 percent the following year. During the 1979–1988 period, the agency increased its fees at an average annual rate of 2 percent (adjusted for inflation) and its fund balances from 18 to 65 percent of annual revenues.

The stable financial history and growing fund balance suggest that Minority Search has solved contingencies associated with marketing services to its particular client population of local corporations. Compared with Christian Therapists, it operates in a very different market and fee environment, which allows it to pursue different management strategies. It defines its central purpose quite narrowly as the provision of a high-quality product (minority talent) to its corporate clients rather than as services to the minority students themselves; it cultivates long-term and institutionally based relationships with fiscally competent, fee-paying clients; it has broadened its relationships with these fee-paying clients to include flat rate donations; and it has maintained control over staff and funding reserves.

Contingencies and Management Strategies

Although the two agencies differ in their programmatic decisions, these strategies only in part reflect deliberate processes. They also reflect differences in the types of service activities the two agencies provide (that is, task

Table 5.1. Strategies for Managing Fees.

Strategic Action	Christian Therapists	Minority Search
Equating Market Niche and Mission	Incomplete	Fully
Structuring Predictable Client Relationships		
Length of relationship	Months	Years
Repeat clients	Few	Most
Fiscal competency of clients	Mixed	High
Dominant client type	Individuals	Corporations
Structuring Control over Other Resources		
Control over staff	Low	High
Staff career ladder	Limited	High
Control client access/management	Staff	Agency

environments); the extent to which clients, staff, managers, and other stakeholders share a basic understanding about what is being provided (degree of domain consensus); and the extent to which the agencies can exercise power in their relationship with clients (extent of asymmetry in the exchange relationship) (Thompson, 1967, p. 28; Coleman, 1982). These are all contingencies that managers must contend with and attempt to control. For the two agencies, efforts to do so manifested themselves in three broad areas of activities: linking market niche and mission, structuring fee relationships, and controlling staff and other resources (see Table 5.1). On all of these dimensions, Christian Therapists faced considerably more difficult challenges than Minority Search.

Equating Market Niche and Mission. One of the major challenges fee-dependent nonprofits encounter is how to link the organization's mission with a particular market niche. Both mission and niche provide organizations with criteria or guidelines for making decisions. The two must be closely linked in order to minimize conflict among goals and reduce the likelihood of organizational crises. For-profit organizations typically equate the two and escape this challenge. However, traditional market adaptations frequently do not apply entirely to nonprofits. Their access to direct or indirect subsidies allows them to escape the full impact of market forces, while their mission statements often direct them to serve impoverished individuals or others with limited ability to pay full market rates. Thus, the organization may find itself unable to fully reconcile pursuit of its market niche with its mission: preoccupation with one of these goals may compromise the other. Christian Therapists and Minority Search illustrate different approaches to the problem.

Christian Therapists—Incomplete Linkage. The constitution of Christian Therapists specifies:

> Christian Therapists shall provide a Christian ministry. . .
> through: (1) individual, marriage, and group counseling;
> (2) educational classes offered to churches, businesses, and com-
> munity organizations; (3) other psychological services such as
> consultation, evaluation, and testing. These services shall be
> provided in accordance with the client's ability to pay. This shall
> be done so that persons who cannot afford the standard cost of
> such services will be able to obtain the needed services [Con-
> stitution, Article 2].

In agreement with its mission, Christian Therapists has attempted to both
serve low-income clients and to secure fee-paying clients. However, in practice
it has devoted only peripheral efforts to the former, while it has pursued its
market niche with such vigor that a decoupling between the two proceeded
unexamined.

   To reach low-income clients, Christian Therapists has sought subsidies
from two different sources. It solicits special offerings and donations from
the Christian Church, affiliated churches, or church members in order to
help serve those with limited means. However, contributions have accounted
for a very small proportion of total revenues and declined in importance over
several years. During the same time, Christian Therapists was very successful
in obtaining new fee-paying clients. Consequently, fees increased dramatically in the early to mid 1980s, and the donative strategy lost its central
relevance. The reduced focus on low-income clients in turn endangered
church contributions.

   Christian Therapists has also sought to develop grant proposals to
public agencies and foundations, to support its work with low-income clients
in a nearby public housing project. However, it did so for only a short time
and relegated the responsibility for soliciting and managing these grants
entirely to one staff member, who also carried the full responsibility for
outreach and the delivery of services to project residents. Grant development
was not treated as a central management task; instead, the fate of the entire
program came to depend on how effectively this one staff member could
raise subsidies and simultaneously provide all the services.

   The staff member had less formal training in psychotherapy and fewer
credentials than most other staff members. She was also female and black
among a staff dominated by white males and ordained clergy. Her own
peripheral status, and the failure of Christian Therapists to assume central
responsibility for the program, meant that the program was also peripheral.
It was the first program to be eliminated when fee revenues began to stabilize
and the agency found itself unable to meet expectations for higher salaries as
staff members obtained advanced degrees.

   In contrast to these halting and somewhat limited efforts, Christian
Therapists pursued fee-paying clients much more aggressively through a
large number of approaches. The agency made itself more attractive and

convenient to clients able to pay the full fee. That occurred when it moved its office to a new attractive building, closer to the lakefront and costing $12,000 more per year than the previous location. It retained its geographical, but not cultural or social, proximity to clients in the housing project.

Christian Therapists restructured its sliding scale fee schedule upward, to cover the substantially greater cost of the new office space (and of new office equipment purchased at the same time). But the move strained the agency's financial ability to subsidize services to public housing residents, once that program lost its outside funding. Other program additions— satellite offices, internship, community education—fared much better in the fight over resources. These additions appeared to serve the dual purposes of augmenting revenues and enhancing the staff's professional and personal interests.

Christian Therapists expanded its referral system and client catchment areas into the suburbs by establishing a number of satellite centers in suburban churches. These centers significantly enlarged the middle-class client base, reduced staff commuting time, and increased fee income rapidly, at least initially. In fact, by 1985 the satellite offices had become so well established that the agency's listing in the 1986 *Human Service Directory* included information (and phone numbers) for *only* the satellite offices and made no mention at all of its central-office location. (This came as a major surprise to its executive director when we pointed it out in 1988.)

Fee revenues peaked in 1987 as the satellite centers matured and became established. However, the period of quiet was short-lived. Staff members seized control of the satellite centers as part of the 1987 contentious settlement between them and the agency's board of trustees. By the fall of 1988, when I sought to contact the organization to ask it to participate in the study, I found that the phone number listed in the 1988 *Human Service Directory* had been transferred to another agency, whose director was one of the resigning staff members.

Christian Therapists attempted to generate access to a steady stream of clients whose fees could be paid in full by third-party insurance companies. It succeeded in establishing one link when it became the exclusive local provider of mental health services for a health maintenance organization (HMO). However, insurance and contract payments provided a diminishing source of revenues after 1985. Agency staff members then sought to convert church donations and special collections into a more predictable funding relationship. Under their proposed group practice model, the Christian Church would cover client payments in full for those members of the congregation who were unable to pay the full rate. In effect, the church would have come to act as a third-party payer. Christian Therapists then could have exercised control over church support by modifying the fee system rather than relying on internal church decisions about when and whether to provide donations. The church rejected these proposals as well as the general shift to a group practice model.

Increasing professionalization of the staff created additional pressure for expansion in order to meet the staff's expectations of status and compensation. The professionalization occurred as Christian Therapists formalized an internship program for psychology and counseling trainees and kept them on as staff members after they completed their degrees. Initially, the internship program kept staff costs down because interns worked for lower pay in return for getting required practice experience under the supervision of a qualified staff member. There are also good reasons for hiring the interns after they finish their training. It prevents the loss of revenues that might otherwise occur if and when interns take positions (and their reputation and clients) elsewhere and ensures a continuing supply of staff known to be qualified and to share the Christian approach. However, over time the practice resulted in an expensive, degreed staff whose costs could be met only through an expanded client base, especially one able to pay close to the full fee. The enhanced professional self-image of staff members who completed their training and internships created additional pressure for such expansion.

The internship program also created an internal market, because interns had to undergo therapy with one of agency's regular staff members for a small fee. These fees were relatively unimportant (about 1 percent of revenues in 1987), but the program established an internal career ladder by acknowledging the superior professional status of senior staff. As a result, staff members came to have a vested interest in the internship program and in an expanded middle-class client base. They received more limited professional rewards from serving low-income clients in the public housing project.

The community education program provided the agency with an alternative model for outreach. Compared with reaching and serving residents of the public housing project, almost all of whom were black and very poor, the community education program had a decidedly middle-class slant. The program consisted of seminars and workshops targeted at the racially and economically mixed broader community and was more professionally rewarding and less demanding on staff than attempts to accommodate the special and difficult needs of project residents. The lone staff member in charge of the public housing program spent part of her time helping her clients shop and otherwise meet immediate needs. Although other staff seemed to respect her "methods," they saw themselves as therapists and her as a social worker. Consequently, when Christian Therapists made the decision to drop the public housing project and limit outreach to the community education project, it also accommodated the professional and personal strengths, possibly preferences, of the bulk of its staff.

Finally, the agency sought to exploit its special market niche, although not as aggressively as it might have. Although there is no shortage of counseling services in urban areas, a niche does exist for meeting counseling and therapy needs among conservative Christians. Theologically conservative

persons are skeptical about securalism and avoid psychologists and counselors out of fear that these professionals will minimize religious and spir-
itual orientations. Christian Therapists provides a "safe" option for such
clients and has a small but probably underserved clientele.

To exploit this niche, the agency advertised its relation to the parent
church, its connection with conservatively oriented counselor-training programs, and the self-definitions of its staff members as Christians providing
psychological services within the framework of contemporary Christianity.
During interviews, staff members stressed the evangelical nature of the
parent church and the Christian orientation of the agency's likely clients; they
defined *Christian counseling* as occurring within a context of Christian teach-
ings and individuals' relation to God, although they acknowledged a
conservative-liberal theological continuum among the staff.

However, the agency did not emphasize its Christian focus in its relatively innocuous name.[2] Nor did Christian Therapists emphasize the number
of ordained ministers on staff. So far as we know, none used clerical titles,
clerical garb, or other identifying symbols. The waiting room and office space
contained no specific religious symbolism, and the radio was not tuned to any
of Chicago's several Christian-oriented stations. Perhaps the diverse range of
Christian orientations among potential clients to which the agency might
cater precluded such display.

Of course, there are also structural limits to pursuing this particular
niche that cannot readily be transcended. Competition from other like-
minded practitioners and agencies exists; individual therapists do advertise
their Christian base; church pastors take pride in their therapeutic skills and
invest considerable time in pastoral counseling; and some churches assign
clergy as in-house therapists. The market niche is also reduced to the extent
that potential clients come to trust and purchase the services of secular
agencies and practitioners. In short, Christian Therapists devoted considerable resources to its efforts to pursuing its market niche, but that reduced its
ability to serve low-income clients.

Minority Search—Tight Bond. In contrast, Minority Search fully equates
its mission and its market niche. It has undertaken a range of efforts to
exploit changing corporate interests in its particular services and explicitly
mimics key aspects of the corporate culture. It has faced increasing difficulties in finding and securing the quality of raw talent that is of interest to
corporations, and has adopted several strategies to deal with these difficulties, but not without some cost to its primary goals.

Minority Search has redefined its mission to match a changing market
niche. The agency emerged out of the 1960s and the enactment of civil rights
and affirmative action legislation by federal, state, and local governments. It
provided minorities with access and career skills for mid-level corporate jobs
while serving closely related and politically salient corporate goals of documenting their affirmative action. Since then, affirmative action goals have

slipped down on the national agenda. Many obvious inequities have faded, and court decisions as well as successive presidential administrations have given lower priority to affirmative action, if not actually opposed it. International competition, corporate takeovers, and the restructuring of the U.S. economy have boosted corporate preoccupation with efficiency more than with achievement of broader social goals of equity and access.

These developments could have presented major threats to Minority Search and the market for its services. However, the aging of the U.S. population and the disproportionate growth of minority groups also mean that corporations increasingly have to recruit employees from among women and members of racial, ethnic, and immigrant minorities. These changes have redefined the market niche of Minority Search. It has adapted its strategies accordingly and articulated them in how it perceives the corporate environment and its own role.

Minority Search describes the corporate environment as being quite different than it was in the past and less interested in minority opportunities as a goal in itself. Instead of meeting equal opportunity or affirmative action goals, as it did in its early days, the agency now defines its particular market niche — and its mission — as meeting corporate needs for high-quality managers and technical personnel in the face of a shrinking supply of white males who traditionally have filled those positions. It emphasizes how its programs help corporations prepare for America's changing demographic structure and increase their ability to perform under "Workforce 2000" conditions.

Minority Search identifies itself with corporate culture. Like other nonprofits, Minority Search provides direct services to individuals (the student interns). However, it does not define the interns as clients or services to them as its primary mission. In fact, when we reviewed some of our financial charts with the exective director, he felt that our graphs inappropriately labeled Minority Search as a "social service" agency. He emphasized that the agency's purpose was to serve its corporate clients, not to provide social services to minority students, although it might do that as a byproduct. Rather, he described the agency as a "nonprofit" business in which student interns constitute the raw material ("talent pool") that it processes (trains) and sells to (places with) corporate clients who need and want the product. This vocabulary illustrates exceptionally well what DiMaggio and Powell (1983) call "organizational isomorphism": the process by which organizations that depend on other organizations for resources come to resemble them in structure, operation, and language.

Minority Search's close identification with the corporate culture has important consequences. If an intern does not perform up to standards, Minority Search insists that the interests of the corporate client take precedence, removes the intern from the program, and supplies the client with new talent. It maintains that such action not only safeguards its own relationship with clients by giving them value for their money but also provides realistic socialization for the interns into the corporate environment and ultimately serves their best interests.

The agency portrays itself also in other ways as operating in the "mean and lean" corporate environment of the 1980s. It points to its own "bottom-line" approach of using explicit performance measures to demonstrate its utility to corporate clients. These performance measures, and the use of a corporate vocabulary, form a prominent part of its presentation of self and of its internal structure and processes. It evaluates individual staff members in terms of how well they meet specific performance standards and employs explicit business principles in its financial management. These practices help Minority Search articulate its familiarity with and sympathy for corporate standards of performance to its corporate clients. They also serve to instill a similar internal culture within the agency and among the talent pool.

By linking its mission and market niche so directly, Minority Search has avoided being captured by a multiplicity of goals that pose management and organizational problems and contribute to the kind of internal conflict found in Christian Therapists. Indeed, when faced with increasing difficulties in obtaining an adequate supply of raw talent to meet the needs and expectations of its fee-paying clients, Minority Search implemented strategies that give primacy to corporate interests. The precollege program and the alumni program effectively impose more stringent criteria on students. The precollege program allows Minority Search to contact potential students earlier, improving its knowledge of potential candidates and selection for participation in the internship program. The alumni program extends contact after the formal completion of the internship, allowing Minority Search to monitor, nurture, and socialize students longer. Both programs increase the likelihood that students will perform acceptably in their internship and that the agency can meet performance standards and document its achievements.

Minority Search has also shifted its catchment area for recruitment to improve the initial quality of the talent pool. It has reduced its efforts to recruit from general inner-city, nonselective, public high schools and given greater attention to minority students in suburban, private, or selective inner-city public high schools. This has allowed it to become increasingly selective in the students it accepts into its college program and to tighten eligibility criteria without greatly expanding its regular screening efforts (or increase production costs). The focus on less risky students of middle-class background probably means that Minority Search has lost some of its immediate value for student participants, although the negative impact may be partially offset by the establishment of the precollege program. However, the strategy is fully consistent with its mission to serve the needs of corporate clients.

The strategy is not without potential liabilities, because the focus on less risky students also means that Minority Search has encountered greater competition in securing minority student candidates. Those who now meet its more stringent selection requirements are likely to have a number of other options available to them and to already be the subject of intense recruitment efforts by prestigious universities and colleges from across the nation. Students that meet these new criteria have other options and may not be willing to commit themselves to the long-term and relatively intense interaction the agency demands.

To overcome student reluctance and maintain a sufficiently large talent pool, Minority Search has had to accept compromises in its relationship with students that could further endanger its ability to provide a quality product to its corporate clients. For example, it no longer refuses to accept interns to attend college outside of the Chicago area and no longer refers them to other affiliate organizations closer to their college locations (thus losing a fee). Instead, the agency now accepts monthly telephone calls from students (and has installed an 800 number for the purpose) in place of personal appointments at its office.

However, the long-distance relationship means that the agency can no longer supervise students very closely or provide intensive support services during the school year. This poses a major dilemma. Either Minority Search must select students who do not need intensive support services or it risks higher placement failures for students in the internship program. If the former occurs, corporations might do as well through their own internal recruitment and mentoring efforts and save the Minority Search fee. If the latter occurs, corporations might decide that the fee is too high for the quality of students it gets.

Finally, Minority Search even views donations as part of its market strategy. It has sought to meet the costs of the precollege program by asking its corporate clients to pay a flat annual donation — in effect, a voluntary, tax-deductible fee. Other affiliates have incorporated the cost of the precollege component into the standard internship fee, but Chicago agency executives felt this would endanger the agency's competitiveness and market share. Instead, they promote the fees and donations as a package deal to ensure a quality product. Of course, only nonprofits with access to fiscally competent clients-customers can effectively link donations and fees so directly to a single product. Most human service agencies (like Christian Therapists) do not seek donations from current clients.

Although Minority Search in principle should be able to encourage donations by providing a quality product, donations declined by 19 percent in actual dollars and by 31 percent in constant dollars over the 1983–1988 period. Linking fees and donations directly may make the services so costly to clients that some avoid paying the voluntary (donation) portion, at least on an ongoing basis. They are free riders who get the benefit of the precollege program without paying the full costs. Corporations are cost-sensitive clients, and Minority Search cannot avoid the tendency for corporations to cut costs and maximize returns in this manner. Intense market competition among them provides additional incentives for accepting the free-rider solution.[3]

In short, although both Christian Therapists and Minority Search depend on fees, they differ in the extent to which they have equated their mission and market niche. Christian Therapists cannot fully equate the two. Its clients reject the traditional market structure of secular counseling, and its donors represent other interests, insisting on service to the poor. Its staff and managers share in this ambivalence, but its preoccupation with market means that other mission goals receive less attention and shape management decisions in ways that endangered staff morale and contributed to a history of fee turbulence. In practice, the agency has come to prefer clients able to pay the full costs, thereby undermining its claim to serve economically diverse groups and its appeal to donors.

Minority Search avoided internal conflicts because it maintained isomorphism with the corporate, market-driven culture of its clients, who were also its donors. Minority Search fully equates market niche and mission, so that the pursuit of one is also the pursuit of the other. The mission mandates services to corporate—profitable—clients. Creating socially desirable opportunities for minority youths is a desirable by-product, but subordinate to the primary mission. By making new program activities complementary to and supportive of the primary mission, Minority Search is able to maximize economic gain without endangering other goals or resources. This has undoubtedly increased its efficiency. However, Minority Search is now effectively captured by the corporate market. Its diminishing benefits for minority students, especially low-income ones, may ultimately endanger its ability to meet corporate interests.

Structuring Predictable Client Relationships. The structure of client relationships forms an important vehicle for managing resource dependencies for fee-reliant organizations. Ideally, agencies apply strategic planning rather than ad hoc adjustments in their efforts to structure such relationships and produce predictable revenue streams. We identified four contingencies associated with such efforts for the two agencies (see Table 5.1): (1) the time frame within which client relationships operate, (2) the opportunity for repeat business and low-cost marketing strategies, (3) the fiscal competency of clients, and (4) the dominant client type. The ways in which market structures are institutionalized along these dimensions limit the range of options available to organizations. Christian Therapists and Minority Search differ in the extent to which their markets are structured along these dimensions and therefore in the extent to which they have opportunities to create predictable client relationships.

Christian Therapists—Mainly Unpredictable Structures. Christian Therapists operates with time-limited client services. Its clients receive individual psychotherapy, the duration of which is unpredictable but usually measured in weeks or months.[4] Should a client miss a session, the agency and the

assigned therapist lose expected income; should a client voluntarily terminate treatment, agency income is also lost; if a client cannot pay for a session,
agency policy prohibits therapists from giving the client additional treatment hours until the agency has received payment for services already
provided. Such a policy may lead to premature terminations of service and
was occasionally violated by therapists.

Second, Christian Therapists has few repeat clients. Individual clients
who complete counseling rarely return in significant numbers, although
strong relationships with other agencies could, over time, serve much the
same function by referring a steady stream of new fee-paying clients. Christian Therapists has maintained contact with agencies that might refer clients,
but these efforts have not generated predictable streams of clients. It has
attempted to make itself known to local Christian churches through workshops, speakers, and outreach in suburban churches. The latter did serve to
channel new clients to the satellite offices, but heavy staff involvement in
establishing the new sites diverted attention from potential clients or referral
sources located close to the main office and truncated the existing referral
network.

Third, Christian Therapists relies on clients with mixed fiscal competency. There are few hard data on the fiscal resources of the agency's clients,
but they seem to vary to a considerable degree. Certainly, both low- and
middle-income clients are likely to have limited discretionary income for
psychotherapy and to require agency subsidy. There is indirect support for
this interpretation for the 1987–88 fiscal year, when the agency billed almost
50 percent of therapy hours at less than the maximum fee and wrote off fees
equivalent to almost 8 percent of all client revenues.

Reliance on direct payments from clients creates inherent uncertainty
unless the agency is assured a predictable flow of clients with equally predictable abilities to pay the fees. These problems are reduced for agencies that
rely on government grants and contracts to cover in part or full the cost of
services for designated clients. Seeking clients with access to third-party
payments serves a similar cushioning function for fee-reliant organizations,
because it reduces the need to subsidize clients directly through sliding fees.

It also allows the agency to develop a more elaborate fee structure than
the individual client market will carry. Indirect evidence suggests that the
agency routinely billed insurance companies at a rate that was significantly
higher than the maximum rate for clients who paid the fee directly. Net
revenues per client hour approached $60 for some therapists in 1987, after
deductions of write-offs and subsidies in the form of sliding fees. Yet related
documentation shows that the full rate for self-paying clients was $45 per
client hour. Either some therapists were in such demand or so well creden-
tialed that clients agreed to pay more than the $45 full fee, or the latter fee
applied only to clients who paid the fee themselves while insurance companies were charged the highest rate allowed under the client's policy.

However, uncertainty is still prevalent because individual insurance carriers do not necessarily cover therapy or provide identical reimbursement rates. As a result, agencies may not know what proportion of a client's therapy fee the carrier will cover until the claim is processed, at which point it may not be possible to retrieve the balance from the client. Although third-party payments may be more predictable than direct client payments, agencies must have a firm handle on policies and procedures of individual insurance companies. All in all, the fiscal resources and competency of clients were problematic for Christian Therapists.

Finally, most clients are individuals. Clients who voluntarily seek therapy make personal decisions to do so. Their decisions might be informed by recommendations from pastors, doctors, and other trusted individuals in their network. But the choice is theirs, not that of a coordinating organization that, through contractual or other arrangements, assigns or directs them to an agency, perhaps in return for subsidizing the services. Christian Therapists' fee revenues, therefore, depend on whether a large number of independent decision makers seek its services rather than on decisions by a few institutionalized actors to subsidize it.

Such multiple and noninstitutionalized funding sources create an environment of inherent uncertainty and lack of control. No organization can easily negotiate such a fragmented system, especially one without effective institutional representatives (whether third-party payment sources or client organizations). Instead, the agency must negotiate with each client and convince the client that it can effectively meet his or her individual needs. Moreover, because the client's service needs are time-limited, the negotiation system itself is fragile and easily interrupted.[5] Consequently, Christian Therapists' market is characterized by reliance on individual clients, few repeat clients, time-limited services, ineffective referral networks, and clients with uncertain fiscal competency. These features make it very difficult to create predictable client relationships and help to explain the fiscal fragility of Christian Therapists.

Minority Search — Mainly Predictable Structures. Minority Search has been able to adopt very different strategies because its service domain allows for very different structures of client relationships. First, it has sought to assure itself of long-term client relationships by charging corporations a flat annual fee per student intern and billing the amount early in the fiscal year to cover costs of intern training during the summer. This allows Minority Search to portray the fees as post-effort payments and to resist requests for refunds if a client rejects an intern during the academic year.

The practice explains why Minority Search received almost half (48 percent) of its total fees for the 1987–88 fiscal year within the first two months, 64 percent within three months, and 81 percent within four months. Such a pattern of early and year-long fee commitments provides a high level of funding predictability for a given fiscal year and allows for flexible fiscal planning and control over management decisions. It resembles the security provided by twelve-month government grants and contracts that we observed for other agencies, but avoids the payment delays and significant cash-flow problems associated with government support.

Second, the agency has also sought to develop repeat clients. Because it requests corporations to agree to support student interns for the entire four-year period of their college studies, it can predict fee revenues reasonably well over several years. Such long-term client relationships easily evolve into repeat business as the corporate clients assess their future needs. In fact, Minority Search assumes that corporations will want to accept new interns in subsequent years, tells them so, and actively exploits the potential of repeat business in a variety of ways, much as would be expected of any good sales organization. It has devised points of multiple client contact to encourage new business by demonstrating how well it responds to client concerns. Consultations during which the agency informs the client about the progress of interns and seeks the client's evaluation of the intern's on-the-job performance provide these opportunities. By institutionalizing regular contacts with its clients in this manner, Minority Search has positioned itself for repeat business.

Third, Minority Search relies entirely on clients with a high level of fiscal competency. They are large corporations with sizable assets and impressive earnings that do not lack financial resources or face unsurmountable fiscal barriers in accessing its services or paying them up front. It does not need to use sliding fee scales or otherwise subsidize clients through third-party payments, donations, or write-offs. Although it requests donations for the precollege program, it portrays them as improving the quality of the product delivered, not as subsidizing corporate clients who cannot pay the standard fees. It has, therefore, a more effective market test of its performance and product value than is available to other nonprofit organizations. The early and prompt payment of fees gives additional validation of how clients value the services.

Finally, the clients are all major organizational actors. They agree to purchase the agency's services after making their own organizational assessment of whether the services will further corporate goals sufficiently to warrant the investment. Individuals within the corporations make the decision, but negotiations about what services to provide, to whom, and at what cost are more formalized, involve fewer actors, and include a broader range of institutional interests than similar dealings with a large number of independent decision makers. In the case of institutional decision makers, the stakes are higher because the outcome affects bigger chunks of resources, but the negotiation system involves fewer actors, outcome is more easily determined, and the basis for negotiation can be broader. The funding system therefore tends to be more resilient and less easily interrupted. Indeed, client type serves as a crucial thread running throughout these two organizations. Having corporations as clients enables Minority Search to pursue a variety of strategies, just as having individuals as clients precludes a variety of strategies for Christian Therapists.

Structuring Control over Other Resources. Creating predictable client relationships emphasizes extraorganizational relations around which strategies may reduce or minimize resource dependency. Alternatively, structuring control over intraorganizational characteristics may reduce environmental dependency and condition the impact of market forces. I review strategies to control the nature of staff interactions with clients, establish and internalize staff rewards (and thus create loyal staff and reduce direct competition from staff members), and limit delegation of control and responsibility for client access and management (see Table 5.1).

Christian Therapists—Incomplete Control. During the period covered by this study, Christian Therapists exercised relatively little control over a range of internal resources (it has since sought to rectify many of these problems). The agency operated with high staff autonomy that limited staff loyalty. On an ad hoc basis, individual staff members at times cut their own deals with the executive director, autonomously created agency-to-agency programs, and frequently served as the exclusive interface with other agencies. During most of the period, staff members also took full responsibility for their clients, subject only to limited supervision by the director and then only in his capacity as senior professional therapist.

The establishment of satellite offices strengthened staff autonomy by allowing linkages between individual clients and therapists to develop outside the confines of the agency itself. The agency would have only good-faith assurance that clients would even know from which agency they received services. When the large-scale staff defections occurred in 1987, the resigning staff members continued to see their clients, but now as independent practitioners.

Staff autonomy is less problematic if the organization in other ways can create staff loyalty or dependency—for example, through internal career ladders or staff training. However, at the time of the case study, Christian Therapists provided few opportunities for staff mobility or socialization. Most of its staff had advanced degrees, and all, including the director, provided therapy to clients. Yet it employed a significant proportion of its staff on a part-time basis. This gave it a more varied staff, improved its ability to match clients' needs, and thus facilitated good staff-client rapport. But these practices limited job security and attenuated staff dependence on the agency. Moreover, because the agency paid its staff a flat hourly fee (after they were fully trained), it could not recognize performance with monetary rewards.[6]

Only the internship program provided an internal career ladder by allowing senior staff to supervise the interns. After the staff resignations in

1987, even this supervisory role disappeared as Christian Therapists contracted with a former staff member to provide the service as part of his private practice. With the exception of professional supervisor-intern relations and occasional retreats, we found no indications of agencywide training programs for staff members to help place the agency's imprimatur on staff activities. As a result, staff loyalty was undeveloped, and the agency was highly fragmented and structurally incapable of responding to problematic or opportunistic contingencies.

Fragmentation is not in itself undesirable, because it allows organizations to operate in the face of internal conflict due to multiple goals (as in the case of Christian Therapists). As Meyer and Scott (1983) point out, by decoupling elements of the organization in this manner, the organization can buffer itself from external jolts and internal contradictions. The absence of a strong staff culture is much more problematic, because, without a unified mode of operation, the agency had no mechanism for ensuring that decisions independent staff members took adhered to the basic goals of the organization.

Finally, and possibly most important, individual staff members controlled access to and management of clients, the agency's key resource. In a very real sense, the bulk of resources flowed through staff rather than the organization per se. The proposal to institute a group practice model would simply have ratified an existing practice. For example, prior to the staff resignations, individual therapists collected client fees directly from their clients. The procedure served practical considerations because therapists counseled clients at night or in satellite locations and it was easier and cheaper for them to collect the fees than for an absent office manager to do so.

This system of locating fiscal management responsibilities with direct service staff paralleled how the agency structured its outreach program to public housing residents. In both cases, the practice left day-to-day decisions about the agency's major resource (clients, donors) and source of funding (fees, grants) under the direct control of individual therapists. In the case of fee-paying clients, staff members determined how much clients should pay on the sliding fee scale and whether to continue to see clients if they failed to pay the stipulated fee.[7] Staff control over client resources surfaced explicitly in the negotiated agreements in 1987 between the agency and resigning staff members when departing staff were allowed to keep the satellite offices as their own units. Christian Therapists could have proclaimed full ownership of the satellites and hired new staff to take over the client population, but it didn't. Rather, the agreement ratified that agency clients indeed "belonged" to staff members. In effect, the agency negotiated away one of its most profitable assets.

These problems of control can be overcome through strong administrative supervision and efforts to contain staff authority. However, the agency's director at the time appeared to think of himself as a colleague-supervisor, not an administrator. In fact, at one point he seriously planned to join a former staff member in a newly created private practice. His status and role relationships were also complicated by the fact that several of the staff were ordained clergy and that he had supervised many of the staff through the internship program.

Minority Search—Centralized Control. Minority Search differs from Christian Therapists on most of these dimensions. First, its isomorphism with and adoption of a corporate culture has served to justify relatively low staff autonomy. This allows it to centralize planning and operate through a predefined division of labor. Management exercises control over subordinates and retains for itself the role of strategic decision making. For example, marketing activities go through the agency's line level, never through staff.

Minority Search has balanced this strategy with staff development efforts and the creation of internal career ladders. It defines staff development as an official agency goal. It provides staff members with a range of formal training programs. The work with student interns also serves as informal training for staff. The focus on staff development derives in part from the agency's central mission, because it parallels the agency's efforts to induce its corporate clients to do likewise. This also serves marketing purposes because it allows Minority Search to point to its own actions as a model and as evidence of commitment to its mission and approach.

The agency has also made explicit efforts to increase internal mobility by reorganizing its thirteen staff members into a five-tier organizational structure (from three tiers). The staff is too small to require such a complex organizational structure for purposes of supervision, but the change made it possible to incorporate more explicit and longer internal career paths and to develop more finely graded levels of compensation. The agency's affiliation with a national network of similar agencies in other cities provides further opportunities for staff mobility. These features allow Minority Search to reward staff for long-term commitment to the agency and to enhance their sense of personal and organizational accomplishments in the face of low autonomy.

Perhaps as important, the agency's work with major corporations allows its staff direct and legitimate access to high-level key corporate actors. These contacts provide other forms of compensation as staff members work closely with corporate personnel directors, professional supervisors of student interns, and, on occasion, top corporate executives. These interactions allow staff members to increase their familiarity with and appreciation for corporate activities and help them perform their jobs. The contacts and skills, which are easily transferable to the corporate clients themselves, also increase the market value of the staff members and constitute a form of personal rewards. Moreover, if most service providers derive status from their clients, the staff of Minority Search have far greater opportunities for this type of status reward than the staff of nonprofit organizations that serve troubled and low-income clients. The agency's decision to define its primary mission as assisting its corporate clients rather than minority students thus also benefits its staff members.

Finally, several structural features have allowed the agency to control access to and management of its clients and to avoid direct competition from its own staff. The central focus on serving corporate clients means that corporate contacts and networks are critical for success. Such contacts and networks are most efficient if they occur at the top of the corporate hierarchy to provide initial entry and approval. Minority Search uses a policy (governing) and an advisory (network) board of top corporate executives to provide access to the corporate market in this manner. The reliance on top-level institutional relationships means that staff members cannot easily create them on their own. These networks and relationships are properties of the agency, not of its individual staff members.

These practices have allowed Minority Search to maintain or develop control over its key organizational resources, especially its staff and market access. It has pursued strategies that promote staff loyalty and structured its key market activities around and through the organization itself, rather than through the independent activities of its staff.

These practices contrast sharply with those of Christian Therapists. There staff members controlled access to clients, recruited clients directly, and engaged them in individualized therapy that required and fostered close client-staff rapport and loyalty. Staff members operated satellite offices outside the agency's confines, determined the level of fees that clients should pay, and collected fees for the agency, but were compensated only in proportion to the number of hours they gave counseling. Under these circumstances, the loyalty of staff members becomes a critical resource: the agency depends more on its staff than they do on it. However, Christian Therapists provided few opportunities for internal staff mobility or other mechanisms for fostering staff loyalty. It lost its battle to maintain organizational control when most of its staff members left and set themselves up as independent therapists or otherwise competed directly with the agency.

Summary

The case studies of these two fee-dependent agencies illustrate the difficulty of categorizing nonprofit organizations as *charitable, commercial,* and *mixed* (Young, 1988b; Hansmann, 1987; Hall, 1988), depending on their funding profiles. Both agencies are commercial in that most of their revenues come from private sector fees. Both give de facto priority to marketing strategies, but neither endorses building budgetary surpluses as a primary goal, as do commercial nonprofit organizations (Young, 1988b, p. 61).

In spite of these similarities, the findings show that the two agencies differ dramatically in their abilities to secure fees on a continuing basis, in their structure, and in their management of change. I interpret these differences as reflecting the extent to which they have linked their market niche and mission, how they have structured their fee relationships, and how they couple these to other agency resources—in short, how they manage their resources and use appropriate contingency responses.

Although the two agencies may represent extreme differences in strategic approaches, their experiences demonstrate the strengths and weaknesses of a variety of strategies to manage contingencies associated with reliance on fee revenues in the social service field. The findings illustrate strategic contingencies associated with the structure of markets and fee relationships over which agencies may have only limited or residual control. Agencies control which markets to pursue and how to establish a particular market niche. However, once that choice is made, they face a set of institutionalized features that structure fee relationships within that particular industry, such as access to third-party payments or the expected duration of services. These features limit further options. Agencies can decide whether to accept a particular structure of fee relationships, modify it within fairly narrow parameters, or forfeit the revenue source.

Agencies have greater control over how to expand the particular market niche they have selected for themselves. However, as the findings show, market decisions may easily detract from efforts to pursue substantive goals articulated in organizational missions. Even when carefully crafted to establish clear priorities, as in the case of Minority Search, organizational missions operate within market parameters. Moreover, as the case of Christian Therapists shows, other organizations (for example, the Christian Church) that provide key resources (flexible funding, legitimacy, leadership) may seek to achieve their own goals by influencing strategic decisions about how the mission is implemented. The case findings show that it is difficult to pursue mission and market niche simultaneously unless the two are fully congruent, as they are for business organizations.

Agencies would appear to exercise most explicit control over a range of internal management decisions about the conditions under which staff interact with clients, the structure of staff positions, opportunities for rewards, the nature of staff supervision, and delegation of control and responsibility. These strategies relate to the administrative structure of the organization. They are less directly linked to market contingencies or other external resource relations, but require a proactive, organizationally directed style of management.

Findings from the two agencies suggest that nonprofits that rely on client-paid fees need to pay careful attention to administrative types of strategies if they are to address problems associated with creating loyal staff and loyal and numerous clients. Such efforts not only retain organizational control over key resources but also may condition the impact of market or other external forces. Even so, the efforts, as well as marketing strategies that seek to convert potentially fragile fee relationships into ongoing and predictable resource bases, may not easily reconcile themselves with manifest organizational goals. The market structure of the social service and community development fields limits the range of available options for achieving these objectives, but less so than is the case for other sources of funding.

Client-paid fee revenues are attractive to nonprofits because such revenues exert less direct control over management and appear more subject to the types of widely used marketing strategies that for-profit organizations employ. Many social service and community development organizations probably resemble Christian Therapists in how they define their missions and structure fee relationships (as did the other three social service agencies with fee revenues). Those that rely heavily on fees and other earned income may therefore experience high rates of transformation and dissolution. To the extent that nonprofit organizations increasingly turn to fees and similar service charges, they may encounter problems that resemble those of Christian Therapists, although probably more gradually and less explicitly.

Notes

1. Portions of this chapter are based on Grønbjerg and Harkins, 1990.
2. At one point, staff members debated whether or not to use a telephone-answering message that stressed the agency's born-again Christian ideology. The theological diversity among staff members appears to have scuttled the idea.
3. As I show in Chapter Seven, donations fluctuate even more for other social service agencies. The focus on institutional sources of donations and on efforts to build these onto existing client relationships may alleviate but not solve the general problem of how to secure donations.
4. The agency does not offer long-term psychoanalytic treatment and has a policy of discontinuing services at the end of the tenth week for clients who do not pay the full fee.
5. This is one reason why client advocacy groups are not likely to come into existence as they do for clients with prolonged or serious conditions (such as developmental disability, mental illness, or old age).
6. The proposed group practice model would have addressed this problem by creating an incentive system for the staff.
7. In fact, after the wave of staff resignations, the agency discovered that some clients owed as much as $800 in unpaid fees that therapists had failed to collect while continuing to see the clients.

SIX

Special Event Fund-Raising: Managing Uncertainty

Special events resemble fees or service charges in that both require marketing products or services to customers who are willing to pay for them. However, fees and service charges usually provide nonprofits with revenues on a fairly continuous basis and require ongoing efforts to develop and monitor core organizational activities. Proceeds from special events are likely to be much more sporadic and to require intensive but episodic management efforts that may well be peripheral to the organization's major purpose. These features create uncertainty and closely related administrative contingencies that nonprofits must address if they are to rely on special events for significant proportions of their revenues. However, they have very high levels of discretion in making such decisions, because few outside organizations impose institutionalized requirements.

Historically, nonprofits have organized special events as a means of generating revenues and as a public relations vehicle for attracting favorable attention (Leibert and Sheldon, 1972). As a funding source, special events generate relatively small proportions of total revenues for most nonprofit organizations, but they have importance beyond their financial role (Mulligan, 1987).

For nonprofit organizations, the work involved in planning and executing events provides numerous opportunities for volunteers to become involved with the organization. The episodic nature of the work, the diverse activities, and the opportunity for leadership, as opposed to more mundane tasks, make events particularly attractive to volunteers. Special events also serve as important occasions for organizations to reward and entertain donors, volunteers, staff, and clients (Liner, 1987) and to cheer their own accomplishments. Preparations for events, as well as participation in them, help create personal contacts and promote a sense of community (Harris, 1988).

These outcomes, as well as opportunities for volunteer leadership, may also directly serve the organization's mission, such as when street fairs help community development organizations promote community pride and co-operation. Indeed, special events are integral to the expressive life of non-profits — allowing their members to celebrate their own achievements, commitment to shared goals, and sense of belonging. Decisions about whether and how to link events to the organization's mission are among the most difficult features for nonprofits in managing special events.

Special events have distinct utilities for other organizations as well, because a large number of businesses and professional consultants earn sizable profits from special events. They benefit from the cloak of legitimacy provided by their nonprofit clients, on whose behalf they organize events or solicit contributions (Montague, 1988, 1989a, 1989b). Special events have collateral value as marketing and promotion tools for celebrities and corporations, who obtain exposure and visibility from sponsoring or participating in events. In fact, corporations increasingly fund their involvement in nonprofit special events from their marketing budget rather than from their charitable contributions budget (Olcott, 1988). This commercialization of special events has recently come under greater scrutiny by the Internal Revenue Service.

For participants, special events also satisfy private interests that have less direct economic value, but for which they are willing to pay. Events have entertainment value and furnish access to leisure activities and interpersonal interaction. They create a safe arena for such activities and have special utility for newcomers and those without extensive personal networks (much as do churches). Special events may also cater to individuals' status aspirations by allowing them to interact with celebrities or explore realms from which they otherwise would be excluded (for example, they might visit the backstage at the opera, conduct the Chicago Symphony Orchestra, or be a school principal for a day). And, frequently, participants receive recognition for their support or involvement to boot.

Management Contingencies

Special events are one of the few sources of earned revenue that are widely accepted as particularly appropriate for nonprofit organizations. A large repertoire of special events, however, presents nonprofit managers with major contingencies. Infinite variations and choices are possible. The market structures through which special events revenues are generated create additional contingencies. As is the case for fees and service charges, special events highlight the trade-off between uncertainty and control.

Varieties of Special Events

Over time, an astonishing array of special events have come into existence and diffused across organizations. Some aim to give participants sufficient entertainment or leisure value for their money to produce a sizable surplus for the organization. That is the aim of such functions as charity balls, fashion shows, art exhibits, bazaars, auctions, fairs, carnivals, house tours, garden walks, theater benefits, bingo, raffles, walk-a-thons, benefit concerts, white elephant sales, celebrity cocktail parties, and cookie sales. Other events highlight the organization itself, such as anniversary celebrations, annual meetings, building dedications, ground-breaking ceremonies, citation awards, testimonial dinners, or open-house tours, but they may create less immediate financial rewards to the organization.

In addition to their diverse content and purposes, special event activities reflect a series of strategies or structural dimensions over which organizations exercise more or less deliberate control. For example, events may be designed to match the major purposes of the organization. (An organization serving the homeless might sponsor a fast for hunger rather than a fancy dress ball.) They may involve only a few events or a large number and diverse set of events. Some organizations now prepare booklets with a full cafeteria of special events, so that customers may select those of particular interest. This allows the organizations to cater to as many different tastes as possible and minimizes the impact of misjudging the attractiveness of any specific event.

Special events differ also in the scope and volume of efforts that they require of staff and volunteers and in how institutionalized they have become and therefore in how persistent a market they have created (for example, the Girl Scouts have undoubtedly created a permanent market for their cookies). They differ in the scope of the customer base and therefore in the type and amount of publicity efforts and marketing required. They differ in the extent to which they require the participation of other institutions (for example, police traffic control and city services for street fairs) and therefore in the nature of interorganizational relationships they promote or endanger.

The Market Structure of Special Events

In contrast to some forms of nonprofit fees and product sales, special events constitute an inherently unattractive market for proprietary businesses, except as the suppliers of necessary input for the events. One reason for this is that special event revenues have intrinsic instability. They involve intense short-term activities with relatively fixed expenses and uncertain payoff. Intense activities mean that labor inputs are high and costly if paid for on the open market. Short-term activities mean that the client market is episodic, unpredictable, and most likely shallow. They also mean that revenues are subject to circumstances over which the organization may have little or no control (such as other competing attractions, bad weather, or late-breaking news) — circumstances that reduce attendance and income but have no similar impact on costs. Nonprofits can offset these liabilities in part because of their reliance on volunteer workers and their access to loyal customers (such as donors and others committed to the organization and its goals). Proprietary organizations have access to few of these resources.

The use of volunteers to perform the work and the marketing of special events to donors and other loyal customers means that special event revenues become a hybrid of earnings and donations. When donors buy tickets or other items associated with special events, they receive something of value (prestige, entertainment, participation) in return for the support. The request for support therefore comes to resemble a normal market transaction, although the monetary value of the product may be less than what the customer paid for it. Perhaps for that reason, people cite special events as the type of appeal to which they are most likely to respond (cited by 51 percent in a Dallas survey; Gagnard, 1989).

From the point of view of both donors and those who dread asking others for donations, the resemblance to market transactions makes special events preferable to donations. Event participants receive something of concrete value in return for their support, and fund-raisers (professional or otherwise) do not have to rely solely on their ability to convey and sell the moral purpose or effectiveness of the organization.

Over time, special events may serve as clever marketing techniques for linking potential donors to an organization (Davidson, 1987). But they may also contribute to a mentality in which supporters want something in return for their money, thus undermining the basis for charitable donations. As a result, special events blur the line between commercial and donative transactions and constitute another set of mechanisms by which for-profit features come to dominate nonprofit ones. There is indirect evidence that this process is occurring. Observers from within the nonprofit sector (McGuire, 1989; Nemes, 1989) are concerned that special events will become less successful because of IRS efforts to disallow the full deduction of charitable donations if a service or product is received in return for the donation (as is the case for special events).

Management Discretion and Uncertainty

Special events provide occasions for nonprofit organizations to package and market a great variety of products, with full discretion over all specific activities and decisions. The success of special events reflects (at least in part) the organization's ability to obtain the necessary input (such as appropriate space or recognizable celebrities). However, it must decide which input to seek, how to organize the work appropriately, and how to balance receipts and outlays. There are few other sources of revenues over which nonprofit organizations exercise similar direct control or have as much management latitude.

The latitude and management discretion, however, are not without their costs. There are no mandatory requirements or guidelines issued by clout-heavy funders or key institutionalized actors about how to select and manage a successful event. Instead, nonprofit managers and volunteer committees must sort among the countless guides and hints to fashion their own event and attempt to make the event as special as possible in order to stand out above the crowd of similar efforts by other nonprofits (Reiss, 1987). Even so, the work and investments may have uncertain payoffs (in addition to other sources of uncertainty described above) because tastes and preferences vary greatly and are notoriously fickle. What works one year or for one organization may not do so again or for another organization. To maximize control over special event revenues, sponsoring organizations must monitor and shape such parameters as event costs, changes in taste or interests of event participants or volunteers, competition for sponsors, and distinctiveness of themes compared with those of other organizations.

Other problems occur because of the heavy reliance on volunteers. Large numbers of volunteers frequently require complex committee structures to complete the work in time (Devney, 1990). Nonprofit managers must be prepared to support volunteers and their committees. Although volunteers may constitute a flexible work force because of the variety of skills and interests they bring and because of the flexible hours they may be available, they are not paid staff. Consequently, the organization has little formal authority over them and has few options available if volunteer performance or attendance falls short.

These management problems help account for why special events have become sufficiently institutionalized to warrant a separate management literature and specialization. For example, Derrickson (1989) and Derrickson and Kurdylo (1990) jointly list seventy-three entries under the heading of fund-raising/special events. Almost three-quarters of these entries (73 percent) consist of manuals and how-to books with guidelines, elaborate checklists, and detailed examples. An additional 12 percent of the entries involve descriptions of some particularly successful event that other organizations might emulate.

The number of professional event managers shows the degree of specialization that the management of special events may require. The Society of Nonprofit Organizations' 1990 National Directory of Service and Product Providers to Nonprofit Organizations lists thirteen national or international consulting companies that are registered with the society as providing services and products for nonprofit special event fund-raising. There are many more local firms and consultants. The use of a professional manager, of course, helps buffer the organization against failure by ensuring that something more than a minimum level of effort is exerted. It also makes it less likely that the organization has to blame any valued or high-status volunteer in case the event fails and provides less than the anticipated amount of proceeds.

Unpredictable Funding Stream

Management discretion also comes at the cost of unpredictable levels of funding. For the eleven case-study organizations[1] in which it was possible to track special events revenues separately, net proceeds fluctuated considerably from year to year. Annual changes (up or down) in net special event proceeds averaged only 18 to 19 percent for Community Renewal and Preservation Council, but they ranged between 32 and 50 percent for Alcohol Treatment, Youth Outreach, Immigrant Welfare League, and Hispanic Youth Services.

Fluctuations in special event proceeds were even more extreme for the remaining organizations. Net proceeds changed by an average of 76 and 350 percent annually for two different events organized by New Town Sponsors, by 149 percent for Hispanic Neighbors (over the 1981–1989 period only), and by 612 percent for United Residents. In a few cases (such as United Residents), large annual fluctuations in net special event proceeds reflect the success of an anniversary celebration that was held only once. However, most of the organizations maintained a fairly consistent schedule of events from year to year, but still experienced large annual changes.

Strategies for Managing Special Events

Findings from the case-study organizations show that special events are widely used among them but are difficult to manage successfully. Executive directors or other key staff members uniformly emphasized the amount of work involved and the unpredictable nature of outcomes. Several expressed specific frustrations about having to manage events that board members or other volunteers became sufficiently enthusiastic about to initiate, but left in midstream. Most, however, emphasized the public relations value of successful events and the more general social, emotional, and celebratory functions of events for volunteers, contributors, board members, and occasionally clients.

For most of the organizations, special events provide only small proportions of total revenues (1 to 5 percent), and strategies to manage them had relatively low priority compared with efforts to maintain other funding relations. Yet, for three community development organizations—Preservation Council, Hispanic Neighbors, and New Town Sponsors—special events constituted a major source of funding. Obviously, large annual fluctuations in special event proceeds become particularly problematic for such organizations. My review of management contingencies and strategies associated with special events therefore relies primarily on findings from these three organizations.

Preservation Council, Hispanic Neighbors, and New Town Sponsors differ in how financially successful their events have been, in the types of strategies they employ for managing the events, and in the degree of uncertainty these strategies create. The strategies influence how the three organizations deal with general management challenges associated with fluctuating streams of revenue and of work intensity; the strategies also determine the mechanisms by which the organizations buffer their central cores from uncertainties associated with reliance on special events.

Diverse Event Parameters

The three organizations received the bulk of their revenues from earned revenues, including those associated with annual special events. As Figures 4.11, 4.12, and 4.13 showed, all three encountered funding turbulence, most of which reflected experiences with special events. However, the sources of turbulence are difficult to compare, because the three organizations differ in their accounting practices (see Appendix A).

The special events presented by the three organizations have some similarities. All aim to attract the general public, take place in outdoor locations, recur annually on a regular schedule, require some level of participation by other organizations, and involve a broad scope of activities. The events themselves have different themes and vary in financial success and how proceeds are used. The three organizations differ also in what they define as the overall purpose of the event and in how central the events are to the core of their activities or mission.

Hispanic Neighbors—Increasing Success, Key Role for Operations and Mission. Hispanic Neighbors reported revenues of about $189,000 in 1989, but actually grossed considerably more than that ($277,000) when gross revenues from its major special event ($181,000), rather than just the net profit, are counted. As Figure 4.12 shows, Hispanic Neighbors experienced major changes in the amounts and sources of revenues, from significant reliance on public funds to very high reliance on special event revenues.

The special event proceeds come from a major ethnic street fair that takes place over several days in late summer. It draws hundreds of thousands of people from all over the city and region and may soon outgrow its current location. The fair includes ethnic music and entertainment by well-known performers; a carnival; booths where beer, food, and products are sold; and a variety of other activities, such as mural paintings. Visitors do not pay to attend the fair. Rather, Hispanic Neighbors gets most of the direct costs underwritten by promotion fees from corporations and by booth rentals from local churches, organizations, and businesses. The organization also receives all proceeds from beer sales staffed by organizations represented on its board and by other organizations if necessary.

As Figure 6.1 shows, Hispanic Neighbors has experienced increasing financial success with the event. Net revenues from the event increased from about $15,000 over the 1974–1982 period to almost $70,000 in 1989 (all in constant 1981 dollars), or from about 10 percent of total net revenues to almost half. Gross revenues have increased even more dramatically, up from 10 to 20 percent of gross revenues from 1975 to 1978, to about half from 1979 to 1982, and to almost 80 percent in 1985, before stabilizing at about two-thirds.

The growth in special event revenues has outstripped growth in events

Figure 6.1. Gross Special Event Revenues and Expenses, 1970–1989, Hispanic Neighbors.

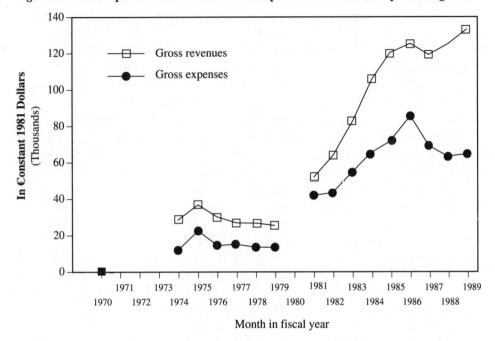

expenditures since 1982, and especially after 1985, when the current executive director was hired, instituted new cost control measures, and encouraged board members to investigate how major special events were organized in another large city. Among other changes, subcommittees now have to prepare and defend their part of the budget for the event, procedures for managing the event have been standardized, and massive notebooks outline all contracts or agreements, budgets, procedures, and time lines for each year. The planning of each event spans the entire year. Some activities even begin before the previous event is over.

The increasing financial success of the event is important because Hispanic Neighbors uses all the revenues it generates exclusively for its own programs and operations, including the cost of leadership training for community volunteers.[2] Hispanic Neighbors cannot easily postpone or reduce these efforts for any sustained period of time without endangering its primary purpose. However, donations from foundations and corporations have also been substantial, covering a minimum of 40 percent of administration and program expenditures. Hispanic Neighbors has well-established relationships with several funders and could undoubtedly make a special effort to request additional funds from them should the event fail.

Although important for meeting operational expenses, the financial success of the event is only part of the organization's goals for the event. The event plays a key role in meeting the organization's mission. It serves as a major vehicle for celebrating the community's ethnic identity and is an

integral part of Hispanic Neighbors' own program activities. This critical role
is reflected in the fact that all event activities require board approval and are
under the direct control of the board.

Consistent with the mission of community organizing, the event provides numerous opportunities for community residents to plan, negotiate
with vendors and other commercial sponsors, and manage the event. More
than 500 local residents are involved in such volunteer activities for as much
as twelve months prior to the event. The organization's director believes that
this involvement provides major opportunities for the community's mostly
low-income residents to practice and experience leadership and to obtain
self-confidence so as to exercise community power in other arenas.

In addition, Hispanic Neighbors has organized the event so that its
affiliated organizations also generate revenues from it. Member organizations have first refusals on obtaining access to booths at the event, in return
for which they operate beer-selling booths for Hispanic Neighbors. (Other
vendors are required to rent booths.) Some obtain considerable revenues
from these activities. By providing these opportunities to other organizations in the community, Hispanic Neighbors ensures their cooperation and
support for its more controversial Alinsky-type empowerment strategies.

*Preservation Council—Sustained Success, Limited Role for Operations
and Mission.* Preservation Council reported net revenues of about $232,000
in 1990 but actually managed $389,000 when both reported revenues from
its major special event ($206,000) and the costs of food and beverages for the
event (more than $120,000) are counted. As shown in Figure 4.11, Preserva-
tion Council has experienced some fluctuation in overall revenues following
the late 1970s, including three years during the 1980s when annual changes
approached or exceeded 25 percent (up or down). Most of these changes
reflected variations in net revenues from the major event because of weather
conditions and other uncontrollable factors.

Net revenues from the event now account for about 80 percent of total
revenues, up from 40 percent in the mid 1980s. This shift reflects mainly a
decline in other sources of earnings. During the late 1970s, Preservation
Council received substantial revenues from tuition payments and rental
income. It lost these sources when it moved to its current smaller facility,
prompting a decline in revenues in 1983–84 and an increasing role of special
event proceeds.

The event consists of an art fair, a two-day, outdoor event during which
artists exhibit and sell art and local businesses sell food and beverages.
Visitors pay an entrance fee and receive a booklet that lists exhibitors and
scheduled events and includes advertisements from local businesses. A jury
of experts selects participating artists from a large number of applicants
from across the country. All applicants must pay an application fee, and all
selected artists must donate an art object to the organization. Most of the
event's revenues come from gate fees, a percentage of gross food and beverage

sales, and auction sales of donated art objects. Preservation Council obtains additional revenues from application fees, booklet advertisements, and sales of posters and t-shirts.

Preservation Council has experienced sustained financial success with the event. As Figure 6.2 shows, gross revenues (including revenues to cover costs of food and beverages) increased steadily but slowly over the years, despite bad weather in 1986. Expenditures have shown a similar pattern, and net proceeds have remained steady at about 50 percent of gross revenues. However, expenditures generally exceed 85 percent of revenues if the costs of food and beverages are excluded from both sides of the equation.

This financial stability reflects the event's long history (it has passed its fiftieth anniversary), well-established reputation (more than 500 new vendors competing for ten to fifteen new openings each year and tens of thousands of visitors), and high level of institutionalization. Like Hispanic Neighbors, Preservation Council maintains massive notebooks with time lines and documentation on all activities, in order to coordinate the work of more than 500 volunteers, who plan and manage the event. Each event chairperson serves for two years, and planning for the event is ongoing throughout the year.

The increased reliance on event revenues suggests that Preservation Council is becoming more vulnerable to events-related conditions. However, its operations are probably not at risk. It has access to a relatively wealthy and active community, to whom it could effectively appeal for special support if the event should fail completely. More important, although net proceeds account for the bulk of all revenues, they are used only in part for operating purposes. In contrast to Hispanic Neighbors' proceeds, net proceeds from Preservation Council's event far surpass total expenditures for operating and administrative expenses (by a factor of two for the average year over the 1981–1989 period). That is because only a relatively small—and declining—portion of expenditures goes for personnel costs, down from 25 to 30 percent in

Figure 6.2. Gross Special Event Revenues and Expenses, 1980–1988, Preservation Council.

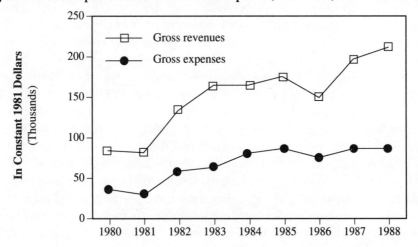

the early 1980s to less than 20 percent in recent years. Together with relatively fixed expenditures associated with its building, these expenses have accounted for less than half of all expenditures in most years.

Instead, Preservation Council uses the net proceeds for a range of optional program expenditures, most of which could be postponed without directly affecting its own operations. Activities such as tree planting and sidewalk repairs account for an average of 20 percent of annual expenses. Donations to other organizations account for more than one-third. A youth club in the community receives the bulk of donations, averaging about 30 percent of all net expenditures for Preservation Council. The donation is in accordance with a long-standing written agreement between the two organizations, which stipulates that the youth club is to receive 40 percent of net proceeds from the event.

The donation has been subject to some debate within the organization because of the large amounts of money involved (now approaching $50,000 per year) and the affluent status of the families served by the club. However, the written agreement between the two organizations, their interlocking boards of directors, and the argument that the youth club attracts and keeps affluent families with children in the community limits any serious efforts to discontinue the practice.

Other local organizations receive much smaller amounts. For example, Preservation Council awards about 2 percent of its net proceeds to an umbrella organization with which it is affiliated, only slightly more than it usually donates to local schools or other organizations in the community (1 percent). It has now established formal procedures for managing these smaller donations, including the use of application forms, funding criteria, and reporting requirements for grantee organizations.

Also in contrast to Hispanic Neighbors, the event has only a peripheral role in meeting the organization's mission. Although at one point the event helped celebrate the community's self-proclaimed artistic identity, currently the art emphasis is at best consistent with several of the organization's other activities. The content and organization of the event have only limited relevance to the organization's major mission of promoting planned development, community preservation, and reductions in congestion. Financial success is the primary goal of the event.

Nor does the event appear to promote organizational development or community cohesion to nearly the same extent as does Hispanic Neighbors' event. Although Preservation Council supports other organizations with proceeds from the special event, these linkages are primarily financial and contractual rather than part of sustained efforts to develop cooperative relationships. Nor are neighborhood residents even the primary source of volunteers. Many volunteers live a considerable distance away and have no involvement with the community other than their participation in the event. In addition, the event operates quite independently from the organization's other activities. Preservation Council's board has no direct control over or explicit involvement in the event, although it has recently voted to require the event's chairperson to be a member of the board for the duration of his or her chairmanship.

New Town Sponsors — Limited Financial Success, Mixed Role for Operations and Mission. New Town Sponsors reported revenues of about $115,000 in 1988. Detailed information on the several special events that the organization managed over several years were not available, but audit statements appear to include both gross revenues and expenditures for the events. As Figure 4.13 shows, New Town Sponsors has experienced major growth and subsequent decline in revenues, reflecting the initiation and subsequent complete elimination of one major event. The organization obtained small amounts of funding from public arts and humanities programs as well as substantial donations from local businesses and investors to undertake the event. These designated grants or donations began at less than $8,000 in 1983, increased to $130,000 in each of the next two years, and reached $162,000 in 1986. At its height, the arts event accounted for more than 60 percent of total revenues.

Several smaller events accounted for about one-quarter of total revenues in 1987–88, consisting of mainly participation fees paid by street fair exhibitors. Other earned income, averaging 14 percent over the period, came from advertisements in a small informational booklet about the community that New Town Sponsors publishes and distributes free of charge to local residents. Together, dues and earned revenues from smaller events or other program activities have accounted for an average of 65 percent of the organization's revenues during the 1983–1988 period.

The major event organized by New Town Sponsors was a cultural event that it began in 1982 and that consisted of several days during which visitors to the community could observe art in the making, rather than just finished products. Artists set up shop on sidewalks or inside commercial buildings with no entrance fee for visitors. Organized activities took place, but the organization did not set up booths or allocate space to other vendors. It sought donations from local developers and businesses to cover the costs of the event. It discontinued the event in 1987 to focus on other, much smaller events, primarily a book fair in which vendors rent booths from the organization.

New Town Sponsors had minimal financial success with the cultural event. It managed to break even in most years (see Figure 6.3), but lost money in 1987, when events expenditures exceeded revenues by 19 percent. Net events proceeds averaged 7 percent of gross event revenues. This is a fairly low level of financial success compared with the events organized by the other two organizations.[3] In contrast, sales of advertisements for the community booklet and other program activities are steady money makers, although averaging only $5,000 to $6,000 in net proceeds per year.

Because event revenues have exceeded expenditures by only modest

Figure 6.3. Net Proceeds from Special Events by Source, 1983–1988, New Town Sponsors.

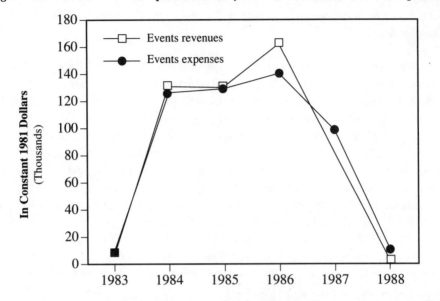

amounts, they played little role in meeting operating expenses. New Town Sponsors has not relied on them to meet its own operating expenditures, as have the two other organizations. Taken together, special events and related program activities usually constituted net costs, meeting only 6 percent of basic administrative expenditures in the best year (1982). The events-related funding turbulence has therefore had only limited impact on basic operating activities, because these have been funded primarily through membership dues. Dues revenues and operating expenditures have remained fairly stable over the years, although dues have declined somewhat in recent years (by an average of 2 percent per year) when adjusted for inflation.

The event has had shifting utility in meeting the organization's mission. New Town Sponsors did not intend for the cultural event to be a financial success or to cover its own operation, although it wanted to break even. Instead, the event's cultural focus, which had some borderline affinity with the community's early association with the printing industry, was designed explicitly to attract people of high income to the area. The developers, financial institutions, and local businesses that control the organization viewed the event as promoting the community and familiarizing potential residents and shoppers with its residential facilities and commercial amenities. This is fully consistent with efforts to overcome negative images of the community, promote it as a desirable residential area, attract new commercial establishments, and safeguard existing investments. New Town Sponsors solicited donations to cover the approximate amount required to cover the event. Local merchants and developers responded in the hope that the event would increase visibility of the community and allow them to recover their cost in the form of future sales.

As the community increasingly established itself, the event lost much of its utility for these donors, and they lost enthusiasm for the relatively high level of sponsorship it required. As it grew in scope and success, it also demanded increasing efforts by the organization's two-person staff and occasional student interns. By 1984, it rivaled the events of Hispanic Neighbors and Preservation Council in revenues, but while the latter two relied on the active and year-long participation of a large number of volunteers, New Town Sponsors had few people resources of this type, and its small staff carried most of the work load. A change in executive director and the difficulty of maintaining a separate accounting system for the event also contributed to the decision to terminate it. Because of the event's financial structure (donations), there were no compelling financial reasons to continue the high level of effort.

Special Event Strategies

The analysis presented so far suggests that the three organizations differ considerably in how they have structured their special events. These differences represent specific management decisions and contingencies. The top panel of Table 6.1 summarizes some of these contingencies along four dimensions: the mechanisms by which event revenues are generated, the structure and amount of work associated with organizing the event, the utility of the event to other organizations, and the utility of the event to the organizations themselves.

Structure of Revenue Generation. The three organizations differ in how they have structured the generation of revenues. Gate receipts, promotion fees, vendor sales, and booth fees differ in the extent to which they are secured up front before the event takes place or are generated during the event itself in proportion to the number of people attending the event. As Table 6.1 shows, both Hispanic Neighbors and New Town Sponsors rely primarily on revenue sources that are secured in advance of the event and escape uncertainties associated with weather conditions. In contrast, Preservation Council obtains the bulk of its event revenues from sources that depend directly on the number of visitors to the event and the amount of money they spend.

Hispanic Neighbors negotiates promotion fees with corporate sponsors and booth fees from commercial vendors long before the event. The vendors retain all earnings (and uncertainties) from the sales. The organization monopolizes the sale of beer, a significant source of revenue that depends on the number of visitors to the event but is a low risk because the unsold beer can be returned to the supplier or otherwise disposed of without loss of investment. New Town Sponsors generated its revenues from donations also secured before the event took place. It has now begun to charge booth fees from participating vendors for its more recent and smaller events.

Preservation Council gets its revenues from gate receipts, a fixed

Table 6.1. Special Event Strategies and Contingencies.

	Events-Reliant Community Organizations		
Strategies	*Hispanic Neighbors*	*Preservation Council*	*New Town Sponsors*
Event Strategies			
Revenue Generation			
Gate receipts[a]	None	Primary	None
Share of vendor sales[a]	None	Primary	None
Product Sales[a]	High	Medium	None
Promotion fees	Primary	Low	None
Voluntary donations	Low	Low	Primary
Booth fees	Mixed	Mixed	Low
Organization of Work			
Range of tasks	Medium	Extensive	Medium
Reliance on volunteers	High	High	Low
Institutionalized process	High	High	Medium
Utility to Other Organizations			
Grants/donations	None	Several/large	None
Earnings/promotion	Members/vendors	Vendors/exhibitors	Vendors/exhibitors
Utility to Organization			
Use of proceeds	Operations	Operations/grants	Little
Link to mission	Integral	Separate	Changing
Uncertainty Strategies			
Resource base	<u>Diversified</u>	Consolidated	<u>Diversified</u>
Financial reserves	Medium	<u>Very high</u>	Low
Organization of work	<u>Structured</u>	<u>Structured</u>	Ad hoc
Revenue risk/return ratio	<u>Min. risk</u>	Max. return	<u>Min. risk</u>

Note: Items <u>underlined</u> designate strategies that minimize uncertainty or reduce its impact.

[a] Relatively uncertain revenue sources.

Source: Case-Study Project.

percentage of net proceeds from food and beverage sales, and auction proceeds for donated art products. The only predictable revenues secured prior to the event come from a small application fee for exhibitors (500 each year) and the sale of posters, t-shirts, and advertisements in the events booklet.

Organization of Work. The three organizations also differ in how they have organized the work. Different types of event revenues vary in the amount, nature, and timing of work that sponsoring organizations must undertake. Prior to the event, Hispanic Neighbors engages a large number of volunteers in carefully structured efforts to negotiate promotion agreements, organize booth locations, obtain cooperation from the city for police control and special electrical wiring, and secure entertainment and related equipment. During the event, responsibilities are relatively limited and involve primarily managing the street itself. Hispanic Neighbors has no booths or gates to operate and no vendors to collect receipts from or monitor in other ways.

Because New Town Sponsors relied on donations for its major cultural event, it also had only few obligations during the event itself. Most of the work consisted of obtaining donations and arranging for proper facilities and accessories for event participants. These efforts were not nearly as institutionalized as for the other two organizations. They did not involve continued and active participation of a large number of volunteers to plan and carry out the event, and the event lasted only four years — probably insufficient time to fully institutionalize the work.

In contrast, the revenue sources on which Preservation Council relies for its special events require it to be directly involved in an extensive range of activities during the event: it must operate the gates, collect receipts from vendors, store the money, conduct auctions, award prizes, and manage the street during the event. It therefore depends on a large and active body of volunteers to work during the event itself. Like Hispanic Neighbors, Preservation Council has institutionalized these activities to a significant extent in order to ensure that all volunteers know what their responsibilities are.

Utility to Other Organizations. The three organizations differ in the mechanisms by which they maintain linkages to other organizations or otherwise seek to build in ongoing support or collaboration. Given the scale of events that the three organizations operate, such support and participation is critical to ensuring that the necessary tasks are completed and that large numbers of people know about and attend the event. Thus, Hispanic Neighbors and Preservation Council both must obtain the collaboration of food and beverage vendors, to make sure that refreshments are available in sufficient quantities to satisfy diverse tastes and large numbers of visitors. In return, vendors get publicity and opportunities for substantial earnings. Preservation Council also expects exhibitors to sell products during its event and uses its own auction of donated products to help generate interest in sales. New Town Sponsors has only recently begun to charge participation fees for vendors or exhibitors and did not use that practice while operating its major event.

Obviously, the more successful the event is in attracting customers, the more vendors and promoters will be interested in participating and the more the sponsoring organization can negotiate advantageous arrangements with them. Hispanic Neighbors seems to provide vendors with the highest return on their efforts, because it charges a flat booth fee per vendor; Preservation Council takes a cut of total sales. The latter practice may provide greater financial benefit to the sponsoring organization but requires it to supervise sales and manage cash flow.

Two of the organizations also provide opportunities for noncommercial vendors to benefit financially from the event. Hispanic Neighbors makes booths available at no cost to its member organizations and to other non-profit or public agencies in return for staffing of its own beer booths. Most depend on these booth earnings for a significant part of their own revenues. Preservation Council uses a substantial portion of its own net proceeds to support other organizations directly in the form of grants. By providing donations, rather than demanding sweat equity, Preservation Council links recipient organizations less directly to its own activities and is less able to ensure their active participation in scheduled activities, but it maintains greater control over the event itself.

Utility to the Organization. Finally, the three organizations differ in the utility of the event to the organization itself and its basic purpose. As noted earlier, the event is central to and has broad utility for Hispanic Neighbors. Net proceeds are used entirely for its own program operations, and their flexibility and unrestricted nature allow Hispanic Neighbors to pursue empowerment and confrontations as part of its organizing efforts. The event forms the basis for other goals as well: instillation of pride in the ethnic heritage of the community, linkage to other community-based organizations, and structured opportunities for leadership and active participation in decision making for community residents. The central importance of the event for achieving these goals helps explain why the organization seeks to exercise direct and extensive control over the event activities.

Preservation Council also relies extensively on proceeds from its major events to cover its own operations and obtains sufficient surplus to reallocate substantial proportions to other organizations. Although it helps draw attention to the community and its attractive residential character, the event is otherwise of limited utility for the organization, separate from its other efforts and not subject to its direct control.

In contrast, New Town Sponsors receives very little financial benefit from the special events it has organized, but it has viewed special events as integral to its major purpose of promoting the community's growing complement of residential and commercial facilities. The small financial stake in the event meant that the demands on time, effort, and funding easily came to outweigh the less tangible benefits of goodwill and other opportunities for long-term returns on investment.

Managing Uncertainty

Organizing special events is an exercise in the management of uncertainty. Organizations must select among a wide range of options to define a special entertainment or other market niche for the event on the basis of incomplete market information. They must carry out diverse and time-consuming activities without access to paid staff who specialize in such work. Although some events are successful (as measured by publicity, amount of gross revenues, or net proceeds), unforeseen circumstances may sharply reduce financial returns.

For organizations that rely extensively on special event revenues, there are additional sources of uncertainty. For example, they must contend with major fluctuations in cash flow associated with the event itself, and also must meet their ongoing obligations associated with operation of the organization. Monthly data on financial activities for Hispanic Neighbors and Preservation Council show intense bursts of monthly outlays and receipts due to the special event activities. Should the events fail totally and unexpectedly, both organizations could curtail expenditures, but only to a limited extent.

By the middle of the 1989 fiscal year, one month before the event itself, Hispanic Neighbors had accumulated a net deficit of almost $40,000 because of ongoing operating expenditures. Over the next three months, it received 70 percent of annual receipts and spent 50 percent of annual outlays. Receipts exceeded $110,000 in August, more than four times the average for the entire year, although the expenditure peak was only at the ratio of three to one.

By the tenth month of the 1990 fiscal year, Preservation Council had accumulated a net deficit of more than $60,000, reflecting outlays for ongoing operations and virtually nonexistent receipts. The last two months of the fiscal year accounted for fully 83 percent of revenues and 64 percent of outlays for the year. Monthly receipts exceeded $300,000 in June but averaged less than $30,000 for the year. Outlays show a similar ten-to-one ratio. Such high levels of cash-flow activity impose equally intense but short-term demands on financial management.[4]

These monthly financial data do not capture the high and fluctuating level of volunteer efforts that the special events also require. These demands are also most intense immediately prior to and during the event itself and probably correspond somewhat to fluctuations in monthly outlays and receipts. Directors of both Hispanic Neighbors and Preservation Council emphasized how intensively volunteers work just before and during the event, putting in eighteen-hour days and collapsing from total exhaustion at the end. Some have even used their experience to become paid special event consultants for other nonprofits. Staff members carry major burdens as well. Both directors emphasized the difficulty of managing the cash flow and keeping committee work flowing, and they recounted harrowing problems of covering for volunteers with major responsibilities who suddenly left town, got ill, or otherwise failed to carry out promised work.

The amount and intensity of efforts involved and level of uncertainty about the outcome explain why most nonprofits do not rely on special events for a significant proportion of their revenues. That is the case for most of the organizations included in the case studies. Those that do must buffer themselves from large fluctuations in revenues. I identified several such strategies (see bottom panel of Table 6.1), some of which relate closely to strategies for managing the event itself.

The most obvious way to buffer organizations against the contingencies associated with special events is to diversify the organization's resource base and avoid exclusive reliance on special events for ongoing operating expenditures. New Town Sponsors and Hispanic Neighbors follow this strategy. The former relies primarily on membership dues to cover its basic activities, and the latter obtains substantial donations from corporations and foundations to supplement its events revenues. In contrast, Preservation Council relies almost exclusively on its event to meet its own operating expenditures.

Alternatively, organizations may develop and maintain large fund reserves because that allows them to continue activities at some minimum level if the event should fail. The analysis shows an inverse relationship between the organization's reliance on special events and the relative size of its fund balance for the three organizations. As Figure 6.4 shows, New Town Sponsors has a small fund balance that has not yet reached 25 percent of yearly expenditures, equivalent to only three months of expenditures. Hispanic Neighbors has a relatively comfortable margin, equivalent to about six months of expenditures (50 percent of annual outlays). In contrast, Preservation Council has a very high and growing fund balance, now approaching twice the level of annual expenditures. Such a high level buffers the organization from its high dependence on the event and the large proportion of event revenues that depend on the success of the event itself. In fact, the buffer is so important that the organization downgrades its size. The manager explained that she never counted the part of the fund balance that would cover next year's expenditures (that is, the first 100 percent) because it would go for operational expenditures should the event fail.

Organizations may also seek to buffer themselves against uncertainties associated with special events by institutionalizing the work involved to

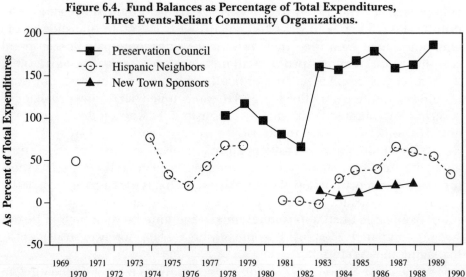

Figure 6.4. **Fund Balances as Percentage of Total Expenditures, Three Events-Reliant Community Organizations.**

Note: Data are missing for some years.

ensure that it gets done in a timely and appropriate fashion. Such a strategy is particularly important if the organization relies extensively on revenues from the event, as do both Hispanic Neighbors and Preservation Council.

Finally, organizations can buffer themselves against uncertainties associated with special event revenues by balancing risks and returns and structuring revenue streams in such a manner that the organization will be guaranteed some revenue whether the event suceeds or not. Hispanic Neighbors minimizes risks by obtaining sponsorship by major corporations and written contracts before the event takes place. It spreads the risk by seeking sweat equity from other organizations while relinquishing a share in gross revenues and some control over the event itself. New Town Sponsors also minimizes risks by obtaining donor commitments in advance of the event. In contrast, Preservation Council maintains much greater control over gross revenues and surplus from the event. It has correspondingly high risks, but can afford them because of its healthy fund balance.

Although the three organizations differ in the specific mechanisms by which they seek to guard themselves against fluctuations in and lack of control over revenues from special events, each employs at least two buffering strategies. Hispanic Neighbors has the most conservative approach: diversified funding base, structured organization of work, and minimized risk. It also has a relatively comfortable fund balance. Preservation Council is at the other extreme: consolidated funding base and maximized but risky revenue streams. However, it balances these uncertainties with a highly structured organization of work and very high fund balances. New Town Sponsors is between the two: diversified funding base, minimized revenue risks, but also low fund balances.

Role of Special Events for the Three Organizations

The three community development organizations are located in very different communities and vary in what they see as their major goals. They demonstrate some of the ways in which nonprofits link special events to organizational goals and activities. Hispanic Neighbors has experienced considerable success, both in establishing its event as a major occurrence in the city and in pursuing traditional goals of empowerment and community organizing. Having access to large amounts of special event revenues has made those efforts easier to undertake and less subject to interference or control by outside forces.

In contrast to other community development organizations, Hispanic Neighbors has escaped the direct consequences of political favoritism or retaliation by public officials and agencies. It does not depend on voluntary donations or dues payments from a handful of local community institutions whose interests it must serve. It has done what funders often tell nonprofit organizations to do: developed its own source of funding and reduced its reliance on outside funding sources. It and its affiliated member organizations control the disposition of the revenues without the involvement of other organizations.

The organization does face some challenges, but these are not critical to its purpose. It has had rocky relationships with several other organizations in the local community. It must locate and hire at least one competent Hispanic organizer, something it has failed to do in spite of sustained efforts. It must decide whether the event can — or should — continue to grow in scale and, if so, how to balance it against the primary goals of community empowerment.

Preservation Council also has a highly successful event with considerable visibility across the city. However, the event operates under a structure parallel to that of the organization, and there are only limited formal links between the two structures. As with Hispanic Neighbors, Preservation Council has a very high level of independence to pursue its activities without the involvement of other organizations. Among all the organizations included in this study, it is the most self-sufficient, independent, even insular organization.

Although its office manager interacts extensively with public agencies, private developers, and local institutions as part of the preservation efforts, these activities appear to be more reactive than proactive in nature. In contrast to other community development organizations examined, Preservation Council does not have its own plan or development projects for the community; does not directly monitor legislative developments, city council meetings, or housing court cases; makes no effort to organize or support local businesses; has little or no interest in seeking stronger alliances with other community organizations, churches, or social service agencies; and does not seek to expand its activities or support beyond its own boundaries.

In principle, the organization would appear to have the resources to undertake some or all of these initiatives. But its resource independence alleviates the need to explore new resource relationships or seek the new alliances that would be necessary. Its formal agreement that the youth club receive 40 percent of the net proceeds of the event and the cost of owning and operating its building limit its immediate options to do so. Even its sizable distribution of donations is so formalized that it does not seem to become the occasion for this organization to interact closely with other organizations.

New Town Sponsors voluntarily terminated its major event when it judged the work and efforts to be too burdensome. The event itself appears to have been successful and attracted citywide attention. The organization used the event directly and specifically to help it accomplish one of its defined objectives: promote the local community as an attractive, interesting place in which to live, work, and play. That done, the organization now relies primarily on ongoing dues from local businesses and real estate managers to carry out its objectives: monitoring city services and new development plans to protect existing investments in the community.

The decision to drop the event may well reflect the emergence of less unified interest groups in the community. Initially, developers in the area could easily agree on the organization's goal: overcoming negative public stereotypes about the area in order to attract initial investments. As that problem recedes, local developers no longer share a single agenda, and the organization may no longer serve as the effective negotiation ground between the competing and increasingly diverse interests in the community. If that should occur, the organization may no longer be able to count on the sustained payment of dues from all its members, just as it could not obtain their unified support for the event.[5]

Summary

Efforts to generate revenues from special events present a number of challenges to nonprofits and their managers that resemble those associated with other commercial sources of revenues, such as sales of products, fees for services, and dues from members. All require organizations to determine and develop a market niche, establish price/cost ratios, and identify and reach customers able and willing to pay for the product. The customer base may be part of the general public (as in the case of street fairs) or have established linkages to the organization (as in the case of member dues).

However, there are also important differences between special events and other sources of commercial revenues for nonprofits. Special events usually demand highly concentrated bursts of activity and large reserves of manpower and financial resources. They require sufficient visibility to entice customers with limited attachments to the organization or its community and depend heavily on effective marketing and promotion. Events also usually limit contacts with customers to short durations (hours) interspersed with long intervals (a year) of no interaction at all and are subject to competition and erosion of interest. Because they are of short duration but also require long-term advance planning and commitments, events are easily affected by the unforeseen. Of course, marketing and related strategies traditionally associated with commercial organizations do provide well-tested techniques for reaching potential customers. Even so, the techniques may be difficult for most nonprofits to employ systematically because of the sporadic nature of the activities and the high reliance on volunteers to perform the work.

These features contribute to high levels of uncertainty associated with special events. Organizations have relatively few opportunities to control the level of funding the events generate. A given level of effort does not necessarily guarantee or promise a particular amount of funding, as is the case with fee-for-service activities, government grants and contracts, and some foundation or corporate support. Instead, special events uniformly require high levels of effort by staff, board members, volunteers, or consultants in return for earnings that are obviously unpredictable. Although the financial payoff may be significant, the balance of advantages and disadvantages is sufficiently precarious for most organizations that special events are relatively minor sources of revenues. Otherwise, organizations need to develop fund reserves, institutionalize the work involved, or seek an optimal balance of risks and returns.

However, special event proceeds have very important nonfinancial characteristics that most organizations find desirable: they are flexible, discretionary sources of income over which organizations exercise full control, in contrast to many types of donations and all forms of public funding. That makes them particularly attractive to organizations that engage in controversial activities for which traditional sources of funding are less available. Special events also help publicize the organization and its purpose and therefore open the door for other sources of funding. They reward and entertain the organization's key constituencies and therefore promote social cohesion.

On occasion, special events may even directly promote the organization's mission. This is easier for community development organizations to do because of how they define their mission. For community development organizations, events may not only provide significant levels of funding but also often serve directly to achieve central organizational goals: celebrate the local community and provide interesting and visible opportunities for community residents to undertake major community projects with immediate recognition of their efforts and accomplishments. Special events are less likely to have similar close relationships to core organizational goals for social service organizations.

Notes

1. It is likely that the remaining two organizations (Minority Search and Economic Development Commission) had such income as well. Both organized events on several occasions, but primarily for public relations or celebratory purposes. Their audit reports do not identify special event proceeds separately from miscellaneous other income sources.
2. Detailed information on expenditures associated with specific programs is unavailable for the 1981–1989 period, but personnel costs (salaries, social security taxes, fringe benefits) account for between 50 and 70 percent of net expenditures for most years, exclusive of costs directly attributable to the event itself.
3. The comparatively high level of revenues relative to expenditures in 1986 (net proceeds of 16 percent) most likely reflected accounting adjustments. New Town Sponsors operates on a cash basis, and its fiscal year ended before the books were closed on the event. Each event therefore straddled two of the organization's fiscal years, and small annual changes in net proceeds may reflect the timing of expenses and revenues from the event, rather than any actual differences.

4. Hispanic Neighbors employs an accountant explicitly for that purpose during the two months immediately prior to and during the event.
5. There are increasing efforts to organize the community around the interests of tenants, local homeowners, and merchants. If New Town Sponsors defines its own interests as that of the community as a whole, it will have to accommodate some of these other interest groups within its own internal structure. Otherwise, it may find itself competing with organizations that pursue their own distinctive goals, some or most of which may not be in the direct interest of New Town Sponsors' members.

SEVEN

Donations:
Balancing Flexibility
and Risks

While reliance on fees and other sources of commercial revenues blurs the distinction between nonprofits and for-profits, donations symbolize their differences. Nonprofits have their origin in philanthropic and charitable efforts to alleviate suffering and promote human welfare (Hall, 1987). They represent the institutionalized form for such activities, and the public interests they serve justify the special tax treatment of donations to them. The receipt of donations in turn provides them with tangible evidence that others endorse their goals and approach. Donations, then, are their most traditional and least controversial source of revenues.

Most types of donations allow nonprofit managers considerable discretion in how to use the revenues. Yet, as the case studies show, the discretion and flexibility may be more imagined than real. Each of the many different types of donations presents complex exchange relationships that may not easily convert into ongoing, predictable funding levels. These management contingencies are further exacerbated by the tendency for most types of donations to fluctuate considerably from year to year. Social service and community development organizations do not have equal access to all types of donations and differ in the nature of exchange relationships they are able to develop with donors. As a result, the two types of organizations face somewhat different contingencies in their efforts to secure and manage donations.

Management Contingencies

Donations are solicited by almost all nonprofit organizations, but they account for a declining percent of revenues. The decline occurs across the board, but it has particular importance for human service organizations. They face increasing competition for donations but are less able than larger nonprofits to reach fragmented donor markets or overcome the lack of institutionalization that characterizes most donor types.

Fragmented Donor Systems

In order to position their organizations for change, nonprofit managers must closely monitor developments that affect different types of donors. This is part of a broader set of management contingencies associated with frag-mented donor systems, in which different types of donors require fairly specialized approaches. The phon-a-thon script that produces support from an individual donor is unlikely to result in a contribution from a local church and will certainly not satisfy United Way membership requirements.

Other problems occur because most people (and even organizational donors) donate on the basis of preferences or idiosyncratic tastes that vary greatly from one donor to another, much as consumers have different prefer-ences for products. However, nonprofits cannot simply advertise their pur-pose in the yellow pages and wait for donors to seek them out, as they can with fee-paying clients who desire particular services or products. Fee-paying clients have specific incentives for identifying appropriate vendors and can be expected to take an active role in the selection process. In the absence of institutionalized solicitation systems (such as United Way organizations) to convince donors of the worth of their cause, individual nonprofits must hustle to get their particular message across, and they have only imperfect access to information about donor preferences.

Some donor systems are themselves becoming increasingly institu-tionalized, making it easier for nonprofits to know whom to solicit for funds and how. Foundations are formal mechanisms for allocating donations, and most now publish annual reports, distribute requests for proposals (RFPs), and operate with formal application procedures. The creation of local councils of foundations reflects broader institutionalization of donor sys-tems composed of large foundations and major corporate giving programs.[1]

Flexibility, Uncertainty, and Management Demands

Although donations demand fund-raising efforts, they are flexible and do not require recipient organizations to use service staff members to generate the revenues directly, as do fees. The donations must be used for charitable purposes, of course, and sometimes come with donor specifications, but the specifications are less restrictive than government grants and contracts. There is little up-front control associated with them; and after they are received, there are few restrictions on how they are used.

Donations expand the range of management options, therefore, be-cause recipient organizations can use unrestricted funding to complement activities covered by restricted grants and contracts or undertake efforts for which there is no existing client market or public funding available. Organi-zations with access to unrestricted funding, such as special events, individual donations, corporate support, or foundation grants, should therefore be able to plan their allocation of resources, staff, space, and activities with some degree of flexibility and direct control.[2]

Interviews with executive directors of Chicago-area social service and community development organizations in 1985 generally confirm the positive assessment of most types of donations. Directors were asked to express their agreement with nine statements about specific funding sources. As Table 7.1 shows, 60 percent or more of the directors evaluated both individual donations and foundation/corporate grants (considered jointly) positively on seven of the nine criteria.

Most of the top-ranked criteria involve specific assessment of these forms of donations as consistent with organizational missions ("does not force into areas of little ability," "allows development of needed programs," "enables serving clients we want") and as flexible funding that is relatively easy to administer and account for. Community development directors were less enthusiastic about individual donations than their social service counterparts for three of the dimensions, but still endorsed these statements by 42 to 47 percent.

United Way funding received high levels of agreement on only three of the nine criteria. However, consistent with United Way funding priorities and reporting requirements[3] that favor social service agencies, social service executive directors expressed more positive assessment of United Way funding than did community development organizations. Differences between

Table 7.1. Evaluation of Donation Sources, Chicago-Area Nonprofit Organizations, 1985.

	Percentage of Directors Agreeing with Statement		
Evaluation of Funding Source	*Individual Donations*	*Corporate/ Foundation Support*	*United Way/ Federated Funding*
Does not force into areas of little ability	82	70	64
Flexible in how and when it can be used	79	62	51[a]
Worth pursuing for effort required	72	89	73[a]
Allows development of needed programs	72[a]	79	56[a]
Enables serving clients we want	69[a]	77	76[a]
Easy to administer and account for	67	72	46
Type of funding would prefer to rely on	61[a]	73	54[a]
Easy to plan for future with	47	33	56
Involves no favoritism	32	21	44[a]

Note: Percentages are based on combined responses from thirty-five social service agencies and sixteen community development organizations. Three items were originally presented with reverse directions (does not force: "forces an organization into areas where it has little experience or ability"; worth pursuing: "generally not worth pursuing, likely return too small for efforts required"; no favoritism: "mainly available to 'favored' organizations that know the right people").

[a] Social service agencies are significantly more likely to agree with the statement than community development organizations are (at .05 level of significance or better).

Source: Urban Institute Nonprofit Sector Project for Chicago, personal interviews.

the two groups were significant for six of the nine criteria (see Table 7.1) and approached significance for another ("easy to administer"). In fact, 60 per-cent or more of social service directors expressed agreement with seven of the nine criteria for United Way funding and endorsed the two remaining criteria ("involves no favoritism," "easy to administer") by a majority of 54 percent.

A majority of community development directors indicated support for United Way funding on only two of the criteria ("enables serving clients we want," "does not force into areas of little ability"), by 53 and 50 percent, respectively. About two-fifths of these directors expressed agreement with two additional criteria ("worth pursuing," "easy to plan with"), while the remain-ing criteria were endorsed by less than one-third.

As these findings show, nonprofit managers generally view donations as having a range of desirable characteristics. Similarly, the nonprofit manag-ers involved in the Case-Study Project acknowledged the important manage-ment advantages associated with donations, especially flexibility and match-ing the mission of the organizations. But they did so with less enthusiasm than I had anticipated.

Instead, the directors emphasized the uncertainty involved in generat-ing donations. This is consistent with the interview data, which showed that only a minority of directors viewed individual donations or corporate and foundation grants as easy to plan for the future with or as involving no favoritism. An even smaller minority of directors viewed United Way as involving no favoritism. Unpredictable funding sources are difficult to plan for the future with, and those that involve favoritism are difficult to anticipate or counteract unless the recipient organization has good connections and can neutralize idiosyncratic decisions by donors. The assessment of dona-tions as unpredictable is also consistent with Figures 4.1 to 4.13, which showed that donations vary considerably from year to year.

More detailed analysis of year-by-year changes also documents very high levels of volatility for most types of donations. The thirteen organiza-tions reported annual data on eleven different categories of donations over varying periods of time for a total of twenty-nine separate donation streams (not all organizations had donations from each of the eleven categories). As seen in Table 7.2, roughly one-third of the streams (9 out of 29) showed annual changes (up or down) that averaged 100 percent or more. Another quarter of the donation streams (7 out of 29) showed average annual changes that range between 50 and 100 percent. These volatile streams account for more than half (55 percent) of all the streams and include individual donations, church contributions, corporate support, foundation grants, or various combina-tions of these types, depending on the accounting categories used.

At the other extreme, about a quarter of the streams (7 out of 29) involve relatively small changes on an annual basis—less than 20 percent. Two of these stable streams include corporate contributions to Minority Search (average annual changes of 9 percent) and individual contributions to

Table 7.2. Volatility in Donation Streams for Case-Study Organizations.

| Donation Stream | Number of Streams by Average Annual Percentage Change | | | | |
	Very High ≥ 100%	High 50–99%	Low 20–49%	Very Low < 20%	Number of Streams
Unspecified/Various	4	3	2	2	11
Foundations/Corporations	3	1	3	–	7
Individual Donors	1	3	1	–	5
United Way/Federated Funding Sources	1	–	–	5	6
All Streams	9	7	6	7	29

Note: Volatility is defined as the change (up or down) in a given source of donation as a percentage of the total donation from that source the previous year. Only those streams for which data were available for a minimum of four consecutive years are included. The "Unspecified/Various" category includes churches.
Source: Case-Study Project.

Community Renewal (average annual changes of 12 percent). The rest are United Way or religious federation streams. Indeed, United Way and feder-ated funding streams are almost entirely very stable. Only one of the highly volatile streams involve United Way funding: Hispanic Youth Services ob-tained two one-year grants from the United Way and then obtained mem-bership just before we began data collection. As a result, its United Way funding changed by an average of 331 percent.

In addition to high volatility, the case-study findings also document high levels of management efforts associated with donations. This is true for all sources of donations. As the example of Youth Outreach in Chapter One shows, the efforts include such activities as monitoring foundation priorities, deciding on how to highlight selected aspects of activities for different types of donors, updating mailing lists, preparing newsletters, meeting with poten-tial funders, as well as making the actual solicitations.

Strategies for Managing Donations

All thirteen organizations have income from donations (see Table 2.2), although Preservation Council averaged less than 1 percent during the 1984–1988 period. Another community development organization (Economic Development Commission) and two social service agencies (Alcohol Treat-ment, Hispanic Youth Services) averaged less than 10 percent in donations during the 1984–1988 period. All three rely heavily on government grants and contracts.

Describing the Strategies

The thirteen organizations use a range of activities to generate donations (see Table 7.3). Most involve attempts to market the organization to a variety of publics that directors or board members think are potential sources of donations. The case-study findings suggest that nonprofits pursue three general types of strategies in their efforts to obtain contributions. These strategies consist of decisions about the range of donors to pursue, how to identify and target specific segments of donors, and how systematically to pursue these efforts.

Spreading the Risk Through Multiple Donation Streams. Three of the four organizations that rely most extensively on donations—Youth Outreach, Immigrant Welfare League, and United Residents—also target the broadest

Table 7.3. Donation Sources and Strategies.

Agency Profile	Individual Donations	Community Entities	Foundations/ Corporations	Churches	United Way
Social Service					
Primarily Public Funding					
Alcohol Treatment	Ad hoc[a]	—	Ad hoc	—	—
Hispanic Youth Services	—	—	Systematic	—	Yes
Primarily Mixed Funding					
Youth Outreach	Network	—	Systematic	Formal	Yes
Immigrant Welfare League	Constituency	—	Ad hoc	Formal	Yes
Primarily Fee Funding					
Minority Search	—	—	Constituency	—	—
Christian Therapists	Constituency	—	Ad hoc[a]	Formal	—
Community Development					
Primarily Public Funding					
Economic Development Commission	—	Constituency	Systematic	—	—
African-American Neighbors	—	—	Systematic	Ad hoc	Yes
Primarily Mixed/Donation Funding					
Community Renewal	Constituency	Constituency[b]	Ad hoc[a]	—	—
United Residents	Constituency	Constituency	Systematic	Constituency	Yes
Primarily Special Events Funding					
Preservation Council	Ad hoc	—	—	—	—
Hispanic Neighbors	—	—	Systematic	—	—
New Town Sponsors	—	Constituency	Ad hoc	—	—

Note: Community entities include businesses, professionals, churches, schools, homeowners associations, and similar organizations. *Ad hoc*: Occasionally pursues source, but not systematically or persistently. *Constituency*: Appeals to a defined constituency for donations. *Formal*: Maintains formal relations with religious congregations/federations. *Network*: Relies primarily on personal networks to obtain access to donors. *Systematic*: Has special and ongoing mechanisms for soliciting donations.

[a] One-time effort.

[b] One Community Institution.

Source: Case-Study Project.

variety of donation streams, a minimum of four (see Table 7.3). All three also use special events as a fund-raising mechanism. However, large volumes of donations do not necessarily require a variety of donation streams. Community Renewal, for example, relies extensively on donations but obtains them from only two sources. It has institutionalized its relationship with one major funder and avoids most of the contingencies associated with managing donations. Similarly, both Hispanic Youth Services and Minority Search match Immigrant Welfare League in the amount of donations they obtained in 1988, but they rely on fewer donor streams. All three had donations of about $100,000, compared with $350,000 for Youth Outreach.

High reliance on donations, then, as opposed to raw dollar amounts, seems to require either firmly institutionalized relationships with a few specific donors (as in the case of Community Renewal) or a generalized effort to play the field. An institutionalized relationship with a donor reduces volatility in individual donation streams by linking the organization tightly to a given funding source. Playing the field allows organizations to cope with the effects of highly volatile donation streams by spreading the risk so that unpredictable increases in one stream may offset equally unpredictable decreases in another stream.

What seems to distinguish organizations with multiple donation streams—at least among social service agencies—is that they tend to recruit board members with fund-raising capacity and interest. For nonprofits that are large enough to have a separate development department, professional staff play a similar role. The two social service agencies with the highest reliance on donations (Youth Outreach and Immigrant Welfare League) depend greatly on their boards for fund-raising, view these efforts as among the board's primary responsibilities, and recruit board members for that purpose. This practice reflects long-standing traditions in the two organizations. They are the oldest organizations included in the study and were established at a time (the 1920s) when government funding was available for very limited activities. (Of the remaining social service agencies, only Christian Therapists assigns a similar role to its board.)

Once initiated, however, the involvement of board members in fund-raising becomes a self-reinforcing process. Board members bring their own interests, networks, and fund-raising experiences to such efforts. Over time, board recruitment and involvement in fund-raising activities can encourage organizations to pursue a growing variety of donation streams and strategies.

Board members are less involved in fund-raising efforts among the community development organizations. In these organizations, boards perform political functions (developing agenda, facilitating compromises), and board members play a primary role in getting local residents, businesses, and other organizations involved in community activities initiated by the organization. This may include asking local residents and businesses to pay their dues. Less frequently, it involves soliciting donations. Community development organizations that seek donations tend to focus on institutional donors outside the local community and rely on staff members to do so.

Once nonprofits obtain donations from a variety of donors, a second self-reinforcing process comes into operation: having multiple donors becomes a source of legitimacy. Donors tend to take some comfort from knowing that the organizations they are being asked to support also have the endorsement of other donors. Support by several types of donors, then, increases the likelihood of obtaining support from others.

In general, donations (or other subsidy funding, such as government grants and contracts) provide nonprofits with evidence of their legitimacy and, indirectly, of their market value to other donors. Most of the organizations that aggressively seek donations highlight the variety of support they receive in their publicity efforts. This is institutionalized in the case of the United Way of Chicago, which requires as a condition of membership that organizations demonstrate some level of community support by obtaining donations.

Identifying and Targeting Marketing Segments. A second general strategy centers on the search for potential donors. The principles by which nonprofits identify donors range from use of personal networks to formalized, systematic efforts to discover and match donor preferences. In some cases, nonprofits have strategic opportunities to develop and cater to already existing constituencies or affinity groups.

Some strategies exploit personal networks. When previous donors already have an established relationship with the organization, they are primary targets for solicitations and tend to bring the highest return for the amount of efforts invested. However, some donors will lapse (die or otherwise cease to donate to the organization), and others may not donate as much as they did previously. Maintaining the donation base, then, becomes a continuing challenge and requires a steady addition of new donors, especially if the organization wants to increase the donor base as well.

Several of the social service agencies rely extensively on their board of directors to generate lists of friends and acquaintances from which to solicit donations or special event sales.[4] Reliance on personal networks of this type solves the problem of locating promising donors. Obtaining a list of individuals, as well as finding an angle that will encourage them to support the organization, is otherwise a costly and complex affair. How is the list to be developed, from which source, at what cost, and with what level of up-to-date addresses? Reliance on networks for new names generates a smaller but usable list of individuals at low costs.

Finding a story that will sell the organization to individual donors is also difficult. Commercially available lists allow nonprofits to identify particular neighborhoods, subscribers to particular magazines, or occupants of particular jobs as targets for solicitation. Knowing the origin of these lists may help in formulating a targeted message. But typically, commercial lists generate small returns for the investment. Respondents in a national Gallup poll ranked telethons, letters, phone calls, television commercials, or advertisements as the types of solicitations to which they would be least likely to respond (Hodgkinson, Weitzman, and the Gallup Organization, 1988). Alcohol Treatment tried to obtain donations by mailing requests to a list of local community residents, but barely broke even and decided not to repeat the experience.

Reliance on personal networks allows for at least some matching of interest with the organization and is likely to be a more efficient fund-raising tool than completely cold approaches. Personal networks also mobilize interpersonal obligations on behalf of the organization. More than two-thirds of respondents to a Gallup poll indicated that they were likely to respond to solicitations by someone they knew well (Hodgkinson, Weitzman, and the Gallup Organization, 1988). Further evidence of this comes from complaints by several directors that board members are reluctant to provide names or make personal solicitations because soliciting friends and neighbors complicates already existing obligations. Most likely, the act of soliciting modifies the existing balance of obligations so as to favor the person being solicited.

Several of the organizations undertake a systematic search for matching interests and explicitly target donors, especially foundations and corporations, that they believe share some substantive interests with them. Using information provided by individual funders or local councils of foundations, they examine annual reports, funding categories, previous awards, or similar information to find out which foundations or corporations have priorities that match their own activities, organizational characteristics, or mission. In turn, many funders use formal criteria and procedures for evaluating requests submitted to them, target certain geographical areas, or limit their funding for unrestricted support or operating expenses. They have adopted more stringent criteria as the number and diversity of nonprofits seeking grants have increased.

The mutual selection process serves the interest of both parties. For funders, self-screening by organizations seeking funding limits the number of requests they must review and reduces their own management efforts, although they must develop and apply the criteria. For organizations seeking funding, self-screening minimizes the number of requests they make and increases the likelihood that they obtain funding that matches their own priorities, although they must invest time in screening potential sources. However, it also encourages them to market themselves aggressively and to be highly selective about how they present themselves to funders, perhaps to the point that the match between funder priorities and their own activities may have less reality than both parties expect.

The organizations included in the case studies vary greatly in how systematically and consistently they undertake these types of efforts. Four of the seven community development organizations have special and ongoing mechanisms for soliciting foundations and corporate giving programs. They target utilities and other enterprises — such as banking, real estate, and financial industries — that have an obvious interest in the vitality of local communities.

Community organizations tend to define these funders as part of their constituency and believe that systematic solicitation helps establish their credibility and creates contacts with important and relevant community actors. Once established, these linkages promote the missions of community development organizations and constitute funding networks that can be activated in the case of unpredictable declines in other types of funding.

Hispanic Neighbors uses systematic solicitation of foundations and corporate giving programs to supplement unreliable special events revenues. Economic Development Commission, African-American Neighbors, and United Residents also solicit foundation and corporate grants for alternative funding because they have all experienced abrupt shifts in public funding sources and view them as fickle and unreliable. The remaining three community development organizations either do not seek foundation support or do so only sporadically because they have access to stable base funding from other revenue sources.

Three of the six social service agencies approach foundations and corporate giving programs on an ad hoc basis. They view themselves as unlikely to obtain foundation or corporate support because of the constituency they serve (Immigrant Welfare League), their focus (Christian Therapists), or their history of stable public funding (Alcohol Treatment). The three remaining social service agencies employ more systematic efforts to obtain foundation and corporate grants. Minority Search targets its fee-paying corporate clients, while Youth Outreach researches a large number of foundations and corporations, maintains extensive records on each, and has a full-time development director who coordinates fund-raising efforts. Hispanic Youth Services has only recently begun to solicit foundations and corporations and has had to hire a consultant to do the necessary research and write proposals.

I speculate that the two latter agencies use more systematic efforts to obtain foundation and corporate grants than the other social service agencies because they have no natural constituencies to whom they can easily appeal. In contrast to community development organizations, the services of Youth Outreach and Hispanic Youth Services are not critical to those with vested interests in local communities. In contrast to the clients of other social service agencies, their clients are too young and poor to make sizable donations.[5]

Identifying Constituencies. Personal networks and systematic efforts to locate donors who share substantive interests with the organization become more effective mechanisms for gaining access to donors if these donor groups also form identifiable constituencies for the organization. Several of the organizations have access to natural constituencies: loyal and fiscally competent clients, people who share the organization's ethnic or religious identity, or groups or individuals who identify with the organization's geographical turf. In some cases, nonprofits deliberately attempt to create constituencies from which they subsequently solicit support. That is the case for most advocacy organizations, but it also characterizes many community development organizations.

Minority Search illustrates the former pattern. It has access to loyal, fiscally competent clients, major corporations, who value its services (as evident in the fees they pay) and from whom it solicits donations systematically. It defines the donations as a form of voluntary fees and promotes fees and donations as a package deal, allowing it to claim that donations recognize its performance (domain efforts). The organization has succeeded in maintaining a very stable level of donations, changing by an average of only 9 percent per year.

Many nonprofits seek to exploit service constituencies of this type, although some wait until the client is no longer receiving the service or solicit family members of current consumers. For example, universities frequently solicit alumni and parents, but rarely current students. The approach is likely to be most successful for organizations that provide a high volume of important services over a sustained period of time to broad segments of the population. The high volume ensures a large constituency, important services promote intense interest among clients, sustained involvement encourages client loyalty, and a broad cross section of clients guarantees fiscal competency. Higher education, disease-related organizations, and arts and culture organizations meet some or all of these criteria.

Other nonprofits use a similar approach when they cater to people's self-interest as future consumers of their services. Disease-related organizations stress how donations to them may help find cures for a disease "within your lifetime." United Way campaigns frequently follow this strategy as well when they emphasize how the United Way services help people "just like you." Such generalized appeals to self-interest may have their limits, however. Controversy surrounding the 1992 resignation of Bill Aramony as president of United Way of America has thrown the legitimacy of the United Way system into question. United Way officials now make frequent and explicit references to "serving the needy," in an apparent effort to reclaim legitimacy by emphasizing explicit charitable purposes.

Other constituencies may have less direct linkages to a particular organization. However, the religious, ethnic, and racial diversity of the United States and of most local communities provides ready-made constituencies for many nonprofits. Some of these organizations, of course, have their origins as self-help organizations of various groups and still obtain donation support on that basis. Christian Therapists is a case in point. It was founded by a local church, with which it maintains close relationships, and has appeal to fundamentalist Christians, especially those residing in the community in which it operates. Other nonprofits with obvious religious identities are likely to have similar advantages.

The name of Immigrant Welfare League specifies the ethnicity of its target group, which is well organized and overwhelmingly Catholic. The agency, therefore, has ready access to ethnic organizations as well as the

Catholic church. It exploits its ethnic niche by maintaining several affiliate chapters that provide the ethnic constituency with membership and other opportunities for social interaction. It also cultivates established ethnic fraternal and mutual insurance organizations and maintains close relationships with the local Catholic Charities and the Archdiocese.

Hispanic Neighbors and African-American Neighbors are also clearly identified with ethnic or racial groups, but neither has sought to exploit these identities in soliciting funds from individuals. They do target major Hispanic and black businesses (or corporations with large numbers of minority customers) as part of their systematic efforts to obtain foundation and corporate grants. Both emphasize the leadership role they play in mobilizing their respective local communities and point to their participation in citywide empowerment efforts on behalf of their ethnic groups. Funders appear receptive to their minority credentials.

Finally, nonprofits may appeal to constituencies on the basis of geographical turf. Because of high levels of residential segregation, geographical areas frequently coincide with racial and ethnic identities. This is especially true of Chicago. Local communities become contested terrains for competing groups, and turf battles play themselves out among and within community development organizations, which need support from local residents to maintain their credibility as representatives of the community. Participation by local residents in rallies, demonstrations, clean-up campaigns, and other collective efforts documents this support. Donations or dues from residents and local businesses provide equally tangible evidence of support. Geographical constituency groups, therefore, are of key importance to community development organizations.

All seven community development organizations make explicit efforts to involve and create interest in community issues among local residents, businesses, independent professionals, schools, churches, civic organizations, hospitals, and so on. Several of them also seek to create local, geographically based constituency groups with sufficient interest in the organization and its activities to provide sustained financial support.

Community development organizations may have greater or more limited opportunities to develop local funding constituencies, depending on the composition of their communities. Some communities are so impoverished that the organization obtains little financial support locally. In other communities, the organization has access to local funding, simply because local residents or businesses possess these resources.

Major community institutions, however, are also important actors for a community development organization. They have vested, legitimate interests in the community, and community organizations cannot oppose or ignore them. The relationship is reciprocal because each sees the other as an opportunity to influence community development without having to take full responsibility for direct action themselves.

Still, relations between community development organizations and important local institutions are rarely neutral, but range from confrontation to cooperation and co-optation. Hispanic Neighbors and African-American Neighbors operate in some of the most deprived areas of the city. The local businesses include many bars, liquor stores, and marginal businesses, most of which the organizations view as part of their problems rather than as a resource. The absence of more legitimate community institutions points to larger structural problems that affect the communities and that must be addressed if conditions are to improve. As a result, both organizations have taken high-profile political roles in citywide politics.

In contrast, New Town Sponsors, Economic Development Commission, and United Residents have access to local banks, larger businesses, major employers, and institutions of higher education. All three have cultivated relationships with these community institutions and developed special mechanisms to facilitate the process of engaging these institutions and to institutionalize funding streams.

Because of the variety of local institutions, these community organizations define their role as one of providing opportunities for diverse interests to be heard and compromises to be reached. Direct political involvement by the community organizations, then, tends to be low key or more explicitly focused on issues of direct local impact around which negotiated positions are developed. Otherwise, the organization risks offending portions of its constituency and the loss of donations.

Community Renewal illustrates the more extreme version of this process and approaches a condition of co-optation. It obtains the bulk of its funding from a single community institution with major investments in the community. The institution has devoted significant resources to expanding and protecting its interests in the community. However, it has delegated much of the visible activities as well as day-to-day operations to Community Renewal rather than to an internal division. Although possibly less efficient than direct actions by the institution, this decoupled structural arrangement ensures that the efforts receive full-time management attention. Had the activities been relegated to an internal division within the institution, they would have absorbed its own management efforts and might have been sidetracked by other considerations.

Community Renewal also serves as a mediating structure with other actors, such as city agencies (the police and other city services), community residents, and other local organizations or institutions. The community institution is likely to encounter numerous occasions where its own direct involvement would be problematic but where facilitators, buffers, or go-betweens can convey its positions and influence decisions more effectively. Community Renewal helps ensure that the interests of the community institution are protected and the community actions are consistent with, if not in total agreement with, those interests. At the same time, it protects the community institution from controversy and risks of failure by separating it from controversial, forceful efforts that might entail substantial financial or symbolic costs.

Only a narrow range of community institutions is likely to have interests in intense relationships with community development organizations to the point of co-optation. Factories, hospitals, universities, major commercial establishments, leading banks, and large corporate headquarters all exercise direct control over sizable local real estate holdings. They have vested interests in self-protection and cannot avoid having a major impact on local communities. Each faces decisions about how broadly to define its community interests and how actively to pursue them.

Two conditions affect the range and nature of community strategies that locally vested institutions pursue and the extent to which they may have specific interests in community development organizations. First, the extent to which the institution's input (suppliers, employees) and output (services, customers, clients) are concentrated in the local community determines whether community actions have direct consequences for its own well-being. A high level of concentration provides incentives for broad and active community involvement. In the absence of major local investments or locally concentrated inputs and outputs, most institutions will define their community interests narrowly, pursue them passively, and maintain a low profile to avoid controversies.

Second, the legal status of the institution (for-profit, public, nonprofit) shapes cultural expectations about the nature and types of roles it can and will play, including those at the local community level. Thus, for-profit corporations face broad expectations of self-interest, which limit the range of community actions their managers can pursue without arousing suspicions about their motives.[6] They may buffer themselves from these suspicions by providing sustained but carefully balanced support for local development organizations, because low-key actions demonstrate their commitment to compromise.

Public institutions that operate in local communities also face structural constraints on the role they can play. Legislative bodies or political authorities circumscribe management autonomy, especially in investment decisions, and constitute pressure points for the institution's adherence to broad but often conflicting "public benefit" goals. As a result, managers of public institutions may find it dangerous to pursue local community action, except when wider political consensus allows them to override special local interests. They may alleviate these difficulties by participating in and supporting local community development organizations, but not the point of playing a forceful or controversial role.

Nonprofit institutions with high levels of local investments have broader opportunities to take direct community action without encountering comparable suspicions or stalemates. In contrast to proprietary institutions, their nonprofit status and explicit goals of promoting general welfare and public benefits accord them some initial goodwill and benefit of doubt about their motives. In contrast to public institutions, they have relative autonomy.

The major community institution that supports Community Renewal resembles a company town (Buder, 1967), because most of its clients and employees live in the community. This fact has encouraged the institution to define its goals and interests broadly to include general community stability and an improved quality of life for community residents, rather than merely making narrow decisions about its own investments. The institution's nonprofit status has enabled it to reject a passive role and engage in a broad range of proactive efforts to achieve these goals. It has done so more explicitly, more aggressively, and for a longer period of time than most other institutions with similar local investments. It took these steps for three reasons: its own investments were seriously at risk; it wanted to maintain nearby residential opportunities for its employees and clients; and it viewed the city's racial and economic transformations as so forceful that only concerted, aggressive action could counteract them.

By doing so, the institution accepted several closely related contingencies. The strategies involved high risks of failure (they attempted to counter "known" ecological imperatives), controversy (forceful actions inevitably hurt some community residents and other community actors), and substantial costs (they required a high level of investment and concerted management efforts to implement). Community Renewal serves as a less visible vehicle for achieving these goals while minimizing some of the risks.

Institutionalizing the Donation Relationship. Nonprofits may be able to formalize the donation relationship if constituency groups have some level of organizational structure themselves. The case study organizations attempted to convert informal contacts with donors (or potential donors) into institutionalized relationships in the hope of making the relationships more predictable and controllable.

United Way membership presents the most obvious example of such efforts for social service agencies. The United Way of Chicago guarantees member agencies a yearly allocation of at least 95 percent of the prior year's allocation. In return, member agencies must adhere to fairly stringent membership requirements about governance, accountability, efficiency, effectiveness, and statistical reporting on service activities and client characteristics (such as race, ethnicity, residence, income status, and now also gender and disability).

During the period covered by the study, United Way passed on new revenues (that is, increases over the previous year) to agencies in almost direct proportion to the size of their base allocation. It provided agencies with increases to their base allocation that varied only slightly according to whether or not they used the allocation for services that the United Way had

given top priority.[7] As Table 7.2 shows, United Way funding has been exceptionally stable for most of the participating organizations.

Affiliations with religious federations, such as Catholic Charities, Jewish United Fund, Lutheran Social Services, or Episcopal Charities, represent
institutionalized mechanisms for securing ongoing support from churches
and congregations. These religious federations obtain support from church
or synagogue collections as well as from their own direct efforts to solicit
fellow believers. Youth Outreach is a member of a religious federation from
which it has received stable support over many years. Immigrant Welfare
League has also received ongoing funding from a religious federation,
although it is not formally a member of the federation.

Some organizations create special structures to maintain ongoing
relationships with donors. Several of the community development organizations use formal membership structures to secure continuing support from
residents, businesses, and other community institutions. New Town Sponsors'
members pay dues on the basis of assessed valuation and amount of front
footage of property owned in the community. Most other community development organizations have less complex dues structures that distinguish
only between residents, businesses, and other community organizations.
Since community development organizations do not strictly enforce membership standards, the distinction between donations and dues becomes
murky.

Two other community development organizations, Economic Development Commission and United Residents, have sought to eliminate the
voluntary aspect of membership support and institutionalize the process by
creating local service area taxing districts. As discussed in Chapter Eight,
property owners must agree to establish such a district and are then legally required to pay a special assessment on their property, but can vote the district
out of existence later. This type of experiment failed for United Residents, but
appears to be succeeding for Economic Development Commission.

In some cases, attempts to institutionalize donor relationships amount
to outright efforts to co-opt donors or their key representatives by creating an
affiliation through board membership. More than half of social service and
community development organizations surveyed in 1984 and 1985 indicate
that their boards include representatives from neighborhood groups (64
percent), corporations (62 percent), religious institutions (57 percent), civic
organizations (55 percent), or professional associations (52 percent).

Efforts to establish these types of affiliations are most likely to occur
when constituency groups have some organizational basis of their own.
Three of the social service agencies (Youth Outreach, Immigrant Welfare
League, and Christian Therapists) have established formal relationships with
sponsoring religious federations or churches in exchange for one or more
positions on the board. Youth Outreach also appoints corporate officers to its
board, with explicit expectation of obtaining ongoing donations from the

corporations. Minority Search employs a comparable strategy to maintain close linkages with its corporate clients/donors. At one point, Immigrant Welfare League attempted to confirm its relationships with three key ethnic fraternal organizations by asking each to sponsor a program to the tune of $25,000 per year in return for appointing officers of the organizations to its governing board. Review of correspondence with donors suggests that the agency routinely offers membership on its board to individuals or organizations that make substantial contributions to it.

Auxiliary boards have similar functions. Immigrant Welfare League has chapters whose members are expected to raise a minimum amount of funding for the organization. Youth Outreach maintains three auxiliary boards that undertake special events. In both cases, the chapters or auxiliary boards have representatives on the governing board.

Most community development organizations pursue co-optation strategies explicitly when they seek representatives from major community institutions to serve as board members or chairs. In this case, the strategy both institutionalizes the donor relationship and affirms the organization's legitimacy as a negotiating arena for diverse and important community interests.

Co-optation through appointment of board members has potential costs as well and creates complex relationships of dependency and control. These board members are able to play critical roles in shaping the organization because of the financial support they bring. For Christian Therapists, board members affiliated with the local church rejected staff members' proposed group practice model. The church provided only a small proportion of the organization's funding, but it was flexible and fairly predictable funding. The church also provided the organization with access to loans.

Community Renewal maintains a more complex but fully institutionalized relationship with the local community institution that helped found it and remains its major constituency, only client, and primary funder. The institution's need to take forceful action, but at high potential costs, helps explain why it has relegated a significant portion of community strategies to a separate organization. The risks involved explain why the institution and Community Renewal both maintain that the latter is an independent organization and that the community institution "does not dictate" Community Renewal's activities as newspaper accounts often claim.

Although Community Renewal is reluctant to reveal exact details about its funding relationships, the community institution retains direct authority over key aspects of Community Renewal's management. The two organizations are tightly coupled, but the relationship does not operate primarily through the board structure. Only thirteen of seventy-five board members and six of twenty-nine honorary life directors have formal affiliation with the community institution.[8] The large board of powerful and prestigious individuals provides the organization with technical expertise, legitimacy for the organization's activities, and access to key decision makers. But board members do not raise funds for the organization or give personal donations to it.

The full board meets only once a year, largely for a ceremonial dinner. It has no formal role in managing the organization, nor does it approve its budget or exercise other forms of control.

Rather, most board functions are vested in an executive committee. In practice, the president of the board, who occupies a key executive position within the community institution, and the executive director jointly make all major decisions, in consultation with the community institution's vice president for external affairs. Their actions are endorsed by the executive committee but are not shared in any detail with the full board. Broader community issues must be channeled through this narrow decision-making structure to gain consideration, ensuring that Community Renewal pursues an agenda that reflects the goals and interests of the community institution, or at least does not conflict with them. The absence of multiple funders or an active board limits opportunities for other interests to be considered.

The community institution maintains tight fiscal control over Community Renewal. For more than twenty-five years, the organization's executive director was on the payroll of the institution. Subsequent directors have also had personal connections with the institution and are listed in its internal phone directory. Community Renewal's annual budget is developed with the help of, and approved by, the community institution. Community Renewal does not receive flat or lump-sum payments from the institution; instead, it receives a monthly stipend for what it needs to meet actual expenditures.[9] This procedure eliminates cash-flow problems, which normally present serious problems for other nonprofits, but makes it impossible for Community Renewal to accumulate a surplus to use for discretionary purposes. It also allows the institution to question expenditures and serves as a constant monitoring of the organization and its management.

The goals and interests of the community institution shape all the program arenas in which Community Renewal is active. This is the most tightly coupled funding relationship among the organizations included in the study. Similar structures may characterize other nonprofits that also depend heavily on a single funding source. For example, organizations that are operated or governed by religious orders or denominations maintain complex and highly institutionalized relationships with their sponsors.

Assessing the Strategies

As the findings show, each type of donation source presents particular contingencies and opportunities for development. Certain types of donors share some similarites in the contingencies they impose, but there are important differences within each of these categories as well. Some nonprofits seek donations from a large number of different donor types; others concentrate their efforts on just a few types. The greater the variety of their donation streams, the more complex are their management tasks. Seeking multiple donors spreads the risk, but nonprofits are likely to be most successful in obtaining donations if they tailor themselves to specific donor interests.

To secure stable donation streams, nonprofits seek to institutionalize their relationships with donors. To do so demands additional management efforts (as in the case of United Way funding) and almost always requires the organization to relinquish some control over its own operations. In extreme cases, the organization may cease to operate as a fully independent entity, as in the case of Community Renewal.

Lack of Overall Growth in Donations. In spite of the level or variety of efforts to obtain donations, few strategies result in growing sources of revenue for the organizations (see Figures 4.1 to 4.13). Only Hispanic Youth Services and Christian Therapists increased their overall donation base during the 1984–1988 period. For the first organization, the success reflects a new and highly polished marketing approach to foundations and corporate giving programs. For the second organization, the increase reflects emergency efforts to keep the organization alive when most of its staff resigned and its access to fee revenues was reduced. Neither of these efforts can be sustained over prolonged periods of time. Hispanic Youth Services cannot forever be the new minority organization on the block, which foundations or corporate grant makers have just discovered as a viable organization. Christian Therapists can appeal for emergency support for only so long before donors return to previous priorities.

None of the community development organizations have experienced sustained increases in the overall level of donations. African-American Neighbors and United Residents had growth in donations for two to three years but then saw equally rapid declines. The donation spurts came in response to emergency appeals that the organizations made when they suddenly lost other sources of funding. Responses to these special requests did not convert to sustained growth in donations. Hispanic Neighbors has maintained a relatively stable level of donations during the last ten years, but only at about half the volume it received during most of the 1970s.

Volatile, Unpredictable Donations. As shown in Table 7.2, individual donation streams change in volatile and unpredictable ways. Only United Way allocations, support from religious federations, operating support by the community institution for Community Renewal, and voluntary fees for Minority Search are stable from year to year. These are the most institutionalized sources of donations encountered among the organizations. The remaining sources of donations appear to be much more difficult to control. Individual contributions, foundation or corporate grants, and special event receipts ranked among the most volatile funding streams and showed major increases or decreases from year to year.

Even efforts to build on natural constituencies are not fully successful.

Minority Search managed to increase its donations from fee-paying corporations, but only temporarily. Some corporate clients have avoided paying the voluntary portion, especially on an ongoing basis. Efforts by Immigrant Welfare League to establish close relationships with its ethnic base also failed. Its affiliate chapters have declined in number and in how much revenue they generate for the agency. Its support from ethnic fraternal organizations was intense but brief (down from $75,000 in 1986 to $15,000 in 1988). The agency's board, affiliate chapters, and fraternal organizations are dominated by second and third generation immigrants, while its clients and staff consist almost entirely of newly arrived immigrants. The two groups have very different experiences, needs, and expectations. By attempting to meet the needs of the latter group (through public funding available for the services needed), the agency alienated the former.

Even Community Renewal may encounter difficulties. Its secure funding allows it to pursue costly strategies of confrontation and to avoid devoting time and energy to fund-raising activities. It has been credited with considerable success in maintaining community stability, but that very success means that its goals and strategies are of declining salience to the community institution. It has so little autonomy and such a limited agenda that it is likely to face antagonism from other local community actors. Because it cannot easily develop alternative areas of interest or a broader resource base, it has few viable options in the event that its relationship with the institution should deteriorate.

Inconsistent Results of Systematic Development Efforts. These fluctuations in sources of donations occur whether or not systematic development efforts are used. Youth Outreach has a professional fund-raiser on staff and engages in systematic development efforts for most donation streams, but has achieved no more stable donation streams than organizations that pursue donations on an ad hoc basis. Its success rate with foundation and corporate grants (about 50 percent of solicitations result in a donation) is at best slightly higher than for other organizations for which I have similar data.

However, a formalized system of solicitation does mean that the organization can solicit a larger number of donors and pursue a greater variety of sources. Youth Outreach generated the largest amount of donations among all thirteen organizations. Nonprofits that hope to obtain large amounts of donations will need to engage in deliberate and carefully targeted efforts to do so, in part because donors, especially foundations and corporations, increasingly demand tailor-made solicitations. The overall competition for donations is likely to favor these systematic efforts.

Summary

Donations have mixed benefit to nonprofits. They tend to involve little up-front control over services or activities and are therefore highly valued. The funding is either unrestricted (individual donations) or comes from targeted sources that match planned activities (such as foundation and corporate grants or United Way support). However, the level of work involved in securing donations requires considerable effort by staff, board members, and occasional consultants. Contingencies and uncertainties associated with most donation streams impose additional constraints. Organizations must be willing to invest time and money in establishing support from donors and must be prepared to absorb major fluctuations. The stability gained by developing institutional relations with donor sources must be weighed against the potential loss of organizational autonomy.

To obtain donations, nonprofits must market themselves to potential donors and convincingly describe the value of their activities. This approach is similar to what commercial organizations do when they advertise their products to customers, but the pitch is different. A nonprofit must either appeal to the self-interest of donors—so that they will want to keep the organization strong in order to serve their needs in the future—or it must sufficiently convey the importance and public benefit of its services to donors—so that they will want to make a voluntary contribution to this agency as opposed to another one.

In either event, fund-raising efforts focus on building access to donors. Staff, board members, or consultants devote considerable efforts to building such access. This explains why more than 80 percent of Chicago area social service and community development organizations reported in 1985 that they had already added or were seeking board members with connections to private funding sources. But access is difficult to obtain. Small, locally based nonprofits are rarely able to develop a "downtown" board or recruit prestigious, well-connected board members. The director of Alcohol Treatment explained that the organization usually did not seek foundation or corporate grants because the neighborhood residents on the board did not have the contacts, status, or self-confidence to make solicitations effectively.

Even if they are able to obtain access to donors, most nonprofits have no effective leverage over them or much ability to generate the funding through their own direct service efforts. In contrast to fees, donations separate customers (donors) from clients (service recipients). Donors then have little or no investment in the organizations itself and are rarely able to determine for themselves whether their donation buys the expected value of services.

This separation is most likely to affect social service agencies, because they rarely obtain donations from clients. In the case of other nonprofits, such as community development organizations, some donors are also clients of the organization and they can assess its performance directly and donate accordingly. However, both social service and community development organizations experience uncertainty and lack of control for at least some donation sources. This explains why the organizations (and especially the executive directors) usually expressed considerable ambivalence about most sources of donations. As the director of Hispanic Youth Services explained, when expressing her dislike for foundation and corporate grants as compared with public funding: "There are no buttons to push, so you can't get to those guys" when they turn down requests or otherwise make unreasonable demands.

The greater ambivalence that social service agencies encounter with their donor sources also explains why donation revenues rarely drive their service activities or programmatic strategies as explicitly or forcefully as do fee revenues or government grants and contracts. Donations operate in such a fashion as to have limited impact on how social service agencies plan their overall allocation of resources or implement donor priorities. Rather than directing new initiatives, donations supplement activities that derive from efforts to generate fees or manage government grants and contracts.

Community development organizations appear to have less ambivalent relations with most sources of donations. They have greater access to a variety of constituency groups that they can cultivate explicitly for purposes of involvement in their core activities. The financial support that this cultivation produces is important, but it is not the only reason for engaging in it.

Notes

1. More recent efforts of foundation councils to provide systematic information about past contributions by members take those developments a step further. However, the experience of the Donor's Forum of Chicago in developing a computerized grant information data base suggests that many foundations and corporate giving programs, especially smaller ones, are not ready or able to participate in such efforts, occasionally because they consider their giving practices or criteria to be confidential information.

2. United Way allocations have similar advantages, although this type of support requires detailed accounting of how the funds are used and for what purposes. The United Way of Chicago sets fairly stringent membership requirements, but it allows member agencies to use their base allocations with only a few restrictions: no more than 25 percent may be used for general administrative expenditures, and the rest must be allocated to one or more of thirty-two different service fields, such as individual and family counseling, information and referral (now combined into fifteen).

3. Community development organizations receive only a small proportion of United Way funding in Chicago (see Chapter Four), and the activities in which they engage traditionally have received low priorities in the United Way system. The reporting system that the United Way imposes is demanding for small organizations typical of the community development field and is geared toward the interests of social service organizations, for example, number of clients receiving day care or counseling and related unit costs.

4. All of the social service agencies and two of the community development organizations with income from special events use this approach to solicit participation in the events.
5. Youth Outreach is affiliated with a religious federation, but its client population does not belong to that denomination.
6. They can also point to their preoccupation with managing competing interests internally and with developing competitive market positions as justifying less than active participation.
7. This priority system has now been replaced with three-year priority grants that are awarded on a competitive basis in five broadly defined problem areas. To finance the grant system, the United Way has temporarily frozen base allocations until the grant system is fully implemented (by fiscal 1992). The new priority grant system has left the base allocation untouched and has made access to new funding in the United Way system more rewarding for some agencies, because it makes it possible to obtain larger amounts of new funding than they would receive otherwise. However, it also makes the new funding less predictable and more volatile than before.
8. Formal affiliation is defined by whether they were listed in the community institution's internal phone directory in 1989.
9. When I attempted to get data on the organization's monthly cash receipts and expenditures to examine the nature of its cash flow, I was given only monthly expenditures and told that they matched cash receipts exactly because that is how the community institution delivers its support.

EIGHT

Public Funding:
A Driving Force

Public grants and contracts resemble donations in that both provide subsidies that allow nonprofits to make services more widely and cheaply available to service recipients than can commercial organizations; but public funding gives more explicit recognition to the public benefits that nonprofits provide, because it indicates that their services warrant the use of government taxing authority to ensure their availability.

Public funding is a major source of funding for most nonprofits and provides them with legitimacy and access to political decision making. However, it is a problematic source because of the management efforts required. In this chapter, I outline management contingencies associated with public funding and briefly review a range of strategies that the case-study organizations use to address those contingencies. The contingencies and available strategies are such that public funding drives nonprofit revenue levels, dominates their external relations, and absorbs their management energies.

Management Contingencies

Nonprofits are intimately involved in a diverse range of public sector activities, for the reasons discussed in Chapter Three. Although it is an important source of revenues, public funding presents difficult management contingencies. It is complex and therefore inherently uncertain, although it is not necessarily unpredictable or uncontrollable. Public funding frequently requires cost sharing and therefore limits other options. It involves complex exchange relationships and explicit requirements of accountability to external agents and therefore limits management discretion over the internal disposition of resources. Not surprisingly, nonprofit managers express considerable ambivalence about it as a funding source.

169

Uncertainties Generated by Political Process

Much of the uncertainty associated with public funding for nonprofits reflects deficits, budget compromises, and policy priorities. The low and declining priorities given to human services (Grønbjerg, 1985) show annually in intense negotiations to overcome the budget constraints under which most levels of government have operated in recent years. Both the city of Chicago and the state of Illinois have faced large budget deficits almost annually since the early 1980s. The difficulty of reaching agreement about possible tax increases or cuts in appropriations means that rival budget proposals frequently survive until the last day of the fiscal year. Last-minute compromises dominate the process and create continuing uncertainty about the level of funding that will be available for particular program areas, especially human services, and for grants and contracts to nonprofits in these fields.

The political process has been particularly intense at the city level, with major implications for community development organizations that receive almost all of their public funding from Community Development Block Grants administered by the city. The Chicago City Council has been beset by warring political factions since the late 1970s[1]; and because community development programs involve geographical targeting of funding (which streets to repair, which housing units to rehabilitate), the budgeting process for these programs has provided numerous opportunities for opposing parties to reward or punish each other and each other's known supporters.

Other sources of uncertainty come from the complex system of intergovernmental relations that characterizes most of the fields in which nonprofits are active. Nonprofits with a stake in grants and contracts must keep well informed about new developments in public policy at all levels. The federal government and most state governments frequently seek to encourage the participation of lower levels of government in policy arenas by making funding available to governmental units for limited purposes. The process involves partial delegation of responsibility for implementing specific policy directives, but with some residual control at higher levels of government. This kind of "government by agency" (Williams, 1980) characterizes most federal programs in the fields of social service, employment and training, housing and community development, and health.

It is difficult to fully document the importance of these intergovernmental relations at the level of local communities, the scale at which most nonprofit organizations operate. Federal support for programs becomes incorporated in public budgets at each level of government involved, the geographical allocation of funds by higher levels of government rarely coincides with local jurisdictions, and fiscal periods may differ considerably among governmental units (Grønbjerg, Musselwhite, and Salamon, 1984).

The best estimates of these structures confirm their complexity. As Table 8.1 shows for the Chicago–Cook County area for 1984, the federal

Table 8.1. Involvement of Federal, State, and Local Government in Public Spending for Fields of Interest to Nonprofit Organizations, Chicago–Cook County Area, 1984.

Service Field	1984 Total $ Spending (in millions)	Percentage of Public Spending by								
		Tax Origin			Disbursement			Control[a]		
		Federal	State	Local	Federal	State	Local	Federal	State	Local
Core Fields										
Social service	324.7	59	35	5	3	64	32	59	76	32
Mental health	94.5	21	73	6	—	86	14	21	94	14
Employment training	85.2	99	1	—	4	11	85	99	33	86
Housing/community development	234.4	97	2	1	1	3	96	97	9	96
Other Fields										
Income support[b]	1,491.6	67	32	1	19	77	3	67	78	4
Medicare	1,262.1	100	—	—	96	2	2	100	2	2
Medicaid[c]	760.5	47	53	—	48	93	7	47	100	7
Other health	472.2	56	16	28	48	18	34	56	22	34
Arts and culture	131.0	8	11	81	7	4	89	8	12	89
Total	4,856.2	70	24	6	36	47	17	70	51	14

Note: (——) indicates less than 1 percent. All amounts are in constant 1981 dollars.

[a] Includes pass-through funding from other levels of government. Totals add to more than 100 percent because funds are counted at each level of government.

[b] Includes only means-tested income support programs (excludes Social Security, unemployment insurance, workers' compensation, and so on).

[c] Includes state-funded medical assistance program for medically indigent.

Source: Urban Institute Nonprofit Sector Project for Chicago, Public Spending Analysis and special analysis.

government is the source of 59 percent of total public spending for social services (and therefore controls 59 percent), yet it disburses only 3 percent directly. The rest is transferred to state agencies or some unit of local government. Consequently, while the state government pays for 35 percent of social services in the Chicago area, it disburses directly 64 percent of the funds (including most but not all of the indirect federal funds) but controls 76 percent (including expenditures passed through to local government and disbursed by them). Local governments contribute only 5 percent to the total costs of social services, but disburse and control almost one-third (32 percent). Figure 1.1 presents a visual map of this intergovernmental funding structure as it looks from the point of view of a nonprofit social service agency with public grants and contracts.

Table 8.1 shows that intergovernmental relational structures differ among service fields. In mental health, the state is the source of most funds (73 percent), disburses most of them directly (86 percent), and controls almost all (94 percent) of them. The federal government provides and controls about one-fifth (21 percent) of the funds; local governments have even less involvement, contributing 6 percent of funds, disbursing 14 percent, and controlling 14 percent. In housing and community development, almost all the funds (97 percent) come from the federal government and go directly to local governments, which disburse (96 percent) and control them (96 percent). The state has only limited involvement in this field in the Chicago area and controls only 9 percent of the spending. For smaller communities, federal funds for these purposes pass through state governments.

In 1984, the year in which the study was completed, the federal Comprehensive Employment and Training Act (CETA) was being phased out and replaced by the Job Training Partnership Act (JTPA) program. CETA funds went directly to units of local government (such as the housing and community development funds), while JTPA funds are allocated to state governments, which in turn redistribute them to units of local government.

Continuity and Predictability of Funding

Uncertainties associated with managing complex funding structures are somewhat alleviated if funding streams are otherwise predictable and continuous. In these cases, recipient organizations learn how to negotiate the systems effectively. Indirect evidence suggests that public funding involves a fairly high level of continuity for social service organizations, but less continuity for community development organizations. Annual changes in public funding for the seven case-study organizations with public funding fluctuate less dramatically than most sources of donations (see Figures 4.1 to 4.13). While about two-thirds of twenty-nine donation streams are relatively volatile, changing by an average of 40 percent or more from year to year, only two of the seven organizations averaged similar shifts in public funding.

Continuity in the Social Service Field. As shown in Chapter Four, public funding is likely to be less volatile for social service agencies than for community development organizations. Immigrant Welfare League had the largest average annual change in public funding (138 percent), but the high turbulence reflects the loss of almost all public funding for one year because of fiscal irregularities. The other social service agencies had fairly small fluctuations with annual changes averaging 23 percent or less.

The continuity in public funding for social services is also supported by an analysis of all grant and contract payments by the Illinois Department of Children and Family Services during the 1985–1989 period (Chen, Grønbjerg, and Stagner, 1992). Only about 40 percent of all agency providers received DCFS funds during each of the five years, but these agencies accounted for 94 percent of all payments in most of the traditional social service categories.

Similarly, directors of the four social service agencies with public grants or contracts in the case-study project emphasized the continuity and predictability of government funding. The director of Alcohol Treatment referred to the agency's major government contract as "money in the bank." The director of Youth Outreach thought that the agency was unlikely to lose any public funds, because it had maintained good performance levels and had a good reputation. The director of Hispanic Youth Services argued that although some public grants or contracts were awarded with specific time-limited commitments, the large ones were safe, especially if they involved state funding. Only the director of Immigrant Welfare League expressed some uncertainty. He thought that public agencies gave priorities to serving low-income populations and racial or ethnic minorities and that the agency's white ethnic target population excluded it from obtaining access to several sources of public funding. However, as Figure 4.4 showed, the agency had been extremely successful in obtaining public grants and contracts.

Detailed analysis of the history of grants and contracts for the case-study organizations provides explicit documentation. As Table 8.2 shows, three of the four social service agencies received most of their public funding during the 1984–1988 period in the form of grants and contracts that were continuous throughout the period, although payment levels changed from year to year. For two agencies (Alcohol Treatment, Youth Outreach), continuous awards accounted for more than three-quarters of public funding. For Immigrant Welfare League, the proportion would have been equally high if it had not temporarily lost one grant because of fiscal irregularities.

Only two of the agencies had any terminated or one-time grants, and these accounted for less than 6 percent of total government funding during the period. The remaining public funding came from new grants and contracts that the agencies gained access to during the 1984–1988 period and expected to keep. In short, the dominant pattern is one of ongoing grants and contracts, with the addition of new funding sources over time. The availability of continuous funding from government grants and contracts is a

**Table 8.2. History of Restricted Grants and Contracts, 1984–1988,
Four Social Service Agencies.**

	Percentage of Grant/Contract Amounts			
Public Grants/Contracts	Alcohol Treatment	Youth Outreach	Hispanic Youth Services	Immigrant Welfare League
Continuing Grants/Contracts	97	73	53	—
Interrupted Grants/Contracts	—	3	—	63
New Grants/Contracts	4	24	41	32
Terminated Grants/Contracts[a]	—	—	6	5
All	100	100	100	100
Large Grants/Contracts	97	60	29	60
Medium Grants/Contracts	—	22	34	23
Small Grants/Contracts	4	18	37	16
All	100	100	100	100
Total Amounts	$1,146,444	$3,055,323	$2,515,520	$660,114
Total Number of Awards	10	52	63	26
Average Award	$114,644	$58,756	$39,929	$25,389

Note: (—) indicates less than 1%. Large grants involve funding at $100,000 per year or more, medium-sized grants provide funding at $50,000–$99,999, and small grants involve funding at less than $50,000.

[a] Includes one-time grants and contracts.

Source: Case-Study Project.

major factor in making public funding a driving force for social service agencies.

Funding Turbulence in the Community Development Field. The community development organizations generally had somewhat greater annual changes in public funding than did the social service agencies. United Residents had changes in government funding that averaged 107 percent per year, and the remaining two community development organizations averaged 33 and 44 percent, respectively, compared with less than 23 percent for three of the social service agencies. Similarly, the directors of community development organizations expressed much greater uncertainty about being able to count on continued funding from public sources and pointed to specific experiences of their own or other organizations.

Some of that uncertainty reflects ongoing efforts by the federal government to reduce spending in the Community Development Block Grant, the primary source of public funding for community development activities in the Chicago area. However, two of the organizations (United Residents and Economic Development Commission) thought that they performed so well on specific contracts that the city would not be able to meet its own objectives without them.

As Table 8.3 shows, the community development organizations received substantial proportions of their public funding during the 1984–1988
period in the form of grants and contracts that were either continuous or only
temporarily interrupted. These awards accounted for between 35 and 52
percent of total public funding for these organizations, notably smaller
proportions than observed for the four social service agencies (53 to 96
percent).

However, the two community development organizations with the
largest amount of continuous public funding (Economic Development Commission and United Residents) also had substantial funding from terminated
or one-time grants and contracts. Terminated funding accounted for 24 and
45 percent, respectively, of all public funding for the two organizations,
compared with none or less than 6 percent for the four social service
organizations. This finding suggests that community development organizations not only encounter greater uncertainty in securing access to stable
public funding but also face occasional challenges to replace the funding
from other sources.[2]

African-American Neighbors illustrates the extreme turbulence that
public funding may present to community development organizations. The
organization had no continuous public funding at all during the 1984–1988

Table 8.3. History of Restricted Grants and Contracts,
Three Community Development Organizations.

	Percentage of Grant/Contract Amounts			
Grant/Contract Experience	*Economic Development Commission (1984–1988)*	*United Residents (1984–1988)*	*African-American Neighbors*	
			(1984–1988)	*(1978–1990)*
Continuing Grants/Contracts	52	51	—	—
Interrupted Grants/Contracts	—	—	35	40
New Grants/Contracts	24	4	65	16
Terminated Grants/Contracts[a]	24	45	—	44
All	100	100	100	100
Large Grants/Contracts	56	41	—	21
Medium Grants/Contracts	17	—	23	42
Small Grants/Contracts	27	59	77	37
All	100	100	100	100
Total Amounts	$1,747,365	$926,837	$713,513	$2,408,391
Total Number of Awards	30	26	33	52
Average Award	$58,246	$35,648	$21,622	$46,315

Note: (——) indicates less than 1%. Large grants involve funding at $100,000 per
year or more, medium-sized grants provide funding at $50,000–$99,999, and small grants
involve funding at less than $50,000.
  [a] Includes one-time grants and contracts.
Source: Case-Study Project.

period, but it also had no terminated grants and contracts. Instead, African-American Neighbors received 35 percent of its public funds from sources that were temporarily interrupted and 65 percent from sources that were added during the period. However, it had experienced considerable turbulence in its public funding in the period immediately prior to 1984, as Table 8.3 indicates. During the 1978–1990 period, only 16 percent of the organization's public funding came from new funding sources, and 44 percent came from grants or contracts that were terminated or were available on only a one-time basis.

These developments are summarized in Figure 8.1, which shows inflation-adjusted changes in the volume of public grants and contracts received by the organization and its affiliated development corporation since 1978 and notes closely related political events. The figure shows the dramatic growth in public funding that the organization experienced in the late 1970s as two new mayors took office in quick succession. The real value of the organization's government funding levels almost tripled in one year and more than doubled again the following year.

Figure 8.1 also shows the equally dramatic decline that began the following year as the organization and its director became involved in political conflicts with Mayor Byrne, culminating in its support for a boycott of a major event sponsored by the mayor during the summer of 1982. Public funding dropped by 72 percent in one year (from $612,000 in 1981 to $173,000 in 1982) and almost disappeared by 1983 (down to $19,000), reflecting a further cut of 89 percent in the second year. The director said that key staff members of city agencies told him they were directed by Byrne to discontinue all funding to the organization. The organization sought support from at least one coalition of nonprofit development organizations to

Figure 8.1. Public Grants and Contracts, 1978 to 1990, African-American Neighbors.

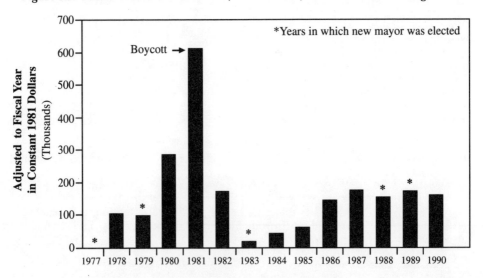

protest the cuts, but it failed to get the coalition or most members actively involved.

When a black mayor (Harold Washington), with whom the organization was closely affiliated, came into office in 1983, the organization was able to reinstitute some of the terminated funding. However, that did not take place immediately, in part because of the lag time in awarding grants and contracts. More important, simultaneous cuts in federal Community Development Block Grants meant that the new city administration was under considerable pressure to maintain funding levels to other organizations and had little excess funds with which to reward African-American Neighbors for its support.

Nevertheless, the organization doubled its public funding by 1984, increased it by another 46 percent the following year, more than doubled it again by 1986, and increased it again by another 20 percent in 1987. As two new mayors have come into office since then, the organization's overall level of public funding has flattened out and fluctuated up or down by 8 to 13 percent per year during the next three years (1988–1990). Overall, this is a much more dramatic pattern of growth, decline, growth, and continuing fluctuations than observed for any of the other organizations included in the study. This is also the only organization for which I can link such changes directly to shifts in local politics.

However, directors of the two other community organizations with public funding also pointed to occasions when they had been caught in the political process. Economic Development Commission, for example, almost lost one public contract because the city department in question had "forgotten" to include the organization's name on the appropriations bill one year. The contract was restored only after vigorous protests by the organization and its local supporters, but not until well into the fiscal year. The director emphasized that he had no specific reason to think the city had done this deliberately, but cited the experience as an example of the uncertainty associated with public funding for the organization.

United Residents encountered serious problems with a Special Service Area taxing district it helped establish to fund local economic and community development under its management. Within a couple of years after the establishment of the district, a small group of local property owners aligned themselves with local aldermen to oppose the district when it came up for renewal. As a result, the taxing district was dissolved, and the organization lost a major source of public funding. That is the main reason the organization had such a large proportion (45 percent) of its public funding in the form of terminated or one-time grants and contracts.

The continuity in public funding among social service agencies and the greater uncertainty that community development organizations face are magnified by the level of funding involved for individual awards. The size of awards is by itself a major reason why public funding is attractive. During the 1984–1988 period, the four social service agencies received 151 awards totaling $7.4 million for an average of $48,900 per award (see Table 8.2). The three community development organizations received $3.4 million through 89 awards during the same period for an average award of $38,100 (see Table 8.3).

Few other types of funders make similar amounts of money available to social service and community development organizations. Thus, none of the seventy-three foundation and corporate grants that Youth Outreach received in fiscal 1988 exceeded $15,000, and all but two were $6,000 or less. Some foundation and corporate grants may approach the size of public awards, but rarely on a continuing basis. Only United Way membership allocations and similar institutionalized donor systems are likely to be comparable to the public funding system in the amount and continuity of funding streams.

Cost Control and Cost Sharing

As shown previously, uncertainties surrounding the political process create difficulties for nonprofit organizations in effectively monitoring public activities and developing appropriate strategic positions. Some of these uncertainties are offset by the tendency for public funding sources to provide continuous funding streams. However, public efforts at cost control and cost sharing generate additional contingencies for managing public grants and contracts. Cost control occurs when public sector agencies limit increases in grants and contracts, perhaps even to levels below increases in operating costs, but require that the same level of services be provided. Cost sharing exists when public agencies require or provide incentives for nonprofit service providers to secure matching funds for program activities otherwise covered by public grants and contracts.

Cost sharing occurs frequently in public grants and contracts. At times, it comes about incidentally as nonprofit contractors compete for limited contract dollars. By accepting payment levels below the actual costs of delivering services, organizations undercut the proposals of other agencies and ensure that their own receive favorable attention. At times, cost sharing is an explicit part of public program policies. The Illinois Donated Funds Initiative (DFI) requires recipient organizations to certify the availability of (in the case of large units of local government) or prepay (in the case of nonprofit organizations or smaller local governments) 25 percent of service costs to the state for designated social services. The state adds the remaining 75 percent from its share of federal Title XX Block Grants for social services and distributes the entire 100 percent in the form of grants and contracts to participating organizations. The DFI program has faced frequent threats to its continuation, but aggressive lobbying by United Way and other nonprofits has kept the program alive. Both the state and participating nonprofits portray the program as leveraging funds from the other sector.

Much of the pressure for cost control and cost sharing originates from the perennial budget problems indicated previously. However, there are also explicit incentives for public agencies to engage in the practice. When public sector agencies leverage nonprofit revenues by requiring or encouraging cost sharing, they can claim credit for a larger volume of services than would be possible otherwise. As a result, the process serves to obscure the low levels of spending for public services. Public officials also argue that cost sharing gives nonprofits a stake in program activities, encourages greater commitment to program goals, and requires less intensive monitoring.[3] The overall result, however, is fiscal uncertainty about the level of funding available for the next cycle of awards and the absorption of other nonprofit resources to meet the full costs of services.

Demanding Management Efforts and Limited Discretion

Relying on grants and contracts to deliver publicly funded human services reduces the effort that public sector agencies devote to managing clients and staff directly and transfers most of these functions to nonprofit subcontractors or grantees. However, public sector agencies seek to control these functions indirectly. In return for the public funding, nonprofit service providers are expected to ensure that their performance of a specified set of activities meets statutory and legislative procedural requirements. Almost without exception, then, public grants and contracts are restricted funding sources for nonprofits.

The receipt of public grants and contracts therefore subjects nonprofit organizations to explicit efforts by public authorities to control and monitor their behavior, limiting the amount of formal discretion that they exercise over internal organizational resources. They must not only manage the direct service efforts but also adhere to the external requirements. The range of agreed-on procedures is extensive and may involve minute details of organizational activities. To demonstrate their accountability, nonprofits are generally required to provide public authorities with assurances that they have spent the funding appropriately, that the agreed-on services have been delivered to eligible clients under suitable conditions, and that they otherwise adhere to appropriate principles of public behavior. These principles may be quite explicit (for instance, "require the organization to certify its refusal to do business with organizations that have economic interests in South Africa"), in accordance with the semiofficial status that the receipt of public funding implies.

There are no adequate data to document whether management efforts associated with government grants and contracts have increased in recent years. Curtailments in the overall level of public spending for human services and the absence of major new initiatives probably mean that fewer nonprofits have experienced rapid growth and the management strains associated with the addition of new public funding sources. However, periods of fiscal constraint may create other management problems, and most of the seven organizations with public funding seem to have experienced increasing management overhead because of how their public funding sources have changed over time.

During the 1984–1988 period, most public grants and contracts show flat or declining grant levels from year to year for the four social service agencies. The year-to-year changes are more variable for the community development organizations, but the dominant pattern is also one of flat or declining levels. These trends do not seem to reflect negative assessments of the organizations' performances: all seven organizations avoided deeper cuts applied to other nonprofits in the same program areas. Meeting ongoing service needs with declining purchasing powers of revenues strains management resources and is an important element in the pattern of cost sharing that characterizes public grants and contracts for nonprofits.

Flat or declining grant levels mean that the overall increase in public funding that most of the case-study organizations experienced (see Figures 4.1 to 4.10) did not come from higher payment levels in existing funding sources. As Tables 8.2 and 8.3 documented, the pattern is one of growth through the addition of new grants and contracts, sometimes from new sources altogether. New funding sources require new reporting formats and program designs and impose additional management efforts, at least temporarily until the organization has learned the procedures.

To examine this argument in greater detail, I looked at the size of the public funding awards.[4] The analysis shows that most of the organizations have experienced increasing reliance on small awards. Table 8.2 shows that all of the social service agencies except Alcohol Treatment received substantial amounts during the 1984–1988 period in the form of small grants and contracts, ranging between 16 and 37 percent. An additional 22 to 34 percent of the funding for these three agencies came from medium-sized grants and contracts. On average, the proportions of small grant awards are somewhat higher for the three community development organizations, ranging between 27 and 77 percent (see Table 8.3).

However, most of the new funding for the social service organizations came in the form of small grants and contracts. Alcohol Treatment added three new public funding sources during the 1984–1988 period, all small grants or contracts. Hispanic Youth Services more than doubled the number of restricted grants and contracts that it managed, from nine in 1985 to seventeen in 1987 and twenty in 1988. Only four of these eleven new funding sources provided medium-sized grants; the rest were small. Of the five new public funding sources added by Youth Outreach between 1983 and 1988, three were small ones and only one was a large grant. Finally, Immigrant Welfare League tripled its public funding sources, from three in 1984 to nine in 1988, but only one new award provided funding at a medium level; the rest were in the form of small awards.

Among the community development organizations, only Economic Development Commission added a new, large funding source during the period. United Residents attempted to do so, but lost the award within three years. Otherwise, the organizations added only small grants and contracts. These trends are important, because each public grant and contract requires a minimum level of management work, irrespective of its size (see Chapter Nine). Reliance on small grants and contracts and the addition of new and smaller grants add disproportionately to management overhead.

Other sources of management overhead have come from the increasingly diverse fiscal periods under which different levels of government operate. The fiscal year begins on January 1 for the city of Chicago, on July 1 for the state of Illinois, and on October 1 for the federal government. The city of Chicago uses all three in its own accounting system: the state fiscal year for all its state grants, the federal fiscal year for most of its federal grants, and its own fiscal year for everything else. Other units of local government have still other fiscal periods. The fiscal year begins on the first Monday in December for Cook County, on April 1 for the Chicago Housing Authority, and on August 1 for the Chicago Public School system. Most nonprofits start their fiscal year on July 1, for reasons of cost, convenience, and need.[5]

However, beginning with the 1987–88 July 1 fiscal year, the city of Chicago shifted all its grants and contracts funded under the Community Development Block Grant program to a calendar year, to match its own fiscal year. This was the second shift in less than five years and required the use of two nine-month program periods each time. As a result, most of the case-study organizations have come to operate with increasingly diverse program periods for their public grants and contracts. Many no longer match their own fiscal years.

By 1988, Youth Outreach and Hispanic Youth Services had close to half of their funding sources and 40 percent of their grant and contract dollars from funding sources that did not match their own fiscal periods, up from none in 1984. Much less dramatic shifts occurred for Alcohol Treatment, which receives the bulk of its public funding (97 percent) from the state's Department of Alcoholism and Substance Abuse and operates on the same fiscal year as the state. Of the seven organizations, only Economic Development Commission had increasing correspondence between its public funding streams and its own fiscal period. It is the only organization that operates on a calendar year and benefited from the city's shift to the calendar year. For the others, operating with multiple fiscal periods complicates efforts to manage and coordinate programs and confounds efforts to budget expenditures, assess program performances, and plan a range of activities.

These patterns of funding continuity, cost sharing, management demands, and limited discretion explain why most nonprofit managers view public funding positively, although with a strong measure of ambivalence. In 1982, more than half (56 percent) of nonprofit managers of Chicago area social service and community development organizations did not believe federal funding distorts their mission or programs (a frequently voiced concern by some policy makers). A substantial majority (72 percent) also believe that government funding causes nonprofits to direct more services to low-income groups, a development that is consistent with the mission of most nonprofits.

This positive view is also supported by interviews with the same directors in 1985, when they were asked for a detailed assessment of five sources of funding. Government funding received a favorable evaluation by at least half of the directors on four of the nine criteria: as being worth the effort (68 percent), not forcing an organization into areas in which it has little or no expertise (58 percent), enabling an organization to serve the clients it wants to serve (57 percent), and not primarily going to favored organizations that know the right people (56 percent). Two of these criteria (not forcing into areas of little expertise, enabling to serve clients) directly assess perceptions of how government funding relates to organizational missions. Government funding was also rated positively by almost half of the directors (48 percent) on a third mission-related criterion: allowing the organization to develop new programs that are really needed.

As expected, a much smaller proportion of the directors rated government funding positively on criteria having to do with predictability (easy to plan for future with, 34 percent), management discretion (flexible in how and when it can be used, 17 percent), and amount of work (easy to administer and account for, 17 percent). Less than one-third (31 percent) agreed that public funding was the type of funding they would prefer to rely on.

The percentage of managers that gave positive assessments of government funding on the nine dimensions is generally smaller than the proportions that gave positive evaluations of other sources of funding on the same dimensions. As Table 7.1 showed, half or more of the directors evaluated each of three major sources of donations (individual donations, foundation and corporate grants, United Way support) positively on seven of the nine criteria. For two sources of donations, the proportions were 60 percent or more. Fees were also evaluated positively on most dimensions.

Table 8.4 presents the average assessment scores for each of the five major funding sources on the nine dimensions on a scale from 5 (agree strongly) to 1 (disagree strongly). It includes an overall score based on the average for all nine dimensions for each funding source. Average scores of 2.5 or higher indicate that the particular funding source is generally viewed positively on that dimension. The underlined and double-underlined numbers reflect dimensions on which the assessment of a particular funding source differs significantly from the corresponding evaluation of government funding.

For most of the criteria, government funding receives a lower assessment score than other revenue sources. Of the possible forty different comparisons between government funding and the other four revenue sources included in the analysis, government funding has a significantly lower assessment than other sources of funding in twenty-four comparisons, is not

Table 8.4. Average Assessment Scores for Major Funding Sources
by Chicago-Area Nonprofit Organizations, 1985.

Criteria	Individual Donations	Corporate/ Foundation Support	United Way/ Federated Funders	Dues/Fees/ Service Charges	Government Grants and Contracts
Discretion					
Flexible in how and when it can be used	4.2	3.3	3.3	3.7	2.0
Work Intensity					
Easy to administer and account for	3.8	3.8	3.0[b]	3.7	2.0
Predictability					
Easy to plan for future with	2.9	2.6[a]	3.4	2.8	2.5
Involves no favoritism	2.7	2.5	3.0	4.4	3.5
Mission Relatedness					
Allows development of needed programs	3.8	3.9	3.5[b]	3.2	3.1
Does not force into areas of little ability	4.2	3.8	3.8	4.2	3.5
Enables serving clients we want	3.8	4.0	3.8[b]	3.1	3.4
General Assessment					
Worth pursuing for effort required	3.8	4.3	4.0[b]	3.8	3.8
Type of funding would prefer to rely on	3.5	3.7	3.3[b]	2.6	2.6
Combined	3.8	3.7	3.5[b]	3.4	2.8

Note: Differences of .45 or more are significant at the .05 level or better. Averages are based on combined responses from thirty-five social service and sixteen community development organizations. Scores reflect ratings on a scale from 5 (agree strongly) to 1 (disagree strongly). Numbers underlined are dimensions on which the assessment of a particular funding source differs significantly from that of government funding. Numbers double underlined are dimensions on which the assessment of a particular funding source is significantly lower than that of government funding. Three items were originally presented with reverse directions (no favoritism: "mainly available to 'favored' organizations that know the right people"; does not force: "forces an organization into areas where it has little experience or ability"; worth efforts: "generally not worth pursuing, likely return too small for efforts required."

[a] Community development organizations are significantly more likely to provide positive assessments than social service agencies.

[b] Social service agencies are significantly more likely to provide positive assessments than community development organizations.

Source: Nonprofit Sector Project, Personal Interviews.

significantly different in fourteen comparisons, and is significantly higher in only two cases.[6]

The favorable assessments occur on only one dimension: government funding is significantly more likely to be viewed as involving less favoritism than individual donations and foundation or corporate grants. Otherwise, government funding is viewed more negatively than all other funding in terms of flexibility, ease of administration, and on the combined score. Public funding is also viewed more negatively than most other funding sources as a preferred source of funding (except for fees), as not forcing organizations into areas where they have little expertise (except for foundation/corporate grants and United Way funding), as allowing organizations to develop pro-grams that are needed (except for fees and United Way funding), and as enabling organizations to serve the clients it wants (except for private dona-tions and fees). It resembles most other funding sources on only two dimen-sions: ease of planning (except for United Way funding, which rates signifi-cantly higher than the rest) and in being worth the efforts (except for foundation/corporate support).

The ambivalence toward government funding revealed in these find-ings is supported by information from the case studies. Most of the managers whose organizations have public funding emphasized the amount of work involved in managing it and the ways in which it limited management discretion. Still, most felt they had mastered the system and that access to public funding on a continuous basis had become critical in enabling their organizations to provide important services without disruptions.

Strategies for Managing Public Funding

A few of the case-study organizations have made deliberate decisions to avoid or severely limit the receipt of public funding in order to minimize possible deflection of the organization's mission. For the rest, management strategies include efforts to cushion the organization against the uncertainties and external control associated with the public grants and contracts system.

Avoidance

We asked all directors of the case-study organizations about their experience with public funding; if their organization did not currently have such fund-ing, we asked whether they had thought about obtaining it. Of the six organizations without public funding in 1988, two (Minority Search and Community Renewal) had never had public funding. The directors of both organizations said that they had made an intentional decision not to seek it, since public funding was too demanding, and sufficient revenues from other sources allowed them to undertake most of what they wanted to do. Minority Search also argued that public funding would interfere with its efforts to maintain a businesslike operation.

Four other organizations had obtained public funding at some point in the past, but no longer did. Hispanic Neighbors had substantial public funding during the 1970s (see Figure 4.12), Christian Therapists obtained one small grant of less than $20,000 in 1986, New Town Sponsors received several grants from the state Arts Council for its major event, and Community Renewal sought but failed to obtain a federal grant to cover the capital costs of a housing development project. All four indicated that they no longer had any interest in such funding, although Hispanic Neighbors just recently obtained public funding for housing rehabilitation. However, the director argued that it was pass-through funding for individual homeowners and therefore not really money going to the organization.

The six organizations expressed a variety of reasons for avoiding or severely limiting the amount or type of public funding, ranging from fear of co-optation (Hispanic Neighbors, New Town Sponsors, Community Renewal), excessive demands on organizational resources (cited by all except Christian Therapists), and difficulties in matching priorities in public funding streams (Christian Therapists, Community Renewal). These themes also surfaced among the seven organizations with public funding and were central to a number of strategies that they employed.

Minimizing Co-optation

Several directors of the community development organizations expressed considerable concern about being co-opted into the political agenda of public agencies or local politicians. Only the director of Preservation Council downplayed the importance of public funding because of the organization's access to substantial funding from special events. Social service agencies rarely expressed such concerns explicitly.

Two of the community development organizations viewed public funding as likely to interfere with efforts to meet the needs of their primary sponsors. The director of New Town Sponsors argued that the organization had to serve the interest of its dues-paying members, that is, local investors and commercial establishments. The director of Community Renewal argued that the organization was established to protect the interest of the local community institution that provided it with the bulk of its funding. In both cases, the interests of the organization's key constituency did not necessarily coincide with those of public officials or public planning efforts, and the directors argued that public funding would compromise their ability to take aggressive stances on some issues.

The director of Hispanic Neighbors was most explicit about the fear of co-optation as a reason for avoiding public funding. She argued that the organization's success with its major special events was critical in allowing it to take strong positions on a number of key issues, although it sought to avoid direct involvement in partisan politics. She recounted how other local non-profit organizations with public funding would refuse to participate or fail to show up for rallies or protest meetings, because they feared funding retaliations or had become too closely aligned with local politicians.

As the funding turbulence experienced by African-American Neighbors demonstrates, these concerns are not unwarranted for community development organizations, especially in low-income, minority communities. In these communities, the local economic infrastructures are fragmented and depleted. The low levels of private investment mean that the communities tend to be greatly affected by—and highly dependent on—public investment and welfare policies. The residents, businesses, and other organizations located in these communities have vested interests in shaping the public agenda but have a limited range of opportunities for doing so. They have insufficient private investment to become major political players on that basis alone, and they rarely occupy top decision-making positions in larger institutions or networks. Instead, they have to seek access to key political power structures through voter mobilization, protest activities, or other actions directed toward institutions outside the community.

Community organization/development organizations can play a key role in these types of activities, as the civil rights movement and the Alinsky movement have shown. However, in most low-income communities, community/organizing development organizations can obtain only limited financial support from local residents, businesses, or other groups. These organizations are particularly vulnerable to discretionary resource decisions by individuals or institutions from outside the community.

The director of African-American Neighbors acknowledged this dependency on outside support but argued that organizations wanting to serve the interests of excluded groups had to take risky but necessary actions and be prepared to deal with the consequences. He explained that the organization had avoided public funding prior to 1978 to avoid any alignment with the first Daley administration. He said the organization's board and staff had recognized that taking positions against the Byrne administration would most likely result in loss of public funding, but decided to do so anyway.

Directors of Economic Development Commission and United Residents minimized the danger of co-optation for their organizations, even though they received substantial amounts of public funding. They pointed to their active boards, consensus mode of operation, and strong support from important local institutions as key factors in their being able to take positions on particular issues. Any threat of major retaliation from public funders could be met by mobilizing local constituencies. Of course, in contrast to African-American Neighbors and Hispanic Neighbors, these two organizations had substantial financial or political support from local constituencies that were important actors beyond the community boundaries as well.

Analysis of newspaper accounts also indicates that the two organizations took less outspoken positions than those in low-income, minority communities. Their cooperative relationships with a full complement of strong community institutions (local banks, larger businesses, major employers, and institutions of higher education) meant that they could not easily ignore or oppose those interests. As a result, political involvement by the organizations is lower keyed or focused on issues of direct local impact.

Buffer from Uncertainty

The complex and large-scale transfer of funds between different levels of government adds cumulative layers of priorities, accountability, and administration structures for organizations with public funding. In order to manage these contingencies, the case-study organizations engaged in a wide variety of activities. They undertook extensive monitoring of public sector actors in order to scan the environment for changes and new opportunities. They sought to develop strategic positions that would allow them to exercise some leverage over public funders and, in two cases, attempted to establish direct control over one type of public funding stream. They strove to maintain their credibility and performance levels to make themselves indispensible to public funders. And they attempted to develop or maintain fund reserves to absorb potential fiscal jolts.

Monitoring and Boundary-Spanning Activities. Nonprofits that receive grants and contracts from public funding sources not only must contend with the consequences of multiple administrative structures but also must monitor all key actors involved, in order to anticipate future policy directions and funding developments. Efforts to monitor public sector activities and position the organization strategically require complex and at times intensive boundary-spanning activities by nonprofits, especially by the executive directors.

Interview data from 1985 reveal that a large majority (68 percent) of social service and community development directors had contacts with public agency officials weekly or several times a month. The proportions of frequent contacts were substantially higher than for foundations (29 percent) and corporate donors (27 percent), but they were comparable to the frequency of contacts with other nonprofit executive directors (75 percent) and staff members (59 percent). Although social service directors appear to have more frequent contacts across the board than community development directors, the differences are not statistically significant.

Almost all directors of the seven case-study organizations with public funding participated extensively in a number of advisory committees, boards, and coalitions, in order to keep abreast of public sector activities. Several sought or held leadership positions. The director of Alcohol Treatment has served as chair of a statewide organization of alcoholism treatment organizations. Directors of Economic Development Commission and United

Residents have both chaired a local association of neighborhood development organizations.

Most also sought to develop and maintain contacts with key legislators
and public agency administrators. For example, at one point the director of
Hispanic Youth Services regularly traveled to Washington, D.C., to maintain
contacts with federal agencies, the Illinois congressional delegation, and the
state's office of intergovernmental affairs. The director of Youth Outreach is
extensively involved in a number of high-powered networks. The agency also
uses its diverse set of assistant directors (one Hispanic male, one black
female, one white male) to broaden the range of boundary-spanning activities in which it is active and to maintain contacts with major political
groupings at the city and state level.

Appointing public officials to the boards of nonprofits provides additional opportunities for contact. About half (52 percent) of Chicago-area
social service and community development organizations reported in 1985
that they had either sought or were planning to seek board members who had
affiliations with public agencies. Among the case-study organizations, Immigrant Welfare League used the personal contacts of one of its several executive directors to secure a high-level city administrator as a board member.
The new board member alerted the agency to possible city funding sources
and was undoubtedly partly responsible for the two city contracts the agency
obtained shortly thereafter.

Strategic Positioning and Leverage. These contacts help keep nonprofit
managers informed about new developments and make it possible for them
to exploit strategic opportunities or exercise leverage and influence. Some of
the leverage resides in core characteristics of the organizations, because
nonprofits have access to public funding streams depending on which populations they target, in which locations, and for what purposes. Public agencies face political demands to be responsive to local needs and to serve
particular constituencies. Nonprofits that position themselves strategically
to meet these demands are likely to be of particular interest to public officials
and to benefit in the allocation of grants and contracts.

The development of strategic positions and leverage operates somewhat differently in the social service and community development fields. The
two fields differ in how dependent public sector agencies are on nonprofit
providers and in the opportunities nonprofits have for exercising leverage or
indirect control over the allocation of public grants and contracts. It is
difficult to document directly their control or influence over public funding
sources. However, the persistent patterns of continuing funding for most of
the seven organizations provide indirect evidence that the process operates.

In the social service field, nonprofits control access to a range of
resources (facilities, staff, expertise) that are critical in allowing public agencies to meet their own legislative mandates and policy objectives (for instance, to secure the safety of abused children). There are numerous examples of the leverage that nonprofit social service agencies are able to exercise

over public agencies. On rare occasions, these generate sufficient conflict to reach the news media.

Two public agencies, the Department of Children and Family Services (in 1987) and the Mayor's Office of Employment and Training (in 1991), sought to employ newly revised criteria in evaluating grant or contract proposals; the application of these new criteria resulted in the acceptance of proposals from several new providers and the denial of some previously funded agencies. In both cases, the agencies that lost out protested vigorously—and successfully—to the governor's office and the mayor's office, respectively. New providers were terminated and previous ones reinstated. In the case of the Mayor's Office of Employment and Training (MOET), the winning agencies obtained additional funding at the expense of MOET, which lost 120 of its 180 employees.

A former director of the Illinois Department of Children and Family Services (DCFS) explained that the state agency is routinely under pressure by large service providers. On one occasion, an official of a large religiously affiliated child-care institution insisted on the right to determine the payment rate at which the state would reimburse it for providing residential services to wards of the state. The official threatened to deposit busloads of dependent children at the Springfield office of DCFS if the state did not accept the principle. The threat did not materialize, in part because DCFS at the time had enough professional staff with access to foster-care homes and residential beds to place a large number of such children on short notice. However, DCFS no longer has this capacity and has little ability to influence nonprofit service providers who control placement slots.

In general, nonprofit efforts to develop strategic positions in social services involve seeking access to public policy makers and administrators while emphasizing service expertise and partisan neutrality. All four social service agencies sought to position themselves strategically for new program developments. The two youth agencies seemed to find this relatively easy to do because of the high priority assigned to their target populations in most public programs. However, Alcohol Treatment decided to add drug abuse treatment to its alcoholism program, at least in part so that it could benefit from the national attention to drug abuse. Immigrant Welfare League did the same when it established a shelter for alcoholic men, but it had little confidence that the approach would be successful in the long run. All four agencies used their access to legislators or public administrators to ensure adequate funding levels for particular programs of interest to them and made explicit efforts to obtain favorable outcomes in specific grant and contract decisions. In most cases, these efforts were successful.

Efforts to establish strategic positions are more complicated for community development organizations because of the marginal value of their infrastructure to public officials, the political salience of their core activities, and the uncertainty of local political alignments. Still, all three community

development organizations with public funding devoted considerable attention to these types of efforts.

African-American Neighbors maintained extensive contacts with
black legislators because the organization and its director viewed black
political mobilization as an important vehicle for improving conditions in
the community. The director had been active in the development of an
independent black political movement in the city and on occasion had
explored political office himself. The director and key staff members had
been active in efforts at restructuring the public housing, educational reform, and increasing minority set-aside programs. These efforts did not yield
sufficient leverage to avoid the major losses of public grants and contracts
that the organization experienced in the early 1980s. However, they were
undoubtedly important in the organization's remarkable comeback in obtaining new public grants and contracts during a period of fiscal constraints
for the city in general.

Establishing Direct Control over Public Funding. Economic Development Commission and United Residents have taken these efforts a step
further and tried to establish direct control over one type of public funding, a
Special Service Area taxing district, for portions of their communities. These
taxing districts require that local property owners agree to a special tax
assessment on property within the district to finance common services
administered by a district commission. In both cases, the services involved
broad efforts at economic development that the two organizations performed under contract with the commissions.

Both organizations worked closely with their respective districts and
viewed them as a mechanism for carrying out their own agenda. Both were
instrumental in building political and community support for the districts,
provided up-front funds for their implementation, invested considerable
time and resources in creating the legal foundation for them, helped
establish the governing structure for the local commissions that govern them,
shepherded the authorizing legislation through the Chicago City Council,
participated in selecting nominees for the governing board of the commissions, and organized and performed most of the activities that the
commissions were mandated to undertake.

The taxing districts provided these organizations with access to a
source of public funding over which they could have considerable control
and which could provide them with ongoing, flexible funding for some time
into the future. However, only Economic Development Commission was able
to maintain the district and benefit from continuing funding. Although the
district was initally established with a renewal clause, the director and the
board of Economic Development Commission convinced local property
owners that periodic efforts to formally renew the district would be too
expensive, since a title search would have to be made of all property in the

district each time. Instead, they argued, the taxing district would simply cease to exist if the governing commission voted its budget out of existence.

United Residents also established its taxing district with a sunset clause of three years in order to make it more appealing to local property owners. The subsequent renewal process provided the opportunity for a group of property owners and two local aldermen to terminate the district. It is difficult to fully establish the reason for this loss. Obviously, the taxing district proved to be a more fragile enterprise for the organization than other sources of public funding, or even donations or membership support from local institutions.

However, several factors appear to have operated. The institutionalization and continued operation of this new type of funding structure require special efforts to build and maintain community consensus about the purpose and effectiveness of the district and its mandate. Such consensus has to be sufficiently strong to overcome persistent pressure to reduce or cap local real estate taxes, especially if assessments and tax rates by other taxing bodies are increasing or if family and business incomes are declining. Both of these trends may have operated in the community.

The directors of United Residents and its affiliated economic development corporation acknowledged that because the taxing structure promised to provide relatively easy access to funding, the organization's staff and administrators lost touch with the business community and other key property owners. This in turn allowed a vocal minority in the community to convince political leaders to abandon the district. Without strong political support it could not continue.

Even the apparent success of Economic Development Commission's local taxing district is problematic. Such taxing districts may face uncertain political futures if their resources begin to rival those available through the city and thus invite vigorous efforts by more centralized governmental bodies to divest them of local control. That has happened to Economic Development Commission. One city agency has claimed the right to approve the budget for the taxing district and to assess the district a fee for the privilege. Certainly, the Chicago City Council tends to accept any available opportunity to extend its control over distribution of resources to local communities. United Residents either did not anticipate the level of efforts required to meet both of these challenges or could not perform at the required level.

Maintaining High Levels of Performance and Credibility. In order to secure continued funding and avoid or minimize cuts, most directors emphasized the need to maintain good performance levels on existing grants and contracts. They sought routinely to exceed contractual specifications and viewed such efforts as providing visible evidence of their organizations' capacity and importance to the public agencies involved. Only African-American Neighbors and Immigrant Welfare League encountered serious problems in meeting one or more of their contractual agreements. The former lost one large contract on that basis; the latter barely managed to avoid a complete loss and renegotiated a contract, but for a much smaller amount.

By exceeding contractual performance standards, organizations not only protect existing grants and contracts but also build credibility and documentation in seeking new funding. In most cases, the organizations sought to expand their existing base within a particular public agency by applying for grants or contracts in a different program area. Such a foot-in-the-door strategy has several advantages. The organizations can (and do) use their existing contacts with the funding agency to obtain relevant and strategic information about new funding opportunities. In some cases, new funding opportunities are managed by public agency staffs that the organizations have worked with in their current grants and contracts. These staff members bring their familiarity of the organization's performance to the new funding decisions.

Less directly, organizations can fine-tune their applications when they know the specific criteria that are likely to be employed, the other organizations that are likely to apply, and the official and unofficial goals of the program. They can increase their chances of success for new funding by providing direct and verifiable documentation of their capacity to perform in a related program area (because it is within the same public agency) and of relevant bureaucratic competence in managing reporting requirements. The process reduces uncertainty for both applicants and funders because it increases their knowledge base.

Similar processes operate, although less explicitly, when organizations pursue funding sources in public agencies with which they have had no prior contact. Reviews of the application process indicate that most of the organizations in these cases seek to build on their credibility and performance achievements in other public grants and contracts. The process operates less efficiently under these circumstances, because both parties have less reliable or trustworthy information about what the public agency is looking for (in the case of the nonprofit organization) or whether the nonprofit organization is likely to perform appropriately (in the case of the public agency). Both Immigrant Welfare League and Hispanic Youth Services sought access to new funding sources in this manner and were quite successful, as indicated by their rapid growth in total public funding.

Establishing Strong Fund Reserves. Finally all organizations with public funding emphasized the need to build strong fund balances in order to manage a variety of fiscal contingencies associated with most sources of public funding. As the experiences of African-American Neighbors shows, public funding may suddenly disappear, leaving the organization with unpaid bills and unpaid staff. Much more frequently, as I demonstrate in Chapter Nine, public funding sources delay approving grants and contracts until political compromises have resolved budgetary crises and routinely pay on a post-effort basis that results in further delays of payment.

However, most of the organizations had only moderate success in securing a high fund balance. The three community development organizations saw major fluctuations in fund balances as a percentage of annual expenditures, occasionally reaching 40 to 60 percent (African-American Neighbors and United Residents). The data are difficult to interpret for Economic Development Commission, because its assets and fund balances include the depreciated value of its share in a joint capital venture. For all three community development organizations, the available cash balances range between 10 and 30 percent of annual expenditures, a cushion of less than three months.

Youth Outreach is the only organization with an endowment; but at less than 20 percent of its operating expenditures, the reserve does not provide much of a cushion. Immigrant Welfare League has experienced a rapid growth in total expenditures, while fund balances have fallen behind and declined from 65 percent of annual expenditures in 1985 to less than 25 percent in 1988. Only Alcohol Treatment and Hispanic Youth Services have succeeded in steadily increasing their fund balances to reach about 35 to 45 percent of annual expenditures in 1988.

Buffer Core from External Control

The external control and lack of discretion that characterize government grants and contracts limit the range of internal management decisions that recipient organizations can make. These features have direct and immediate management implications for nonprofits. The case-study organizations used a variety of administrative strategies to manage external control by public agencies. For example, to minimize conflicting demands on service staff and to facilitate reporting efforts, most adopt a high level of specialization. They assign service staff members to only one public grant or contract if sufficient funding is available to cover the staff member's salary. As a result, the organizations have very complex organizational structures, which largely parallel their public funding streams.

Specialization occurs also along functional lines, with centralized and unique mechanisms for maintaining client or program data bases and preparing financial reports or similar documentation. The mechanisms vary considerably, depending on whether the organization must report on clearly separable activities for each funding source or on overlapping efforts to multiple funders. For example, Immigrant Welfare League and Alcohol Treatment have mutually exclusive client categories for their public grants and contracts and maintain separate data bases for each.

In contrast, Hispanic Youth Services and Youth Outreach direct a variety of services to the same client population. The former centralizes all reporting systems, to make sure that particular service activities are sorted among multiple funders so that program reports match as closely as possible the performance level that each grant or contract specifies. This improves the agency's ability to claim 100 percent of each grant, allows for tight coordination of efforts to manage multiple grants and contracts, and presents a consistent front to funders.

Youth Outreach operates with an explicitly decentralized structure, in which teams of service staff members are responsible for coordinating a variety of services in their respective outposts and complete their own program performance reports. Youth Outreach acknowledges that this decentralized administrative structure makes it impossible to extract all possible dollars from public funding sources, because of unavoidable slack and incomplete coordination of activities and reporting efforts. However, Youth Outreach argues that the structure allows it to present performance statistics with full confidence in their integrity and ensures high credibility with funding sources. The bottom-up structure also allows central administrative staff to incorporate into grant proposals program features that address needs and problems identified by the service staff.

Public Funding: A Driving Force

Public funding is a driving force for nonprofits. It provides sustained funding for most of them and is a major factor in their growth or decline. It involves them in complex political processes that require high levels of monitoring. It absorbs and directs organizational energies and reduces internal discretion, but it also allows them to develop strategic positions and exercise leverage. Public funding provides sustained funding for most organizations, but it requires a high level of management efforts and reduces internal discretion.

Driving Revenue Levels

For the seven case-study organizations with revenues from public grants and contracts, Figures 4.1 through 4.13 showed that their overall growth or stability conforms closely to their experiences with public funds. This is documented more dramatically in Table 8.5. In seven out of seven cases, the correlations between government funding and total revenues are positive and significant. As expected, correlations are high and positive for the three organizations that rely heavily on government funding (Alcohol Treatment, Hispanic Youth Services, and Economic Development Commission). However, government funding is also positively correlated with total revenues for the four organizations where it averaged only about 50 percent of total revenues (Youth Outreach, Immigrant Welfare League, African-American Neighbors, and United Residents). The finding holds even for Hispanic

Table 8.5. Direction of Significant Correlations Between Specific Funding Sources and Total Revenues, Thirteen Case-Study Organizations for Various Years.

Organizations	Public	Donations	United Way	Fees	Dues	Events	Other
Social Service Agencies with Public Funding							
Alcohol Treatment	+	··	NA	··	NA	NA	··
Hispanic Youth Services	+	+	··	NA	NA	NA	+
Youth Outreach	+	··	··	+	NA	··	··
Immigrant Welfare League	+	··	··	+	NA	··	+
Community Development Organizations with Public Funding							
Economic Development Commission	+	··	NA	··	··	NA	··
African-American Neighbors	+	··	··	NA	NA	··	··
United Residents	+	··	··	··	··	··	··
Other Social Service Agencies							
Minority Search	NA	··	NA	+	··	NA	+
Christian Therapists	NA	··	NA	+	NA	··	··
Other Community Development Organizations							
Community Renewal	NA	+	NA	NA	NA	··	··
Preservation Council	NA	··	NA	··	··	+	··
Hispanic Neighbors[a]	NA	··	NA	NA	NA	+	··
Hispanic Neighbors[b]	+	+	NA	NA	NA	+	+
New Town Sponsors	NA	··	NA	··	··	+	··

Note: (+) indicates that the correlation between a given funding source and total revenues is positively related at the .05 level of significance or better. (··) indicates that the correlation is not significant. (NA) indicates that the organization has no funding of this type. The number of years vary among the organizations. For specific years, see Figures 4.1 to 4.13.

[a] Analysis for 1980–1990 period.

[b] Analysis for entire period.

Source: Case-Study Project.

Neighbors when one considers the entire period for which financial information is available. Hispanic Neighbors relied heavily on public funding during the 1970s but had none in the 1980s.

No other funding source approaches the importance of government funding in influencing the overall level of revenues. Fees come closest, with four out of ten correlations being significant. Two of these reflect the expected pattern for organizations that rely heavily on fees (Minority Search and Christian Therapists). Revenue from special events presents a more extreme version of this pattern: it is correlated with total funding for only the organizations that receive most of their funds from special events.

In contrast, although all thirteen organizations had donation revenues, donations correlated with total revenues for only three organizations, including Community Renewal, which relies almost exclusively on donations from one single donor. None of the significant correlations came from other organizations with donations as a significant funding source. These findings corroborate the earlier finding of high levels of turbulence associated with donation revenues.

Moreover, my analysis earlier in this chapter shows that the overall growth or stability of the seven case-study organizations with public funding conforms closely to their experiences with public grants and contracts. The three stable organizations—Alcohol Treatment and Youth Outreach among the social service agencies and Economic Development Commission among the community development organizations—had the highest proportions of continuing grants and contracts in their respective fields. The four turbulent organizations experienced considerable changes in their public grants and contracts. They either added a significant level of new funding sources (Hispanic Youth Services, Immigrant Welfare League) or had a relatively large number of terminated grants and contracts (United Residents, African-American Neighbors).

Dominating External Relations and Absorbing Management Energy

When making their infrastructure available to public agencies in return for funding, nonprofit social service and community development organizations become deeply entrenched in the complex political processes that characterize U.S. welfare policies. These processes, and the resource relationships that connect public and nonprofit organizations, provide structured opportunities for nonprofits to exercise leverage over activities of direct interest to them. Such opportunities rarely exist for most other types of resources to which nonprofits have access.

The leverage and influence have their costs. They require intensive monitoring efforts and careful development of strategic positions to avoid co-optation. Perhaps more importantly, the coupling of public and nonprofit activities allows the public sector to externalize some of its structural problems onto the nonprofit sector. For example, problems of coordinating multiple levels of public programs surface at the level of individual nonprofits when they seek to deliver various combinations of services. Legislative efforts to address concerns of local constituencies take mainly symbolic expression when carried out through nonprofits, unless these organizations are accountable to the same constituencies. These legislative actions may favor some nonprofits, but they may also change as constituencies realign themselves. Finally, the public funding system easily obscures inadequate levels of expenditures for public sector activities, and simultaneously imposes cost sharing on nonprofits. At times, public funding comes to absorb nonprofit resources available through other revenue streams.

The complexity of these contingencies increases the need for non-profits to monitor public sector developments, engage in extensive boundary-spanning activities, and create flexible and carefully crafted strategic positions. In short, the public grants and contract system is a greedy institution (Coser, 1974), absorbing and directing organizational energies and enticing nonprofits with substantial amounts of funding, high levels of funding continuity, and explicit opportunities to exercise leverage and control.

The greater continuity in and predictability of public grants and contracts (compared with donations and fees) make them particularly attractive to nonprofits—especially in the social service field, where government dependence on nonprofit social service agencies is most extensive and where the dominant pattern is one of ongoing grants and contracts. However, as I show in the following chapters, the complexity and amount of effort involved in securing and managing public grants and contracts pose high overhead costs. As a result, government funding comes to dominate nonprofit activities, even if the organization also receives sizable amounts of funding from other sources, such as donations. The intricacy and timing of these efforts also complicate the ability of organizations to engage in effective planning and program development of their own.

Summary

Nonprofits that want to obtain government funding must be willing to play by the rules of the game. The benefits are significant: sizable and fairly predictable funding and legitimate access to the political process where priorities are negotiated and budget compromises reached. The costs are correspondingly high: monitoring the fallout from budget negotations and shifting priorities, tracking the consequences up and down the paths of intergovernmental transfers, surviving cost control and cost sharing, meeting reporting requirements, and adhering to rules and regulations that limit internal management discretion.

Some nonprofits simply avoid public funding for these reasons. Those that do not avoid it pursue a variety of other strategies. Some strategies focus on the external environment. Organizations may seek to minimize risks of co-optation, but community development organizations in low-income minority communities may find that difficult to do. Organizations can attempt to buffer themselves from uncertainty by becoming better informed about public sector developments, by pressing for strategic positions, or, in rare cases, by exploiting new governance structures to establish direct control over public funding. Other strategies are aimed more directly at internal structures. Organizations may seek to maintain high levels of performance to safeguard their credibility with public funders, aim for large fund reserves to deal with cash-flow problems, and structure their core activities and reporting systems in such a fashion that they are buffered from external control.

Few other sources of revenue available to small and medium-sized social service and community development organizations provide them with the level of funding that public grants and contracts do. This explains why public funding drives overall revenue levels. The efforts to obtain the funding are so intensive that public grants and contracts dominate external relations and absorb management energy.

Notes

1. At that time it was described as "Beirut on the Lake" by the *Wall Street Journal* (Helyar and Johnson, 1984, p. 13).
2. In the case of Economic Development Commission, most of the terminated funds involved a one-time capital grant from the federal government and did not require the organization to seek replacement funding in order to maintain its operations.
3. This is similar to the argument by professional counselors that clients must pay something in order to have vested interests in the therapeutic relationship and participate actively and constructively in their own treatment.
4. I arbitrarily defined grants as large if they provided funding at the rate of $100,000 or more per twelve-month period ($8,333 or more per month), medium-sized if they provided funding at the rate of $50,000–$99,999 per twelve-month period, and small if they provided funding at less than $50,000 per twelve-month period ($4,166 or less per month). I did not adjust for inflation because of the complicated time periods involved. Some awards covered only a couple of months, some up to eighteen months.
5. The last six months of the calendar year is a relatively slow period for accountants and nonprofits can negotiate advantageous fees for the preparation of their financial statements and tax returns if they use something very different from a calendar year. Illinois nonprofits that receive public grants or contracts for social service activities also have explicit incentives for using the state's July 1 fiscal year period because the state administers most social service programs directly. Finally, most United Way organizations require member agencies to use a July 1 fiscal year.
6. In four comparisons, the differences reach borderline (.06 and .07) levels of significance. For three of these cases, government funding is marginally lower than other funding sources; in one case, it is higher.

PART THREE

Putting it All Together: Managing Tasks, Planning, and Resources

The first two sections approached the problem of how nonprofit social service and community development organizations manage funding relationships by examining each major type of funding in some detail. By drawing on illustrations from the case-study organizations and on more representative findings from several surveys, I sought to explain how these organizations experience and manage fees, special events, donations, and government grants and contracts. In this section, I turn to how individual organizations manage multiple funding sources: how all the contingencies and tasks come together, what the work is like, how the tasks are coordinated, and how organizations go about meeting internal and external challenges.

NINE

Restricted Grants and Contracts: Complex Paths and Management Burdens

Major changes in one or more primary funding sources are most significant for program-specific funding that directly links the receipt of revenues to the performance of particular activities. Such is the case for fee income, most foundation and corporate grants, United Way support, and especially government grants and contracts. In each case, the revenue is contingent on whether and how the organization provides particular services.

Year-to-year changes in these types of funding depend on how organizations address contingencies associated with each of the sources discussed in Chapters Five through Eight. In each case, the outcome reflects a series of complex and interdependent decisions made by recipient organizations and their funders: a given nonprofit organization decides to pursue a particular funding source; funders or clients accept the services of the organization; and both parties agree on what constitutes an acceptable level of funding or payment for the particular activities. Decisions made by either party influence how the other responds.

This chapter examines these decision-making processes from the point of view of recipient organizations by documenting the amount and type of work involved in coordinating and managing restricted grants and contracts. Because government grants and contracts and United Way funding are significantly more restrictive than other types of nonprofit funding, they pose special problems for the organizations that receive them. Most of the analysis is therefore based on the seven case-study organizations with extensive funding from these funding sources. However, I include comparative information on foundation or corporate grants where appropriate.

The coordination of these funding sources presents a thicket of practical problems and adaptations with which nonprofit managers must cope. The challenges depend on the amount of external control to which organizations subject themselves when they seek restrictive funding and on the degree of the grants' competitiveness. They also depend on the accessibility of the source (for instance, the level of government involved), the number of outside agencies that handle the funds before they are received, and the nature of political involvement in funding decisions. These challenges are not separable but buried within the experience of individual nonprofits. They are problems with definite organizational consequences because of the large number of nonprofits involved with these types of funding sources.

Complex Funding Paths

Most nonprofit social service and community development organizations participate in the complex system of restricted grants and contracts that characterizes the human service field in the United States. Data from the case studies show how interorganizational funding paths link federal, state, and local governments to one another and to nonprofit and proprietary service providers in complex patterns. The structure also includes other organizations when nonprofits are connected to private funding sources. Most, if not all, of these funding paths include expectations about service efforts.

The Service System

The funding paths constitute the service network to which individual nonprofits belong. The Chapter One vignette on a year in the life of Youth Outreach and Figure 1.1 illustrate the network for Youth Outreach and highlight the agency's complex connections to multiple levels of government and to a large number of private funding sources. The management of such a complex funding and service system requires extensive planning and coordination. It also demands intensive monitoring of intermediary and direct funding sources and at least some effort at tracking decision making at more distant funding levels.

Youth Outreach (like the other case-study organizations) obtains most of its restricted grants and contracts from private funding sources. However, private funding paths are among the least complicated in the service system, since they involve only one level of decision making before reaching the organization. So do direct federal grants. In contrast, most other public grants and contracts pass through multiple levels of government and involve decisions of at least two different organizations before they reach the organization that actually delivers the services. In some cases, the paths cross as many as four separate intermediary organizations.

Multiple Transactions. Youth Outreach's funding network (shown in Figure 1.1) is more complex than the network for the other case-study organizations. Its restricted grants and contracts from public and federated funding sources involve an average of 2.3 transactions.[1] This means that each award has been processed by an average of more than two organizational actors before reaching Youth Outreach. Table 9.1 shows that among the seven organizations with public funding, two other social service agencies (Alcohol

Table 9.1. Structure of Interorganizational Funding Relationships, 1988–89.

Profile	Average Transactions per Public/United Way Grant	Number of Organizations Linked by Funding						
		Total	Federal Agency	State Agency	City Agency	Nonprofit Administrator	Nonprofit Subcontractor	Foundation/Corporation
Social Service								
Alcohol Treatment	2.1	10	2	2	2	1	—	3
Hispanic Youth Services	1.6	55	5	6	3	3	1	37
Youth Outreach	2.3	99	6	7	5	5	2	73
Immigrant Welfare League	2.1	29	4	3	3	4	—	15
Community Development								
Community Renewal	1.0	1	—	—	—	1	—	—
Economic Development Commision	1.8	30	2	1	4	—	—	23
United Residents	1.7	68	2	1	5	1	—	59
African-American Neighbors	1.6	30	1	—	6	2	—	21

Note: "Average Transactions per Public/United Way Grant" is the sum of individual paths that link these funders to the actual provider of services, divided by the number of grants. The analysis excludes grants from foundations and corporations, listed in the last column. "Nonprofit Administrator" refers to the number of nonprofit organizations that fund or subcontract to the agency. "Nonprofit Subcontractor" refers to the number of nonprofit organizations the agency subcontract services. "Foundation/Corporation" refers to the number of corporations or foundations that supported the agency through donations (and/or membership fees for community organizing/development organizations).

Source: Case-Study Project.

Treatment and Immigrant Welfare League) have funding networks that are almost as complex, averaging 2.1 transactions per grant or contract. Hispanic Youth Services and all three community development organizations average between 1.6 and 1.8 transactions per public or United Way grant.[2]

Yet the average number of transactions per funding stream is actually higher than the data in Table 9.1 indicate. The table estimates fail to consider the extent to which each funding stream that passes through a state (or city) agency represents a separate program at the federal (or state) level and therefore involves separate transactions at the higher level of government as well. Incorporating this assumption into the calculations increases the average number of transactions for all the organizations to between 2.3 and 2.8 transactions per funding stream[3] for all but Community Renewal, which has no public grants or contracts.

The overall efficiency of the system depends critically on how these exchanges operate. The structure imposes obvious transaction costs, since each organizational participant adds its own layer of objectives but must track decisions at all other levels in order to determine its own resource opportunities. The case-study organizations attempted to monitor the participants in their own funding networks, especially public funders and nonprofit intermediaries. As Table 9.1 shows, networks for each social service organization with public funding ranged between seven and twenty-six organizational participants (not counting corporate and foundation sources, which ranged from three to seventy-three). As I show below, the complexity and amount of efforts involved in securing and managing each funding stream impose additional overhead costs on nonprofit service providers.

Table 9.1 also shows the extensive involvement of state agencies in funding networks for social service agencies, which reflects the high level of control that state agencies exert over public spending for social services in Illinois noted in Table 8.1. Nonprofit social service agencies also have frequent contractual relations with one another, often acting as intermediaries for public agencies. State agencies and nonprofit intermediaries are much less likely to be involved in funding networks for community development organizations.

Organizations active in the two fields therefore differ considerably in how extensively they must monitor funding opportunities at different levels of government and in how much they need to direct similar efforts at other nonprofits. Because state activities are critical to social service agencies, statewide coalitions are salient, active, and important for them. These statewide coalitions tend to be dominated by social service agencies that are themselves statewide in scope or serve major regions of the state (Catholic Charities, the Jewish Federation, Lutheran Social Services of Illinois); and small, locally based social service agencies may find it difficult to get their own slant on state activities.

For community development organizations, city agencies are far more prominent in the funding networks. That accounts for their careful attention to local politics. Their claim to represent the interest of a geographical community further propels them into political involvement. Geographical turf battles may also explain why community development organizations do not subcontract public funding from other nonprofits, as do the social service agencies. To do so would subject them to the authority of another nonprofit with potential claims to the turf and weaken their ability to negotiate directly with the city on issues of concern to local residents or businesses. When community development organizations get funding from other nonprofits, it comes in the form of United Way allocations, special support for community empowerment by a church-based organization (African-American Neighbors), or the type of client-state relationship that characterizes Community Renewal and its interaction with a major community institution.

Decoupling and Planning Problems. In addition to high transaction costs, these intricate funding structures also create significant planning problems. Although linked through the exchange of funds and formal grants or contractual agreements, the organizational participants operate with relative autonomy and are decoupled from one another. No single authority system connects them into a coherent service system. Contacts and exchanges of information may be intense, but they are also limited in time, place, and content. Each participant in the service system is guided by internal organizational imperatives: seeking to minimize its own uncertainty, maximize its own flexibility and discretion, and protect itself against outside challenges to its legitimacy. In the case of funding paths involving public agencies, the result is a "hollow state" (Milward, Provan, and Else, forthcoming), where organizations with official responsibility for ensuring that mandated activities are undertaken have little direct control over the activities. They may be several organizations removed from the actual delivery of services.

In general, intermediary organizations, notably state agencies, often add some of their own revenues to the funds they receive from primary funders. In other cases, especially city and nonprofit agencies, intermediaries simply administer the funds for a higher-level organization, adding no resources of their own. In either case, intermediary organizations have explicit opportunities to add program criteria and reporting requirements to those demanded by primary funders.

I did not directly compare the criteria to which the intermediary organizations themselves are accountable with those they impose on nonprofit providers and cannot document the extent to which they do impose additional layers of accountability or program requirements. However, I have indirect evidence that it occurs—the city of Chicago imposes a standard set of documentation on all recipient organizations, regardless of where the funding originates.

This uniquely uncoupled structure allows for considerable flexibility, but at the risk of disengagement by any of the participants. The addition of program objectives and reporting requirements at each transaction point increases the likelihood that the service system assumed to exist may bear little relationship to the one that actually does. The system is so complex that it defies description, let alone systematic assessment or control by public and private policy makers. It creates corresponding problems for individual nonprofits to develop a coordinated, integrated service system of their own.

Phases of Grants and Contract Work

Although important, monitoring funding networks and tracking potential sources of new grants and contracts take less time and effort than managing the individual grants and contracts. Detailed analysis of restricted grants and contracts that were active during the 1988 or 1989 fiscal year documents the high levels of management efforts involved, especially for public and United Way funding streams.

For the nonprofit service provider, each funding relationship involves interactions and time frames that reflect the joint program agreements and activities of itself and a specific funder. Funders exert the greatest up-front control over the relationships. They decide at will or on the basis of legal requirements which activities to support, what level of funding to make available, when proposals are due, when to announce awards, what types of programs or fiscal reports to require, and when and how to make the payments. Nonprofits are left to determine whether and how they will adhere to funder criteria, although they may control decisions about the actual activities involved. I focus on how nonprofits manage the funding relationships, rather than on how they deliver services or other activities.

Foundation and Corporate Grants

The type and amount of work and the nature of decisions nonprofits face in managing funding relationships differ considerably, depending on how restrictive the funding source is and also on whether the contract or grant is new or continuing. Most private funding sources are relatively undemanding. In the case of direct client fees, service charges, proceeds from special events, and solicitations for individual donations, the tasks are flexible and more or less under the unilateral control of the organization itself. The organization decides what is to be done, when, and how. Foundation and corporate grants involve more institutionalized processes. Nonprofits seeking this type of support must adhere to specific procedures, although most are fairly simple.

We reviewed a number of foundation and corporate grant files for each of the case-study organizations but did not undertake a complete and systematic examination of them all. In almost all cases, the documentation consists of several letters and a copy of the organization's financial statement. We were told, and observed directly in a number of cases, that managing foundation and corporate grants rarely involved more work than this. The organizations frequently used the same basic letter for several different funders, although large grants might require more formalized application packages and more frequent reporting.

For most foundation and corporate grants, applications consist of letters that occasionally but not always follow formats or address topics specified in grant application packages. They rarely exceed three to four pages and usually contain only limited information about the organization and a brief description of the program activities for which it is seeking support. At times, a copy of the organization's audit report and other publicity material are attached. Final reports generally consist of a letter with a description of activities performed during the grant period, a statement of expenditures associated with the grant, and a copy of the organization's most recent audit. The final report may also include copies of any news media coverage about the organization and the activities supported by the grant.

The extent to which these tasks are fairly simple and few in number is most clearly indicated by the fact that several of the case-study organizations do not maintain separate files for each foundation or corporate grant they receive. Indeed, Immigrant Welfare League filed all foundation and corporate grant documentation in a single chronological file that contained all the agency's other correspondence as well, including my letter seeking the agency's participation in the study and letters to creditors explaining necessary delays in paying certain large bills. Only if organizations have ongoing relationships with a particular funder did they establish a separate file for it.

This system contrasts dramatically with the multiple and voluminous files we encountered for each of the public grants and contracts and in most cases for United Way funding as well (occasionally a full file drawer for a single funding stream). Not surprisingly, directors of both the social service agencies and the community development organizations uniformly report that the amount of work involved in securing and managing foundation and corporate grants is significantly less than for government funding and United Way support.

Public/United Way Grants and Contracts

Seven of the thirteen case-study organizations had active government grants and contracts or support from a federated funding source during the fiscal year that preceded our study of them. To understand better how these complex service systems affect nonprofits and their management, we undertook a systematic analysis of each award that overlapped part or all of their most recently completed fiscal year (see Appendix A). We included grants and contracts that the organizations had applied for, even if the application was not accepted.

These funding sources totaled eighty-six for the seven organizations, ranging from a high of twenty-two for Hispanic Youth Services to a low of five for Economic Development Commission and four for Alcohol Treatment. The remaining organizations fell at two intermediate levels. Youth Outreach and African-American Neighbors had seventeen and fifteen such funding sources, respectively, and United Residents and Immigrant Welfare League had twelve and eleven sources, respectively.

In order to describe the work involved in managing the eighty-six grants and contracts, I found it useful to identify two major phases in the funding relationships and to look at a number of key tasks or dimensions in each phase. The proposal and contract phase involved such features as proposal lead times and complexity, funder review and approval times, and the characteristics of final, legally executed contracts. The operating and reporting phase had four concurrent dimensions. I paid little attention to the (1) actual performance of activities or service tasks, although that is what the funding relationship is all about. Instead, I looked at (2) whether contracts or tasks are revised from what both parties originally agreed to and who initiates the revisions, (3) the frequency and contents of program and fiscal performance reports, and (4) the frequency and form of payment systems. For this fourth dimension, I distinguished between grants, reimbursement contracts, and performance contracts.

These phases and associated tasks or work dimensions rarely coincided for the different funding sources, although the level of government involved does affect several features. Nor did they relate in predictable ways to the size of the grant. This diversity constituted a central aspect of the complexity that nonprofit managers face on a continuing basis. It also complicated my description and presentation of the data. There are interesting stories and issues associated with each of the funding relationships.

Proposal and Contract Phase. Interactions with funders during the proposal and contract phase reveal the variety of mechanisms by which nonprofits gain access to the restricted grants and contract system. These interactions are integral to the complex negotiations that pervade funding relationships, but they develop under circumstances that create uncertainty and other planning problems for the nonprofit participants.

Relatively Closed Funding Systems. Some funders, such as the United Way, formally restrict funding to a limited number of predesignated organizations. During the period of this study, for example, more than 95 percent of all funding from the United Way of Chicago was allocated to about 135 organizations. They had at some point in the past applied for membership in the United Way and had been certified as meeting membership requirements, accepted as members, and awarded a base allocation; and they still retained their membership. Obtaining full membership is usually a four-year process: one year for the application process to be completed and three years to meet all membership requirements while maintaining the status of provisional member. Provisional members receive a base allocation and must follow procedures normally required of organizations with full membership.

Few other restricted funding sources operate with a similar degree of formal closure, although many public funding sources approach it. They do so in part because the range and structure of tasks during the operating phase encourage the development of particular patterns of accommodation between funders and providers. However, the structure of the proposal phase also creates significant barriers to entry for new organizations. Analysis of the proposal and contract phase confirms my previous observation that public funding sources tend to provide social service agencies with predictable resources. That is less clearly the case for community development organizations.

Of the eighty-six proposals that the seven organizations submitted for public or United Way funding during the 1987–88 or 1988–89 fiscal years (depending on when we undertook the fieldwork), twenty-eight (or 33 percent) were either preapproved or the funder did not issue a formal request for proposal (RFP) (see column 2 in Table 9.2). In these cases, the case-study organizations were fully justified in expecting the funding decision to be relatively automatic and to focus primarily on the specific level of funding and the service plan involved.

This pattern of relatively closed funding streams was much more prevalent among the social service agencies (43 percent) than among the community development organizations (9 percent). Nonprofit funding sources (80 percent primarily the United Way) and state agencies (12 percent) also used this practice more extensively than city (11 percent) or federal agencies (25 percent). The one federal source that fell in this category was a Department of State program operated through the International Rescue Commission. The latter had a verbal agreement with Immigrant Welfare League to pay a flat client fee for each eligible refugee the agency processed.

Building on Existing Funding Relationships. Although impressive, these summary statistics underestimate the strength of existing funding relationships. Most of the proposals (70 percent) were for continued funding for ongoing program activities. The case-study organizations generally expected these proposals to be approved, although they were less certain about the level of funding they would receive. All proposals for renewals were approved, although African-American Neighbors lost one performance contract during the fiscal period following the one we examined, because of its failure to meet specified performance levels.

Of the eighty-six proposals, twenty-six (or 30 percent) were new in the sense that the case-study organizations did not have prior funding for these purposes from the particular funding organization. Almost all (twenty-three) of these new proposals were submitted by the four organizations initially categorized as having turbulent funding patterns. As I showed in Chapter

Table 9.2. Characteristics of Grant and Contract RFPs and Proposal Lead Times.

Profile	(1) Number of Proposals for Fiscal Year	(2) Percentage Preapproved or no RFP	(3) Percentage New	(4) Percentage Denied	(5) Average Size of RFP/Guide (in pages)	(6) Median Lead Time (in weeks)
By Case-Study Organization						
Alcohol Treatment	4	**25**	—	—	17	6
Hispanic Youth Services	22	**32**	**41**	4	46	4 +
Youth Outreach	17	**56**	**18**	6	32	4
Immigrant Welfare League	11	**55**	**64**	9	28	2
Economic Development Commission	5	—	—	—	45	7
African-American Neighbors	15	**13**	**20**	13	25	6
United Residents	12	**8**	**33**	25	24	4 +
By Service Field						
Social service	54	**43**	33	6	36	4
Community development	22	**9**	22	16	28	6
By Resource Dependency						
Mixed funding	40	41	38	12	39	4
Public funding	46	22	26	6	41	6
By Turbulence/Stability						
Stable	60	40	**11**	4	**45**	5
Turbulent	26	27	**40**	12	**38**	5 +
By Funder Administrative Level						
City administration	47	**11**	28	11	34	**6**
State administration	20	**42**	25	10	40	**4**
Federal administration	4	**25**	75	—	56	**6 +**
Nonprofit administration	15	**80**	40	7	13	**7**
By Final Award Size						
$100,000 or more	12	50	8	—	49	5 +
$50,000–$99,999	11	36	27	—	22	6
Less than $50,000	55	26	27	—	33	5
No award made[a]	8	25	100	100	18	5
All Proposals	86	33	30	9	33	5

Note: (—) indicates less than 1 percent. Column 1 gives the number of proposals submitted during one fiscal year. Column 2 shows the percentage of proposals that were preapproved or for which funders did not issue a RFP. Column 3 shows the percentage of proposals submitted to a new funding source. Column 4 reports the percentage of proposals that were denied. Column 5 shows the average number of pages of RFP or proposal guides. Column 6 gives the median number of weeks of lead time for submitting proposals. **Boldfaced** numbers indicate dimensions where grants and contracts differ significantly according to specified characteristics at the .05 level of significance or better.

    [a] Excluded from statistical analysis.

Source: Case-Study Project.

Eight, these organizations also had the smallest proportion of public funding from continuing funding sources during the 1984–1988 period. The patterns that gave rise to their history of funding turbulence were evident for this one-year period as well.

Immigrant Welfare League had the largest proportion of new proposals (seven out of eleven, or 64 percent). However, two involved in-kind allocations of food that the agency automatically became entitled to when the city approved funding for a shelter for homeless men. If these two are excluded, Immigrant Welfare League approximates the level of new proposals submitted by the other turbulent social service agency, Hispanic Youth Services (45 and 41 percent, respectively).

Both vigorously pursued new funding sources that they thought might be available to them. Immigrant Welfare League focused its attention on the city where its ethnic population plays an important political role. Hispanic Youth Services devoted most of its efforts to tracking developments at the federal and state levels. The director explained that she preferred federal funding because "the feds leave you alone," but that the state was where the money was for this type of agency.

The seven organizations were remarkably successful in obtaining new funding sources. None of the social service agencies had more than one proposal denied, although two of the community development organizations had several failed proposals. (All denied proposals were for new grants or contracts, not continuing ones.) Even for the two community organizations, this is a higher success rate than what they had with foundation or corporate grants.

The two community organizations emphasized that they did not necessarily expect their new proposals to be accepted, given federal reductions in Community Development Block Grants. However, they argued that it was important for them to submit proposals to maintain visibility (and legitimacy) with city administrators and aldermen. They also argued that even failed proposals helped build the case for subsequent efforts to enter new program areas.

More generally, the organizations argued that their high success rates reflected funder recognition of their performances, although they also pointed to their grantsmanship skills more generally. There is some support for these claims. In a number of cases, the organizations either undertook extensive efforts to secure the success of proposals or made effective use of existing knowledge. For example, Hispanic Youth Services sought and obtained endorsements from congressional representatives and the state's liaison office in Washington for its two proposals for direct federal grants. Immigrant Welfare League sought funding from a city agency for which its executive director had previously worked and where he had been responsible for development of program guidelines (and therefore was intimately familiar with priorities and criteria used in the process).

In other cases, proposals went to funding sources that had previously funded the organization and where the organization therefore had contacts, some experience with procedures, and a track record. This was the case for most of the new proposals submitted by the community development organizations and for several of the social service agencies.

However, specific incidents surrounding some proposals, especially those involving new grants or contracts, suggest a more complex interpretation. They show how existing funding relationships provide agencies with leverage in securing continuing funding and access to special funding opportunities, and how they serve to create a system of mutual dependency between funders and providers. Thus, Youth Outreach got caught in the political fallout that resulted when the state's Department of Children and Family Services (DCFS) attempted to open its existing funding relationships for rebid in the counseling program for the Chicago area. As described in Chapter Eight, existing providers with low-scoring proposals were terminated, and higher-ranked proposals from new providers, including Youth Outreach, were formally approved. When the terminated agencies took their complaints directly to the governor's office, DCFS canceled (by telegram) Youth Outreach's approved proposal (and that of all other "new" providers) less than twenty-four hours before the scheduled start of services.

Some of the new providers had hired additional staff and rented office space in anticipation of their expanded activities. They were caught with financial obligations for which funding would not be available. Their protests over the last-minute cancellation did not receive the same level of official attention as that of the previously terminated providers, and the action stood. Youth Outreach escaped these problems. It planned to start the program slowly and had not committed new resources to it. The example shows how difficult it is to break into existing funding streams and how effectively nonprofits are able to defend continuing relationships with public funding sources.

The strength of existing funding relationships also provides nonprofits with access to special funding opportunities. For example, Youth Outreach obtained a new grant when another state agency, with which it had two contracts and a good service record, contacted and awarded it a small grant, verbally, on the last day of the state's fiscal year. The grant served to obligate funds available to the state agency before the end of the fiscal year and thus strengthened the state's own argument for increased funding for the new fiscal year.

The other three social service agencies had similar opportunities. Also toward the end of the fiscal year, Hispanic Youth Services received notification from two of its funders that small amounts of extra funding were available for specific activities. All three proposals had very short lead times (one to two weeks), and the agency was successful in two of the three cases. The losing proposal had a maximum award of just $500 and was the only one of the agency's nine new proposals that failed.

Immigrant Welfare League benefited informally from extensive contacts with the city's Department of Human Services (DHS) when it sought city funds to establish a shelter for homeless men. Subsequently, DHS staff informed the agency that unobligated funds were available in the Community Service Block Grant program and helped it design a proposal to the city for a counseling program for battered women. The proposal was approved.

Similarly, Alcohol Treatment had previously obtained funding for an alcoholism prevention program for youths when an organization that administered a local Youth Service Board notified it that a small amount of funding was available if the agency was willing to undertake the activities. Alcohol Treatment accepted the invitation but now fully expects the Youth Service Board to continue the funding relationship over subsequent years as long as any funding is available, because the latter initiated the relationship.

These examples suggest that the proposal experience takes place in two different environments. Under one set of conditions, organizations submit proposals to funding sources where the process of review and approval is a relatively open one. Most federal programs operate in this competitive manner (as do most larger foundations and corporate giving programs). Under these conditions, proposals stand and fall on their merits and on the characteristics of the organization making the proposal, such as its credibility or its prior relationship with the funding source. These were the conditions under which Hispanic Youth Services submitted its two proposals for direct federal grants.

The creation of an open competitive process is likely to take place when the funding source is under pressure to document that it has sought to allocate funds to the most effective program plan and without favoritism. Large foundations with professional staff (who may pride themselves on designing and implementing funding criteria) and the allocation of funding for research or demonstration projects illustrate these conditions.

The competitive process is also likely to operate when a new pot of money becomes available to a funding source, because then the turf is relatively free of prior claimants. This was the case when Youth Outreach and several other organizations applied to the United Way for funding that had become available for redistribution when another organization lost its membership in the United Way.

However, state and local governments have created few new funding streams in recent years, and existing streams have a full cast of participants. Under these conditions, funding relationships operate in a different environment, because they are conditioned by the system of competitive providers already active in the program area. Although the proposal process is still competitive, it operates as a relatively closed system. In the social service field, an additional consideration lends strength to the closed system: the claim that clients benefit from continuity of care. This argument allows existing service providers to argue that any changes in service providers will disrupt and therefore impair the quality of services that clients obtain, much as defense contractors point to national security to justify their continuing contracts.

Analysis of the grants and contracts system of the Department of Children and Family Services confirms the existence of such a closed system, at least for DCFS (Chen, Grønbjerg, and Stagner, 1992). Although new organizations may enter the system, they do not stay for long (about one-quarter of the DCFS agency providers were in the system for only one out of the five years) or obtain large amounts of funding.[4] Clearly, incremental budgeting rather than an open competitive system dominates the public grants and contracts system.

A closed funding system has obvious attractions to both parties and helps cement a relationship of mutual dependency. For funders, it reduces the amount of effort they must devote to notifying potential applicants, providing technical assistance about the application process, screening applicants, and processing awards. It allows them to use any leftover funds to complement activities they are already supporting and to do so quickly. Timeliness is important, especially toward the end of the fiscal year, because public agencies that fail to use their appropriations in full endanger their claims to higher allocations for the next fiscal period. For recipient organizations, the system provides a high level of certainty about continued funding and more than occasional opportunities for special considerations. However, newcomers gain access only under special circumstances or with considerable difficulty.

In general, the funding relationships appear to allow organizations to build their reputations, provide them with information about other programs, and, together with the use of external networks, help them fine-tune their approach to new sources. Social service agencies, and to a lesser extent community development organizations, appear fully justified in thinking of public and United Way funding as ongoing, once they become part of the funding streams.

Short Lead Times and Complex Proposals. Under optimal conditions, the proposal system allows funders to assess how well a potential (or previous) provider understands the service system and is likely to meet the specific program needs the funder has identified (Rehfuss, 1989). For the same reasons, the process of writing proposals serves to force agencies to clarify goals, specify strategies, and articulate expected outcomes.

However, the circumstances under which organizations actually write proposals impede their realization of these benefits. Thus, the formal RFPs or similar instructions are frequently voluminous and complex (some RFPs consisted of 157 single-spaced pages). As Table 9.2 (column 5) shows, the average number of pages ranged from a high of forty-six for Hispanic Youth Services to a low of seventeen for Alcohol Treatment.

The length and complexity of RFPs is important because the organizations must usually submit proposals very quickly (see Table 9.2, column 6). About one-fourth of the proposals had lead times of three to four weeks, but some had less than that—occasionally only one day, as noted previously. In fact, in more than two-fifths (42 percent) of the cases, the organizations had to complete proposals in four weeks or less, and only 13 percent allowed as much as two months or more. The latter category includes all United Way funding streams and all direct federal grants.

Short lead times are most problematic for new proposals. In case of renewals, the organization can rely on what worked last time and incorporate feedback from the funder. Short lead times also create difficulties for organizations that submit proposals in multiple and highly diverse program areas, because program descriptions and client characteristics are likely to be dissimilar and the organization cannot easily use the same material in several proposals.

Immigrant Welfare League and Hispanic Youth Services illustrate opposite points on this dimension. Immigrant Welfare League submitted one proposal in each of five diverse program areas: counseling program for battered women, employment services for official refugees, legalization of undocumented aliens, employment and training of older workers, and needs assessment for an older, ethnic population. It submitted two other proposals for a homeless shelter for alcoholic males. In contrast, Hispanic Youth Services submitted three proposals for employment training of minority youths, four proposals for drug prevention of minority youths, and five for pregnancy prevention among minority teenagers, in addition to several proposals for community organizing and for literacy services for minority youths.

Many proposals are also lengthy and involve many separate items. The eighty-two proposals for which information is available averaged thirty-two pages and ten separate items (see Table 9.3, columns 2 and 3). However, the range is much greater than that. A couple of funding sources required no proposals or only verbal agreements, and Hispanic Youth Services' application for a direct federal grant consisted of 229 pages and forty-five separate items. Thirteen of the proposals exceeded fifty pages, including six that exceeded one hundred pages.

The length of the proposals usually reflects a long list of required attachments that are standard for most city agencies, but varies otherwise. For example, all proposals to the city of Chicago must include a board member list (with gender and race indicated), the organization's charter and bylaws, documentation of tax-exempt status (official IRS letter), the most recent audit report, the most recent tax return, documentation of insurance coverage (with the city listed as coinsurer), disclosure of ownership status, anti-apartheid affidavits (agreement not to do business with South Africa and Namibia), religious/denominational institution agreements (agreement not

Table 9.3. Characteristics of Grant and Contract Proposals.

Profile	(1) Number of Proposals for Fiscal Year	(2) Average Size of Proposal	(3) Average Number of Items in Proposal	(4) Percentage of Proposals Complex	(5) Median Time Approved (in weeks)	(6) Median Time Finalized (in weeks)
By Case-Study Organization						
Alcohol Treatment	4	**13**	5	25	+ 4	− 4
Hispanic Youth Services	22	**55**	16	77	+ 1	− 2
Youth Outreach	17	**33**	9	65	+ 1	− 3
Immigrant Welfare League	11	**25**	10	27	+ 1	0
Economic Development Commission	5	**44**	12	—	− 3	− 6
African-American Neighbors	15	**16**	8	13	+ 3	− 7
United Residents	12	**18**	7	8	+ 2	− 4
By Service Field						
Social service	54	**39**	10	59	+ 1	− 2
Community development	22	**21**	12	9	+ 2	− 6
By Resource Dependency						
Mixed funding	40	32	**8**	38	+ 2	− 2
Public funding	46	26	**12**	43	+ 2	− 4
By Turbulence/Stability						
Stable	60	28	9	46	+ 2	− 4
Turbulent	26	44	11	38	+ 2	− 3
By Funder Administrative Level						
City administration	47	**25**	10	28	+ 2	− 5
State administration	20	**50**	11	50	0	− 5
Federal administration	4	**94**	24	50	0	− 1
Nonprofit administration	15	**15**	7	67	+ 5	+ 1
By Final Award Size						
$100,000 or more	12	45	14	67	+ 0	− 5
$50,000–$99,999	11	51	17	64	+ 3	− 2
Less than $50,000	55	28	9	33	+ 2	− 3
No award made[a]	8	16	6	25	NA	NA
All Proposals	86	32	10	41	+ 2	− 4

Note: (—) indicates less than 1 percent. Column 1 reports the number of proposals for one fiscal year. Column 2 shows the average number of pages in the proposal. Column 3 shows the average number of items in the proposals. Column 4 shows the percentage of proposals that were judged to be complex. Column 5 shows the median numbers of weeks before (+) or after (−) the start of the program period that the proposal was approved. Column 6 shows the median number of weeks before (+) or after (−) the start of the program period that funders signed the official contract. **Boldfaced** numbers indicate characteristics where the proposals differ at the .05 level of significance or better.

[a] Excluded from statistical analysis.

Source: Case-Study Project.

to bar access to program facilities if located in such institution), and agreement to support minority or women's business enterprises. City departments vary in the number of copies of the proposal that agencies must submit; these departments also may request additional types of attachments (such as organizational charts). State and federal agencies have their own requirements. In addition, the organizations often submit additional material, such as letters of endorsement or publicity material.

To get a better estimate of how difficult or complex the proposals were, we made our own qualitative assessment based on the level of detail in the proposal itself and the variety of material included. We then reviewed these assessments with agency staff members. Overall, 41 percent of the proposals were judged to have a high level of complexity (see column 4 in Table 9.3) because of the detailed documentation or estimates required. For example, one funder required Youth Outreach to estimate the number of worker hours to the closest one-tenth of an hour for a year of services that were not to start for another two to three months.

Complex proposals were much more prevalent among social service agencies (59 percent) than among community development organizations (9 percent). The high degree of complexity among social service agencies reflects the very high levels of complexity for Hispanic Youth Services (77 percent) and Youth Outreach (65 percent). The former submitted a large number of new proposals, which are inherently more difficult. The latter had a large number of programs with a clinical content that required specifications of client diagnosis and treatment.

The low degree of complexity among the community development organizations reflects primarily the fact that all receive most of their restricted grants and contracts under the Community Development Block Grant program and have done so for several years. They have extensive experience with the programs and an established routine for documenting performance and future service expectations. They also benefit from the city's use of similar procedures for all grants or contracts.

This type of standardization helps explain why only 28 percent of proposals to the city were judged complex, compared with 50 percent of those to state and federal agencies. The high degree of complexity of proposals to nonprofit funders reflects mainly the extensive amount of work associated with United Way annual budget submissions. The United Way demands a program budgeting format with estimates of costs, funding sources, and work units for each program field for which the organization plans to use United Way funds (up to thirty-two fields in all). Accurate estimates are important because United Way evaluation procedures penalize organizations for deviating very much from budget plans.

Several funders also required some of the case-study organizations to submit multiple budget proposals for the same program. In one case, Immigrant Welfare League was asked to submit three different budgets simultaneously: a no-change budget, a 10 percent cut, and a 25 percent cut. In a

different example, Youth Outreach was asked to submit a budget with a 4 percent cost-of-living increase; three weeks later, a no-change budget; and one
month after the program start, a budget at 2 percent less than the previous
year. Not surprisingly, this particular award was not finalized until twenty-one
weeks into the program period.

These types of practices provide funders with considerable flexibility
in seeking an optimal match between last-minute changes in appropriations
(as budget negotiations intensify at the end of the fiscal year) and their own
assessment of the service capacities of delegate agencies. The case-study
organizations generally interpreted these multiple requests as serving to
strengthen the position of public officials in *their* efforts to obtain higher
appropriations from the legislature. The organizations saw these demands
as serving their own interests as well and did not complain about the amount
of work involved. These examples typify the mutual dependencies that
develop between funding sources and provider organizations in the public
funding arenas.

More generally, short lead times and complex proposals protect existing funding relationships against intrusions by competitors. A comparison
of column 2 in Table 9.2 and column 4 in Table 9.3 suggests that there is an
inverse relationship between proposals that are pre-approved or involve no
formal RFP and the complexity of the proposals.

However, these same features also have potentially negative implications for effective decision making, needs assessment, or strategic planning.
In order to submit proposals in a timely and appropriate fashion, organizations must manage the proposal work centrally and at the management
level. Under these conditions, field staff, who actually provide the services,
have limited opportunities to furnish feedback on client needs or even review
or comment on proposal drafts. In these cases, knowledge of client needs
may inform the organization's proposals or its planned allocation of resources to only a limited extent, unless the organization makes concerted
efforts to maintain effective internal communication. This is most critical for
larger organizations in which service staff do not perform any management
functions. Additional problems occur because due dates for proposals for a
single fiscal year typically span as much as twenty-one months. Under these
circumstances, organizational planning may become equally fragmented, if
it occurs at all.

Delays in Approving and Finalizing Awards. Although funding sources
gave the case-study organizations an average of 5.8 weeks' lead time for
submitting proposals, they took an average of 7.8 weeks to decide whether to
accept the submitted proposals. As a result, funding sources rarely approve
proposals or finalize contracts before the start of the program period.

In all, funding sources approved just eight of the proposals (9 percent)
more than six weeks before the start of the program; the median was only two
weeks before.[5] As column 5 in Table 9.3 shows, programs administered by

nonprofits gave longer advance notices than other types of funding sources. This pattern reflects the coding of United Way funding as approved by the time the organization submits its proposal, because member agencies are guaranteed a new allocation of no less than 95 percent of what they received in the current year, as long as they meet reporting requirements in a timely fashion.

Otherwise, almost two-fifths (38 percent) of the proposals were not approved until after the official start of the program period and some not until well into it. The most extreme case was a proposal from Immigrant Welfare League that was not approved until fourteen weeks after the official start of the program. This was a refugee employment service that the Jewish Federation administers for the state. The federation only approved the proposal from Immigrant Welfare League when it had received its own contract from the state.

The patterns of delay were even more extreme for getting final signatures on contracts: only three of the seventy-eight awards (4 percent) were finalized as much as six weeks before the start of the program period; the rest, later than that. The median was four weeks into the program period, with ten awards exceeding twelve weeks into the period, including four that were not legally executed until five to six months into the program. As shown in column 6 of Table 9.3, community development organizations received the final contracts a median of four to seven weeks into the contract period, mainly because of delays at the city level of administration.

Only two of the four extreme cases reflected special problems with a given contract. In one case, a proposal for employment training had initially been rejected by the city, but Immigrant Welfare League protested the decision and eventually (twenty-nine weeks into the program period) negotiated a much-reduced award. By then, six months of the program year had passed. Because Immigrant Welfare League had not dared to hire new staff for the program without having the funding in place, it failed to meet performance standards and was uncertain whether the contract would be renewed. The other special delay occurred when the city "forgot" to include Economic Development Commission's usual grant for technical assistance to business groups in the annual appropriations bill. The organization was assured this was an oversight, but had to wait for a special appropriations bill to get passed in order for the contract to become legal.

Planning and Cash-Flow Problems. Although many of these delays are more technical than substantive, they pose management problems for the organizations. As long as funding sources do not approve proposals, organizations do not know at what level of staff positions and salaries they will be able to operate during the coming program period. And, as the experience of Youth Outreach illustrates, approval of new awards can be withdrawn, even at the last minute, leaving organizations uncertain about how much of the start-up activities they should undertake until they have the last signature on the dotted line of the final contract.

In addition, as long as funders have not finalized grants and contracts, organizations cannot lay legal claim to the funding. This presents a cash-flow problem. They must maintain the expected service activities (and pay their rent and staff) in order to meet overall service expectations for the grant. However, funding sources, and especially their respective comptrollers, will not release payments until the grants or contracts have been finalized.

These delays reflect in part the fiscal constraints under which the funding sources themselves operate. Public agencies usually cannot finalize awards until their own appropriations have been established by the respective legislative bodies or they themselves have received formal notification of grants and awards by other levels of government. The result approaches a game of musical chairs. In recent years, both the state and the city have experienced considerable fiscal difficulties and associated political conflicts. As a result, public budgets have rarely been passed until just before the new fiscal year starts.

Uncertainties About Final Contract Amounts. In trying to assess the patterns by which funders accepted the funding level originally proposed by the organizations, I compared the amount contained in the original (or first proposal) and the final amount that the funder actually paid out for the award. Column 2 in Table 9.4 shows that organizations requested an average of $67,300 for the seventy-eight funded proposals, but that an average of $18,100 (or 27 percent) was cut from the originally requested amounts at some point (see column 3). The gap between the requested and actual amount was particularly large for Alcohol Treatment (a cut of 76 percent), with Hispanic Youth Services at the other extreme (a cut of 3 percent).

These differences coincide with distinctive strategies with which the organizations approached their funding sources. Three of the social service agencies (Hispanic Youth Services, Youth Outreach, and Immigrant Welfare League) appeared to pursue a pattern of accommodation. They sought to build credibility for their programs and for themselves as responsible, cooperative funding partners by seeking detailed information from funders about what level of funding would be appropriate and possible. Although they argued that actual costs often exceeded these funding levels, they accepted the funders' suggestions and used them in developing their proposals.

By developing "responsible" budgets in this way, they increased their own certainty about the actual level of funding they would obtain and reduced at least one potential source of conflict with the funder. As shown in column 3 of Table 9.4, the final awards obtained by the two youth agencies deviated by an average of only 3 to 6 percent from the amount they had proposed. The average loss is quite high (27 percent) for Immigrant Welfare League because of the agency's difficulty with the employment and training

Table 9.4. Grant and Contract Proposal Amounts and Revisions.

Profile	(1) Number of Awards for Fiscal Year	(2) Average Amount Requested	(3) Average Amount Changed	(4) Percentage with No Change in Amount	(5) Percentage Contracts Amended	(6) Percentage Amended by Funder
By Case-Study Organization						
Alcohol Treatment	4	$283,325	– $214,539	—	25	25
Hispanic Youth Services	21	47,799	– 1,561	52	45	18
Youth Outreach	16	82,205	– 5,101	44	41	29
Immigrant Welfare League	10	51,886	– 13,996	54	36	9
Economic Development Commission	5	52,400	– 9,388	20	—	—
African-American Neighbors	13	51,763	– 10,475	8	40	—
United Residents	9	36,448	– 12,807	11	17	8
By Service Field						
Social service	51	78,386	– 21,814	46	40	20
Community development	27	46,776	– 11,051	11	25	3
By Resource Dependency						
Mixed funding	35	62,067	– 9,623	39	32	18
Public funding	43	71,442	– 24,978	30	37	11
By Turbulence/Stability						
Stable	25	108,423	– 39,469	32	31	23
Turbulent	53	47,532	– 8,004	35	37	10
By Funder Administrative Level						
City administration	42	48,739	– 9,173	33	30	2
State administration	18	103,897	– 45,564	33	55	40
Federal administration	4	119,125	– 21,316	50	50	—
Nonprofit administration	14	60,661	– 8,586	36	20	20
By Final Award Size						
$100,000 or more	12	218,309	– 64,747	17	58	42
$50,000–$99,999	11	75,402	– 5,035	27	46	18
Less than $50,000	54	32,096	– 10,713	38	33	9
No award made[a]	8	62,176	NA	—	NA	NA
All Awards	78	67,302	– 18,089	34	35	14

Note: (—) indicates less than 1 percent. Column 1 reports the number of active awards during the fiscal year. Column 2 shows the average amount requested in funded proposals. Column 3 shows the average amount by which that amount was adjusted. Column 4 reports the percentage of proposals for which the final amount equaled the proposed amount. Column 5 shows the percentage of active awards that were amended during the program period. Column 6 shows the percentage of awards amended at the initiative of the funder. **Boldfaced** numbers indicate characteristics where the proposals differ at the .05 level of significance or better.

[a] Excluded from statistical analysis.

Source: Case-Study Project.

contract and because it ended up with only a fraction of the clients it had originally anticipated under the amnesty legislation for illegal aliens. The latter was consistent with national patterns, but it also reflected unexpected competition from another organization that decided to serve the same ethnic population. As column 4 in Table 9.4 shows, a large proportion (44 to 54 percent) of proposals by these three organizations were accepted with no change in funding. Note, however, that an equally large proportion were not accepted at the proposed funding level.

The three community development organizations pursued very different strategies. As a comparison of columns 3 and 4 in Table 9.4 indicates, the average size of their final award amounts were 18 to 23 percent below the amounts they had originally requested for the funded proposals. All three routinely submitted proposals that substantially exceeded (by as much as 100 percent) the amounts they were currently receiving for the same activities. They rarely got such increases. In each case, only one proposal was accepted at the proposed funding level.

These directors generally explained their practices as useful for building the organization's case with the funding source. Requests for high funding levels, they said, documented the actual costs of program activities and established the organization's capacity to undertake significant levels of program activities. Of course, the latter also served to legitimate the organization as an important community actor. In addition, requests for high funding levels placed the organization in an advantageous position should extra funding become available, because the funder might simply go down the list of those with claimed capacity for expansion. The strategy protected the organization against hard-luck stories of competing organizations by demonstrating that it had substantial funding gaps as well.

Whatever the reason, the strategy is much more confrontational than the one of accommodation pursued by the three social service agencies described previously. The two types of strategies match the different organizational environments in which the two types of organizations operate. However, the fit is not perfect. Alcohol Treatment was closer to the aggressive approach of the community organizations than to the accommodative strategy of the other social service agencies. Two of its final awards were 76 and 88 percent below the proposed amounts, a third was 39 percent lower, and the fourth was 10 percent lower.

In one extreme example, Alcohol Treatment requested $1 million for its basic alcoholism treatment and prevention program. If the request had been approved, the amount would have quadrupled the grant itself and tripled the size of the organization in one year. The director argued that such an increase was justified because the funding source had requested grantees to submit a budget to cover what they needed and wanted to do. The budget, he claimed, was not frivolous, since it included only appropriate activities. He did not expect to get anything but a modest increase over the previous year but wanted to make the case for the organization. Quite possibly, the funding source might also have wanted to use such documentation to make its own case for increased funding with the state legislature. Realistically, of course, the organization would have found such major expansion difficult to carry out.

The Operating Phase. The several concurrent activities required during the operating and reporting phases impose their own management demands and contingencies. As noted previously, I paid little direct attention to how the organizations actually deliver the services or other activities for which they receive the grants and contracts. Instead, I focused on contract or grant amendments and revisions, program and financial reporting requirements, and payment systems.

Many Revisions or Amendments. Several of the organizations experienced numerous revisions or amendments to their grants or contracts (see column 5 in Table 9.4). Although Economic Development Commission had no revisions at all, more than one-third of all finalized contracts were revised at some point during the program period, some as many as four times. Several were initiated by funding sources, especially state agencies, and involved large contracts or grants (see column 6 in Table 9.4).

Some of the revisions involved technical changes, as when funding sources extended the time period for a given contract or reduced the overall funding level because of its own fiscal constraints. Several such changes became necessary when last-minute budget negotiations failed in the state legislature and state agencies could not provide the cost-of-living increases they had encouraged nonprofit providers to incorporate in budget proposals.

In other cases, the organizations themselves requested line-item adjustments within the overall grant amount. The analysis suggests that organizations that rely extensively on public funding to cover most of the program expenditures, or that combine several line-item grants for one service area, may need a relatively large number of such contract amendments.[6] Otherwise, they cannot recover full grant amounts and reduce or eliminate salvage. For example, all but one of the nine contract amendments of Hispanic Youth Services involved line-item adjustments requested by the agency, and these adjustments left the organization with virtually no leftover funds in any grant or contract.

Alcohol Treatment and Economic Development Commission also relied heavily on public funding sources, but they did not seek budget amendments to the same extent. Alcohol Treatment seemed to have sufficient flexibility within its major grant to alleviate the need for amendments. Economic Development Commission deliberately did not request any line-item modifications. Its staff members argued that leaving some salvage in the grant helped the agency validate its claim to good management. It may also have provided it with some goodwill and bargaining power, because it increased the city's flexibility to meet special needs in other areas.

Only one example of a contract revision involved a reduction in performance goals without a corresponding cut in funding level. This occurred when Youth Outreach could not deliver the volume of services specified in a contract because it had to replace several low-cost student interns with a smaller number of more expensive regular staff members. It sought an amendment to change the unit cost so that it could recover the full contract amount. The agency attributed the funder's acceptance of the change as reflecting its good working relationship with the funder.

Only one amendment increased the amount of funding over the previously approved funding level. This occurred when Hispanic Youth Services exceeded its previously approved service level for a performance-based employment training program. The city approved the request, but it took nineteen weeks to do so, and did it just before the end of the program period. Presumably, the city did not know until then what amount of salvage other subcontractors would leave in their awards and how much it would have available to meet the request of Hispanic Youth Services.

Other revisions involved changes in payment structures (from line-item to unit cost) and in reporting formats. All were instituted by the funders, and all imposed special management burdens on the organizations. They had to implement the changes and train staff. I found no contract revisions that reflected changing client needs.

Need for Internal Grant Monitoring. Contract amendments, whether imposed by the funder or initiated by the organizations themselves, require considerable management efforts to implement or anticipate. If the amendments are imposed by the funder, the organization must quickly determine what the consequences will be — for example, whether they may contribute to an overall budget deficit. If so, it needs to tighten cost-control or intensify fund-raising efforts.

To anticipate potential problems, the organization must monitor its own efforts on an ongoing basis, to determine whether any contract amendment is likely to be needed — specifically, whether cost-control efforts or other developments endanger the organization's ability to reach performance goals. For example, Youth Outreach encountered some difficulties in meeting performance goals in several grants and contracts when it was barred access to its office space because of one of the periodic teachers' strikes. The organization operates most of its programs in donated space in public schools and depends on the cooperation of teachers and school administrators. It made a policy decision to refrain from crossing picket lines, although that decision endangered its ability to meet required performance standards.

Even without contract amendments, agency executives uniformly expressed considerable concern about meeting the numbers in the formal agreements, which were usually based on their own proposals. They empha-sized the need to estimate correctly their own performance capacity in the proposals, because funders compared these estimates with actual perfor-mances as one way of measuring the agency's effectiveness. Failure to meet their own standards therefore endangered their service records and im-paired their competitive strengths in future grant and contract awards. Consequently, they sought to monitor their performance sufficiently well to incorporate appropriate changes in the program plan for the following program period.

Demanding Program Performance Reporting. Most grants and contracts also require organizations to submit numerous and complicated reports on their program activities. As shown in column 2 of Table 9.5, a large propor-tion of funders (43 percent) required such reports on a monthly basis. These requirements were much more prevalent for awards from city (60 percent) and state agencies (39 percent) than from federal (none) or nonprofit funders (7 percent). Moreover, the majority of reports (57 percent) were due within one week after the end of the reporting period (see column 3 in Table 9.5). Awards from city agencies were especially likely (88 percent) to have such requirements, compared with other types of funding sources (22 to 29 percent. These one-week reporting requirements therefore affected commu-nity organizations more extensively (82 percent of awards to these organiza-tions) than social service agencies (46 percent).

These patterns of frequent performance reports within very short time limits help explain why organizations uniformly cited federal and nonprofit funders in particular, and also state agencies, as much less demanding than city agencies. Fortunately, the city usually did not require very detailed reporting formats. As column 4 in Table 9.5 shows, only 14 percent of awards from city agencies were judged to require a high level of detail, compared with about half of awards from other funding sources. However, some reports required considerable detail (see column 4 in Table 9.5). This pattern was more prevalent for social service agencies (40 percent) than for community development organizations (11 percent) and for larger awards (73 percent), compared with medium-sized (36 percent) and smaller ones (20 percent).

Youth Outreach had the largest (69 percent) proportion of demanding performance reports. One of the more complicated formats required Youth Outreach to submit monthly reports on the number of minutes of service units provided to each client by three predefined service categories. For each client that received services during the previous month, the agency also had to submit a daily service confirmation log signed by the client, a case recording sheet, an interagency referral form (if appropriate), transporta-tion referral control forms (if appropriate), a termination summary report form (if appropriate), and other documentation on follow-up and service outcomes.

Table 9.5. Characteristics of Performance Reports and Level of Difficulty
for Grants and Contracts.

Profile	(1) Number of Awards for Fiscal Year	(2) Performance Reports Percentage due Monthly	(3) Performance Reports Percentage due Within One Week	(4) Performance Reports Percentage with High Details	(5) Percentage of Awards with Difficult Requirements
By Case-Study Organization					
Alcohol Treatment	4	100	**75**	**25**	**25**
Hispanic Youth Services	21	40	**35**	**35**	**60**
Youth Outreach	16	44	**47**	**69**	**56**
Immigrant Welfare League	10	36	**54**	**10**	**18**
Economic Development					
Commission	5	40	**60**	—	—
African-American Neighbors	13	46	**92**	**18**	**15**
United Residents	9	22	**78**	**8**	**11**
By Service Field					
Social service	51	45	**46**	**40**	**47**
Community development	27	37	**82**	**11**	**11**
By Resource Dependency					
Mixed funding	35	36	57	**40**	33
Public funding	43	48	60	**21**	36
By Turbulence/Stability					
Stable	25	52	54	48	40
Turbulent	53	38	60	21	32
By Funder Administrative Level					
City administration	42	**60**	**88**	14	31
State administration	18	**39**	**22**	47	39
Federal administration	4	—	**25**	50	75
Nonprofit administration	14	**7**	**29**	50	29
By Final Award Size					
$100,000 or more	12	67	50	**73**	67
$50,000–$99,999	11	54	46	**36**	64
Less than $50,000	54	35	62	**20**	22
All Awards	78	43	57	30	35

Note: (—) indicates less than 1 percent. Column 1 reports the number of active grants during the fiscal year. Column 2 shows the percentage of awards with monthly performance reports. Column 3 shows the percentage of awards where performance reports are due within 1 week. Column 4 gives the percentage of performance reports with high or very high levels of detail required. Column 5 gives the percentage of awards that were judged to have high or very high levels of performance difficulties. **Boldfaced** numbers indicate characteristics for which the performance reports differ at the .05 level of significance or better.

Source: Case-Study Project.

Obviously, Youth Outreach would have had to develop a full complement of customized computer forms and an intricate coding scheme to
integrate these reporting requirements into an overarching data base on all
its clients. To complicate matters, the funding source changed the reporting
formats and contents three times during the program period, adding further

to the grant's management requirements. The performance report averaged five pages per month for the first seven months, but seventy-eight pages per month for the last five months.

Several other funding sources also imposed new reporting formats that required organizations to train staff members in midstream. I was even told about one case during a previous program period where a funding source had imposed a change in reporting format *retroactively*. Under the new format, the agency would have had to locate previous clients (with whom it no longer had any contacts) and obtain new personal information from them. The agency submitted the new reports to the funder with the requested level of detail. Reporting requirements of this type, and unreasonable changes in them, give organizations almost an open invitation to provide less than accurate or verifiable reports. These practices contribute to an atmosphere of informal accommodation that surrounds most relationships with restricted funding sources.

Some reporting requirements reflect federal mandates. For example, the Mayor's Office of Employment and Training (MOET) requires a very high level of documentation for all Job Training Partnership Act contracts. These are performance based and pay according to the employment or educational goals achieved by a designated number of clients. They require organizations to obtain signed documentation by the employer or school principal certifying the clients' employment status or school attendance records in addition to staff assessments and reports. Thus, Hispanic Youth Services' $8,000 summer youth employment program required two reports averaging 184 pages each.

In another example, Youth Outreach was required to submit monthly reports that consisted of an average of 110 completed op-scan sheets, one for each client, using a range of demographic and clinical categories. Similarly, most of the Community Development Block Grant awards required summary statistics on clients or activities by a number of predefined demographic and residential characteristics.

Demanding Data Management Requirement. The work involved in submitting required reports on time and in appropriate formats imposes high data management burdens on these organizations. The organizations had to devote considerable efforts to develop and maintain accurate, up-to-date, and easily accessible client and staff files. In principle, this would seem to constitute a challenge that any organization must meet in order to track its own performance. However, in practice, organizations are likely to find it difficult to create a single overarching data base to document their overall performance and from which to extract appropriate service statistics for each funding source. That is because each funding source usually requires its own distinctive reporting format and content. Documentation on the reporting formats required by each funding source shows that few if any of these were exchangeable or even used consistent categories.

Obviously, organizations that manage a wide range of grants and contracts with distinctive reporting forms, as do most of the social service agencies, will find it difficult if not impossible to integrate their data bases. Such comprehensive data bases would have to include all types of information that any funder might require (now or in the future) for all clients and activities, including data that will never be used or analyzed. Only Youth Outreach maintained a comprehensive client data base.

Organizations are likely to find it much easier to develop separate data bases on clients and activities for each major funder. This was the preference of the six remaining organizations. However, a disaggregated data system greatly complicates the challenge of tracking the organization's overall performance, whether by the organization itself or by any outside monitoring authority. The organization must either preassign staff to specific funding streams or divide a pool of staff activities among appropriate funding streams afterward.

The former practice is simple to administer and easy to document and was used by Youth Outreach. However, under this format, closely cognate services (for example, teenage pregnancy prevention in different locations) may be performed under different funding streams by different staff members using separate reporting formats that prevent any overall assessment of the entire program area. The practice also means that an otherwise limited staff problem, such as illness or turnover, may have a major effect on one grant or contract.

Hispanic Youth Services used the practice of pooling data on program activities and then distributing them among funding sources to match expected performance standards as closely as possible. This required intense, centralized management efforts but allowed the agency greater flexibility and increased its ability to salvage the entire grant amount. However, such an approach raises the possibility that some activities get left out and are not covered in any performance reports, or that some get double-counted because they are included in several different ones. Neither of these practices allows organizations to easily or effectively use their performance data to monitor their own efforts so as to develop more effective service approaches.

These data management problems are of immediate concern to organizations that rely on a variety of restricted funding sources or whose funding sources change over time. However, they also raise a number of important policy issues, especially in the social service field. Many social service agencies combine funding from several different funding sources to serve the same pool of clients. The lack of standardization in reporting formats among different funding sources means that policy makers will be unable to assess the joint impact of different policy initiatives. Nor will they be able to develop or monitor integrated or coordinated service efforts across a range of different problem areas. At best, they may be able to determine some limited accomplishments of a particular program.

Under current reporting formats, therefore, neither nonprofit social service agencies nor their funders can separate the effects of a specific funding program from the effects of other services that clients may receive, even from the same organization. Given the complex problems that many lower-income clients face, the specific combination of service efforts that a particular organization obtains by pooling different funding sources may be at least as important in determining client outcomes as any particular approach required by a single funding source.

Less Demanding Fiscal Reporting Requirements. Recipients of restricted grants and contracts usually must also prepare fiscal reports or otherwise account for how they spend the funds. In the case of performance-based contracts, such as employment training programs administered by the city under the Job Training Partnership Act (JTPA), organizations usually do not have to report on program expenditures. Instead, documentation of performance achievements triggers the appropriate level of payment.

Performance-based contracts are designed to provide delegate subcontractors with incentives for selecting the most efficient service approaches for achieving overall program goals. Yet the system provides even stronger incentives for service providers to select clients that will allow them to meet performance goals quickly and with a minimum of effort. Creaming clients in this way minimizes program costs and translates into greater surplus for the organization. Similar benefits are realized if organizations can operate performance-based programs in conjunction with other contracts that cover program costs. Hispanic Youth Services operated several JTPA programs along with various prevention programs. Its annual surplus correlated closely with total JTPA contract amounts.

Grants and other contracts usually require fiscal reporting of expenditures by line item. The frequency and formats of these reports vary among different types of funders. Federal agencies usually require quarterly reports on estimated expenditures for major line items, due within four weeks after the end of the reporting period. State agencies require such reports on a monthly basis. The United Way wants only quarterly assurances that the organization has paid withheld federal income taxes on time, but then requires an extensive year-end report on program expenditures and a copy of the organization's audit, due fifteen weeks and six months after the end of the fiscal year, respectively.

The city of Chicago relies on its own peculiar and cumbersome system of tracking expenditures through a detailed reimbursement system that amounts to preauditing all expenditures before issuing payments. The city requires organizations to submit canceled checks, paid invoices, bank payroll statements, valid insurance policies, or similar proof of expenditures before it approves reimbursements. Such a system provides numerous opportunities for problems to develop and for payments to be delayed.

For example, Immigrant Welfare League and Alcohol Treatment both obtained their first city grants shortly before we included them in the study.

Both encountered major problems with the reimbursement system. They complained about the apparent arbitrariness with which specific expenditure items were challenged, the lack of explanations for why these actions were taken, and the delay in informing them about potential problems, usually three to four weeks. Immigrant Welfare League compared this system with the much more congenial and informal process used by the Jewish Federation in the refugee programs.

Almost all the organizations with city contracts experienced problems with rejected vouchers because of technical questions of whether they had submitted proof of payment. Several of the organizations had vouchers rejected because their insurance company had failed to send a copy of a renewed policy to the city. Some vouchers were rejected when organizations had obtained approval for contract amendments that involved changes in line-item allocations if the requested amount exceeded the original allocations. Either the approved amendments were not passed along to the city's voucher staff or the documents were not consulted. As a result, the organizations had to resubmit vouchers with the necessary proof of expenditures for those items that were challenged, along with a copy of the approved contract amendment, and payment of the amounts that were not challenged was delayed.

The more experienced organizations had developed a highly specialized vouchering system to manage these contingencies. They submitted separate vouchers for each major line item (such as salaries, rent, supplies, and transportation). That increased the number of vouchers they had to submit. But, they argued, simple, homogeneous vouchers were easier for city staff members to review, were processed more quickly, and did not affect payments for other items if challenged. This was particularly the case for payroll expenditures, which required only bank payroll statements. The organization could therefore submit requests for reimbursements for the major part of the grant almost immediately after issuing paychecks without having to wait for canceled checks to be returned.

Overall, about half of the awards required monthly vouchers or fiscal reports (see column 2 in Table 9.6). These requirements were especially frequent for awards by city agencies (71 percent), compared with state agencies (44 percent) and especially federal (none) or nonprofit funders (14 percent). Fiscal reports had fairly liberal time limits (see column 3 in Table 9.6), with only 18 percent due within one week, compared with 57 percent of performance reports. Most fiscal reports or vouchers averaged only a few pages, especially those to state, federal, and nonprofit funders (see column 4 in Table 9.6). However, some performance contracts exceeded 150 pages per submission and brought the average size for city funders to 32 pages of vouchers and fiscal reports combined.

Post-Effort and Delayed Payment Systems. Almost all public funding sources pay after the fact rather than up front to help organizations meet

Table 9.6. Characteristics of Fiscal Reports, Vouchers, and Payment Times.

Profile	(1) Number of Awards for Fiscal Year	(2) Percentage due Monthly	(3) Percentage due Within One Week	(4) Average Total Pages	(5) Percentage Fixed/Flat Payment	(6) Percentage Four Weeks or More Pay Time
By Case-Study Organization						
Alcohol Treatment	4	**75**	**50**	8	**50**	**50**
Hispanic Youth Services	21	**35**	**10**	36	**60**	**40**
Youth Outreach	16	**50**	—	11	**62**	**50**
Immigrant Welfare League	10	**50**	**30**	8	**30**	**60**
Economic Development Commission	5	**60**	—	27	—	**100**
African-American Neighbors	13	**69**	—	15	**15**	**85**
United Residents	9	**44**	**83**	12	**11**	**56**
By Service Field						
Social service	51	46	14	21	**54**	**44**
Community development	27	59	28	16	**11**	**78**
By Resource Dependency						
Mixed funding	35	49	26	10	40	**49**
Public funding	43	52	11	26	38	**62**
By Turbulence/Stability						
Stable	25	56	9	14	48	60
Turbulent	53	48	22	22	35	54
By Funder Administration Level						
City administration	42	**71**	**33**	32	**7**	**80**
State administration	18	**44**	—	4	**72**	**39**
Federal administration	4	—	—	4	**75**	—
Nonprofit administration	14	**14**	**8**	9	**79**	**21**
By Final Award Size						
$100,000 or more	12	67	8	34	50	50
$50,000–$99,999	11	54	9	20	46	55
Less than $50,000	54	47	23	16	36	58
All Awards	78	51	18	20	39	56

Note: (—) indicates less than 1 percent. Column 1 reports the number of active grants during the fiscal year. Column 2 shows the percentage of awards with monthly vouchers or fiscal reports. Column 3 shows the percentage of awards where vouchers or fiscal reports are due within one week. Column 4 gives the average number of pages for vouchers and fiscal reports combined. Column 5 shows the percentage of awards with fixed or flat payment schedules. Column 6 shows the percentage of awards when payment delays exceeded four weeks. **Boldfaced** numbers indicate characteristics where the reports differ at the .05 level of significance or better.

Source: Case-Study Project.

ongoing expenses.[7] Less than half (43 percent) provided any advance payments to help organizations meet expenses up front. However, even if referred to as advance payments, they rarely are. That is because funding sources in most cases do not authorize advance payments and comptrollers do not release them until the program proposal is approved and the contract finalized. As indicated above, proposals are rarely approved much in advance of the program start, and contracts almost never are. As a result, "advance" payments may arrive several months after the program starts. Some organizations borrow funds commercially, using their official award letters as collateral.

Only small grants are likely to be prepaid fully or in part. The United Way also provides early support by issuing checks at the beginning of the month. Some of the state funding sources have a temporary delay in payments until the contracts are finalized but then revert to a flat monthly payment schedule, with checks arriving at the beginning of or during the month for which they are designated.

Performance contracts, by their very nature, delay payments until after specified goals have been achieved. Similarly, the city's system of preauditing all expenditures necessarily results in payment delays for recipient organizations. As column 6 in Table 9.6 shows, payments for about half of the awards administered by the city arrived four weeks or more after the organizations had requested payment, and one in five (20 percent) arrived more than two months later. These delays, of course, are in addition to the time lag that organizations encounter in obtaining the required documentation for submitting vouchers. As a result, payments may not arrive until eleven to fifteen weeks after organizations incurred the expenditures.

There were examples of extreme delays in payments. The exact status of Youth Outreach's contract with the Chicago Board of Education had not been resolved when we reviewed the files, three months after the end of the program period. The contract amount exceeded the limit under which the board could process payments without obtaining approval of the finance committee, and Youth Outreach was uncertain about when, in what form, and even whether it would receive any payment at all under the agreement.

Similarly, Youth Outreach also experienced sizable delays in payments under another program. When we interviewed staff members in early May 1988, the organization had only two months previously received the last payment for a contract that ended in June 1987 (eleven months previously) and had not yet received any payments at all for the program period that started in July 1987. At one point, Youth Outreach considered legal action to force payment, but the nonprofit agency that administered the program blamed the city for the delay in payments. Payment delays of this scope create obvious cash-flow problems with associated management contingencies for the organizations to address.

Summary

I have reviewed the variety of tasks involved in managing the proposal and operating phases of the restricted grants and contract system in considerable detail because the complexity of these funding relationships is not well understood and has not previously been fully documented. Strict limitations

on line-item expenditures and program requirements about staff qualifications or eligible clients impose additional management challenges not fully
detailed here.

As these findings show, not only does the restricted grants and contract
system require a large number of demanding management tasks, but each
funding relationship involves a particular set of interactions and timings that
reflect program agreements and actions of specific funders and the respective service providers. It is a difficult management system to learn, and the
closed funding relationships that it fosters create other barriers to entry for
new organizations.

Many of these relationships seem almost to take on a life of their own,
and their patterns are not easily explained. For example, such institutional
characteristics as the level of government that administers the award appear
to shape most fiscal aspects and a range of administrative procedures.
However, some features vary among funding sources within the same level of
government, and some even differ from one delegate organization or subcontractor to the next for the same program and funding source.

As a result, the structure of management efforts that these funding
relationships impose is likely to vary significantly among individual organizations. Of thirty-eight different characteristics on which I have systematic
information for individual proposals or active grants and contracts, twenty-
one dimensions (57 percent) show significant differences among the seven
organizations. One additional dimension has borderline significance. This
pattern of diversity reflects the idiosyncratic configurations of funding
sources that the organizations manage. Although some management knowledge is general, other knowledge is specific and may not easily transfer from
one organization to the next. The skills are so costly to acquire and the
relationships so complex to manage that organizations are reluctant to lose
the investment and shift to other funding sources with different learning
curves.

Several additional points stand out. First, in spite of the general
pattern of idiosyncratic funding relations, there are some systematic differences between the two service fields. On sixteen of the thirty-eight dimensions (42 percent), grants and contracts differ to a significant extent among
social service and community development organizations. For six additional
dimensions, the patterns border on statistical significance. These findings
confirm the importance of organizational environments for understanding
nonprofits.

Second, with few exceptions, the stability or turbulence of organizational funding histories and their specific types of resource dependency have
little or no impact on their relationships with restricted funding sources.
These two characteristics were significantly related to the thirty-eight dimensions in only six cases each; respectively, four and three additional dimensions had borderline significance. This is fully understandable because most

of the dimensions reflect funder-imposed requirements over which individual organizations have little control. The requirements hold whether the organizations rely primarily on public funding or on a mix of donations and public grants and contracts. They hold whether the organizations have a history of funding stability or turbulence. The few occasions where funding histories or resource dependencies make a difference reflect primarily characteristics over which organizations have some control (for instance, whether to submit new proposals for funding).

Finally, the amount of work involved is not predictably related to the size of the grant or contract. Small awards may be as demanding as larger ones. The size of the final award is significantly related to only three characteristics (the amount requested, how much the final amount was different from what was requested, and the size of performance reports). Only the last feature does not have any built-in association with award size. Four additional characteristics have borderline relationships with size of award (number of items included in the proposal, level of detail in performance reports, level of difficulty in performing grant or contract activities, and delays in finalizing the contract).

For all other features, the size of the award made no difference in the amount or type of management work. This is an important finding. It means that the relatively large number of small awards that characterize the restricted funding system, at least for the types of medium-sized organizations included in the case-study project, adds disproportionately to the amount of management effort that organizations must exert per dollar received. So does the increasing tendency for these types of organizations to obtain new, small awards in recent years (see Chapter Eight).

Coordinating large numbers of restricted funding streams imposes transaction costs and creates problems of decoupling and incomplete planning. The actual management work involves fairly simple, limited tasks for foundation and corporate grants, but complex and demanding ones for public and United Way funding. For these latter types of funding sources, the overwhelming pattern is one of relatively closed funding systems in which organizations that have managed to enter the system are able to build on their existing funding relations, protected by short lead times and complex proposal requirements.

However, delays in approving and finalizing awards impose cash-flow and planning problems on recipient organizations. During the operating phase of grants and contracts, organizations are also faced with numerous revisions and amendments that require them to monitor closely their own performance levels, but on a piecemeal basis. They must submit many demanding program and fiscal reports and deal with major payment delays. These challenges appear to be endemic to the public and United Way funding system: they do not vary by the amount of the award or by the organization's own track record as reflected in its funding history.

Instead, the tasks are imposed by funders and restrict internal management discretion for the organizations that receive the funding. The particular figuration of tasks varies considerably from one nonprofit to the next, because each organization has its own peculiar funding network. Because funding sources tend to bundle by service field, there are also notable differences between social service agencies and community development organizations. However, the funding is substantial, organizations learn how to work the system, and their managers are able to predict fairly well the level of funding they will receive from year to year.

Notes

1. Transactions were computed by dividing the number of arrows in the chart by the corresponding number of final funding streams reaching the agency.
2. If funding from the United Way and federated funders were excluded from these calculations, the average number of transactions would increase slightly for all but Alcohol Treatment and Economic Development Commission.
3. These estimates fail to include the indirect connections between each of the organizations and other service providers with which it shares funding sources.
4. During the 1985–1989 period, DCFS had contractual relationships with about 38,400 different providers, including 1,200 social service and day-care agencies (most of the rest—32,300—are individual providers). Depending on the type of service involved, 25 to 40 percent of the participating social service agencies received funding on a continuing basis from DCFS over the five-year period, but these continuing providers account for 94 percent of all funds.
5. I use the median as a summary statistic here because it is less affected by a few extreme values than the mean.
6. Organizations will not need budget amendments if contract amounts are small relative to the actual line-item expenditures, because they can recover the entire contract amount without requesting transfers among budget lines.
7. In contrast, most foundation or corporate grants pay up front at the time of the award or the beginning of the program period.

TEN

Handling Coordination,
Uncertainty, and
Transaction Costs

This chapter explores how the magnitude and complex timing of tasks involved in managing restricted funding sources create problems of task coordination. The restricted grants and contracts system also contributes to cash-flow problems, personnel turnover, and management uncertainty. These features add to the transaction costs for both recipient organizations and funders. Some of these costs are obvious and well recognized. Others are less apparent but occur when the restricted funding system encourages recipient organizations to operate with disjointed decision-making structures that impede strategic planning. These problems have important implications for funding organizations, especially government agencies, and raise closely related questions about the cost and effectiveness of the broader structure of human services in the United States.

Problems of Overall Coordination

Such tasks as the preparation of vouchers and program reports create major challenges for nonprofits because of the level of detail required. The number, diversity, and idiosyncratic timing of management tasks that the restricted grant and contract system impose create additional complexity and problems of developing coordinated, effective decision-making structures.

Large Number and Idiosyncratic Timing of Tasks

The overall level of management overhead that the restricted funding system imposes is quite difficult to determine (see Appendix A). It was only possible to count the number of management tasks described in detail in Chapter Nine. All require management decisions and coordination. For example, the receipt of RFPs or notifications of renewals involve decisions about whether and how to respond to the funding opportunity. The analysis includes tasks associated with denied proposals, because the development of new funding sources is part of the normal set of tasks that organizations undertake on an ongoing basis.

Table 10.1 shows the monthly distribution of these tasks for Youth Outreach as they relate to restricted funding sources for which program periods coincided with or overlapped the agency's own 1987–88 fiscal year. The fiscal period itself is shown in **bold**. The agency performed more than 409 tasks for the sixteen public or United Way grants and contracts that were active during the period. As noted in the table, the agency had not completed all reports and vouchers for these funding sources at the time we terminated the data collection. The count therefore underestimates the number of tasks involved. Even so, the table shows that these tasks spread over more than thirty months and averaged twenty-four tasks per awarded grant or contract.

Table 10.2 summarizes the results of similar analyses for all seven case-study organizations with public and United Way funding. The average number of tasks per restricted funding source is well over twenty for all but Immigrant Welfare League. This agency was unusual in that it received several automatic awards for commodity foods when it was awarded funding for a homeless shelter. These awards had no application process and very low reporting requirements. The large number of tasks for African-American Neighbors reflected its practice of submitting separate vouchers for each line item expenditure in order to minimize cash-flow problems.

Table 10.2 underestimates tasks for all the organizations, because it excludes activities relating to licensing requirements (Hispanic Youth Services, Alcohol Treatment) and the development of foundation grants, corporate support, individual donations, or special events. During any given period, nonprofits also manage activities related to the much larger number of restricted grants and contracts that span three consecutive program cycles. They are winding up reporting and reimbursement activities for the most recently completed period; delivering services, reporting, and tracking contract performance for the current period; and preparing proposals for funding for the next period.[1] A complete list of tasks over the entire thirty to thirty-six month period would have included the full range of activities relating to both the prior and subsequent fiscal periods. Conservatively, the total number of tasks during any given fiscal year is probably at least twice the number documented here.

Task Coordination

Having a large number of required management tasks to perform appears to be one of many contingencies associated with reliance on restricted funding sources — contingencies that nonprofits seem willing to accept because they also have management advantages. However, nonprofits must ensure that the full range of tasks is performed and coordinated in a timely fashion. Of course, not all tasks are equally demanding, but some invoke penalties if not

Table 10.1. Monthly Work Flow for Fiscal Year 1988 Grants and Contracts: Number of Management Tasks, Youth Outreach.

Month	RFPs/Guides Received	Proposals[a] Submitted	Proposals[a] Approved	Awards Finalized	Programs Started	Program/Client Reports	Fiscal Reports	Vouchers Submitted	Total Number of Tasks
1986–87 Fiscal Year									
July	1	—	—	—	—	—	—	—	1
August	—	—	—	—	—	—	—	—	—
September	—	1	—	—	—	—	—	—	2
October	—	—	1	—	—	—	—	—	—
November	1	—	—	—	—	—	—	—	1
December	—	1	—	—	—	—	—	—	2
January	1	1	—	—	—	—	—	—	2
February	2	2	2	—	—	—	—	1	7
March	3	1	2	—	—	—	—	1	10
April	—	5	3	2	1	—	—	—	17
May	—	1	3	1	—	1	1	6	16
June	1	—	—	2	2	1	1	5	—
1987–88 Fiscal Year									
July	—	**4**	**2**	**1**	**6**	**3**	**1**	**6**	**23**
August	**2**	—	**1**	**1**	—	**5**	**4**	**6**	**19**
September	—	**1**	**1**	**1**	**1**	**6**	**5**	**8**	**23**
October	**1**	**4**	**3**	**3**	**2**	**6**	**4**	**11**	**34**
November	—	**2**	**4**	**3**	**2**	**6**	**7**	**9**	**33**
December	—	**2**	**1**	**1**	—	**6**	**5**	**9**	**24**
January	—	**1**	**3**	—	**2**	**7**	**6**	**9**	**28**
February	—	**1**	**1**	**1**	—	**8**	**6**	**10**	**27**
March	—	—	**1**	—	—	**7**	**5**	**10**	**23**
April	—	—	—	—	—	**8**	**8**	**7**	**23**
May	**1**	**2**	**1**	—	—	**6**	**7**	**8**	**24**
June	**1**	**2**	**2**	—	**1**	**6**	**5**	**7**	**24**
1988–89 Fiscal Year									
July	—	—	1	1	—	10	7	7	26
August	—	—	—	—	—	4	4	6	14
September	—	—	—	—	—	2	2	2	6
Total	14	31	32	17	17	92	78	128	409

Note: The count of tasks is incomplete for the 1988–89 fiscal year and should have extended through February 1990 for an estimated additional twenty-five tasks.

[a] The number of proposals submitted (column 2) and approved (column 3) includes both preproposals and full proposals, as well as proposals for contract or grant revisions.

Source: Case-Study Project.

Table 10.2. Estimated Management Tasks for Public/United Way Funding Sources.

Case-Study Organization	Total Number of Public/ United Way Sources		Total Number of Management Tasks	Average Number of Tasks per Award
	Awarded	Denied		
Social Service Agencies				
Alcohol Treatment	4	—	118	30
Hispanic Youth Services[a]	21	1	423	20
Youth Outreach[a]	16	1	409	26
Immigrant Welfare				
League[a]	10	1	153	15
Community Development Organizations				
Economic Development				
Commission	5	—	168	34
United Residents	9	3	218	24
African-American				
Neighbors	13	2	575	44

[a] Count of tasks is incomplete because some program periods extended beyond completion of data collection.
Source: Case-Study Project.

performed on time, and funding sources may use their timely completion as an easily established criterion for deciding whether to renew an award or change the funding level.

The timely execution of these tasks is difficult. There are no common funding cycles around which organizations can structure the tasks, funding sources are frequently late in notifying nonprofits about revised grant or contract specifications, and lead times are extraordinarily short in most cases. The variety of documentation that nonprofits must provide as part of the proposal processes or contract negotiations also requires careful attention to coordination and detail. Similarly, the diverse types of service or client statistics that these organizations must collect as part of program performance reports place considerable strain on data collection, management, and analysis.

The diverse activities and long time spans involved also create problems in training staff members, especially in organizations that experience vacancies or changes in key staff positions. It takes time for individual staff members to cycle through and learn the entire process, especially since the individual grants and contracts may be at different stages of their respective task schedules at any given point in time.

General Contingencies and Uncertainties

Managing the restricted grants and contracts system also creates several technical problems for nonprofits and closely related contingencies for funding sources. I identified several issues relating to fiscal contingencies, personnel turnover, and ambiguities in developing clear understandings of funder expectations.

Fiscal Contingencies

Nonprofits encounter a variety of fiscal contingencies in managing restricted grants and contracts, especially from public funding sources. As noted earlier, delays in finalizing contracts mean that organizations cannot bill for their services until they receive the legally executed contract. Even after contracts are signed and implemented, organizations must often wait as much as two months before they receive payments for services rendered and billed. This is particularly problematic for performance contracts and for grants and contracts under the type of voucher system used by the city of Chicago.

In general, the delayed payment systems that funding sources impose on their nonprofit collaborators result in major cash-flow problems. I found specific evidence of these problems from an examination of monthly cash-flow data and cumulative cash balances over the fiscal year and from an analysis of accounts receivables over the same period. All seven organizations with public funding maintained records on monthly cash flow, but some did not have the data available for consecutive months over the full fiscal year. Only four of the organizations had data on monthly accounts receivable.

Cash Flow. Cash receipts fluctuated unpredictably and widely, frequently by a factor of 3 or 4. Figure 10.1 shows monthly cash receipts during one fiscal year for the four social service agencies. All had major fluctuations from month to month. For example, Youth Outreach averaged $114,000 in monthly cash receipts over the one-year period, but received only $60,400 in July and $67,300 in February. On the other hand, it received $167,000 in March, $163,000 in June, and $154,000 in May, more than twice the amounts received in the months with low receipts. Similar fluctuations were also typical among the community development organizations.

Alcohol Treatment relied mainly on one single state agency for its funding. Its pattern of cash receipts, therefore, shows how individual funding sources may affect nonprofits. As Figure 10.1 shows, Alcohol Treatment had considerable fluctuation in its cash receipts during the early part of the fiscal year and much greater stability over the last seven months of the fiscal year. It averaged $27,000 in cash receipts per month over the entire period, but it got only $4,000 in November and $11,000 in September, and received $52,000 in August and $44,000 in October. The amounts received in the two high months were more than six times the amounts received in the two low months.

The director referred to the early part of the fiscal year as white-knuckle time, when he was waiting for the state's Department of Alcoholism and Substance Abuse to finalize the contract for the fiscal year. Only then would the agency receive any payment on the contract, covering the first two to three

Figure 10.1. Monthly Cash Receipts for Four Social Service Agencies.

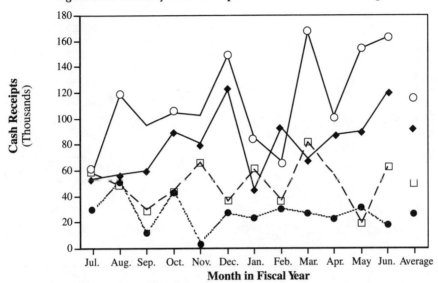

—O— Youth Outreach —◆— Hispanic Youth   —□— Immigrant Welfare ---●--- Alcohol Treatment

months of services. The director worried about meeting the monthly payroll if the payment was delayed and sought to postpone optional expenditures to the extent possible. By December, however, the contract was fully in place, and the state resumed its practice of flat monthly payments. That explains why cash receipts fluctuated only between $31,000 and $23,000 for the December to May period. Most of the remaining fluctuations reflected the three smaller grants and contracts the agency had with other funding sources.

Figure 10.2 shows monthly cash outlays for the four social service agencies over the same period of time. A comparison with Figure 10.1 demonstrates that cash outlays were much more stable than cash receipts. For example, monthly outlays for Youth Outreach ranged between $88,000 and $138,000, a ratio of only 1.6 to 1 compared with a 2.6 to 1 ratio for cash receipts. For Alcohol Treatment, the monthly outlays ranged between $21,000 and $42,000, or by a factor of 2, compared with the ratio of 6 to 1 between the highest and lowest monthly cash receipts. Stable outlays are not surprising, since personnel costs account for the bulk of expenditures for most social service agencies. For all but one of the organizations (Preservation Council), personnel costs accounted for at least 60 percent of total expenditures, usually more than 75 percent.

Several additional points are important. First, only one of the agencies, Hispanic Youth Services, persistently had cash receipts that exceeded outlays almost every month. That is also reflected in average monthly receipts ($81,000), which were substantially higher (by 25 percent) than average monthly outlays ($65,000). As a result, the agency ended the fiscal year with a net surplus of $194,000, equivalent to its total income from donations and United Way support that year.

Figure 10.2. Monthly Cash Outlays for Four Social Service Agencies.

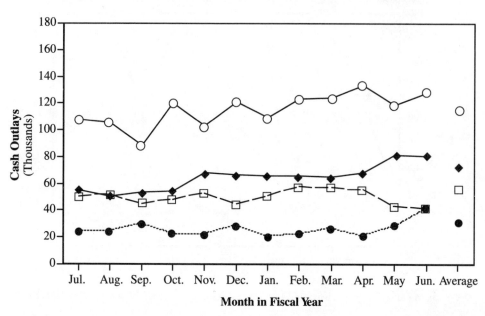

Month in Fiscal Year

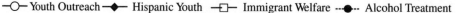

—○— Youth Outreach —◆— Hispanic Youth —□— Immigrant Welfare --●-- Alcohol Treatment

It is difficult to sort out how the organization managed to maintain such a persistent surplus, given its substantial reliance on government grants and contracts, most of which were directly tied to expenditures. However, the agency received substantial funding from JTPA performance contracts ($183,000), which did not require documentation of expenses, only of service outcomes. Possibly, part of the costs of delivering these services might be covered by other grants and contracts.

Second, most of the remaining agencies showed clear evidence of adjusting their cash outlays to match cumulative receipts. Major curtailments in outlays are difficult, since payroll costs cannot easily be postponed if the agencies want to keep their staff members, although several deliberately did not fill staff vacancies in order to avoid deficits. However, as Figure 10.2 shows, monthly outlays fluctuated somewhat for Youth Outreach during the early part of the fiscal year and seemed to be related to its timing of payments to two subcontractors. If so, the adjustments allowed Youth Outreach to meet its own payroll and other obligations in a timely fashion.

Similarly, Immigrant Welfare League substantially curtailed its expenditures during the latter part of the fiscal year, when it became clear that donations would not reach the budgeted level and that several performance contracts would also fall short. The agency even developed a contingency plan to postpone paychecks for the top administrative staff in order to avoid borrowing funds. It did not have to do so when payments from the city arrived in time to meet payroll expenses, but it did have to cash in some certificates of deposit prior to the maturation date.

On the other hand, Alcohol Treatment increased its expenditures during the last two months of the fiscal year when its director realized that the organization would end the year with a surplus. The increased outlays appeared to reflect a combination of making purchases that had been postponed previously and of increasing transfers to a reserve fund for equipment. As a result of such efforts, these three agencies ended their fiscal years with very small surplus levels.

Overall, most of the agencies had several months in which their cash inflow was substantially lower than their cash outflow. Some of them never recovered from these periods of low receipts. Table 10.3 summarizes data on the ratio between monthly cash receipts and outlays for the seven organizations with public funding. Each had at least one month in which cash receipts covered less than 70 percent of outlays during a given month, and three had periods in which receipts were less than 50 percent of their outlays.

Several managers explained that cash-flow problems of this magnitude occasionally forced them to resort to costly procedures to meet payroll expenditures in a timely fashion. Five of the seven organizations did so during the fiscal year in question. Some cashed in certificates of deposit prior to the maturation date. Others borrowed funds, either from their endowment (Youth Outreach) or from banks or commercial lenders. In the latter case, the organizations used their approved grant proposals from public agencies (African-American Neighbors) or outstanding vouchers from public grants and contracts (United Residents, Economic Development Commission) as collateral.

These practices appear to be fairly common among nonprofits. A 1991 survey of 475 nonprofit human service organizations in Illinois (including social service and community organizations, but excluding hospitals and schools) found that almost one-fifth (18 percent) had borrowed funds over the previous twelve months to cover temporary cash shortfall due to the timing of government grants and contracts (Grønbjerg, Nagle, Garvin, and Wingate, 1992). This is the most frequent reason for borrowing funds. About 12 percent said they had borrowed funds to cover other emergency cash-flow needs, but two-thirds of this latter group had also borrowed because of the timing of government grants and contracts. Overall, 23 percent reported borrowing for either of these two reasons, and about 32 percent reported borrowing for any reason, including building-related projects.

The proportion that had borrowed to cover temporary cash shortfall due to the timing of government grants and contracts or to cover other emergency cash-flow needs did not differ among social service and community development organizations (25 to 26 percent). However, the proportion was especially high (44 percent) among organizations that received half or more of their funding from government sources. Most of the seven case-study organizations with government grants and contracts fell into this category.

The survey also examined where these organizations borrowed funds. Of those that borrowed any funds at all, 70 percent borrowed from banks or

Table 10.3. Distribution of Ratios Between Monthly Cash Receipts and Cash Outlays for Seven Organizations.

Monthly Receipts as Percentage of Monthly Outlays	All	*Number of Months in Each Category*						
		Alcohol Treatment	*Hispanic Youth Services*	*Youth Outreach*	*Immigrant Welfare League*	*Economic Development Commission*	*United Residents*[a]	*African-American Neighbors*
170+	6	2	1	—	—	1	2	—
150–169	1	—	1	—	—	—	—	—
130–149	8	1	2	2	2	—	—	1
110–129	20	2	5	3	3	4	1	2
90–109	**17**	**4**	**2**	**2**	**3**	**2**	**—**	**4**
70–89	11	—	—	3	1	1	2	4
50–69	13	2	1	2	2	2	3	1
30–49	5	1	—	—	1	1	2	—
Less than 30	2	—	—	—	—	1	1	—
Total Months	83	12	12	12	12	12	11	12

Note: **Boldfaced** numbers are for months in which receipts closely matched outlays (within ten percentage points).
[a] Data not available for June.
Source: Case-Study Project.

commercial lenders. This was a much higher proportion than the proportion of those that borrowed from any other type of lending source, such as affiliated organizations (16 percent), endowments (13 percents), or foundations (10 percent). Most likely, banks and commercial lenders impose higher interest costs than would these other lending sources.

All the case-study organizations complained about unpredictable and extensive payment delays by public funders. Those that had to borrow funds commercially faced increased expenditures in the form of interest payments. Those that had to borrow against their own savings or endowments lost interest income they would have earned if they had not been forced to take such actions. Unfortunately, the lack of details in most of the audit reports did not allow me to identify interest costs associated with managing cash-flow problems separately from other direct or implicit interest expenditures.

Accounts Receivable. The implicit loss of interest income is even greater if one considers lost interest income from the substantial amounts that public funding sources owed the organizations each month. To examine the fiscal impact of these practices, I tracked outstanding vouchers that organizations had submitted to public funding sources but that had not been paid. When paid, they convert to cash receipts for the organization. However, as noted in Chapter Nine, more than half of public funding sources delay payments by at least four weeks, sometimes much longer. Idiosyncratic variations in when funders pay outstanding vouchers therefore help explain the large fluctuations in cash receipts noted above.

Four of the organizations maintained information on their outstanding vouchers as part of their monthly statement of fund balances. The analysis shows that monthly accounts receivable were quite large relative to the size of the organizations involved, roughly equivalent to 90 to 120 percent of monthly expenditures or about 10 percent of total annual expenditures. However, the outstanding amounts frequently exceeded a value equivalent to 150 percent of average monthly expenditures.

I computed the implicit loss of interest income the organizations experienced as a result of having outstanding vouchers of such magnitudes.[2] The loss ranged between $2,200 and $7,100 per year for the four organizations for which sufficient information was available, or equivalent to about half of 1 percent of total expenditures. This may seem to be a relatively small amount, but it is equivalent to annual surplus or deficit levels for several of the case-study organizations.

These are minimum estimates. The actual loss is greater, because the organizations often had to wait until they had received canceled checks back from the bank before they could issue vouchers for city grants and list the amounts as accounts receivable. The post-effort and delayed payment systems thus provide fiscal relief and interest-free loans to public treasuries.

These fiscal practices by funders place a premium on access to endowments or reserve funds, especially for nonprofits with high reliance on public funding. This means nonprofits will likely use more flexible funding to supplement the efforts that are mandated under highly restricted grants and contracts. In effect, private funding and the nonprofits themselves subsidize the public sector.

Smaller or less cash-flush organizations may face considerable difficulty in managing the month-to-month funding turbulence they will almost inevitably encounter if and when they enter the restricted grants and contracts system. The turbulence may become the occasion for nonprofits to go out of business, or it may aggravate other crises if it coincides with other difficulties that organizations might otherwise survive.

These problems are most visible in the case of public funding sources precisely because nonprofits know when they have money coming to them and how much. It was possible to document the contribution that public revenue sources make to agency cash-flow problems only because the post-effort payment systems create sizable and visible paper trails in the form of accounts receivable.

Similar difficulties may be equally prevalent but less evident in many unrestricted funding sources, especially donations. Nonprofits rarely know for sure if or when they will receive contributions or grant awards from private funding sources. Even if they get foundation and corporate grants up-front and use them for designated expenses, the funds are not due them as are the payments under the public grants and contracts. The predictability of public funding, even with delayed payments, serves as one of the major attractions of such funding to nonprofit agencies—that and the likelihood that the grant or contract will be renewed for subsequent program periods.

Costs and Benefits of Personnel Turnover

I found several instances in which the case-study organizations used staff turnover to deal with cash-flow and other budget problems. In some cases, organizations had to fire staff when grants were reduced or cut altogether. African-American Neighbors laid off several staff members when it lost most of its city funding in the early 1980s. It also laid off staff when it lost a training contract right after we terminated the data collection.

In other cases, organizations exploited staff resignations. Immigrant Welfare League left the position of assistant director vacant for more than eight months in order to curtail expenditures. Youth Outreach delayed the hiring of a team administrator for two months in order to avoid a deficit at the end of the fiscal year and frequently allowed some time to pass before filling vacancies when they did occur. Most of the other organizations reported similar practices in prior years.

The organizations acknowledged that leaving positions vacant in this manner meant that some planned and important activities did not get done and that other staff members occasionally had to accept more responsibilities than they were able to handle effectively. However, using staff vacancies in this manner is a tempting strategy because ongoing personnel costs account for the bulk of monthly outlays and cannot easily be postponed otherwise. Several of the organizations also appeared to rely on staff resignations as one of the mechanisms by which they could match staff skills with changing program demands associated with the grants and contracts system.

The high rate of personnel turnover that generally characterizes the nonprofit sector thus serves several management functions. However, the turnover is costly in terms of finding and training new staff (both major problems) and becomes an additional cost of managing restricted funding sources. Moreover, if organizations curtail staff costs to meet cash-flow problems, they may also fail to meet the service numbers in the contract. In turn, that may endanger both their ability to recover the full grant amount as well as their overall performance record and hence also their bargaining strength for future grants and contracts.

Uncertainties and Informal Accommodations

Although public agencies (and federated funding sources) provide ongoing funding with some measure of predictability, there are also specific conditions of uncertainty beyond those associated with cash-flow problems, especially for public grants and contracts. Numerous revisions in proposals and contracts introduce a layer of complexity and ambiguity in the relationship between funding sources and nonprofit subcontractors or grantees. Nonprofits may expect that their final contract amounts will be less than they were encouraged to submit in the proposals that public agencies requested from them. But they do not know for sure by how much, nor are they certain that further cuts may not come their way.

Frequent revisions in proposals, contracts, and reporting requirements reflect more general patterns of accommodation and informal understandings between funders and nonprofits. There appears to be more or less implicit understandings about acceptable shortcuts or solutions that the organizations could take without the likelihood of being challenged. Several examples of such practices are given in Chapter Nine. Although it is difficult to document them systematically, there are good reasons for believing that these practices exist. Most organizational analysts expect that informal accommodations to formal rules and requirements will develop when people interact with one another as part of complex organizations. Indeed, without such accommodations, work flows might suffer. Several studies have also documented that extensive bargaining takes place when formal agreements are hammered out (Bernstein, 1991; Cooper, 1980; DeHoog, 1984; Kettl, 1987; Nakamura and Smallwood, 1980).

As examples from the case studies show, bargaining and informal accommodations do not end once the contract is signed, but continue throughout the program period. They are promoted by the pattern of unpredictable enforcement and monitoring efforts that most restricted

funding sources practice, directed mainly at fiscal accountability and technical compliance with reporting obligations. Few funders, public or otherwise, seem able or inclined to fully evaluate service performances, even for
the subset of activities they fund.

In fact, most funding sources had only sporadic contact with the
nonprofits they supported and had limited opportunities to ensure compliance with their own requirements. That was also the case for the United
Way, which in Chicago undertakes a comprehensive evaluation of member
organizations only every third year. But even this evaluation does not involve
any systematic audit of service activities. Perhaps more important, the resources of the funding sources themselves, especially in the case of public
funders, depend on avoiding visible failures in the contractual service system. Under normal circumstances, it is in everybody's interest to presume
that work is being done appropriately, even if it is not.

Occasionally, public scandals may force funders to undertake more
systematic reviews. Thus, former staff members of one organization (not part
of the case-study project) were cited in local newspaper articles as claiming
that the organization's reports on service activities to public funders were
grossly inaccurate. The reports indicated that the organization was delivering mental health counseling services in facilities that turned out to consist of
empty, locked warehouses. The former staff members claimed that these
practices were of long standing and that they had sought to alert the organization's public funders about the problems on several occasions, but the
funders did not act to investigate the charges. The newspaper reports provided the necessary incentive.

Although this example may represent an extreme case, informal understandings about what level of accountability is possible and acceptable are
likely to develop among the respective parties. Because they are informal and
perhaps unspoken, such understandings can easily be challenged for political or other reasons without recourse to an appeals process for the organizations involved. Nonprofit service providers, then, may face considerable
ambiguity about important aspects of their funding relations, especially with
new funding sources.

Transaction Costs: The Cost of Doing Business

The restricted grants and contracts system constitutes a special type of transaction system. All organizations engage in wide variety of transactions on a
continuous basis. External transactions occur when organizations obtain the
necessary resources to conduct their activities and when they seek to shape
an appropriate market in which to dispose of products or services. Transactions also occur within organizations when goods and services are transferred across organizational units that have distinctive technological bases
(Williamson, 1981). All such transactions involve costs because they require

time and efforts to undertake. They may also result in conflicts, misunder-standings, and other malfunctions that impose additional costs and delays.

I focus here on costs attributable to the transactions that occur when nonprofits provide specified services in return for funding by other organizations, especially public agencies and federated funders. A full accounting of these costs is essential if one is to assess the impact of increasing privatization of government services in the United States and elsewhere (Savas, 1982; Straussman and Fairie, 1981; Orlans, 1980; Bennett and DiLorenzo, 1989).

The previous discussion of management tasks and contingencies associated with the restricted grants and contract system suggests that these transactions involve complex costs. The costs accrue to both recipient organizations and funders, although they may have different bases and magnitudes depending on which side of the partnership is being examined. Some of the costs are expected and relatively well recognized by both parties. Others are more indirect, unexpected, and difficult to assess.

Costs to Recipient Organizations

The types of transaction costs documented for the case-study organizations are very similar to what Hartogs and Weber (1978) observed in the early 1970s for social service agencies affiliated with the United Way and located in New York City. They examined problems of cash flow, conflicting guidelines, budget reductions, bookkeeping and accounting adjustments, start-up costs, waiting periods, reporting requirements, waivers and violations, and so on. The similarity of these topics to the types of issues identified in this volume is striking and suggests that the costs are ubiquitous at least with respect to public funding sources—they transcend time and place.

To develop a clearer perspective on these costs, I divide them into direct, expected costs and uncertain, unexpected costs. It is particularly difficult to develop good estimates of the latter, and most nonprofits may not recognize all of them as part of the costs of doing business with government agencies or other restricted funding sources.

Cost Sharing—Direct and Expected. Most funders demand or expect nonprofits to make additional financial commitments from their own re-sources to the programs or services for which they receive funding. The reasons they do so range from their own budgetary constraints to more philosophical arguments. Managers of public agencies and other institu-tional funders have explicit incentives, because requiring subcontractors or grant awardees to supplement awards makes their own resources or appro-priations go further for a given volume of services. Requiring service pro-viders to have a vested interest in the programs they operate may also reduce the need for in-depth monitoring by funding sources and encourage pro-viders to operate programs more effectively and efficiently.

The financial commitments demanded of nonprofit participants in the restricted grants and contracts system may take a variety of forms, ranging from a specified percentage match as a condition for the award, agreement to provide supplementary services (necessary or otherwise), exclusion of non-allowed expenses, limits on certain allowed expenses, or unit costs in pur-chase of service agreements that fail to cover known costs. Although these may not be transaction costs in the formal definition of the term, they are all direct costs of accepting a given award and should be considered as such.

Without exception, all proposals to public funding sources indicated that the services to be provided would cost more to deliver than the amount of the award. The difference constitutes the official match. Except for pur-chase-of-service agreements, organizations were required to document how they derived the cost estimates and to specify from which sources the match would be met. Frequently, matches appeared to come from other public funding sources, but occasionally they also came from private donations.

The case-study organizations differed considerably in the principles by which they derived the full cost estimates, although a full documentation of this was beyond the scope of the project. For example, there were several instances where organizations changed the cost accounting in successive versions of the same proposals or where certain costs and resources were included in one funding cycle and excluded in another for the same pro-gram. The reasons for these variations were not always obvious.

The variations were sufficiently pronounced that I have little confi-dence in the cost information. Certainly, directors and key staff members emphasized how difficult it was to balance the need to portray the true cost of services with the need to keep unit costs low. The former had the advantage of setting the stage for negotiating increases in awards, the latter of maintaining their competitive edge vis-à-vis other service providers. Indeed, organiza-tions may not be able to accurately determine the true amount of cost sharing they provide. It is difficult to keep track of the special rules that may apply to a particular contract, and there may be several acceptable options for computing the costs. Only accountants may fully appreciate the range of choices—and then disagree about them.

Deliberate efforts to underbid competitors are presumed to be com-mon in the for-profit sector, even to the point of taking a loss on a contract in order to ensure market share, longer-term profits, or other explicit advan-tages. It is less certain, however, that for-profit organizations would be equally willing to accept the principle of a required match on an ongoing basis. The expectation was almost universal among the nonprofits examined.

Opportunity and Other Costs—Uncertain and Unexpected. In addition to these known costs, the restricted grants and contracts system imposes other costs that are less certain and more difficult to document or estimate. Some are specific to new programs: start-up costs in finding additional space, hiring and training staff, establishing new procedures, developing a client base, and solving the unanticipated problems that always accompany the implementation of new activities. Others pertain to both new and ongoing programs: direct and indirect costs associated with cash-flow problems and outstanding vouchers, problems in maintaining adequate staffing levels, and costs associated with managing required tasks. Developing proposals, meeting reporting requirements, and coordinating data bases on clients, funding, and programmatic activities all require staff time, as do struggles to compensate for delays in finalizing awards or adjust to changes that funders impose on existing awards. Other costs accrue from boundary-spanning activities to maintain contact with key actors in funding systems and relevant policy arenas.

To compute the costs of these activities would require documentation of the staff time and direct expenses necessary to complete these tasks in a timely fashion. Larger organizations will most likely assign specialized staff to these activities and recognize them as direct and expected costs of participating in the restricted funding system. The more typical small and medium-sized organizations examined here would find it much more difficult to cost out the amount of staff time devoted to the specific tasks. Few of them could do so without imposing additional data management costs; they seem to largely ignore or discount the costs.

There are also opportunity costs in the form of other funding sources that are not pursued because of the demands imposed; planning costs in the form of piecemeal, uncoordinated planning; and efficiency costs because the restricted funding system may prevent an optimum allocation of resources. The amorphous atmosphere of uncertainty discussed earlier imposes its own costs. Opportunity, planning, efficiency, and uncertainty costs are far more difficult to determine than staff time, but are important nevertheless. I review them in more detail below, when I consider implications for decision-making structures.

Costs to Funders

The restricted grants and contracts system imposes a parallel set of transaction costs on funders. As with large nonprofits, many of these costs are easy to determine because they are contained in separate administrative units. Others are less visible and more difficult to estimate. I have no direct information on any of these costs, but I generalize on the basis of the interaction patterns observed between the case-study organizations and their public funders. The observations are consistent with the work of public administration analysts (Rehfuss, 1989; Straussman and Fairie, 1981). I also draw on a larger study of the contract system under which the Illinois Department of Children and Family Services delivers the bulk of services under its auspices (Chen, Grønbjerg, and Stagner, 1992; Grønbjerg and Stagner, 1992).

Processing Grants and Contracts—Direct and Expected Costs. Most of the management tasks that the restricted funding system imposed on the seven nonprofits (see Chapter Nine) consists of preparing and submitting different types of information to funding sources. The funding sources demand this exchange of information as a condition of making the awards in order to track the activities of service providers and plan their own activities.

Institutional actors that rely on other organizations to carry out activities for them in return for specified funding must develop appropriate infrastructures along these lines in order to manage the funding relations. Establishing and operating such an infrastructure constitute the direct, expected costs that the transactions impose on funders. In the most narrow definition, these expenses involve the direct (salaries) and indirect (space, fringe benefits, supplies, supervision) cost of employing staff members directly involved in managing the grants and contracts system.

The specific tasks and associated costs may vary a great deal, depending on the amount of subcontracting and the degree of formalization with which funders pursue the process. Private funders may operate quite informally and have limited direct transaction costs of these types. However, public funders are likely to be under pressure to maintain a formal process that can be defended under public scrutiny. Consequently, most public funders would need to allocate special staff to design and operate the contract system. This includes efforts to prepare RFPs or similar notifications of available funding, evaluate submitted proposals and the capacity of service providers, recommend changes in proposals, finalize awards, receive and review submitted reports, monitor adherence to standards and outcomes, revise or amend contract agreements, and authorize and track payments.

These are well-recognized costs that public administration analysts have long sought to determine and develop parameters for (Orlans, 1980). Rehfuss (1989) cites several studies of the costs of implementing and monitoring subcontracting in public administration, on the basis of which he estimates that direct monitoring costs amount to about 5 to 10 percent of total contract awards. The costs are higher if performance levels are difficult to measure and evaluate, because then monitoring must be more intense (for example, counseling or community organizing compared to street cleaning).

Opportunity and Other Costs — Uncertain and Unexpected. In addition to these direct costs, the restricted funding system also imposes more indirect and less certain costs on funders. These are likely to be similar to those described for nonprofits. However, public funders may also encounter other types of transaction costs that are even more difficult to recognize or compute, such as costs associated with potential political fallout from the occasional but inevitable failures of the provider system. Only a much more extensive and expensive monitoring system than currently exists could safeguard against the likelihood that nonprofit service providers will on occasion mismanage funds, endanger clients, fail to perform, or all three.

Other inefficiencies originate with the long-term funding relationships that are especially prominent in the social service field, and with the political favoritism that exists, albeit with less prevalence, in the community development field. Well-established funding relationships of these types are difficult to break, as the case studies show, even if logic and performance assessments dictate otherwise. And establishing relationships with new providers involves start-up costs for funders as well.

Public funders may find these features more problematic when dealing with nonprofit subcontractors than other subcontractors, because nonprofits carry built-in legitimacy. They can claim to act with moral purpose for the greater public benefit, allowing them to resist funder actions with greater effectiveness than most for-profit organizations. This argument is consistent with Rehfuss's assessment that public administrators find it less desirable to contract with nonprofits than with private firms or other governmental units. He argues that while nonprofit subcontractors give priorities to client welfare, use quality volunteers, and have community support, they need close monitoring and are not sufficiently competitive to maintain strong business management practices.

A full understanding of the costs involved in delivering public services would need to take into account not only the direct outlays for the services but also the transaction costs involved in managing the grants and contracts system on both sides of the relationship. These costs are very difficult to determine, especially for smaller nonprofits, but they are likely to be substantial. To the extent that costs on the nonprofit side of the transaction are covered by donations, they involve indirect public spending in the form of forgone tax revenues. When the transactions are with public funding sources, nonprofits in effect collect additional taxes from donors to support publicly mandated services.

Strategic Planning and Decision Making

The complexity, timing, and efforts involved in securing and managing government grants and contracts impose large overhead costs on nonprofits that strain their internal communication and threaten their decision-making structures. If good communication is not in place or operating well, proposal and contract characteristics may bear little relationship to service needs or activities, and services or activities may operate with minimal coordination within or across organizations. The restricted grants and contracts system, then, may impede rather than promote strategic planning and effective coordination of activities at the service delivery level.

The transaction costs associated with the restricted grants and contracts system place a premium on effective internal administrative structures and decision-making processes. To some extent, these are normal problems of management that all organizations face. However, the case studies indicate that organizations differ in whether top administrative staff members are able to maintain close contacts with the service delivery system. This linkage is important if organizations are to transcend fragmented funding structures, coordinate service activities for the benefit of clients, and ensure a close match between program designs and program executions.

The case-study analysis suggests that three features impede strong communication systems along these lines: structural characteristics of key funding sources, diversity of program activities, and size of organization. Characteristics of funding sources involve two dimensions: restricted versus discretionary funding sources and multiple versus single funding sources. Reliance on restricted funding sources limits management discretion, while multiple funding sources create problems of coordination. Diverse program activities encourage specialization and related problems of coordination, while larger organizations accommodate a higher level of division of labor and specialization and require taller hierarchical structures, both of which complicate communication and coordination.

The Imperatives of Primary Funding Sources

Organizations that rely mainly on flexible, self-generated funding sources are relatively free of having management demands imposed on them by other organizations. However, they must develop effective mechanisms for conducting the income-generating activities, and their patterns of decision making must accommodate other contingencies that funding sources may present. Certainly, the five case-study organizations with primary reliance on fees and special events showed systematic differences in decision-making structures that reflected structural characteristics of their funding sources (see Chapters Five and Six).

For example, Christian Therapists relied on individual fee-paying clients and operated with a decision-making structure that was equally decentralized and flat. Minority Search, in contrast, relied on long-term institutional customers and had developed a highly structured, hierarchical system of decision making that matched those of its customers.

Two of the organizations with major funding from special events required a high level of participation by volunteers in order to carry out the events. Their decision-making processes involved complex committee structures and large numbers of volunteers on each committee to ensure that all tasks were completed. They needed numerous leadership positions to encourage volunteer participation with corresponding problems of coordination across and within committees.

Tasks may be numerous and demanding for such organizations, but the organizations and their leadership have full authority over the coordination and timely execution of tasks. They are influenced by external forces in how they resolve these challenges to the extent that they must attend to customer interests and demands. Otherwise, they cannot generate sufficient revenues to stay in their chosen line of business. They must therefore develop strong internal systems of communication, with client feedback, so that they can direct organizational activities appropriately.

Managers may encounter few obstacles to these efforts if customer interests and demands are relatively uniform or if customers are individuals rather than institutional actors. Institutional customers tend to have distinct preferences for interaction that conforms to norms about organizational behavior. Indeed, they may require such behavior as a condition of establishing contractual relationships (DiMaggio and Powell, 1983). Public and United Way funders represent the more extreme versions of these tendencies.

Organizations that rely mainly on one single funder or a homogeneous set of institutional funders may face externally imposed demands of these types, but only one set of demands. They can therefore structure themselves to match those demands as closely as possible. Under these circumstances, close communication with customers or clients is also relatively easy to establish and maintain. As Baum and Oliver (1991) conclude, nonprofits that develop and maintain institutional linkages benefit from the legitimacy that these linkages provide and increase their likelihood of survival.

Thus, Community Renewal coupled its decision making very tightly with that of its single, major donor. The organization operated with a narrow, top-down channel of communication, which provided few opportunities for lower-level staff or even board members to exert influence over the organization. However, the executive director was in direct and close contact with the customer-donor. That was also the case for New Town Sponsors and its membership of relatively homogeneous local developers. Nevertheless, the multiple membership structure of the latter prevented the same level of tight coordination as for Community Renewal.

Coordinating Across Multiple Funders and Diverse Programs

Organizations with major reliance on multiple restricted grants and contracts face the usual problems of how to interact with institutionalized funding sources. However, they must also address the more difficult problem of how to manage and coordinate activities in the face of multiple, at times contradictory, management requirements that these external funders impose and of the variety and scope discussed in Chapter Nine.

By virtue of having multiple, restricted funding sources, these organizations usually operate diverse programs. That is the easiest way of ensuring that the various funder requirements are met in a timely and appropriate fashion. In fact, most of the case-study organizations with restricted grants and contracts have created organizational structures that mirror or coincide with specific funding sources. (The only exceptions to this pattern are Youth Outreach and Hispanic Youth Services. They are discussed later.)

Alcohol Treatment provides only treatment for alcoholism and substance abuse and receives almost all of its funding from one single public funder. Nevertheless, it maintains two separate divisions, one for adult substance abusers and one for youths. The separation has some basis in different service needs for the two groups but also accommodates other considerations. The agency's alcoholism treatment license and its major public funding are limited to adult substance abusers, and other grants are restricted to substance abuse among youths. The dual structure allows the agency to manage distinctive reporting requirements with relative ease, but it impedes coordination of service activities for individual clients, especially if other family members are in need of services as well.

Problems of coordination become both more difficult and less immediately pressing if diverse program and funding structures target non-overlapping target populations with distinctive service needs. This was the case for Immigrant Welfare League, which targeted very diverse groups (elderly, alcoholic homeless males, battered women, illegal immigrants, and officially recognized refugees), each with its own complement of funding sources.

Such diversity encourages organizations to develop a corresponding level of staff specialization or divison of labor in order to ensure that the necessary tasks are performed. Diverse programs of this type provide a logical framework for establishing an organizational structure with a horizontal list of distinctive program components, but with few tiers and few management functions allocated to specialized staff. However, unless coordination occurs among program areas, organizations may easily end up with unrelated activities that take on a life of their own and develop in relative isolation from one another. The result may be not only lack of planning at the organizational level but also failure to meet client needs for comprehensive, integrated services.

Immigrant Welfare League demonstrates additional problems of communication that some nonprofits may face if they serve client populations with distinctive cultures. On the one hand, the agency's director controlled key agency decisions and most interactions with external organizations, except for those related to specific service issues. The lines of communication were short to the various program activities, and the director managed most grants and contracts, wrote all grant proposals, and handled most fundraising activities. Only the director (and later also the associate director) attended board meetings.

On the other hand, in spite of these structural advantages, the executive director faced considerable difficulties in maintaining strong lines of communication with program activities and was limited in his control over decision making. He and the supervisor of employment services were the only staff members who were not bilingual, while most clients did not speak English well or at all. As a result, most service activities took place in a language the director did not understand, and the other staff members often interacted with one another in that language as well. By default, the agency operated with a decentralized, decoupled decision-making structure that excluded the director from full participation.[3]

Maintaining Communication Across Hierarchies

Problems of coordination and adequate attention to client demands or needs become especially difficult in larger organizations. They tend to have multiple restricted funding sources and diverse program activities simply by virtue of being large, because they accumulate new funding sources and new program activities as they grow in size. Funders who administer restricted grants and contracts also tend to favor larger organizations because they look and act like the funding sources themselves: they meet institutional expectations about proper organizational behavior.

However, size encourages further specialization and the establishment of additional hierarchical levels to maintain an effective span of control. Both features are likely to increase the social and communication distance between central administrative staff responsible for coordination, planning, and proposal development and lower-level staff members who actually deliver the services and have direct contacts with clients.

These problems appear to be much less prevalent in smaller organizations. None of the organizations participating in the case studies were very large, and among the smaller organizations executive directors frequently provided direct services in addition to performing central administrative functions. Similarly, staff members with primary responsibility for the delivery of services often participated in the writing of proposals. These features ensure that those who formulate programmatic features in grant or contract proposals do so on the basis of their own direct knowledge of programmatic activities.

Although these conditions do not guarantee coordination and effective decision making, they do facilitate the achievement of such goals within the limits of available resources. Of course, multiple responsibilities of this type may also prevent smaller organizations from developing a high level of grantsmanship or operating services or activities as efficiently as possible. In fact, several of the directors complained about not being able to devote sufficient attention to these efforts.

Larger organizations tend to have diverse target populations and numerous programs. The two largest organizations included in the case study, Hispanic Youth Services and Youth Outreach, targeted a single, relatively homogeneous population: minority youths. Although they operated diverse program components and had multiple restricted funding sources, all of these were directed at the same client population, and both agencies emphasized the need to coordinate service activities across programs and funding sources.

In spite of this advantage, both faced problems of internal coordination and decision-making structures similar to those of larger organizations with a specialized management staff. The two agencies also illustrate diverse approaches: Hispanic Youth Services relies on a centralized decision-making structure and top-down communication system, and Youth Outreach devotes very high levels of effort to internal communication and coordination.

Hispanic Youth Services was small enough that it could maintain a fluid administrative structure with relatively few tiers and several people reporting directly to the director. The focus on a narrow age range of clients residing in a single local community meant that there were no natural administrative units for the agency as there were for other organizations participating in the study, or for most large organizations. In addition, the director conceptualized or marketed the agency's activities differently for different funders in order to match funder criteria as closely as possible. A fluid, shifting structure allowed the director considerable flexibility in portraying the organization's activities,[4] and the marketing strategy discouraged the development of a more formalized structure.

The director also maintained close control over key activities. The agency centralized all reporting systems, including service statistics, the completion of staff time sheets, and client files. The director wrote all new public grant proposals and was the only staff member to formally represent the agency to the outside. The board appeared to participate only sporadically in fund-raising and public relations efforts, and the director was the only staff member to participate in board meetings.

For the same reason, staff members had few opportunities to participate in program development, and board members could not easily develop detailed knowledge of program operations. The director viewed centralized control as essential for managing the agency's complex operations and funding systems. However, it also served to confirm and protect her position within the agency.

Centralized control over resource relations and communication allows nonprofits to meet the demanding time constraints that the restricted grants and contracts system imposes. However, it limits them to the range of contacts that directors can maintain, leaves them with few resource relations during a change in directors, and provides only limited opportunities for staff members to develop a full range of management skills. It also raises questions about the extent to which grant and contractual agreements are fully consistent with organizational activities or service needs among clients.

Youth Outreach differed from this structure in several respects. The largest of the thirteen organizations in level of revenue and size of staff, it had the most educated staff, especially in terms of professional social work training (42 percent had advanced degrees). These features accounted for both the autonomy of the organization's staff and its fairly elaborate administrative structure.

Youth Outreach had a five-tier administrative structure: an executive director, three assistant directors, five team administrators, service staff, and student interns organized into geographically based teams and special projects. Each team provided a range of service activities, so that the basic administrative unit was based on geographical rather than programmatic activity. The agency also had a central staff for administrative support and development efforts.

The agency provided staff members with explicit, structured opportunities to participate in decision making. The team structure decentralized some program decisions, because teams coordinated a variety of services in their respective outpost, but members participated in joint weekly meetings to review program activities and brief the executive staff on problems encountered. The agency referred to this as a "client-driven" process of decision making, because the weekly meetings focused on client issues. The team concept allowed the agency to provide its staff with a form of bounded autonomy and to decentralize a number of program decisions to the outpost level. On the other hand, client data and program proposals were handled centrally by the executive staff.

The emphasis on staff autonomy and decentralization of control also emerged in the agency's broad range of interactions between staff and board. It had an annual staff and board retreat, and the full executive team and team administrators participated in board meetings, as did a number of student interns. The interns, executive staff, and team administrators also worked with individual board committees, team members briefed the board on team activities, and individual board members were expected to visit at least one of the outpost sites each year. This amounted to a much broader and denser range of staff-board interactions than were evident in most of the other social service agencies participating in the study. As a result, board members appeared to be relatively well informed about the agency's programs, and the agency's middle-management level participated in at least some important agency decisions.

It is my impression, although I cannot fully document it, that these features were important in shaping the agency's programs in existing outposts. However, other decisions, such as expansion into new sites, were made at the top executive level and reflected efforts to exploit available funding opportunities. The agency's director and assistant directors acknowledged that these other developments were spreading staff members thin and impeding the development of more comprehensive efforts in existing programs. Yet they pursued these openings because they provided opportunities for growth and visibility.

Even so, the coordination efforts required a high level of investment. Twenty percent of the agency's staff resources — one full day per week — were devoted to a mixture of completing reporting requirements and maintaining the broad communication and decentralized decision-making structures. The agency's elaborate organizational structure is typical of larger nonprofits. However, I have not elsewhere encountered similar levels of efforts devoted explicitly to creating coordination and communication across service units and hierarchical levels. This type of approach might not be feasible for still larger organizations because of the number of persons who would be involved.

Summary

Sheer diversity of funding sources and special problems associated with the restricted grants and contracts system pose major challenges to nonprofits. They must coordinate the large number and idiosyncratic timing of management tasks, survive fiscal contingencies (especially cash-flow problems and large accounts receivable), weigh the costs and benefits of personnel turnover, and negotiate informal accommodations with funding sources.

These are some of the normal costs of doing business with restrictive funding sources for nonprofit social service and community development organizations. There are other transaction costs as well: required or necessary financial investments as well as planning, opportunity, and efficiency costs that both parties to the transaction experience but may not fully recognize. For nonprofits there are additional challenges in how to structure decision-making structures so as to accommodate the imperatives of major funding sources, coordinate across diverse programs, and maintain communication across hierarchical levels within the organization. In spite of these costs and challenges, the restrictive funding system appears to be well entrenched among nonprofits in these fields. The overall advantages outweigh the disadvantages or are at least more obvious and certain than for alternative funding sources.

However, the complex transaction costs for both public funders and their nonprofit counterparts have important implications for the nature of service provisions. Nonprofits that participate in the restricted grants and contracts system under public auspices serve as the de facto executors of public policy. They provide the locations, the staff, and the infrastructure for a significant proportion of the services that are being delivered, especially in the social service field. By default they become responsible for merging and coordinating priorities that are formulated under public auspices at all levels of government.

It is not surprising that a considerable amount of attention has been paid to the problem of ensuring service coordination (Gilbert and Specht, 1977; Aiken and others, 1975; Benton and Millar, 1978). Most of this attention has been directed at coordination or collaboration among organizations, which is generally viewed as highly desirable but is rarely accomplished (Aiken and others, 1975; Benton and Millar, 1978; Gilbert, 1972; Haveman, 1977; Peterson and Greenstone, 1977; Vanecko, 1969; Weiss, 1988).

Much less attention has been paid to the extent to which coordination occurs within organizations across different funding sources. I have argued in this chapter that the restricted grants and contracts system operates in such a manner as to make strategic planning, coordination, and effective implementation of services difficult at best, and impossible at worst, even at the level of individual organizations.

The manner in which these funding relationships operate creates a world of uncertainty and ambiguity that easily lends itself to goal displacement and may compromise the nonprofits themselves, their missions, and funder objectives. Individual funding relationships do shape organizational missions and vice versa, but not always in planned or recognized ways.

Notes

1. Some of these additional tasks are included for funding sources when two consecutive program cycles overlapped the organization's own fiscal year. This affected the total number of tasks but not the average number of tasks per award, since each program period was counted as one award.
2. The computation assumes that accounts are paid within four weeks. This is a reasonable assumption, but not always a realistic one, because several funders took six to eight weeks to process payment requests. I also assumed that the organizations could have earned 5 percent per year in interest on the funds if they had been placed in an interest-bearing bank account.
3. The director has since resigned, in part because he recognized these problems. His replacement shares the ethnic and linguistic background of the agency's clients. Some of the administrative problems identified here may no longer pertain.
4. We found several different organizational charts in the organization's files. The director and staff members explained that none of them were wrong but that each was designed to highlight some aspect of the agency to a particular funding source.

ELEVEN

The Challenges of
Managing Organizational Resources

So far, I have pointed to a number of organizational problems that nonprofit social service and community development organizations face when they attempt to manage their funding relationships and to participate in the delivery of publicly funded human services. There are specific contingencies associated with each of four major nonprofit funding streams (Chapters Five through Eight) and special problems connected with the restricted grants and contracts system (chapters Nine and Ten).

This chapter summarizes and reviews more general strategies and patterns of adaptation that nonprofit organizations pursue in managing broader contingencies associated with their funding relationships. Most of these emerged directly from the case-study project, although they do not have equal salience to all the organizations, nor do I have systematic information on all of them. Some reflect more accidental observations in my wider fieldwork. Although I have some documentation for all of the strategies discussed in this chapter, I present them as types of adaptations that on occasion go beyond what I observed in the individual agencies.

Strategies and Patterns of Adaptation

Nonprofit service organizations must address a number of general challenges in order to manage effectively their funding relations and other resources. These challenges include how to structure internal resources to be most consistent with demands from the environment and how to monitor the environment and position the organization to make most effective use of resources controlled by forces external to the organization (Tung, 1979). These two sets of challenges are interdependent so that efforts to address one set of issues may limit the ability to solve other problems.

Note: Portions of this chapter are reprinted with permission from *Human Services as Complex Organizations*, edited by Yeheskel Hasenfeld. Copyright 1992 by Sage Publications, Inc.

The challenges and strategies examined in this chapter are not an exhaustive analysis. I ignore other challenges, such as how to manage organizational facilities, meet licensing requirements, deliver specific services, and reach primary target groups. However, the problems I examine are among those that appear to warrant widespread attention from organizations and individuals that provide technical assistance to nonprofits. As seen in Table 11.1, general problems of organizational management and leadership have attracted well over half of the eighty different technical assistance providers who advertise at the national level in each of four service areas. Some of these have detailed subcategories (column 2). Other technical assistance focuses more explicitly on internal organizational operations, such as personnel, office operations, and financial management and control.

Technical assistance for managing relationships with the external environment is also widely available, especially in the area of fund-raising and development (55 percent of the providers and thirty-nine distinct service categories), interorganizational relations (52 percent of providers), and marketing (46 percent of providers and twenty-seven service categories). Of course, most technical assistance providers operate mainly in local markets and are not included in this analysis.

The variety of service categories, the number of detailed categories for each, and the extent of participation by technical assistance providers indicate the extent to which management problems of these types have become institutionalized and recognized in the nonprofit sector. Some of the detailed categories are quite specific (for example, the ever popular "mail fulfillment" subcategory under mailing lists).

Challenges in Managing Internal Resources

I focus on three major problems in managing internal resources that affect the ability of organizations to meet external demands: how to match staff skills with program demands, establish organizational leadership and structure, and develop a coherent organizational philosophy and culture, including a defined role for the board. Table 11.2 summarizes specific strategies (and their respective limitations) for meeting each of these challenges.

Match Staff Skills with Program Demands. Restricted grants and contracts usually require nonprofits to meet specific program demands, and the flat or declining values of public funding payments compromise their ability to compete for high-quality employees in the market place. In addition, organizations that change or expand their services (whether in response to new grants or contracts or to changing market niches in the case of fee-paying clients) must either hire new staff to perform the new or changed activities or make their current staff members more productive.

Broader environmental developments are likely to intensify these types of staff problems, especially for smaller nonprofits. The supply of

Table 11.1. Distribution of National Technical Assistance Providers
and Diversity of Services, by Type of Service.

Type of Service/Product	Percentage of Technical Assistance Providers (N = 80)	Number of Technical Assistance Subcategories
Management and Leadership		
Organizational management	69	28
Organizational governance (boards)	55	20
Volunteers (nonboard)	52	18
New organization formation	51	11
Operations		
Personnel	62	30
Office operations	34	29
Financial management and control	28	38
Information support systems	28	24
Legal	18	17
Facilities	15	15
Fund management and investment	14	13
Insurance services and products	11	15
Security	5	4
External Relations		
Fund-raising/development	55	39
Interorganizational relations	52	11
Marketing	46	27
Public relations	26	11
Promotion/advertising	25	10
Publishing/printing	25	15
Mailing lists	19	11
Government relations	16	10
Audio video, film, multimedia production	8	10
Other		
Meetings, conferences, conventions, and expos	66	15
Education and training	60	4
Publishers and distributors	19	9
Total	80	434

Source: Developed from the Society for Nonprofit Organization's *1990 National Directory of Service and Product Providers to Nonprofit Organizations*, 1989.

suitable workers is shrinking and the demand for them is intensifying. Major public school systems are faltering in their capacity to educate a literate, trainable work force and meet the demand for skilled workers. National projections show that the college-age population will decline until at least the mid 1990s (Atkinson, 1990).

These trends will affect all but the smallest, least sophisticated nonprofits, since 79 percent of program specialists in nonprofits already hold college degrees (Technical Assistance Center, 1988). The more specialized skills that nonprofits seek are also likely to be in short supply. Current

Table 11.2. Challenges, Strategies, and Caveats in Managing Internal Resources.

Challenge: Match Staff Skills with Program Demands

Strategy	Caveats
Hire clients to reduce barriers	May not have adequate technical and reporting skills
Hire staff with multiple skills	Expensive if high technical competency
Hire temporary staff with special expertise	Difficult to use for program services
Use volunteers or interns	Fluctuating numbers, uneven qualifications
Train, develop, and upgrade staff	Difficult to get trainable, appropriate staff
Exploit staff turnover	Difficult to find and train new staff

Challenge: Establish Internal Leadership and Decision Structures

Strategy	Caveats
Centralize control in director	Problems of time, attention, director turnover
Decentralize control and decision making	Requires coordination, integration, strong communication

Challenge: Develop Philosophy and Role of Board

Strategy	Caveats
Create professional, independent board	Requires large, active board, independent leadership
Create limited, specialized boards for fund raising, leadership	Problems of identity and internal reward system
Use boards for symbolic value	Problems of purpose and involvement
Use boards as service component	Requires strong but invisible director control

Source: Case-Study Project.

projections indicate that the number of job openings for human service workers will increase by 45 percent over the next ten years, and for social workers by 29 percent. Both trends far exceed the projected overall employ-ment growth of 15 percent (Silvestri and Lukasiewicz, 1989).

Nonprofits will be hard pressed to obtain their share of qualified staff members because of the lower overall salary and benefit levels they provide their workers compared with the public and for-profit sectors (Hall, 1990; Barbeito, 1990). In 1987, the average salary for nonprofit workers ($15,938) was only 75 percent of average wages in the public sector ($20,064), and even smaller (72 percent) in comparison to average wages in the for-profit sector ($21,995) (Hodgkinson and Weitzman, 1989). More detailed studies for the New York region indicate that these differences persist for most job positions, except perhaps for secretaries, receptionists, and other support staff (Ben-Ner and Hoomissen, 1989; Bailey, 1990).

In all likelihood, then, nonprofits will find it increasingly difficult to attract staff members who will allow them to meet service specifications or further develop their service capacities. This will affect smaller nonprofits most severely, because they have fewer opportunities for staff promotions and less adequate resources. These problems are also likely to be more problematic for social service agencies than for community development organizations because the former tend to require professional or other specialized skills, such as drug abuse counseling. I encountered several strategies that nonprofits appear to use in their efforts to match staff skills with program demands, especially among the social service agencies. Each has important limitations.

Hire Clients. Organizations may hire current or former clients to deliver services. This may serve to reduce cultural or other social barriers between clients and program staff and result in more effective services. However, unless clients are already well educated and highly skilled, nonprofits have to expend considerable resources on training them in technical services or reporting requirements. This strategy is therefore most likely to be available to organizations that either do not aim to provide a broad range of technical or professional services or whose clients already possess such skills. Community development organizations may find this strategy relatively easy to use, because they have access to local community residents with interests in and knowledge about local conditions.

Seek Staff with Multiple Skills. Organizations can choose to hire (or develop) staff with multiple skills who can assume new responsibilities as programs or funding change. There are obvious costs to this strategy because individual staff members who have a broad range of skills may either command high salaries or not have in-depth expertise. This strategy will therefore be problematic for organizations that require very high levels of technical competencies.

Hire Temporary or Part-Time Staff with Special Expertise. Organizations may hire consultants or short-term staff members with special expertise. Several of the case-study organizations used consultants to conduct board retreats or staff training sessions, produce development plans, or deliver services for which no trained staff was available. Hiring short-term staffs may also allow organizations to institute new management procedures that can subseqeuently be carried out by other, less qualified staff.

However, temporary or part-time staff members are likely to have fragile and easily disrupted relationships with the organization, as the case of Christian Therapists shows. Their departure can therefore produce major disruptions if they abandon activities that are part of the organization's central core efforts, such as the delivery of program services or the establishment of ongoing relationships with clients or funders.

Use Volunteers and/or Interns. Organizations may use volunteers or student interns to complement the efforts of regular staff and provide special expertise. Immigrant Welfare League used volunteers with special language skills to start a low-budget literacy program for which no public funding was available, but for which the agency expected public programs to be developed. Similarly, organizations may use student interns to deliver services in collaboration with experienced staff, undertake special management projects, or provide staff support for board committees at a lower cost than would be possible with regular staff. At times, Youth Outreach had more than twenty student interns working in the agency in both administrative and clinical service positions.

These approaches provide organizations with flexibility and additional resources. They also serve as effective recruitment strategies for securing new staff that will need only a minimum of orientation to the organization. However, the number and qualifications of available volunteers or student interns tend to fluctuate considerably over time. In the case of Youth Outreach, the strategy appeared to interfere with the agency's ability to maintain performance standards and created difficulties in living up to contractual service obligations.

Develop and Train Staff. Organizations may train, develop, and otherwise attempt to upgrade their existing staff. This strategy may take several forms. If the organization already has some staff with the necessary expertise or can hire consultants, the training and development can occur internally within the organization. In this case, training and debriefing sessions can also provide feedback about problems encountered in the field and serve as an informal needs assessment process.

Otherwise, organizations can pay partial tuition and professional membership fees for existing staff members, which adds to operating costs. Youth Outreach used both of these approaches. However, even with such staff development efforts, organizations encounter difficulty in securing trained staff, especially service staff with appropriate language skills or with ethnic or racial backgrounds that match client characteristics. These problems are particularly acute when organizations cannot pay competitive salaries, as is frequently the case for smaller nonprofits in the human service fields.

Exploit Staff Turnover. Finally, as noted in Chapter Ten, organizations may use staff turnover (deliberately or opportunistically) to deal with cash-flow problems and other budget problems and to meet changing program demands associated with the grants and contracts system. However, the turnover is costly in terms of finding and training new staff. All of the social service agencies emphasized the difficulties of finding staff members with appropriate skills, except for Christian Therapists, which had developed a special recruitment pool of interns.

Establish Internal Organizational Leadership and Decision Structures. As shown in Chapter Ten, restricted grants and contracts require a high level of management efforts within short time frames. These demands and the nature of transaction costs associated with the restricted funding system have major implications for the structure of internal organizational leadership, decision making, strategic planning, and coordination of efforts. There is an extensive literature on the development of nonprofit leadership types and structures and on the need for strategic planning. However, most of it is prescriptive rather than descriptive or analytical (Heath and Associates, 1988; Knauft, Berger, and Gray, 1991; Bryson, 1988).

Perhaps for that reason, there is also considerable disagreement about how well nonprofits are managed. Some (for example, Drucker, 1989, 1990) claim that nonprofits are likely to be managed better than other types of organizations because they are directed more explicitly by the organization's mission (see also Steinberg, 1987). This is consistent with Wood's (1981) finding that leaders of nonprofits can lay claim to special sources of legitimacy when they are able to link their actions explicitly to the organization's central values as expressed in its mission.

Others (for example, Bennett and DiLorenzo, 1989) argue that nonprofits are managed less well than other types of organizations because managers and directors do not have adequate incentives for implementing effective and efficient strategies. Bryson (1988) takes a somewhat different approach by emphasizing the difficulties of strategic planning in nonprofits, a conclusion that is consistent with my observations. He argues that the diverse constituencies and broad organizational goals of nonprofits (and of public agencies) make it difficult to apply strategic planning approaches from the business sector and that few alternative models exist.

Two sets of issues are involved: (1) the structure of decision making among the organization's staff members and (2) the extent to which the organization's board exerts effective influence over strategic decisions. My findings suggest that the way in which these problems are resolved differs by service field. In the social service field, the provision of ongoing services to a client population and the frequent access to reliance on centralized and institutional funding sources mean that administrative control easily reverts to executive directors or key administrative staff members. As a result, the agency's board members, volunteers, or program staff are left to play more peripheral or adjunct roles (see also Hartogs and Weber, 1978).

As argued in Chapter Ten, some of these tendencies toward centralized control are counterbalanced when organizations operate diverse program activities and have a large number of staff members. These features require some degree of internal delegation of authority to mid-level staff members. That reduces the direct control of executive directors, but it increases the likelihood that internal coordination may falter.

In community development organizations, similar tendencies toward centralized control exist, especially if they rely on institutionalized funding sources. But for community development organizations, they are attenuated by the need to validate the organization's claim to represent residents and institutions in a particular geographical area. This mandate forces the organization to pay greater attention to a broad range of outside actors, including some who do not provide ongoing funding. The need to incorporate broader community interests provides greater leverage and more clearly defined functions to the organization's board. Board members also have more explicit vested intersts in moving the organization in specific directions to meet their own interests than is likely to be the case for social service agencies.

Centralize Control. As Chapter Ten showed, organizations may deliberately employ a highly centralized structure with full and explicit control in the hands of the executive director in order to coordinate boundary-spanning activities and ensure a consistent image of the organization with outside decision makers. Among the social service agencies, Hispanic Youth Services and Minority Search illustrate this pattern. They have the most explicit entrepreneurial approach among the case-study organizations, and both emphasized the need to maintain a well-articulated image in order to position themselves in their respective funding arenas.

Similar motivations account for the centralized control exercised by Community Renewal. It emphasizes the need to coordinate its activities with the interests of its primary donor. African-American Neighbors also maintains a relatively high degree of centralized control, in this case justified by the need to direct the organization through the perilous waters of local politics and race relations.

Less deliberate examples of centralized structures develop by default when most outer-directed, nonservice tasks gravitated toward the director because the organization is not sufficiently large or well organized to delegate these tasks to others. Immigrant Welfare League exemplifies this pattern among the social service agencies. Alcohol Treatment also falls into this category, most likely because its stable reliance on one major source of public funding means that its environment is stable, predictable, and easy to manage centrally.

The three organizations relying mainly on special events (Preservation Council, Hispanic Neighbors, and New Town Sponsors) fall into this category among the community development organizations. All three had very small staffs (one to three persons) who ended up with responsibilities for central coordination of activities. That was especially important for the first two of these organizations because most of their activities involved extensive reliance on numerous volunteers.

The centralization strategy can work well in terms of securing ongoing funding, but it becomes problematic if directors or key staff members do not devote enough time to some of these central functions, cannot do them systematically, or encounter difficulties in maintaining or creating external contacts. Director vacancies and turnovers may create especially difficult problems under this strategy.

Decentralize Control. Organizations may implement a decentralized organizational structure in order to ensure that specialized programs are operated appropriately and that supervisors have a narrow enough span of control. In more elaborate formats, decentralized control involves the use of team structures or group decision making at some or most levels of the organization, ranging from client contacts to program decisions and networking with the larger community. The latter approach allows organizations to tap into a large number of different networks and to build consensus about difficult decisions, such as selecting staff for vacant or new positions and developing new program or funding initiatives.

Youth Outreach (with its team structure of decision making) and Christian Therapists illustrate this approach among the social service agencies. The former used the process deliberately as a mechanism for attending to client needs and staff participation in decision making. The latter allowed the same approach to develop by default when it vested control over key resources in the hands of individual staff members.

Two of the community development organizations had fairly elaborate structures of decentralized organizational structures. In Economic Development Commission, the executive director limited his involvement to part-time in order to serve as consultant to private funders and other community organizations. To do so, he transferred authority to several assistant directors and encouraged them to develop their own direct relationships with funding sources. United Residents operated with two executive directors and complex, overlapping board structures. These features allowed the organization to incorporate wide participation by diverse community interests.

However, decentralized control requires careful attention to coordination and integration to ensure that the diverse efforts cohere with overall organizational goals. It also requires intense levels of communication among the various administrative levels (up and down) and a commitment to joint decision making. In addition, as staff members develop networks and boundary-spanning abilities of their own, they become highly attractive to other organizations, and the organization may lose their expertise when they are hired away.

Develop Philosophy and Role of Board. The internal structure of decision making also has important implications for closely related questions about how organizations develop and maintain service philosophies and what role their boards play in developing initiatives. Nonprofits do not have owners who are legally liable for the actions of the organization, as do private business organizations. Nonprofit articles of incorporation specify the mechanisms by which the organization establishes formal responsibility for ensuring that it continues to qualify for tax-exempt status. Most formal organizational charts for nonprofits indicate that boards of directors are vested with responsibility for establishing overall policies and for ensuring that the organization's mission and philosophy are articulated and implemented (Carver, 1990; Herman and Van Til, 1989).

However, as noted previously, social service agencies with a high reliance on public funding or other institutionalized funding sources tend to centralize these decisions in top management staff and allocate a more peripheral role to the board. This assessment is confirmed by Hartogs and Weber's (1978) conclusion that one of the ways in which government funding affects nonprofit social service agencies is by reducing the leadership role of boards. It is also consistent with the high priority that technical assistance providers give to the need for board development and the widespread concern about management by default and ineffective boards (Carver, 1990). There is considerable uncertainty, then, as to when or whether boards do perform leadership functions.

In spite of the small number of organizations included in the case-study project, I was able to identify a variety of board structures and functions. A few of the boards appeared to approach the standard model in which boards exercise at least some explicit policy functions. However, other patterns were more prevalent: limited and highly specialized function (primarily for fund-raising), symbolic role in maintaining legitimacy, and as a direct tool for achieving the organization's mission. I review each of these strategies.[1]

Create Professional Board with Independent Functions. The traditional model of nonprofit boards vests them with primary responsibility for setting policy and exercising oversight. Under this model, boards represent community interests and serve as a forum for these interests to be negotiated and eventually incorporated into organizational activities. In practice, boards do include members with connections to a variety of potential funding sources (corporate, ethnic fraternities, foundations, public funding), substantive experience and interest in the organization's program fields, and expert knowledge in fiscal, legal, and management matters (Carver, 1990).

The model requires a relatively large board to ensure the necessary range of expertise and constituency groups, active committee structures to make effective use of diverse board expertise, participation of key staff in board meetings to maintain full communication with operations, and development of ongoing relationships between individual board members and key staff members on particular issues. In principle, the structure allows the organization to secure ongoing private funding, undertake new program initiatives with the active support of the board, and promote consensus about new directions. To be effective, the strategy requires board leadership that is relatively independent of the executive director.

Only two of the case-study organizations, Youth Outreach and Christian Therapists, approached this model. In both cases, there were occasions during which the boards exercised strong policy roles. For example, Youth Outreach implemented a major new program component at the direct initiative of a board member, and the board of Christian Therapists rejected the staff's proposed group practice model, which would have resulted in a major restructuring of the agency. However, these occasions were episodic and rare, and most initiatives came from staff members, although they were undoubtedly shaped by how staff members expected board members to view particular developments. The case studies suggest that an independent board role will be difficult to implement for organizations with high reliance on government funding, because of the time frames and mutual dependence associated with that type of funding.

Several boards experienced problems of inactivity or conflict over the organization's direction. These occasions appeared to coincide with rapid growth, the development of major new program directions at the initiative of the executive staff without board involvement, and serious problems in meeting funder requirements with a loss of ongoing funding. Persistent conflict or inactivity also occurred among organizations that incorporated multiple or split client constituencies on the board. In these cases, the organization may face a board where some members become alienated or find themselves excluded from program decisions. The result may significantly affect the organization's subsequent ability to secure funding, especially private funding. Several of these features were present for Immigrant Welfare League.

Create Limited, Specialized Boards. Several of the organizations used specialized structures in the form of auxiliary boards for accomplishing limited tasks related to fund-raising, special events, and other resource mobilization. This is a traditional part of board structures and operates in tandem with the type of independent board described above. Generally, auxiliary boards have representatives on the governing board, but are otherwise formally excluded from participating in policy decisions.

Both Youth Outreach and Immigrant Welfare League had auxiliary boards of this type. The former agency had three affiliated boards composed mainly of young corporate executives and professionals who organized special events for the agency: a large and active predominantly white board, a small, but relatively active Hispanic board, a very small and struggling African-American board. Immigrant Welfare League had three operating auxiliaries, down from five several years earlier. Each was expected to raise $10,000 for the organization through special events but rarely did so. The vast volunteer committee structures used by Preservation Council and Hispanic Neighbors as part of their special event activities approximate the role of auxiliary boards, but they were not given that title.

The use of auxiliary boards can be most effective if they establish a separate identity and internal reward system. Preservation Council and Hispanic Neighbors appeared to have done so for their volunteer commit-tees, as had Youth Outreach with its largest auxiliary. However, the latter agency's two other auxiliaries and those of Immigrant Welfare League were less successful—they found it difficult to attract and keep active members.

If successful, auxiliary boards may also serve to develop leadership for broader organizational or community activities and create a symbolic role for particular constituencies who otherwise have little opportunity to partici-pate in or occupy top leadership positions in governing boards. That strategy may explain the prevalence of women's boards in many large nonprofit institutions. It was the explicit reason why Youth Outreach developed its Hispanic and black auxiliary boards. In these cases, auxiliary boards also serve as a basis for recruitment to the governing board and provide a structured opportunity for expanding the overall diversity of the board.

Use Boards for Symbolic Value. Whatever the specific utility of individual boards, nonprofits need boards for their symbolic value. Boards serve to certify to the general public, and the Internal Revenue Service in particular, that the organization has established formal mechanisms for ensuring that it operates appropriately and continues to deserve its status as a tax-exempt organization, especially if also eligible for receiving tax-deductible dona-tions as a charitable organization. Indeed, this symbolic role may be the primary function of the board. Three of the case-study organizations approx-imated this model.

Community Renewal (as described in Chapter Seven) had a very large board (more than seventy-five members) of prestigious and clout-heavy indi-viduals. The organization's close affiliation with the equally powerful and prestigious community institution justified their involvement. The board served to provide legitimacy and had considerable symbolic value, but it was not a governing board by any definition of the term. Nor did it participate in any direct fund-raising activities. Most likely, the organization was able to maintain such a large and prestigious board because it demanded very little from board members in return for listing their names on its letterhead.

Alcohol Treatment and Immigrant Welfare League also approximated this model, but not so explicitly. Both executive directors expressed some frustration in having to work with board members who did not fully under-stand the agency's programs or purposes. In the case of Alcohol Treatment, the board was composed of local residents who rarely had other positions of leadership or much experience with the organization's programs. The board of Immigrant Welfare League was composed of second- and third-generation immigrants, while clients and staff were almost entirely first-generation im-migrants with very different experiences and expectations.

In both cases, board members seemed to face problems of purpose and involvement. In their search for purpose, they made considerable de-mands on staff members and on the director's time, energy, and patience.

Occasionally, the directors viewed these demands not only as interfering with the more pressing work of serving clients and meeting funder requirements, but as inappropriate or even self-serving and misleading.

The preoccupation with board development that is evident in the technical-assistance literature (Carver, 1990) suggests that these types of problems may be fairly typical in smaller, less sophisticated nonprofits, especially if they are also rooted in local neighborhoods or minority populations. Larger, more prestigious nonprofits are likely to have much greater access to "downtown" board members with extensive board experiences and practice in exercising leadership. Youth Outreach had such a board, allowing it to approximate the independent board model described previously. Hispanic Youth Services was moving in that direction at the time I finished the data collection.

Use Boards as Program Component. The final model I encountered involved defining board activities as an integral component of or instrument for accomplishing the organization's primary purpose. This model seemed most congruent with how directors of community development organizations viewed their boards, with the exception of Community Renewal and its symbolic board. However, it also characterizes two of the social service agencies.

Six of the community development organizations, as well as Hispanic Youth Services, viewed the involvement of community institutions on the board and the use of community sites for organizational programs or activities as an important part of linking the organization to the community. Most took the argument a step further and defined these links as mechanisms for instituting structural change at the community level and engaging in the difficult task of community building. Most of the community development directors and board chairs explicitly acknowledged community linkage as a major goal of the organization and viewed the board as one of the most important mechanisms for achieving it.

Minority Search seemed to fit this model as well, although it did not articulate it as explicitly as the other organizations. Nevertheless, Minority Search argued that the governing and advisory boards served as major vehicles for making corporations aware of the agency's services and for recognizing their own needs to recruit and train minority managers. Efforts to create such awareness were integral to the organization's major purpose. By adding new corporations to these boards, Minority Search expanded its opportunity to make its message heard and obtain access to new placements.

In all cases, someone in a key leadership position, usually the executive director, exercises strong control over the organization but with the active cooperation of at least some members of the board. The director's work with the board becomes effectively another program of the organization. However, it is a difficult role for directors to play. On the one hand, they must involve diverse constituency groups and give each a sense of purpose, participation, and leadership. That means they must create leadership opportunities and attribute leadership to others. On the other hand, directors must also ensure that the organization maintains direction and sufficiently unified leadership to avoid internal power struggles and stalemates. That means they must exercise leadership directly themselves. The balance is difficult to maintain.

Challenges in Managing the External Environment

Organizations must also address contingencies associated with particular funding sources and seek to manage their external environment more generally. They must decide how to link the priorities of funding sources to organizational missions and client or community needs, how to develop resource flexibility and cushion themselves against funding jolts, and how to engage in networking and other boundary-spanning activities in order to develop and maintain resources. Table 11.3 lists these challenges and the associated strategies and caveats.

Link Funding Priorities to Mission and Client/Community Needs. The effective delivery of human services requires fairly tightly coupled relationships between nonprofit service providers and public funders, in order to ensure that funder priorities reflect client or community needs as closely as possible and that the organization's mission is consistent with both of these. The case studies suggest that such coordination and linkages are especially difficult to create if organizations rely on a variety of funding sources or on multiple restricted grants or contracts.

Although all of the organizations had problems along these lines, they appeared to be more prevalent among the social service agencies. These agencies have access to ongoing funding from external organizations, especially public agencies, and may therefore easily encounter disarticulation between funder priorities and their own mission. The community development organizations were less likely to view public funding sources as equally secure. They were more likely to expect continuing support from groups with vested interests in the organization and its activities, increasing the likelihood of a tight fit between the priorities of funding sources and the primary purpose of the organization.

The Bottom-Up Approach. Organizations may seek to use a client-driven approach, in which they attempt to maintain close communication between service-level staff and the key administrators who have central responsibility for developing grant and contract proposals. Such communication structures may counteract the tendency to decouple the delivery of services from the maintenance of funding relationships. Short lead times associated with

**Table 11.3. Challenges, Strategies, and Caveats Associated with
Managing External Resources.**

Challenge: Link Funder Priorities, Mission, Needs

Strategy	Caveats
Bottom-up, client-driven approach	Easily disrupted or subverted
Marketing approach to repackage activities	Costly if revealed to funder
Selection approach to match mission	Threatens missions, client needs, resources
Accidental approach	Unanticipated directions

Challenge: Create Flexibility, Cushion Funder Jolts

Strategy	Caveats
Develop private funding	Uncontrollable donations
Seek markets for commercial services	Secure organizational control
Expand existing public funding	Requires funder trust
Combine grants/contracts	Requires narrow, priority target populations
Centralize control over reporting	Encourages errors or abuse
Disaggregate files, customize reports	Staff training, assessments, abuse
Cash-flow crisis procedures	Cost, long-term impact

Challenge: Expand Networking, Boundary-Spanning Activities

Strategy	Caveats
Seek political contacts	Requires legitimacy, high-level efforts, may backfire
Seek contacts with funder staff	Requires competent staff
Seek referral networks with other nonprofits	Demanding if fully implemented
Create joint programs with other nonprofits	Complex, difficult to evaluate
Copy features from other nonprofits	May not meet client needs

Source: Case-Study Project.

grant and contract work can otherwise interfere with using more formal needs assessments (or other mechanisms for determining client needs) to guide decisions about how to restructure proposals for existing funding relationships or develop approaches to new funding sources.

Even so, the bottom-up approach seems to be followed intermittently, at best, and is easily compromised. It requires a high level of commitment to maintain effective communication and to share decision making. It also consumes a great deal of staff time. Youth Outreach could do so because it had unrestricted private funding available and could also use such funds to initiate new program developments. Most of the other organizations did not show a similar level of formal commitment to assessing client needs. The analysis of restricted grants and contracts revealed no contract amendments that reflected changing client needs, and most proposals seemed to contain only minor modifications of the previous proposal for the same program.

The Marketing Approach. In one version of the marketing strategy, the organization takes what it is currently doing and repackages it with new terminology that fits "hot" funder priorities or emerging market demands. Several of the organizations pursued this strategy with funding success in terms of increased funding, and Hispanic Youth Services did so systematically. If centrally controlled without the involvement of service staff, the approach may have little impact on what the organization actually does. Although perhaps preserving the mission of the organization, new funder initiatives or program developments may be new in name only, not in approach, service structure, or client outcomes. To the extent that organizations follow this approach, funders will find it difficult to accurately assess the effectiveness of new program initiatives. There are limits to how far nonprofits can take this approach, because funders may withdraw their support if they find that their priorities are implemented in name only.

The Selective Approach. In the more common version of the marketing strategy, the organization uses its perceptions of market demands by funders or fee-paying clients to select among the array of funding possibilities. In principle, the organization ought to use its mission to guide its choices, but my review of the case-study data suggests that this type of marketing approach may easily take on a life of its own. Although this approach is likely to be successful at least in the short run, organizations seem to find it difficult to maintain the primacy of their mission, and the strategy can endanger both mission and ability to meet client needs. Either or both of these failures may threaten the organization's access to other resources, such as client referrals or community support. Youth Outreach and Immigrant Welfare League illustrate this approach.

The Accidental Approach. Organizations may simply happen to be in the right place at the right time — for example, serving ethnic groups with large numbers of illegal aliens eligible for publicly funded legalization services, as was the case for Immigrant Welfare League. Or organizations may obtain funding before their programs have been fully developed, because they have access to inside information or similar opportunities coming their way. This was true for both Immigrant Welfare League and Youth Outreach. As a result (and similar to the second version of the marketing approach), the organization can find itself pursuing new directions with which its staff and board may feel uncomfortable. The strategy can also create problems in meeting funders' expectations about program performance.

Provide Flexibility and Cushioning Against Funding Jolts. Fiscal contingencies associated with the restricted grants and contracts system place a high premium on access to flexible funding and reserves to cushion against funding jolts (Meyer, 1982). Differences in the predictability and controllability of funding sources also mean that nonprofit managers must continuously explore a variety of short- and long-term resource strategies. I identified several such strategies, ranging from attempts to increase nonpublic funding sources to efforts to overcome specific problems associated with government grants and contracts.

Develop Unrestricted Private Funding. Most of the organizations sought to use unrestricted private funding to subsidize public grants and contracts, to compensate for their failures to claim the entire contract amount (eliminate salvage), as bridge funding, or to support efforts for which no public funding is available. However, the case studies show that organizations often have limited success in controlling donations and that even sophisticated and formalized donation strategies may not result in predictable revenues.

One reason for this is that corporations, foundations, individual donors, and other sources of private donations are not usually subject to outside control (except through access to volunteer decision makers). In contrast to public funders, donors are not legally mandated to ensure that specific service efforts continue. As a result, they have less reason to provide ongoing funding or impose detailed management tasks on grantees. Organizational leverage, at least for social service agencies, originates less in their own service efforts than in the contacts they can establish with outside resource decision makers who have little or no investment in them or their capacity beyond the donation itself. For community development organizations, this pattern may also apply to funders from outside the community.

Staff, board members, or consultants devote great efforts to building access, but uncertainties and high failure rates encourage organizations to insulate their central core from these fund-raising activities. Social service agencies in particular tend to relegate donation efforts to special subunits within the organization (development departments) or to more peripheral untis (consultants, auxiliaries, or busy board members), or engage in them only sporadically.

Seek New or Predictable Markets for Commercial Services. Organizations may seek fees or other forms of earned revenues to reduce the impact of high failure rates of private fund-raising or the up-front management efforts associated with public grants and contracts. Fees and earned income also provide organizations with a market test of their services and exploit their service capacities to generate resources directly. Management practices and efforts associated with fees are less obviously shaped by institutional actors outside the organization than is the case for government grants and contracts and are therefore less standardized and more closely intertwined with internal features of the organization.

The analysis of two fee-dependent social service agencies (see Chapter

Five) reveals dramatic differences in their ability to secure fees on a continuing basis and in the extent of related programmatic and structural changes. Their experiences demonstrate the importance, as well as the difficulty, of linking missions and market niches and of creating loyal clients and staff in order to secure organizational control over this particular revenue source.

Seek Expansion of Existing Public Grants and Contracts. Organizations use a variety of mechanisms to seek expansion or prevent reductions in existing grants and contracts with public agencies. All seven of the case-study organizations with public grants and contracts submitted proposals that would have increased funding levels over the previous year. Most of these expansion proposals were fairly close to previous-year funding levels for the social service agencies, although Alcohol Treatment submitted a very ambitious proposal that would have more than tripled the contract and its own size. All of the community development organizations submitted proposals with significant increases in funding levels. These expansionist efforts were rarely successful, but administrators thought of them as strategies for preventing cuts and as bases for future negotiations with the funding source by building a claim for increased client needs and higher levels of service capacity.

A closely related strategy involves attempts to manipulate unit costs of services and therefore the organization's competitive edge in future grant and contract proposals. This strategy includes decisions about the qualifications and costs of staff to be used, how broadly to define program efforts (and thus costs), and which overhead costs to include. In all cases, the analysis suggests that organizations must cultivate relationships with funders over a period of time in order to develop sufficient trust and credibility to succeed in these strategies.

Combine Grants and Contracts. Organizations may combine grants from several sources by packaging them around concepts that appear to be salable to a variety of funders, so that services will be provided consistently even if a funder drops the program. This is easiest to do if the organization focuses on narrowly defined target populations with high funder priorities (such as low-income, minority youths, as in the case of Youth Outreach and Hispanic Youth Services). It is a much more difficult strategy to follow if the organization aims to serve a variety of different, nonoverlapping client groups with different service needs (for example, battered women, older alcoholic males, illegal aliens, and officially recognized refugees, as in the case of Immigrant Welfare League).

Centralize Control over Reporting. Organizations may institute systems of centralizing control over reporting, to ensure that it matches funder expectations and contract requirements as closely as possible. This allows the organization to overcome a variety of common problems, such as changes in the

levels of funding or service activities required by other contracts, staff vacancies, or events that bar access to program facilities (such as fires or strikes).
The strategy is most likely to be needed if the organization has a very high
reliance on very restrictive funding sources. However, very centralized systems of reporting are difficult to carry out conscientiously because of the
complexity of reporting requirements. Centralization is therefore subject to
error.

Disaggregate Reporting and Data Files. Whether or not organizations
choose to exercise central control over the actual reporting, they can maintain separate files and reporting systems for each funding source in order to
customize funding relationships. This practice has special implications for
how staff are trained to report and file service statistics and may prevent the
organization from developing a coherent perspective on its own activities.
Like centralized reporting, disaggregated reporting will impede the ability of
a funder to determine how its funded activities relate to the organization's
other activities, and, in extreme situations, open the door to abuse.

Establish Cash-Flow Crisis Procedures. Organizations can develop crisis
mechanisms for dealing with cash-flow problems, such as postponing the
payment of bills, establishing a line of credit, delaying paychecks selectively
for some staff members (usually central administrative staff), and borrowing
against endowments. However, these solutions are likely to have adverse long-
term impacts, such as limiting opportunities for future credit, creating
disaffection among staff, and reducing earned interest.

Some organizations see the development of marketable products or
services as a strategy for ensuring relatively stable cash flow. Another strategy
is the purchase of real estate to house the organization itself as well as rent-
paying tenants. However, each of these efforts involves direct expenditures,
expands the range of tasks and scope of management responsibilities, and
may detract from efforts to meet client needs and pursue organizational
missions.

Expand Networking and Other Boundary-Spanning Activities. To develop
and maintain resources, nonprofits must maintain accurate and current
information about the institutional environment in which they operate. The
large number of organizations active in the human services field, the multiple sources of funding available, and the short response time that many
funders impose make networking and other boundary-spanning activities
especially important. Most of these activities center around efforts to protect
existing funding relationships and develop opportunities for new ones. I did
encounter some networking and other boundary-spanning efforts aimed at
developing coordination and integration of services, but these were fewer
and less vigorously pursued.

Seek Political Contacts. Organizations may attempt to develop contacts that serve the explicit purpose of providing information about new funding and protecting existing funding relationships. For public funding, these efforts appear most effective if they involve contacts with elected officials who can pull the right strings. Legislative bodies exert resource control over public agencies, making them vulnerable and subject to this form of nonprofit leverage.

However, the competition for influence is great, and only a few nonprofits can successfully and persistently use political contacts for these purposes. The strategy also requires high-level efforts, usually those of the executive director and more rarely board members. It therefore serves to maintain central control and power in the hands of the director and leaves the organization vulnerable to turnovers in executive directors — as the director leaves, so do the contacts.

As the cases of African-American Neighbors and United Residents show, political influence may require perilous direct involvement in local politics. African-American Neighbors lost favor with the mayor and almost all its city grants and contracts. United Residents failed to maintain the support of a local alderman and key constituency groups and saw its Special Service Area taxing district voted out of existence.

Seek Contacts with Funder Staff. Organizations may focus on developing working relationships with the staff of funder organizations, usually at the program level. This strategy establishes the credibility and legitimacy of the organization's performance of services and serves to forewarn an organization about impending changes in funding levels or program requirements. These contacts also facilitate the resolution of problems that occur in documenting the organization's performances. However, it requires a relatively high level of competency among staff members to ensure that these contacts with funders enhance rather than endanger the organization's credibility.

Seek Referral Networks with Other Nonprofits. Organizations may seek to establish networks with other nonprofits for referral purposes. Networking is required or strongly encouraged by some funding sources in the social service field. Some social service agencies see them primarily as pro forma requirements that they need to document in order to have access to resource opportunities. It is unclear how much referral actually takes place in any event. Several studies suggest that few organizations are likely to fully implement effective referral networks. The fragmented service system requires extensive efforts to ensure that clients actually received the services for which they are referred, and effective referral systems threaten professional autonomy (Jacobs, 1990; Bush, 1988).

Develop Joint Programs with Other Nonprofits. I encountered several examples of joint programs, especially in the form of subcontractual relationships.

Most joint program structures are very complex and appear difficult to evaluate, especially if created specifically to secure a particular funding source. The relationships may be easiest to institute if the participating organizations have unrestricted funding available and do not need to secure funding at all costs.

Youth Outreach engaged in several such relationships with smaller agencies and viewed most of them as successful. It saw these efforts as strengthening the nonprofit sector and as part of its own service to the larger community. In contrast, Hispanic Youth Services resisted these types of relationships except for the explicit purpose of allowing it to provide the full range of services that it was required to make available to clients as part of its own contractual obligations.

Copy Features from Other Nonprofits. Several organizations adopted program models or administrative features from other organizations. This strategy appears to be effective if used carefully. For example, it may be easy to adopt a particular fee schedule from an agency that provides similar services, but more difficult to replicate a program from an agency that serves a different ethnic group. This strategy requires organizations to know about available models and to choose to adopt or adapt appropriate models developed by others rather than formulate their own. The approach provides organizations with ready-made legitimacy of service models and thus strengthens their efforts to secure resources, but it may also encourage them to adopt models that do not necessarily meet the needs of their own clients.

Summary

I have described the strategies available to nonprofit social service agencies and community development organizations in addressing several major organizational challenges and identified some of the limitations associated with the strategies. Some challenges derive from efforts to use internal resources effectively to match staff with program demands, establish internal organizational leadership and decision structures, and develop the philosophy and role of the board. The strategies that nonprofits use to address each of these challenges do not appear to differ systematically between the two service fields, although some are likely to be more easily available to larger and more established organizations than to smaller and newer ones.

Other challenges relate to organizational efforts to manage funding relationships and other external resources in order to link funder priorities to missions and community or client needs, provide flexibility and cushioning against funder jolts, and expand networking and other boundary-spanning activities. These challenges are more explicitly related to the industry in which organizations are active, because they involve service needs and funder priorities. As expected, on several of these dimensions, there are important differences between social service agencies and community development organizations.

The difficulty in using these strategies effectively and the differential ability to avoid problems associated with them help account for why the thirteen organizations included in the case studies had such diverse experiences with overall funding stability. Several of the organizations maintained overall stability in their funding sources. These organizations pursued the least risky strategies, balanced a mix of strategies, or paid special attention to the limitations of the strategies. They saw themselves as facing major problems in meeting the need for services and in maintaining their own infrastructure, but did so against a backdrop of funding stability that provided a measure of security.

Other organizations have grown rapidly by pursuing some of the funding strategies aggressively. Although each pointed to its growth as a major accomplishment and as recognition of its importance in the eyes of funders, it was also clear that the rapid growth imposed costs. Frequently, staff development, decision-making structures, and the maintenance of organizational philosophy lagged the rapid growth in funding and became sources of conflict and strain. In fact, most of the organizations that experienced rapid growth had also experienced dramatic declines in total funding during the period examined: Christian Therapists (in the mid 1980s), African-American Neighbors (in the early 1980s), and Hispanic Neighbors (during the 1970s). Immigrant Welfare League has done so recently (early 1990s). In each case, the decline illustrated drawbacks and limitations associated with the particular strategies the organization had pursued as part of its growth phase.

Note

1. The data are limited because I had most extensive contacts with executive directors and key staff members. The observations may therefore reflect management perspectives more than those of board members.

PART FOUR

The Impact of Complex Funding Patterns on Nonprofit Organizations

Drawing on in-depth case studies, survey findings, public spending analysis, and a range of conceptual approaches, this book has examined contingencies and strategies associated with different nonprofit funding sources, with special attention to the restricted grants and contract system and the implications of this system for management, planning, and general resource development. I began by asking what happens to organizations that appear to escape the discipline of market processes because they have access to subsidies in various forms, as nonprofit organizations do. The short answer is that donations and government grants probably do not substitute for market processes. Market systems are prevalent, but as normative models for nonprofit behavior rather than as descriptions of their actual behavior.

Instead, nonprofit social service and community development organizations are captured by resource relationships that depend critically on the reputations they maintain. However, the script that satisfies one type of funder may not meet the expectations of another or transfer from one field of service to the next. The overall system is dominated more by regulations and informal expectations of organizational behavior than by market processes linked to production or service activities. This argument might well extend also to for-profit organizations.

Several more specific findings also emerged. First, one of the persistent findings is that once nonprofits hit on a particular mix of funding sources, they tend to stay with that mix (Chapter Four). Variations in the number and types of funders drift over time because of changes in the environment to which managers may be more or less attuned. Some funding changes can be dramatic; but, on balance, nonprofit managers return, year after year, to the same funders. Continuity of funding allows the organization to routinize tasks. Establishing a new funding stream imposes a steep learning curve, high overhead costs, and risk of failure.

Second, some nonprofits are so tightly bound to a single funder that the nonprofit organization comes to function like a for-profit subsidiary—

serving primarily or entirely the interest of those who control its resources. The tight coupling encourages the nonprofit to adopt goals, structure, and vocabulary that mirror those of its sponsor. One of the case-study organizations—Community Renewal—exemplifies this model (Chapter Seven). Two others—Minority Search (Chapter Five) and New Town Sponsors (Chapter Six)—approach it.

Third, social service agencies and grass-roots community organizations that serve a range of clients and state their mission primarily in the language of philanthropy—serving the common good—generally seek a mix of funding sources in order to spread their bets and dampen the impact of fluctuations in any single funding stream. Most of the remaining case-study organizations fit this model. Individual funding streams can be quite volatile, especially most forms of donations (Chapter Seven), followed by special events (Chapter Six), fees (Chapter Five), government grants and contracts (Chapter Eight), and United Way support—in approximately that order. The absolute magnitude and relative stability of each funding stream determine how attractive it is to nonprofits. Smaller and/or less stable streams may nevertheless be appealing when they provide discretionary income. Fees, individual donations, and foundation grants are among the least restrictive funds that traditional, philanthropic nonprofits can pursue. Government contracts are the most restrictive (Chapter Nine).

Fourth, public funding is the driving force for many nonprofits active in these two fields. Because of its relative magnitude, it easily comes to govern the core activity of organizations that obtain it (Chapter Eight). Because public grants and contracts demand high levels of management efforts, other activities are often subordinated to them or brought into a division of labor dictated by the structure of public contracts (Chapter Nine). A few nonprofits may evolve toward a specialized niche where they serve only public funders. There are countervailing reasons, however, for most nonprofits to avoid complete dependency on government contracts. Such funding is stable over the near term, but subject to drastic interruptions on political grounds or changes in policy priorities. Government funding also contributes to cash-flow and other financial contingencies that nonprofits must counteract by seeking other revenue sources or accumulating reserves (Chapter Ten).

Fifth, the relationship between nonprofits and their funders is reciprocal in the sense that each depends on the other (Chapter Three). The terms of the exchange relationship, however, are not that of simple mutualism. Tightly bound nonprofits that are virtual extensions of their funders are heavily dominated by their funders and voice the same ideology. The more participatory community organizations have to balance their responsibility to local residents against their responsibility to funders, especially if they are located in a poor residential area (Chapter Eight). Community organizations located in more affluent areas often have the best of both worlds (Chapter Seven). Their clients are their primary funders although the exchange is couched in terms of broad community goals rather than narrow personal interests. Funders from outside the area add an increment of discretionary income that helps make the generalized pattern of exchange work.

The terms of exchange between social service agencies and their funders are often murky and subject to continual negotiations. Relationships with public funders can approach mutualism, but on occasion will be subject to political contingencies that cannot be controlled by either nonprofit managers or accessible political leaders. Individual donors are quite unpredictable for these organizations, although some can be co-opted into the nonprofit organization as board members and regular supporters. Access to the United Way system is difficult, but once such access is obtained, this system probably becomes the most reliable and constant source of funds for social service agencies. Special events and fees give fiscal latitude within which the agencies may negotiate special agreements with more institutionalized funders. The challenges of managing external funding relations are further complicated by the need to structure internal resources appropriately (Chapter Eleven).

In this concluding section, I elaborate on the conceptual framework that emerged from the analysis. I also examine implications of the findings for theory, research, practice, and policy.

TWELVE

Assessing the Structure and Management of Nonprofit Funding Relations

The findings presented in this book point to three broad conclusions about nonprofit management of funding relations. First, detailed analysis of fees, special events proceeds, donations, and government grants and contracts shows that major nonprofit funding sources vary notably in their structural characteristics and in the management contingencies they present. Second, the extent to which any given funding source exhibits a particular set of structural characteristics or contingencies varies among service fields. Third, conceptualizing and measuring outcomes for individual organizations require careful attention to how organizations manage environmental contingencies.

Assessing the Approach

The broad sweep of these conclusions makes it important to acknowledge the strengths and weaknesses of my particular approach. I draw on a wide range of research findings about nonprofits, including several carefully designed surveys. However, I rely most extensively on in-depth case studies of how a baker's dozen of accessible, medium-sized, nonprofit organizations with distinctive funding profiles in two fields of service have experienced and managed their funding relationships over time.

This approach emphasizes in-depth analysis of complex, dynamic forces but requires extra care in generalizing the findings to other nonprofits (smaller or larger, located in other communities with different traditions of nonprofit-public relationships, active in other fields of service, relying on different combinations of funding sources, or with other patterns of funding stability and change). My strategy for picking organizations for the case studies explicitly acknowledges the importance of several of these features; that is, the organizations were selected so that they would differ systematically in field of activity, major funding sources, and funding stability.

The underlying conceptual model views service fields and funding sources as independent but interacting conditions that influence funding stability (the dependent variable) through the intermediary variables of strategic management. A rigorous statistical test of this hypothesis is not feasible, because it would require longitudinal data from a large number of diverse organizations. Even if feasible, it would not be appropriate, because such a deductive approach would inevitably overlook important dynamic forces at work. An interactive model requires a grounded theory approach (Glaser and Strauss, 1967), to allow a careful examination of dynamic processes and to generate new insights and conceptual clarity. Thus, the longitudinal focus for the case studies and the variety of data sources examined allow me to track and analyze organizational experiences with specific funding sources over time. This, in turn, makes it possible to assess and interpret mutual interactions between these experiences, external conditions or events, and internal management structures and decisions.

The grounded theory approach also does not require organizations participating in the study to fit perfectly the conceptual profiles, as a true experimental design would. The organizations approximate the profiles but do not match them fully. I use the selection criteria mainly as heuristic devices for ensuring sufficient variations among the organizations to allow for systematic comparisons of contingencies associated with different funding sources and varying environmental conditions.

To examine how these contingencies affect organizations also requires attention to their size and location. The former shapes internal capacity, and the latter constitutes a part of the environment. All the case-study organizations are of medium size in terms of revenues, and all are located in the Chicago area. My decision to limit the selection of organizations in this manner in part reflected a number of practical constraints,[1] but there are also good conceptual and theoretical reasons for making these choices.

Medium-sized organizations are not so large that their sheer size and complexity impose more than a minimum division of labor, formalization, and adherence to bureaucratic procedures. They are not so small that they become a direct extension of a single staff member or small group of volunteers. A focus on medium-sized organizations therefore allows for a more systematic examination of the range of mechanisms by which the imperatives of funding sources affect implementation of organizational goals, structures, and management strategies.

Similarly, a fuller understanding of how funding dynamics operate in one community, in this case Chicago, makes it possible to generalize to other communities as long as key underlying theoretical dimensions are clearly articulated and incorporated into the analysis. I have sought to do that by emphasizing the distinctive relationships that characterize nonprofit-public interactions along two major conceptual dimensions: the presence or absence of direct public dependence on nonprofits and of strong proprietary sector activities.

In Chicago, the absence of a strong proprietary sector in social services has allowed public agencies to maintain a long history of close and direct relationships with nonprofits, so that the latter provide the bulk of publicly funded services. In other communities, public sector agencies may be less dependent on nonprofit service providers, because public agencies themselves deliver much higher proportions of social services or because proprietary service agencies are more prominent. The reasons for these variations most likely involve complex combinations of historical traditions, timing, definitions of acceptable service standards, and relative cost of operations.

In Chicago, the clout of powerful private interest groups and the persistence of residentially and turf-based local politics and patronage systems have created a mixture of mutual exploitation and cooperation between nonprofit community organizations and the public sector. In smaller communities, direct citizen participation in local politics might alleviate the need for formal community organizations to play this type of symbiotic or intermediary role.[2]

In short, it is in local communities that nonprofit service fields take on their specific environmental characteristics. My characterization of the social service and community development fields in Chicago most likely applies to other communities as well, although the degree of public dependence on nonprofits may be higher or lower and the presence of proprietary interests stronger or weaker in these other communities. Certainly, other service fields vary along these dimensions as well. If so, structural characteristics of particular funding sources should vary in predictable ways among communities or service fields along the lines discussed throughout this volume and summarized here. By relating the findings to the structural characteristics of the environment in which individual nonprofits operate, the analysis achieves broad relevance to the full range of nonprofits.

Elaborating on the Conceptual Framework: Three Conclusions

This conceptual framework embraces the three broad conclusions identified previously. The first two form the driving force for the entire analysis and draw on most of the findings presented in this book. That is, I specifically set out to examine how structural differences among funding streams and environmental variations among service fields jointly affect strategic management of nonprofits. Each of the three has important implications for theory and research.

Diverse Characteristics of Nonprofit Funding Sources

The resource dependency perspective on organizations — namely, that organizations depend on the exchange of financial and other resources for their continued operation — forms the basis for my analysis. Most of the literature on resource dependency focuses on how the exchange of such resources translates into degrees of interorganizational power and control (Pfeffer and Leong, 1977; Pfeffer and Salancik, 1978; Provan, Beyer, and Kruytbosch, 1980). Resources that are relatively uncertain, irreplaceable, and account for a disproportionate share of all resources will exercise the highest level of influence and absorb most of the energy devoted to resource relationships.

The locus of control over external resource relationships has corresponding implications for the internal distribution of power (Pfeffer and Salancik, 1978). That is because individuals responsible for maintaining those external relationships that provide the most critical resources for the organization will be able to exercise the highest level of power in the organization, especially if they are able to reduce the amount of uncertainty associated with the resource. They have internal leverage because they can deprive the organization of access to the resources by how they manage the exchange relationship, whether by design or default.

My findings support these expectations and the general argument that an organization that depends heavily on an exchange relationship with one particular funding source will be subject to considerable influence from that source. As a result, the organization most likely will seek to reduce its dependency on the source, minimize uncertainty by linking itself closely to the source, seek to gain some control over the source, or otherwise buffer itself from adverse actions or other developments originating with the source. Correspondingly, the organizational units responsible for maintaining the exchange relationship will command power in the organization.

These principles of resource dependency are likely to apply to all organizations, whether operating under proprietary, nonprofit, or public types of auspices. However, the case-study findings show that not just the relative amount of dependence and associated uncertainties are important. Resource relationships have qualitative attributes. They may be characterized along a number of separate dimensions, each of which has special implications for efforts to control and reduce resource uncertainty. In principle, although not always in practice, these qualitative aspects operate independently of the relative amount of funding involved. They reveal themselves most clearly when they are examined from the vantage point of nonprofits, because of the diversity of resource streams to which they have access.

Here I review five broad dimensions that have emerged from the analysis of individual funding sources described in Chapters Five through Eight and discuss their general application. Although the dimensions may be related to one another in predictable ways for specific funding sources, they need not be, and should be examined separately. Nor are they necessarily related to the relative degree of resource dependency. Rather, they describe contextual characteristics of funding sources that combine to form special funding arenas and establish distinctive parameters for organizational actions and control. In contrast, measures of resource dependency describe the relative success of individual organizations in manipulating these parameters, reflecting such characteristics as organizational size (and therefore organizational slack, expertise, and visibility), boundary-spanning activities, and strategic management.

Simplifying the Exchange Relationship Through Market Transactions. Resource relations differ in the extent to which they involve straight market transactions of goods and services for private (divisible) consumption or subsidy transactions in which public (indivisible) goods benefit broader or different population groups than those who pay for them. In market transactions, consumers of goods or services purchase them from producers who sell them in the open marketplace (perfect or otherwise) at a price that approximates the cost of production. Dues, fees, or sales receipts from consumers who pay the full cost of goods and services fall at one end of this dimension. Donations, grants, or third-party contracts that fully subsidize costs for consumers fall at the other end. Special event revenues are intermediary between these two extremes, because they involve a mix of market and subsidy transactions.

Market exchanges link revenue streams directly to what organizations produce and to the tastes and preferences of the consumers they serve. Producers can influence these exchanges, and hence their volume of revenues, by manipulating the quantity, quality, and price of what they produce and by targeting niches of consumers with particular types of preferences. Marketing efforts may achieve the same results by modifying how consumers perceive product characteristics.

Subsidy exchanges provide fewer opportunities for increasing revenue streams by manipulating consumer preferences, because third parties underwrite the production of goods and services but do not necessarily consume them. Under these conditions, consumers may not participate in the exchange decision at all. Rather, producers must satisfy subsidizers who have little opportunity to assess the relative merits of what they are subsidizing. Producers may therefore face contradictory incentives for manipulating the characteristics of their products, because subsidizers and consumers most likely differ in their preferences for specific services. In a more technical formulation, the organization's domain efforts (decisions about productivity and market niche) do not necessarily have direct implications for generating revenues.

Seeking Self-Similar Exchange Partners. Other complications arise from the fact that not all participants approach a given resource exchange in the same way. The findings on fees and donations show that organizations may find individual customers or donors more difficult to anticipate or control than organizational ones. Individuals differ from organizations on a number of traits that influence how exchange relations develop or operate—in the

multiplicity of interests to which they are accountable, the volume of resources to which they have access, the degree of formality and structure with
which they approach exchange relationships, and the processes by which
they make decisions about exchanges. Exchange relationships are likely to be
more isomorphic (self-similar) when both parties are organizations (especially similar types of organizations), because then mutual expectations will
be fairly clear-cut and understandable to participants. Exchanges linking
individuals and organizations (dimorphic relations) are subject to greater
uncertainty.

On this dimension, isomorphic versus dimorphic exchanges, lack of
isomorphism (DiMaggio and Powell, 1983) among exchange participants
confounds their ability to communicate or control the exchange relation.
These problems are widespread across all organizations, although partial
solutions do exist—most notably, in the large body of contract law. To
manage uncertainties associated with dimorphic exchange partners, organizations may use specialized marketing efforts that train and educate customers in making "wise" consumer decisions. These practices are institutionalized in consumer fraud legislation, small-claims courts, and other less formal
complaint structures through which individual customers can protest exchange relationships that fail to live up to their expectations. The safeguards
also protect those delivering goods or services by limiting grounds for
appeal. Similar safeguards exist for exchange relations among organizations
but are less well developed. Organizations are expected to know (and do
know) how other organizations operate, and the balance of power is more
evenly distributed. The expectations themselves are institutionalized, especially within organizational types.

Benefiting from Pervasive Exchange Relations. The nature of the exchange relationship (market versus subsidy) interacts with the characteristics
of the exchange partners themselves (isomorphic versus dimorphic). Some
participants limit themselves almost entirely to certain types of exchange
relations; for example, business organizations engage primarily in market
transactions, although some may also grant subsidies to nonprofits. In other
cases, the exchange can occur only in one particular direction; for example,
by law, only charitable nonprofits can receive tax-deductible donations. As a
result, business organizations, public agencies, nonprofits, or individuals are
likely to differ in whether, when, or with whom they engage in particular
types of exchanges.

On this dimension, common versus rare exchange relations, all business organizations have experience with generating earned revenues, but
relatively few have practice in managing subsidy revenues. If they do, it is
mainly from organizational units to which they are formally linked by
ownership and control within the same corporate framework. In contrast,
most government agencies and nonprofits have experiences with subsidy

revenues from outside bodies; somewhat fewer are likely to have practice in obtaining self-generated revenues.

As these examples suggest, the prevalence of any given revenue source is likely to vary for organizations under different types of legal auspices. For that reason, there may also be special patterns of prevalence in particular service fields, because some fields are dominated more by certain types of organizations than others. For example, the health field is overwhelmingly dominated by market exchanges, so that even subsidy relations (such as Medicare and Medicaid) operate under a market model, albeit with institutional control by those providing the subsidy. Only government agencies and nonprofit community development organizations are likely to have any experience with managing Special Service Area taxing districts, but it is a rare revenue source even for these types of organizations.

The prevalence of certain types of exchange relationships is important in part because it relates in obvious ways to the level of experience and expertise that organizations may have with managing particular funding sources. In turn, that may affect their success in generating revenues from the source. In part, prevalence creates normative expectations about the types of exchange relationships in which organizations, at least of this type, should engage.

Normative expectations facilitate processes of decision making because they identify tested and well-worn paths of action. For that reason, organizations also may find special opportunities in pursuing exchange relations that are rare among their counterparts, because they can create new structures for doing so with few obstacles in the form of institutionalized, external expectations. Of course, they may also encounter higher failure rates, because there are also fewer institutional safeguards in place.

Minimizing and Simplifying Competition. The degree and type of competition reflect several different forces, including how crowded the field of competitors is, how consolidated or institutionalized the funding sources are, and how open the competitive field is to new entrants. These characteristics establish the conditions under which individual organizations may then compete for specific funding sources and obtain a smaller or larger share of the pie.

The competitive field may be crowded or thinly populated by other organizations. The prevalence of a certain type of funding is closely related to the relative number of other actors who are competing for that type of revenue. Most nonprofits seek support from individual donors, making this a very crowded competitive arena. Somewhat smaller proportions pursue donations from foundations or corporate giving programs, special events, public funding, or fees and other commercial types of revenues, making these competitive arenas thinly populated.

Organizations can exercise control over this aspect of competition by focusing on funding sources for which there are few competitors or, alternatively, by increasing their share of crowded markets. Under the latter strategy, they try to strengthen their own appeal to exchange partners or undermine the appeal of competitors. When nonprofits describe the good things they accomplish for needy and deserving clients, they seek to enhance their appeal to potential donors. When their solicitations provide occasions for mentioning membership in the United Way, grants from major foundations, or involvement with government contracts, they trade on the recognition implied by such support and undermine the appeal of competitors who lack similar evidence of legitimacy.

Just as the number of organizations competing for a particular type of funding is important, so is the extent to which there are few or many specific sources (streams) for a particular type of funding. Revenue sources differ in the extent to which they are consolidated among few streams or fragmented among many. Individuals (donors, clients, or special events participants) constitute a highly fragmented funding source, with as many substitutes available as there are persons with suitable characteristics in the catchment area. In contrast, United Way organizations form a highly consolidated source: only one stream per community. Similarly, although several government agencies may purchase residential care and a few fund psychiatric care, many private health insurance programs cover psychiatric care. In this case, there are many more potential funding streams from which to generate subsidies for psychiatric care than for institutional care for children.

The more fragmented a funding source is, the more cumbersome it is to develop detailed information about all the potential streams and the less likely organizations are to know much about their competitors, because they tap different streams and do not encounter one another's claims. Both increase funding uncertainty. On the other hand, fragmented funding sources increase the opportunity to substitute one stream for another of the same type. This reduces the ability of a particular funding stream to dictate terms of the exchange, since it is not the only game in town.

A closely related aspect is whether the competitive process is protected or open. If competition is crowded and funding sources fragmented, new organizations may find it relatively easy to obtain access to the funding stream. Of course, the competitive process is rarely entirely open. Licensing requirements, legal definitions of charitable purposes, product safety regulations, or legally mandated funding criteria may limit opportunities to participate in a given resource exchange. Even so, many organizations, especially business organizations and others engaged in market transactions, obtain resources under relatively open competitive processes. They can enter into new resource relationships with relative ease, depending mainly on their expertise with the type of funding transaction and their appeal or familiarity to exchange partners.

However, a large or persistent influx of new competitors means that organizations already active in the exchange system will face escalating competition and therefore increased uncertainty in their existing resource relationships. To counteract such uncertainty, organizations may seek to create a protected competitive process, in which formal (or informal) arrangements ensure the continuity of the resource relationship and/or limit access for new entrants—a cartel. Membership in the United Way of Chicago gives member agencies a binding claim to available base funding, barring nonmembers from accessing the funds. Complex application processes ensure that government funding for social service agencies operates as a protected competitive system. Foundation or corporate support or government funding for community development organizations appears to operate like more open systems.

Under cartel-like structures, competition becomes a two-stage process: obtaining access to the cartel and increasing the share within the cartel. Competition exists, but with distinctive dynamics for each of these stages. Cartels are generally frowned on in the for-profit sector as interfering with open competition in the market. However, they develop there as well— through informal accommodations and agreements or through formal claims to special circumstances (for example, national security justifies limited competition in the case of military research and procurement contracts).

Systems of protected competition serve to reduce funding uncertainty by increasing the leverage that exchange partners exercise over one another. These systems reflect complex, highly institutionalized patterns of interdependencies and are clearly evident in subsidy exchanges between government agencies and nonprofit social service agencies for the provision of entitlement services to eligible clients. Perhaps these services are so important that they cannot be left to the open competitive process. More likely, nonprofit human service organizations have succeeded in establishing protected competitive systems because their focus on substantive goals and claim to mission-driven activities allow them to escape even symbolic adherence to the open competitive process.[3]

Maximizing Internal Discretion. Finally, exchange relations differ in whether they allow extensive or restricted internal discretion. Under cartel-like structures, those paying for the goods or products (whether through market or subsidy exchanges) cannot easily withdraw from the exchange. As a result, they cannot use such withdrawals (or the threat thereof) to exercise control over their exchange partners. That limits the range of direct actions they can take to ensure that the exchange continues to meet their interests or needs. Funders may use past performance to decide whether to expand or reduce the scope of future exchange agreements, but they need to consider the impact of such decisions on other members of the cartel and on their own long-term interests. Cutting off one subcontractor may make the funder more dependent on the remaining ones and less able to trade them off against one another. In the case of subsidy exchanges, funders may also lack direct knowledge of the quality or even quantity of services provided and therefore be unable to use such information effectively to control the resource relationship.

Under these types of limitations, funders resort to more direct efforts to ensure that proper procedures are followed or that specified activities are undertaken. That is what happens in the case of government grants and contracts and to some extent United Way funding as well. As my findings show, these funders place limits on acceptable expenditures, require particular types of procedures or staff qualifications, and demand idiosyncratic and highly detailed reporting systems (see Chapter Nine). These requirements restrict options and discretion for nonprofit managers who participate in the system and increase the amount of effort they must devote to managing funding relations.

These limitations on internal discretion provide government agencies with opportunities to monitor activities for which they are responsible but over which they have no direct control because they are removed from the actual delivery of services. The limitations and restrictions satisfy their need to document performance and accountability to legislative bodies and other sources of funds. For nonprofits, the management contingencies constitute trade-offs for operating within the security of a relatively protected competitive system.

In contrast, unrestricted donations for operating support, special event revenues, and most types of fee revenues (except when under institutionalized control, as in the case of Medicaid or Medicare) provide extensive latitude for nonprofit managers to structure internal organizational activities. Although all these types of funding sources may involve highly intensive management efforts to obtain and maintain, they maximize internal management control and freedom of choice.

Different types of funding sources reflect key underlying resource dimensions that point to mechanisms by which organizations may achieve funding predictability, control, and interdependence (leverage). The organization's degree of reliance on specific resources is important for such efforts, but so are contextual characteristics of the resource relationships. These include the nature of the exchange itself and its linkage to organizational domain efforts, the similarity of exchange partners, the pervasiveness of the exchange, the number of competitors involved, the consolidation and institutionalization of funding sources, the openness of the competitive process, and the level of discretion over internal management activities.

These resource features shape nonprofit management contingencies and strategies, because the characteristics and underlying dimensions become incorporated into the specific funding relationships. Consequently, they shape internal organizational structures, including the locus of control (especially the relative power of executive directors and board), the nature and intensity of management efforts, and the extent and nature of planning.

They also set parameters for interorganizational dependencies and control mechanisms. To the extent that funding sources reduce internal or external resource uncertainties, organizations will find them attractive in spite of the control, management difficulties, and work they impose.

Diverse Characteristics of Nonprofit Industries

The case studies illustrate general problems in controlling client-paid fee revenues and the trade-offs required for generating special events proceeds. They also demonstrate the volatility of most forms of donation revenues in contrast to the greater continuity in and predictability of United Way and government funding. However, in spite of these general observations, the case studies also reveal that similar funding sources may differ in the extent to which they fall at one or the other extreme of the resource dimensions discussed previously. These differences are shaped by a broad range of environmental contingencies that merge into systematic patterns according to the service field in which organizations are active. An adequate understanding of funding relationships therefore requires systematic attention to how structural characteristics of funding sources differ among service fields.

This argument has most direct relevance to service fields in which nonprofits are active, although I speculate that it has wider applicability. Proprietary organizations may also find that certain sources of revenue exhibit combinations of resource characteristics that vary according to the economic sectors in which they operate. However, proprietary organizations have access to a narrower range of funding sources than nonprofit ones. A narrow range is likely to favor the development of transferable, institutionalized approaches that can be promoted through management training programs and business schools. As a result, proprietary organizations may find greater continuity and consistency across revenue sources to which they have access than do nonprofits.

My documentation comes from a comparison of funding relations in the social service and community development fields. However, other nonprofit fields are likely to present their own combination of variations. As I show below, each of these service fields constitutes a somewhat distinctive organizational environment.

Nonprofit organizational environments differ on several key dimensions that may influence resource characteristics of funding sources. The nature of the activities themselves is important, but so are other features. I discussed two of these in Chapter Two when I argued that nonprofits are intimately linked to two driving forces in U.S. society: the scope and structure of public sector activities and the dominance of market models. These forces have special applicability to nonprofits and set broad parameters for their actions, but they do not operate uniformly across service fields. Several other aspects of organizational environments also differ among service fields. I discuss each of these in turn.

Nature of Activities: Client Services Versus Group Cohesion and Change.
Relatively few nonprofits are involved in the processing of raw materials or
other kinds of manufacturing activities. As most observers have noted, these
kinds of activities allow for tight coupling of organizational activities,
straightforward documentation of productivity, and therefore relatively un-
ambiguous measures of performance.

Instead, most nonprofits provide more or less intangible services, such
as day care, education, health care, counseling, community organizing, advocacy, and sociability. By definition, each of these activities constitutes a
separate service field. However, beyond this obvious point, the activities sort
themselves out along broader and more inclusive dimensions. The fields
range from those that depend heavily on a highly specialized, professional
labor force (for example, health or higher education) to those with few such
workers (for example, day care or community organizing). The more professionalized the service field, the more likely it is that organizations must
adhere to institutionalized, outside standards on a wide variety of criteria
(DiMaggio and Powell, 1983; Meyer and Scott, 1983). That limits internal
management discretion.

The activities differ also in the extent to which they can be assessed
against clear standards of performance and how easy it is to measure productivity. When performance standards are difficult to establish and observe,
market transactions take place under high levels of uncertainty that favor the
more trusted nonprofit service providers (Weisbrod, 1975, 1977).

For fields where activities involve direct client services, performance
standards may not be sufficiently well developed to determine the quality of
services, but the volume can be established. Counting the number of people
who have been processed by the organization (for example, those who have
been provided with days of day care or hours of counseling) makes it possible
to tie revenues directly to some type of productivity measure. Revenue
sources may therefore take on some aspect of market transactions, whether in
the form of direct client fees and service charges, third-party payment
systems, grants and contracts to subsidize volumes of service activities, or
donations from grateful recipients of past services (for instance, alumni).

In other fields where nonprofits seek to promote group cohesion (for
example, through community organization) or social change (through advocacy), standards of performance are very ambiguous. That makes it very
difficult to link revenue streams directly to performance or other measures of
productivity. Indirectly, a link may exist when the activities create and mobilize constituency groups whose loyalty and dedication to the organization
constitute critical resources. For example, community organizations define
their primary purpose as representing the interests of residents and organizations located in a particular geographical area. To the extent that organizations can identify and cultivate such constituency groups, they may secure
stable sources of subsidy revenues.

Direct Public Sector Dependence: Low Versus High. Other differences among service fields reflect the influence of two driving forces in U.S. society: government and business. Public sector activities in the United States vary greatly in scope and structure across different service fields. There are also local variations within specific service fields, reflecting timings, patterns of settlement, and other special circumstances. Nevertheless, for historical and ideological reasons, the public sector has been involved earlier, more exten-sively, and more directly in the provision of some services than others. For example, the public sector took early and full responsibility for elementary education and directly operated schools and closely related institutions, such as libraries. Over time, these direct responsibilities have expanded to include higher education, previously controlled entirely by nonprofits.

The United States has been a much more reluctant welfare state in assuming responsibilities for health and social services and for job training. In these fields, public efforts are limited to special groups that meet particu-lar eligibility requirements. The United States assumed these responsibilities later, less extensively, and with considerable reliance on nonpublic service infrastructures that were already in place at the time. In social services, the infrastructure was largely controlled by the nonprofit sector. In health, the infrastructure was controlled by a combination of nonprofit and for-profit entities, respectively hospitals and medical practitioners. In job training, the infrastructure was located mainly in for-profit organizations that trained their own workers, although the capacity for job training of most direct relevance to low-income or other specialized groups was located in public schools or nonprofit social service agencies.

In still other fields, such as environmental control, arts and culture, civil rights, housing, and community development, public sector responsibil-ities are even more recent and limited in scope. As a result, they have not been fully institutionalized and are still subject to considerable debate. These debates focus on the proper role of government vis-à-vis that of the private sector. Nonprofits are more actively involved in shaping the debate than in providing the public sector with access to service infrastructures. (Arts and culture may be an exception to this pattern, perhaps because public sector involvement is extremely limited and relatively unimportant.) Finally, public sector activities are more or less completely absent from such fields as philan-thropy and religion.

These variations in the scope and structure of public sector activities reveal the wide variety of relationships that nonprofits may have with public sector organizations. Nonprofits either compete with public sector organiza-tions (education), operate in partnerships with them through subsidy rela-tions (social service, health), define them as forces to be mobilized (civil rights, environmental issues, community development), or view them as alien to the primary purpose of the organization (philanthropy, religion).

Correspondingly, public sector dependence on nonprofit infrastructures may be low and limited to reducing public sector outlays (education); direct and high (social service); direct and mixed with dependence on for-profit infrastructures (health, job training); or low, indirect, and limited to setting and shaping agendas (civil rights, community development). These types and degrees of dependence determine whether and how much public sector funding is available to nonprofits as well as the leverage that nonprofits are likely to have over public sector agencies.

Funding is extensive and nonprofit leverage is direct in social services because the public sector has high, direct, and primary reliance on nonprofit infrastructures. The funding is high and nonprofit leverage is direct but lower in the health care field because the public sector relies extensively on nonpublic infrastructures but not exclusively on nonprofit ones. The funding is low and nonprofit leverage is indirect and highly politicized in community development, civil rights, and environmental issues because the public sector seeks to induce actions in the private sector and does not require direct access to service infrastructures. The funding is low and nonprofit leverage is minimal in education because the public sector maintains its own infrastructure.

These different patterns of relationships to the public sector help account for otherwise contradictory findings from various service fields. Geiger (1986) observes systematic and sizable differences between public and nonprofit institutions of higher education that coincide with their reliance on different funding sources. Hollingsworth and Hollingsworth (1986) reach the opposite conclusion — that nonprofit, public, and proprietary hospitals have become increasingly similar.

In other societies, the scope and structure of public sector activities, and therefore the leverage that nonprofits have over the public sector, may take different forms across the various service fields. For example, in societies with a state religion, the relationship between nonprofit churches and the public sector is likely to shift from one of alienation to one of competition. In societies with direct public responsibilities for all important social services, the relationship between nonprofit social service organizations may shift from one of partnership to one of competition, perhaps to the point of nonprofit irrelevance.

Relationship with the Private Sector: Limited Versus Complex. As this discussion suggests, service fields also differ in the type and range of relationships that exist between nonprofits and private sector organizations. In some service fields, notably education and social services, public and non-profit organizations dominate the service fields, and for-profit organizations have a very limited role. They may provide funding for nonprofits in the form of donations and other subsidies, because they view themselves as benefiting from the array of services that nonprofits provide in these fields. However, for-profit organizations do not have direct vested interests in these service fields. That is, they rarely compete directly with nonprofits, nor do nonprofit actions or services often affect directly their own critical resources. Their funding for any specific nonprofit organization is therefore likely to be episodic, uncertain, and difficult for the nonprofit organization to influence or control.

In other service fields (for example, health and job training), non-profits compete directly with for-profit organizations or engage in horizontal integration of services with them (for-profit health clinics refer patients to nonprofit hospitals, nonprofit job training agencies seek private sector placements for their trainees). The for-profit sector therefore has a vested interest in nonprofit activities, and the relationship between the two sectors takes on greater complexity. Moreover, in fields where the for-profit sector is actively involved in providing goods and services, it tends to dominate and impose marketlike transactions on nonprofits as well. As a result, even subsidy relations tend to take marketlike forms in these fields. For example, the Medicare and Medicaid systems both incorporate critical elements of consumer choice, while the Job Training Partnership Act uses a performance-based payment system.

In still other service fields, such as housing and community develop-ment, environmental control, and civil rights, the for-profit sector also has a vested interest in nonprofit activities. However, the basis is not direct com-petition between the two sectors, but the likelihood that nonprofit actions in these fields may affect the proprietary sector's own productive capacity, discretion, and access to critical resources. That is the case when nonprofit community organizations oppose (or support) private sector development projects, when environmental groups seek restrictions on industrial pollu-tion, or when civil rights organizations press for affirmative action in private sector employment.

Under these circumstances, relationships between nonprofit and for-profit organizations become highly complex, with either party viewing the other as potential opponents, constituents, or customers. To the extent that for-profit organizations become constituents or customers of nonprofits, they are likely to be stable, fairly controllable sources of market transactions or subsidies for nonprofits.

Organizational Structure of Environment: Complex Versus Simple. There are also differences in the organizational structure of the various service fields, such as the number of organizations involved, their size and geograph-ical scope of operation, and the extent and nature of interorganizational relations. For example, an elaborate effort to portray the nonprofit sector in the Chicago metropolitan area in 1982 found more than 3,000 culture and human service organizations (including a handful of health care clinics), about 800 nonprofit elementary and secondary schools, but only 102 non-profit hospitals and 67 colleges and universities (Grønbjerg, Kimmich, and Salamon, 1985, p. 9). At the time, there were only three to four proprietary and four public hospitals in the area. There were a few proprietary elementary or secondary schools and no for-profit institutions of higher education, but a large number of public schools and several public institutions of higher education. The number of proprietary arts and culture or human service organizations is more difficult to establish, but there were only a few public agencies.

Of course, the 3,000 organizations included a wide variety of organizations. An estimated one-quarter were social service agencies, one-fifth were arts and cultural organizations, another one-tenth were education/research organizations, with health services, institutional/residential care, and housing/community development organizations each accounting for about 5 percent of the total. Organizations providing legal services/advocacy, mental health services, and employment/training/income support were somewhat fewer in number (3 to 4 percent each), with 15 percent defined as multiservice organizations because they had no single primary service field. As these figures suggest, certain types of service fields have a much denser population of organizations than others, although service specializations and definitions of geographical catchment areas may reduce direct competition to a significant extent.

There are also major differences in the economic structures of service fields, including the overall value of their economic products and the prevalence of very large organizations. The 102 nonprofit hospitals accounted for total revenues of about $4.1 billion in 1982, and the 67 colleges and universities had combined revenues of $1.3 billion, suggesting that hospitals on the average were twice as large as universities and colleges (average revenues of $40 million versus $19 million). Other nonprofits are even smaller. The 3,047 nonprofit culture and human service organizations jointly accounted for $2.5 billion, and the 806 nonprofit elementary and secondary schools had combined revenues of only $478 million, or averages of only $820,000 and $600,000, respectively.

More recent analysis suggests that human service organizations themselves have highly skewed distributions of revenues. The Illinois facilities project shows that about one-third of Illinois nonprofit human service organizations have revenues of less than $100,000, and 70 percent have revenues of less than $750,000. These smallest 70 percent of organizations jointly account for only 9 percent of total revenues, and the 10 percent of organizations with revenues of $3.3 million or more account for 69 percent of total revenues (Grønbjerg, Nagle, Garvin, and Wingate, 1992).[4] Nonprofit hospitals, institutions of higher education, and elementary and secondary schools are likely to have less extreme disparities in size.

Level of Institutionalization: High Versus Low. These variations in the organizational structure of service fields are likely to coincide with differences in the degree of institutionalization that characterizes interorganizational relations and internal management structures. Nonprofit social service agencies experience some pressure toward consistency from their widespread and extensive dependence on public funding, the central position of a handful of state agencies, and the relative absence of proprietary competitors. However, opposite forces toward diversity come from the large number of organizations in the field and their great variations in size and funding patterns.

These variations make it difficult to institutionalize funding strategies among nonprofit social service organizations so that they become part of a ready-made vocabulary and conceptual formulation. In the absence of institutionalized approaches, organizations are likely to engage in a serial search for solutions, action by reaction, and general reliance on opportunism and accidental approaches. Evidence for this comes from the wide variety of accounting methods and categories, unstandardized client definitions (for example, no equivalence to "FTE student"), and idiosyncratic data-base structures that social service agencies use. The permeability and flexibility of their program definitions and difficulties in developing a simple taxonomy of service activities are also indicative of these forces.

In this respect, nonprofit social service agencies are halfway between the health and education fields, on the one hand, and community, advocacy, or similar organizations, on the other hand. Health (especially hospitals) and higher education both tend to be characterized by large organizations, standardized relations with clients or customers, minor variations in organizational and management structures, highly institutionalized revenue structures, and standardized products and rates. Under these conditions, management and resource strategies operate under highly constrained conditions and are much less likely to show the great variety that I found for social service or community organizations.

At the other extreme are community organizations. These are typically very small organizations (about half have revenues of less than $100,000). They tend to be highly politicized, rooted in particular communities, subject to the interests of local constituencies, and with few direct competitors because of their focus on a specific geographical turf. These features constitute pressures toward diversity and lack of institutionalization. So does the structure of public funding for these organizations, even though it is available mainly from very few sources and therefore might be thought to promote uniformity and institutionalization. However, in contrast to social services, the public funding for community organizations is not designed to purchase standardized services for eligible clients but to secure the organization's capacity to organize and develop a particular, idiosyncratic, local community. That allows organizations to operate with and emphasize unique attributes.

Complexity of Assessing Organizational Outcomes

The third major contribution of the conceptual framework, that outcomes or performance measures for individual organizations are difficult to assess, also is not unforeseen. In previous analysis (Grønbjerg, 1986), I found that nonprofit human service organizations were much more likely to report expansions of service activities than reductions, and did so even in the face of declining revenues. Either nonprofits have much greater success in increasing efficiency than they generally are credited with or revenues are not good predictors of service efforts. I also observed a high incidence of substantial funding turbulence from year to year, raising additional questions about the linkage between revenues and service activities.

Recognizing External Bases for Assessing Outcomes. Assessing organizational performance levels is difficult because multiple factors influence organizational outcomes. Diverse resource characteristics of many different revenue sources interact with equally diverse features of various service fields to create a complex set of environmental forces. A full assessment of organizational outcomes must judge the outcomes against the contingencies created by these combinations, but that is rarely done because their complexity makes it difficult to do so systematically.

These external conditions set parameters for the range of options available. Organizational outcomes then reflect the extent to which nonprofits and their managers position themselves strategically with respect to these external conditions. How closely they link themselves to key institutional systems may be especially important. For example, intense and prolonged relations with institutionalized funding sources give nonprofits opportunities to learn how to negotiate the system and circumvent or adjust to customer or funder demands. The three social service agencies with high reliance on government funding or other prolonged relationships with fee-paying organizations had consistent surpluses and growing fund balances. The other organizations were more likely to show deficits or closely balanced revenues and expenditures and small or declining fund balances. I interpret these findings as reflecting the benefits associated with opportunities to centralize organizational control over long-term, institutionally based resources.

Organizational outcomes reflect how and whether the organizations solve the full range of organizational challenges described in Chapters Ten and Eleven. Some of these involve internal management decisions. Others are conditioned by external features over which organizations may have little or no control. Efforts to assess organizational performance generally assume that organizational outcomes can be attributed to internal characteristics. Observers also view these as of primary interest because they are most amenable to direct control by managers. However, my findings suggest that an exclusive focus on internal sources of outcomes is likely to miss important pieces of the picture, possibly even the most interesting ones.

Using Qualitative Measures of Performance. In addition to problems in determining how broad a set of features to consider in assessing organizational outcomes, there are more explicit and technical difficulties in arriving at appropriate performance measures. Traditional measures of performance have focused on economic, quantitative indicators. They reflect the rational preoccupation with financial success that characterizes market economies. However, these measures are frail and have uncertain relationships with qualitative assessments of how robust or effective organizations are. Of course, for major corporations with sales in the billions of dollars and managers with eyes fixed firmly on next quarter's profits, small changes in economic performance are important, whether measured in gross sales, profit margins, asset ratios, returns on investments, or the like. For them, a preoccupation with short-term financial success is understandable if not adequate or fully appropriate.

Researchers who want to assess organizational performance use similar measures of economic performance on an annual basis. The measures have important advantages: they can be linked directly to economic theory, have very high salience to the organizations themselves, are readily available, and allow for easy comparisons across industry, time (with proper adjustment for inflation), and location. However, they are neither sufficient nor appropriate measures of performance, especially for nonprofits. At the theoretical level, economic performance measures cannot be linked directly to incentives for organizational behavior because nonprofits cannot distribute profits to owners. Moreover, because nonprofits have access to subsidy revenues they can escape the full rigors of the traditional market test. These characteristics weaken the theoretical underpinnings for relying on economic measures for assessing the performance of nonprofits.

At the technical level, my findings show that annual measures of economic performance are unstable and not very sensitive indicators of the level of service efforts or performance more generally. As Chapter Four shows, annual measures of economic performance are subject to considerable turbulence with widely divergent patterns of growth, decline, and stability. These findings suggest that cross-sectional analysis that relies on single-year revenue data to measure organizational performance may incorporate spurious, unstable variations that reduce the reliability of the measures. This conclusion comes from analysis of nonprofit human service organizations, most of which were relatively small. I have no corresponding information for organizations of similar sizes in the public or for-profit sectors. Consequently, I do not know whether the high degree of turbulence observed reflects the small size of organizations rather than the nonprofit auspices under which they operate. Both may be important.

Perhaps more important, the individual case studies demonstrate that divergent patterns of funding turbulence frequently cannot be linked directly to immediately prior actions or service efforts (except perhaps for fee income). Annual measures of economic performance may be not only unstable but also of questionable validity in assessing overall performance levels, because they do not direct attention to long-term strategies or "positioning." The latter requires systematic attention to organizational robustness and

effectiveness, but that is difficult to do because it involves qualitative judgments. For example, "robustness" includes assessments of the extent to which
organizations are able to cushion themselves against environmental jolts,
maintain responsiveness to environmental conditions, and make appropriate internal adjustments to ensure overall coordination of activities. These
are all conditions that are not subject to short-term assessments, because they
surface only against the backdrop of specific events and may not be evident at
all times.

In addition, meeting one of these conditions may make others difficult
to attain. For example, being responsive to environmental conditions may
place organizations in the position of benefiting from new resource opportunities and result in high levels of performance on traditional economic
measures. But organizations that grow rapidly may find it very difficult to
make appropriate internal adjustments to maintain overall coordination. All
of the case-study organizations that had undergone sustained and rapid
growth showed evidence of internal strain, whether in the form of board
divisions, board-staff conflicts, or difficulties in maintaining internal communication and quality control. Other research supports this observation as
well. Conflict is more likely to be found among nonprofits that grow than
those that decline, whether growth is measured as program starts and expansions (rather than curtailments and terminations; Grønbjerg, 1986) or as
change in revenues (Galaskiewicz and Bielefeld, 1992).

Assessing the effectiveness of services is also very difficult. It requires
attention to whether the organization has an impact in terms of its primary
purpose or mission. Evaluating the achievement of normative, substantive
goals is much more difficult than establishing that the organization maintains a given level of productivity (as reflected in volume of service statistics)
or that it operates with economic efficiency (as measured in unit cost and
annual surplus levels).

I have found no easy way to measure effectiveness, except to conclude
that it requires a qualitative approach that pays attention to long-term
developments (see also D'Aunno, 1992; Cameron, 1986; Connolly, Conlon,
and Deutch, 1980; Zammuto, 1982, 1984). In practice, the difficulty of
evaluating effectiveness results in the use of stand-in measures that reflect
little more than reputations, legitimacy, and credibility or image (Herman
and Van Til, 1989). This is an important point because the strategies by which
organizations obtain and secure funding, and hence meet economic measures of success, favor those with well-defined identities, strong reputations,
good marketing efforts, and highly developed and easily activated networks.
These resources are not equally available to all nonprofits and are not
necessarily closely related to program effectiveness. Having access to such
resources may make program effectiveness easier to achieve, but that is an
empirical question that needs to be examined, not an assumption to be built
into the measurement of effectiveness itself.[5]

Implications for Theory, Research, and Practice

In this final section, I briefly summarize some of the more specific implications of these three general conclusions for theory and research in several different arenas. I also identify a number of practical issues that the study raises for nonprofit managers and funders.

Theory and Research

The findings and conclusions have a variety of implications for organizational and management studies. I have discussed specific issues on several occasions throughout the volume. I do not want to repeat them here. Instead, I limit myself to some broader observations as they apply to specific theoretical perspectives and methodological approaches.

Organizational Theory. At the most general level, my findings confirm the overwhelming need to use an *open systems approach* in the study of organizations. Certainly, it is not possible to understand the behavior of nonprofits, including their internal structures and processes of decision making, without paying careful attention to the complex organizational environments in which they operate and with which they interact on multiple levels.

In addition, the fact that all the case-study organizations maintained overall patterns of funding reliance and stability over time confirms a key tenet from *ecological theory*—namely, that organizations rarely undergo major transformations. Rather, once organizations establish basic structures for interacting with their environment, these structures tend to persist. To the extent that adaptation occurs, it takes place primarily in peripheral characteristics, such as modifications to existing service activities or the pursuit of funding sources similar to those already in place.

As the comparison of social service and community development organizations shows, organizational environments are not uniform, but differ systematically along several structural dimensions. These differences create distinctive management contingencies that influence the relative success of strategic responses. This general observation supports a basic tenet from the *institutional theory* of organizations—namely, that the external environments in which organizations operate take on institutionalized forms (Zucker, 1988) that contribute to the formation of distinctive organizational cultures. These institutionalized forms vary by the specific population of organizations under consideration.

This point also supports the importance of giving full consideration to *contingency theory*; that is, organizations have only limited control over their environment, although specific sources of uncertainty vary from service field to service field. Entrepreneurship, boundary-spanning activities, skillful manipulation of strategic opportunities, and careful attention to potential limitations may counteract some of the sources of external control but will not eliminate them.

Finally, as discussed above, my findings give broad support to the *resource dependency model* and the tremendous utility of examining resource exchange relations in the study of organizational behavior. However, not only is the relative degree of resource dependency important, but so are the structural characteristics of the funding sources themselves. These structural dimensions establish broad parameters against which organizational actions and contingencies must be evaluated.

Management Theory. The argument that specific resource streams differ on qualitative dimensions and that these intersect in distinctive ways with contingencies associated with industry or field of operations has implications for management theory in general and for the management of nonprofits in particular. If this argument is valid, there may be severe limits to the utility of teaching generic management skills. Although some skills may be transferable across industries and organizational types, others may not be. Instead, managers need specialized skills and strategic understandings of the complex set of contingencies that organizations may encounter, depending on the kinds of environmental and resource factors discussed here.

Organizational Research. My findings also have implications for research on organizational behavior. I have already discussed several of these. Specifically, cross-sectional studies of organizations may not easily allow for systematic attention to the complex environmental contingencies, implicit structures of decision making, and other key processes that influence organizational behavior. These efforts require more of a longitudinal focus, examination of a wider variety of data sources, and more in-depth attention to qualitative characteristics of organizational behavior than are found in most organizational studies. The combination of case studies with broader survey findings on organizations presents a useful solution to the dilemmas of qualitative versus quantitative measures and of depth versus breadth of analysis.

Organizational researchers also need to pay systematic attention to basic organizational types and dimensions. That is, they need to recognize the importance of auspices and fields of service or industry, so that we can establish more clearly the parameters for organizational behavior. For example, do the funding patterns I found for social services and community development operate differently in other service fields, as I hypothesize? Do specific funding streams operate differently for organizations that are not independent nonprofits (for example, nonprofits under religious auspices, members of umbrella organizations, or for-profit organizations under different types of ownership)?

We also need to direct attention to the diversity of resources and their qualitative aspects. I have discussed the dimensions that emerged from the case studies, but I have no adequate documentation on how they manifest themselves across a broader range of organizations. In addition, the analysis of the government grants and contracts system suggests the need for careful attention to transaction costs associated with different types of resources and for both parties to the resource exchange relationships.

Practice

I have demonstrated key features associated with how nonprofit social service and community development organizations manage their funding sources. The success of specific strategies depends on the extent to which funding relations follow the patterns described in this book. The funding relationships are close, complex, and dynamic, reflecting joint as well as independent decisions by interconnected organizations. They involve both the service delivery organizations and their respective funding sources in a set of contingencies and mutual dependencies, which either party may only reluctantly attempt to escape, and then at some costs. These findings have a number of practical implications for public and private policy makers and the managers of nonprofits. The findings also raise broader questions about social policy in the United States.

Implications for Public and Private Funders. The types of funding relationships examined here form the primary mechanisms through which public and private policy makers implement program decisions and attempt to achieve their own goals. If they are to assess their own performance, funders, especially public ones, must concern themselves with how nonprofits solve the problems I have examined in this book. They need to understand how diverse funding sources and equally diverse service fields combine to create highly specific management contingencies for nonprofits. Otherwise, they will have unrealistic expectations about how their own policies and priorities have an impact on recipient organizations. Few funders understand these features. Specifically, donors, especially foundations, need to recognize that one-time grants or demonstration programs are unlikely to have significant impact on organizational activities unless a subsequent sponsor is secured by prior agreement.

Funders must also know and understand the specific funding context of the individual organizations that they fund—what other services these organizations provide, to which other clients or groups, and with which other funding sources—if they are to assess how the programs they fund are implemented at the service delivery level. This will require much more comprehensive reviews of activities and overall capacity of the recipient organizations than the usual paper audits and limited program reviews. Few funders make such efforts.

In addition, managing the complex system of grants and contracts under which human services are delivered in the United States (with both public and private sources of funding) involves large transaction costs. These costs are largely hidden and unrecognized, but they have major consequences for the human service system, especially for planning and coordination of services. These costs require systematic efforts to prevent their shift to lower levels of organizational participants, where they are likely to impede the delivery of services. Few funders are likely to make aggressive efforts to prevent these shifts because to do so would increase their own transaction costs.

Finally, although individual funders may facilitate simplified and coordinated management tasks for nonprofits, these efforts will remain ineffective until implemented on a centralized basis by the full range of public and private funding sources. Possible options include the following:

- Establishing time frames for proposal development that allows for coordination across different funding sources
- Processing proposals and final contract agreements in a timely fashion before the start of the program periods
- Developing a centralized and standardized depository for commonly requested documentation to reduce paperwork and simplify compliance reviews
- Standardizing taxonomies of client and service categories to simplify data management tasks
- Implementing standardized, monthly payment systems
- Minimizing contract amendments and revisions and increasing flexible allocations of line-item expenditures

These options would require fairly minor changes in the grants and contracts system. They are consistent with recommendations for state and local action on a nonprofit policy agenda (Koch and Boehm, 1992).[6]

Implications for Nonprofits and Their Managers. Previous chapters have reviewed and documented strategies available to nonprofits for managing specific costs and complexities associated with major funding sources in two different service fields. However, there are other general implications for nonprofits and their managers. Nonprofit managers must be prepared to deal with inevitable cash-flow problems. This will require access to funding reserves that match the organization's growth and/or reliance on unpredictable funding sources (such as donations) or unreliable payment streams (such as voucher-based public grants and contracts). Managers must also recognize that the complexity of managing different funding sources, especially public grants and contracts, puts a high premium on effective internal communication in order to articulate program and client needs in funding proposals and maintain overall coordination and integration of services.

In addition, nonprofits need to pay careful attention to how their substantive goals (as expounded in mission statements) articulate with direct and indirect consequences of their efforts to manage funding relations. This is most explicitly a problem with fees and other commercial sources of revenues, but it also occurs for government grants and contracts. Specifically, as nonprofits obtain more diverse funds, they obtain more goals. Too many goals may make them seem (and become) diffuse and opportunistic.

Finally, the three broad conclusions discussed as theoretical constructs have their counterpart for nonprofit managers. To understand funding sources and act strategically in managing them, managers must recognize the nature of exchange relationships to which they commit the organization when they seek particular types of funding—the fairly simple exchange involved in market transactions or the more complex ones that characterize subsidy exchanges. They must understand what moves and motivates different types of exchange partners. They probably will discover that the more different exchange partners are from themselves, the more likely some misunderstanding or problems are to occur.

They must accept the fact that funding sources that are pervasive among organizations of their ilk become funding sources they are expected to use themselves. Although they may know more about how to interact with these sources, there may be fewer opportunities to develop new innovative approaches. They must understand the degree of competition they are likely to face when pursuing different funding sources: how crowded the field is, how fragmented or consolidated, how protected or open. They must also be aware of the extent to which funding sources restrict their internal management discretion.

They must also be intimately familiar with the structural characteristics of the service fields in which their organizations are active—that is, how easy it is to assess and document performance levels, what the relationship is between the public sector and nonprofits in the field, and to what extent (and by what mechanism) it is possible to develop leverage and influence over public sector decisions. They need to know what opportunities exist for developing relations with the private sector in the field and what the structure of the field itself is: how many nonprofits, how large are they, and how institutionalized are the relationships with other organizations?

Ultimately, nonprofit managers must contend with the complexity of assessing the outcomes of their organizations—indeed, their own performance. They must recognize that most observers will go no further than easy, familiar, quantitative measures of economic outcomes. However, managers will find that these types of measures are incomplete, because they do not systematically incorporate the impact of external constraints. The measures fail to capture some of the most important aspects of what their organization does. They need to find ways to articulate their robustness and effectiveness on a more qualitative basis, but few in the audience are likely to be attuned to them when they do.

Notes

1. Excluding larger organizations made it feasible to manage the data collection effort for the thirteen organizations within a reasonable time period. Even so, the work took more than two years and involved sixteen graduate students in the data collection and analysis. By limiting myself to organizations located in the Chicago area, I could more easily gain access to them because of my name recognition from previous research (and also minimize conflicts with competing job and family commitments). Even so, I encountered some difficulties in gaining access (and did neglect other responsibilities).

2. This argument is supported by the Illinois facilities project, which found that over half (55 percent) of 501(c)(3) charitable community organizations were located in Chicago, compared with 30 percent of all 501(c)(3) human service organizations in the state (Grønbjerg, Nagle, Garvin, and Wingate, 1992).

3. An analysis of payments to DCFS providers shows that the amount of funding providers receive has some relationship to their market characteristics: the type of expertise they have and whether they target children, youths, and their families. However, their ability to influence DCFS is at least as important: the legitimacy to which they can lay claim because of their nonprofit status, age, expertise with public funding, and links to nonprofit networks (Grønbjerg, Chen, and Stagner, 1992).

4. The Gini index of income concentration for this sample is .77, higher than the corresponding index for the for-profit service industry (.64), although otherwise comparable to the level of concentration among U.S. corporations. The Gini index of income concentration varies between a high of .94 for both the transportation/public utilities and the finance, insurance, and real estate industries and a low of .64 for the service industry (computed from U.S. Bureau of the Census, 1991, pp. 449, 522).

5. Some approaches to measuring effectiveness rely explicitly on this assumption by arguing that the subjective assessment of effectiveness by stakeholders in the organization may be the only way to document effectiveness when outcome measures are difficult to measure and organizational goals are diverse (D'Aunno, 1992; Cameron, 1986; Connolly, Conlon, and Deutch, 1980; Zammuto, 1982, 1984).

6. Recommendations for reform of nonprofit contracting include getting state and local governments to implement standard compensatory systems; securing payment alternatives to avoid payment delays; coordinating mechanisms for reporting purposes; providing technical assistance to nonprofits; and evaluating outcomes, not only service delivery (Koch and Boehm, 1992, pp. 2–3).

EPILOGUE

Implications
for Public Policy

For policy analysts, the findings in this book raise a number of broad questions about the role of nonprofit service providers in the delivery of human services in the United States. The system is one in which some public goods are delivered under the private auspices of nonprofit organizations. How large a role can and should these mediating institutions play in the provision of public goods? Obviously, the nonprofit sector is too small and fragmented in most developed nations to singlehandedly address the widespread economic and social insecurities associated with advanced, industrial economies. Only coordinated public action in the form of monetary, fiscal, and regulatory policies can hope to do so. How, then, do public policies affect nonprofit organizations? And how do the special resource constraints under which they operate affect their ability to participate in the delivery of public services?

Public Policies as Demand Structures for Nonprofit Action

The nature of federal monetary policies and the structure and size of tax systems indirectly modify demands for nonprofit services. Monetary policies influence the general state of the economy and therefore overall employment and wage levels. The very wide wage gap in the United States (Phillips, 1990) is unchecked by central planning or wage policies and leaves increasing proportions of the population in low wage jobs. The structure of tax systems affects the volume of discretionary income available to different income groups, and the relatively regressive tax system in the United States disproportionately targets low-income groups (Reynolds and Smolensky, 1977; Edsall, 1984; Grønbjerg, 1985), further reducing their economic well-being.

The amounts, purposes, and forms of public spending directly shape the community needs and service demands that nonprofits encounter, whether or not they have any public funding themselves. The United States

315

has a fairly limited definition of public goods, lags most other industrial nations in the proportion of gross national product allocated to public welfare spending, and is almost unique in lacking universal health insurance or family allowance programs (Palmer, Smeeding, and Torrey, 1988). Almost two-thirds (63 percent) of public welfare spending goes to income insurance programs (such as Social Security) or for medical benefits. These expenditures have grown rapidly in recent years (even adjusting for inflation and population growth) to benefit primarily the elderly and those who have experienced long-term unemployment. By contrast, means-tested income assistance programs (such as Aid to Families with Dependent Children) and other services for the poor have increased only modestly and account for only about one-tenth of total public welfare spending. These low levels of spending for traditional welfare purposes mean that nonprofits must try to accommodate a wide range of needs that are not directly addressed by public spending.

The form that public spending takes is also important. Direct public provision of services (public schools, hospitals, health clinics, residential care) is of interest to nonprofits primarily if the spending occurs in fields where they are active. In this case, the public services substitute for their own (primary education) or compete for potential fee-paying clients (higher education, hospitals). Those who endorse strong public sector mandates favor the direct provision of services by public agencies, because this form of spending locates the greatest direct control in the public sector. Nonprofits have a vested interest in limiting the scope and quality of direct public services.

Public spending that takes the form of direct payments to individuals (public aid, Social Security payments) or vouchers that individuals exchange for specified services (food stamps, student loans, Medicare, Medicaid, Section 8 housing vouchers) also affects nonprofits. This spending system gives individuals discretion over where to obtain the service in the private or nonprofit market. However, it is usually viewed with ambivalence in the United States when applied to low-income groups and is of limited direct interest to the types of nonprofits examined here.[1] Under either of these two spending systems, nonprofits must compete with free public services (in the case of direct public provision) or with each other and for-profit organizations for fee-paying or credit-bearing clients.

Nonprofits benefit most directly from public spending if it takes the form of direct public subsidies to them or other nongovernmental entities. In this case, public spending converts to grants and contractual arrangements between consenting organizations. To the extent that these arrangements favor nonprofit service providers, public spending transforms itself into a nonprofit revenue stream and directly expands the range and volume of nonprofit resources. As discussed in Chapter Four, this type of spending pattern has been of major importance for nonprofit social service agencies and is of growing significance for community development organizations as well.

Nonprofits prefer this type of public spending because the subsidies benefit them directly. The limited support for public welfare activities in the United States has favored nonprofits by encouraging a grants and contract system through which public spending is channeled, as opposed to expanding public sector infrastructures or leaving decisions entirely in the hands of the poor. The contract system also appeals to market goals of efficiency by forcing the public sector to exploit available (nonpublic) infrastructures and avoid the creation of new public infrastructures at taxpayers' expense. These entrenched ideologies are at the root of continuing efforts to curtail public spending and privatize public services in the United States.

The existing spending structures are also strengthened by the dynamics under which public-nonprofit resource relationships play themselves out in the political arena. Once a nonprofit-public funding relationship is established, public agencies purchase more than service capacities or access to infrastructures, and nonprofits obtain more than revenues. The relationship comes to involve an exchange of a broader range of resources, such as legitimacy, influence, and knowledge (Saidel, 1991). The system carries major advantages for both participants, because the formal agreement between them strengthens the claim to legitimacy for both, reduces the need for either to accept responsibility for failure (Sosin, 1990), and expands their spheres of influence.

For government agencies, reliance on nonprofit service providers reduces their own visible role, because services occur in locations and under auspices that are not public. This obscures public responsibility for failures by providing government agencies with some other organization to blame. It reduces program start-up costs by accessing existing extragovernmental infrastructures, increases flexibility by making it easier to reallocate resources, and maximizes control over resources while minimizing responsibilities for direct administrative supervision (Rehfuss, 1989).

The use of nonprofit providers allows government to document its adherence or attention to local control, because nonprofit boards are presumed to represent local interests. It also expands opportunities for government agencies to influence the political process, because they can mobilize the prestige and influence of nonprofits and their coalitions to defend joint service structures from legislative or administrative hostilities. Finally, by specifying which types of services they are willing to fund and by incorporating nonprofit service organizations into the policy debate, public agencies influence the structure and development of nonprofit service delivery systems beyond the portion that they fund directly.

For nonprofits, public funding confers formal recognition of their service capacity and strategic importance. Directors of the case-study organizations spoke with visible pride about new public grants and contracts they had received and frequently found occasions to mention these events in requests for other types of funding, such as foundation grants or corporate support. The contractual relationships and exchange of critical resources represent formal recognition of the value that legislative bodies — and in turn public sector agencies — bestow on individual nonprofits. The relationships document that nonprofits perform tasks and activities for which there is sufficient political consensus to demand the allocation of scarce tax dollars — they contribute directly to "collective goods" (Douglas, 1983, 1987). Donors may be equally concerned about supporting public benefit activities when they award grants or approve membership in the United Way, but these decisions are made privately, are not subject to public scrutiny, and have less prima facie credibility.

Public funding also shields nonprofits from failure, at least to some extent. Should problems in service delivery occur and come to public attention, nonprofit subcontractors can almost always point to inadequate public funding levels, arbitrary decisions by public authorities, burdensome reporting requirements, or some degree of breakdown in communication or interaction on the part of public agencies. Finally, public funding gives nonprofit organizations legitimate access to the political arena. They participate (at least indirectly) in key decision-making structures and have nontrivial opportunities to shape public policies and service delivery structures. They have vested interests in their own rights, but also argue on behalf of their clients for whom the public spending is designated. The annual crisis surrounding the adoption of the Illinois state budget routinely finds representatives of a large number of nonprofit human service organizations and coalitions present in Springfield, ready and eager to testify about the impact of proposed cuts in spending.

Such opportunities are important to nonprofit service providers. On occasion, they express resentment when public officials fail to enlist their active support. That was the case in 1992, when private social service agencies threatened to refuse to accept new children into foster-care placement, reportedly — at least in part — because the director of DCFS failed to ask them to play a larger role in lobbying the state legislature for more money (Karwath, 1992). The director subsequently resigned.

Nonprofits have relatively easy access to this process of interest-group politics (Lowi, 1969). They view themselves as promoting the public good and can point to their tax-exempt or charitable status as documentation of the claim. Those who have public funding have additional advantages. They have expert knowledge about clients and services, they can provide detailed documentation of how policy changes have direct effects on specific clients and their own organization, and they can mobilize their boards or other networks to help argue their cases. They become, therefore, difficult for politicians to dismiss or ignore and are frequently included in the planning stages of public policy formulation as well. The participation in turn increases their visibility and legitimacy. In the absence of effective political parties at the state and local levels, nonprofits become one of the mechanisms by which segments of the population have some representation.

The Role of Nonprofits in the Provision of Public Goods

The involvement of nonpublic organizations in the provision of public services raises fundamental questions of whose interests are being served and where accountability is located under these funding structures. These questions are most obvious when public agencies subcontract with proprietary corporations, but they are no less important in the case of nonprofit organizations. When nonprofits earn commercial revenues, they inevitably serve private interests. When they obtain access to subsidies that either reduce (donations) or absorb (public grants and contracts) tax receipts, some accountability to the commonwealth must be assured. Each of the major sources of funding examined in this book touches on one or both of these dilemmas.

Private Interests and Public Goods

Nonprofit reliance on commercial revenues raises the question of how public and private interests coexist in a single organization. From one perspective, the question is moot, because public interests are served when private interests are met. The driving force of capitalism in U.S. society promotes an economic system in which market transactions are fully institutionalized and widely encouraged. Under this economic model, nonprofit market transactions are desirable to the extent that they solve problems of contract and market failures in the private market (Hansmann, 1980, 1987; Weisbrod, 1988, 1989), subsidize the development of new markets until commercial enterprises can exploit them, and encourage nonprofits to become more efficient.[2]

Indeed, some argue that well-developed fee systems among nonprofit organizations might serve public policy functions directly as well. For example, Rose-Ackerman (1983) proposes that payment standards for public grants and contracts to nonprofit organizations should be pegged to the fee levels that each organization is able to obtain in the private market. The system would force nonprofits to provide competitive services and eliminate arbitrary levels of public payments by using private consumers as proxies for welfare clients. Effectively, private consumers would control the level of payments nonprofits would receive from public grants and contracts. Of course, the model presumes that a significant proportion of nonprofits have private sector clients, so that appropriate price levels can be established — an assumption that may not be warranted in several nonprofit service fields.

These perspectives reflect a traditional economic model, in which market organizations are defined as primary and government and nonprofits play secondary and supportive roles. In fact, the increasing emphasis on privatization and curtailment of government functions is justified not simply on the basis of cost containment but as part of a general mimicry and celebration of the private sector that culminated in the Reagan legacy of the 1980s.

These same basic premises have roused an outcry over the "encroachment" and unfair competition (Bennett and DiLorenzo, 1989; U.S. Small Business Administration, 1983) that nonprofit commercial transactions might pose to the viability of small businesses and free market capitalism. These critics argue that nonprofits hurt private businesses because they have significant cost and price advantages over for-profit businesses.[3] Nonprofits are also thought to be inherently inefficient, because donations and other subsidies allow them to distance themselves from profit incentives and escape the discipline of the free market (Douglas, 1983), even if they engage in commercial transactions to a significant extent. For similar reasons, nonprofit managers are often portrayed as lacking the skills or profit motives needed to undertake successful commercial transactions (Perlmutter and Adams, 1990).

Traditionally, a perspective that focuses more explicitly on the public goods role of nonprofits themselves has also served to justify their receipt of commercial revenues. Under this model, nonprofit fees and commercial revenues directly support their charitable purposes by allowing them to cross-subsidize their own services and expand the range of public goods they can provide. That occurs when nonprofits can charge sufficiently high fees in one service arena or for one client population to underwrite in full or part the costs of providing less marketable services in other fields or serving client populations that lack the ability to pay. Models of cross-subsidization (James, 1986) form the theoretical basis for sliding fee scales.[4]

However, even these more "benign" perspectives on fees have met with controversy, especially from within the nonprofit sector itself. Some argue that increased dependence on commercial types of revenues will undermine the rationale for nonprofits and threaten their legitimacy (Weisbrod, 1989). Nonprofit reliance on commercial transactions may also blur the boundary between the nonprofit and private sectors, and pits the achievement of substantive goals against the attainment of rational economic gains, profit maximization (Kalberg, 1980; Rushing, 1976; Rose-Ackerman, 1986; Weisbrod, 1989), and private benefits.

This argument is consistent with expectations based on the resource dependency perspective, which suggests that if nonprofits rely on commercial transactions, they are likely to let market forces drive organizational decision making. They may therefore lose their charitable character or find that commercial activities conflict with or subvert the substantive goals articulated in the mission. Certainly, organizations that rely on fees are much less likely to serve low-income clients (Grønbjerg, 1990a). The case-study findings on fees (Chapter Five) support this latter interpretation and also the notion that nonprofits may help create markets for commercial enterprises.

The findings on special events (Chapter Six) raise similar issues. Special event revenues also have a somewhat problematic status in terms of public utility. Like fees and other commercial types of revenues, special events have distinct private utilities. They benefit those who consume the services or product as well as the full array of entrepreneurs and commercial businesses who profit from catering to these types of nonprofit activities. Special events provide relatively small proportions of total revenues for most nonprofits and therefore have more limited economic value than fees and other commercial revenues. But like cross-subsidization from fees and service charges, they allow nonprofits to expand the range and volume of public goods.

Yet both types of revenues do so less explicitly than donations or government grants and contracts, and they are subject to only minimal oversight or other forms of public control. Absent outright fraud, nonprofits can use these funds entirely as they see fit for purposes that may or may not have public goods value. Any source of funding, of course, may be used to subvert charitable objectives, and no funding source can ensure that nonprofits will actually provide public goods. However, donors and government agencies have opportunities to exercise control and maintain the value of nonprofit public goods when they require nonprofits to engage in particular types of activities in return for the funding or withhold funding from those judged to pursue less appropriate goals. Even so, they depend mainly on nonprofits themselves to maintain a commitment to public interests, raising the equally difficult problem of how to ensure accountability to these goals.

Accountability to the Public Interest

In a democratic society, anyone can give money to an organization or person of his or her choice, limited only by individual proclivities or preferences and by the amount of surplus income available. In the case of commercial transactions, an exchange of goods and products takes place in return for the payment. In other cases, the payment falls under the category of contributions, because it provides mainly intangible rewards in return for the exchange. Such is the case when people drop a quarter in the hat of a street musician or when they write a check to the Salvation Army.

However, some contributions are more equal than others, at least for tax purposes. Giving money directly to homeless or other needy individuals receives no official encouragement, while the same support does if it is channeled through a charitable organization. Contributing to an organization that is formally incorporated and officially recognized by the Internal Revenue Service as charitable in character can reduce the donor's taxable income dollar for dollar (within certain maximum limits). The resulting lower taxes constitute a powerful incentive for making donations in this form.

The lower taxes mean that donations also leverage public support in the form of forgone tax revenues for the public sector. Tax expenditures of this type therefore constitute a form of voluntary taxation, but one that gives the donor-taxpayer rather than legislators or public administrators discretion over how public funds are used. Private donors who paid for the restoration of the Statue of Liberty reduced their own taxable income to the extent that they channeled donations through a recognized charitable organization (as most did). American taxpayers picked up part of the tab, but without any opportunity for public officials or legislative representatives to consider the relative merits of the tax expenditures, once the IRS accepted the general purpose as being charitable in nature.

Giving special tax treatment to donations is justified on the grounds that nonprofits (and donations to them) provide a mechanism for expanding the range and quality of collective goods. If the political process accords low priority to the allocation of public funds (taxes) for the production of certain collective goods, donations allow nonprofits to provide such goods for at least subsectors of the population (Rose-Ackerman, 1986; Hansmann, 1980, 1987; Weisbrod, 1975, 1977; Douglas, 1983, 1987; Olson, 1971). For the same reason, nonprofits are thought to have greater capacity for innovation, because they do not require broad political or social consensus to implement new initiatives.

Yet, even if nonprofits play these important functions, there are no effective structures of accountability in place to ensure that they do so. Many nonprofits operate on a precarious financial basis and frequently must balance special donor interests against broader organizational goals. The complex resource dependency relations that result may require nonprofits to restrict their activities to those that fit conventional expectations of mainstream funders (DiMaggio and Powell, 1983; Bush, 1988; Commission on Private Philanthropy and Public Needs, 1975).

Moreover, nonprofit efforts to meet specific demands or preferences by subgroups of the population invariably mean that other subgroups or demands are ignored (Sosin, 1990). As Odendahl (1990) and Schiller (1989) point out, donations encourage nonprofits to focus disproportionately on elite interests. The control that donors exercise over tax expenditures and the composition of nonprofit boards give added significance to such "nonprofit failures" (Salamon, 1987). Although these concerns have considerable validity, the findings in this book suggest that neither donors nor board members exercise extensive control over nonprofit activities, at least in the two service fields examined here. When donors do so—rarely—they are primary and continuing funders and have institutionalized relationships with the recipient organization. When board members exercise control, the organization is likely to be either small or involved in mobilizing constituencies, or the control is sporadic and limited to certain arenas.

Indeed, nonprofits may be actively involved in the responsible provision of public goods, but this occurs most explicitly when they provide publicly funded services under contract to public agencies. Even here, special constraints limit their role, although there are major costs and benefits of such a service system to all participants. For example, the high level of transaction and planning costs associated with the current system raises important questions about whether it is possible to systematically implement new policies and assess the impact of existing ones.

The diverse funding structures under which nonprofit human service organizations operate raise important questions, therefore, about what services are available, to whom, and at what costs. Inevitably, services are unevenly available to different clients, irrespective of client needs or public mandates. Inevitably, the costs are high, because they include not only direct tax dollars used for the purchase of goods and services but also the loss of unrealized tax revenues from the exclusion of donations on individual and corporate tax returns used to support or supplement these services. The costs also include the direct and indirect administrative and other transaction costs associated with the complex system of grants and contractual relationships.

Finally, the findings suggest that although public funding shields and benefits nonprofit organizations in the short run, they may over time, as participants in "third-party" government (Salamon, 1981, 1987, 1989a, 1989b), easily come to share in the broad decline of public confidence in government. They become part of the "hollow state" (Milward, Provan and Else, forthcoming), in which public agencies are able to externalize their problems onto the nonprofit sector, including fiscal shortfalls, staff turnover, limited career mobility, and visible responsibility for the (often inadequate) funding and delivery of mandated public services (Sosin, 1990). Nonprofits that rely heavily on government grants and contracts risk becoming part of an organizational sink in which government submerges its problems. As the general public comes to recognize this, nonprofits may be unable to attract other sources of funding, especially from donors with a moral commitment to the collective good.

Notes

1. The voucher system represents a partial adaptation to market structures while maintaining public control. It allows vendors to compete for cash or credit-bearing customers, but it limits the range of goods that customers can purchase (in contrast to cash payments). The restrictions are justified by the argument that low-income customers are not sufficiently responsible to manage their finances or other circumstances appropriately (as evidenced by their need to rely on public benefits; Tropman, 1989).

2. Commercial transactions are thought to stimulate efficiency, because organizations that rely on commercial revenues must meet or modify consumer demands in order to be competitive. In contrast, donations and public grants and contracts diminish leverage by consumers.

3. Included are exemptions from income, sales, or real estate tax obligations; lower postage rates; exclusions from certain government regulations; and market advantages from the presumption (possibly inaccurate) of providing quality services.
4. Panel data from 1985 showed that more than half (56 percent) of social service and community development organizations in the Chicago area use sliding fee scales. This includes 21 percent that use both sliding fee and flat-fee scales. Only 11 percent use flat-fee payments only; but 33 percent are at the other extreme, with no fee income at all.

APPENDIXES

APPENDIX A
Methodology

Any analysis of the nonprofit sector or of nonprofit organizations is beset by major data problems. There are only limited national and aggregate-level data available, no complete listing of nonprofit organizations, or even any agreement about how to categorize their activities or employ standard definitions of such basic characteristics as revenue sources. As a result, the Case-Study Project posed several methodological challenges: how to document macro-level trends in nonprofit service fields at the national or regional level to serve as a backdrop for the case studies, how to identify appropriate organizations to represent the organizational profiles, what types of data to collect, and how to solve problems of missing, incomplete, and noncomparable financial data for the selected organizations.

Problems of Macro-Level Data

The overall pattern of growth and stability of the nonprofit sector is difficult to determine because the sector lacks an adequate historical data base. That is the case whether the analysis focuses on revenue streams as they leave the originating source (fee-paying client, donor, government agency) or as the streams reach the nonprofit organizations. The problems are even more problematic for any regional-level analysis.

National Trends

Given the symbolic, political, and economic importance of nonprofit organizations in the United States, the available data bases are remarkably primitive and incomplete.[1] Data from originating sources and from recipient nonprofit organizations have major gaps and lack critical detail.

Certainly, no sources provide reliable data on the volume of purchases that consumers make directly from nonprofit organizations as opposed to for-profit organizations. Businesses do not routinely track (or report) whether the services they purchase are produced by nonprofit or for-profit organizations. Nor do national analyses of money flows require financial institutions to record whether the financial accounts they manage are owned by private households or nonprofit establishments.[2] Similarly, government agencies rarely distinguish among subcontractors that are for-profit, nonprofit, or other government agencies. In fact, the development of such a data base is sufficiently complicated to be highly limited in time and place (Grønbjerg, Musselwhite, and Salamon, 1984).

Only the volume of donations has been tracked reasonably well over time from tax-return data. However, by definition, donations must be identified as such on tax returns to be included, and the data are therefore highly sensitive to tax policies and changes in tax regulations. For example, donations made by individuals who do not itemize returns are excluded for most years as are donations from individuals or firms that donate amounts in excess of certain limitations. Moreover, tax-return data may identify donations by source (individuals, corporations, foundations), but not by type or purpose of recipient organization.

Obtaining usable data from nonprofits themselves is also difficult. The census of service industries, which is most likely to capture nonprofit funding streams at the receiving end, has been conducted every five years since 1967 and at varying intervals prior to that since 1929. However, the census generally does not include information on detailed sources of revenues and includes only those establishments that report payroll expenditures. As a result, the large number of nonprofit organizations that rely entirely on volunteers are excluded, as are those that do not have regular payrolls or do not report wage expenditures.

There are other problems as well. The census surveys have at varying times excluded certain types of establishments with large numbers of nonprofit organizations (for example, eliminating hospitals, educational institutions, labor unions, and political organizations in 1982). At other times, the census has grouped certain types of governmental units with tax-exempt organizations (for example, not distinguishing between public and nonprofit hospitals in 1987).

More important, the Standard Industrial Classification system (SIC), which is used to categorize establishments in terms of service activities, lumps very different organizations together under one code. For example, religious press houses and environmental advocacy groups may all be classified as publishing organizations under the SIC system because that is their one activity that most closely resembles commercial transactions. This makes it very difficult to undertake any systematic analysis of specific nonprofit subsectors, except for service fields in which there are large numbers of for-profit establishments and where the SIC categories therefore have been most fully developed (health, day-care, residential services).

Data from tax returns (990 Forms) filed by tax-exempt organizations are even more problematic and biased in favor of large establishments. Only a small proportion (about one-quarter) of tax-exempt organizations actually file returns. Many organizations are not required to file: those with revenues below a certain amount, operating under religious auspices, or covered under returns filed by an affiliate organization. Analysis of survey data from the Chicago area suggests that 45 percent of nonprofit human service organizations and 35 percent of their revenues may not be included in the IRS tax files of charitable organizations for a given area (Grønbjerg, 1992).

Even if tax returns are filed, the data are not easily available for more than a few organizations at a time (copies of filed returns have to be requested from the IRS for each organization separately). Access to computerized IRS tapes may not be satisfactory either if there are substantial errors introduced in the data entry process. Because the IRS does not collect taxes from these organizations, the agency has few incentives for devoting major resources to alleviating these types of problems.

More detailed data bases exist for some nonprofit subsectors for which specialized surveys have been conducted regularly over time. However, only those sectors with the largest and most institutionalized organizations, such as hospitals and institutions of higher education, have developed relatively complete and consistent data bases. Other specialized surveys—for example, surveys by the American Family Service Association of its member organizations or surveys for research purposes—suffer from serious problems of sampling bias, geographical coverage, timing, and comparability of data collection instruments.

Local Trends and Patterns

The analysis presented in this book draws heavily on a panel study of nonprofit organizations in the Chicago area conducted during the 1982–1985 period for the Urban Institute's Nonprofit Sector Project, for which I served as the Chicago field associate. I also draw on selected findings from two statewide surveys I directed in 1991 of service providers involved with the Department of Children and Family Services (the DCFS provider project for the Children's Policy Project at Chapin Hall Center for Children at the University of Chicago) and of nonprofit human service organizations in Illinois (the Illinois facilities project for the Illinois Facilities Fund).

Chicago-Area Panel Study. The Chicago portion of the Urban Institute's Nonprofit Sector Project initially surveyed a 28 percent random sample of nonprofit organizations in the Chicago metropolitan area in 1982, with a response rate of 49 percent (Grønbjerg, Kimmich, and Salamon, 1985). The multiple listing from which the sample was drawn (see Grønbjerg, 1989a) excluded hospitals, universities, fraternal and veterans organizations, foundations, federated funding organizations, and churches. Eventually, nonprofit elementary and secondary schools were also eliminated because other sites participating in the national project did not have fully comparable samples.

The data include responses to two waves of mail surveys (in 1982 and 1984) with questions on services, client characteristics, and sources of revenues. A third wave of personal interviews with a subsample of executive directors (in 1985) focused on how nonprofit organizations evaluate funding sources, modify their missions, restructure their programs, and relate to low-income or minority clients. A fourth wave of data collection in 1986 sought to update expenditure information for 1985 and 1986 through a brief telephone survey.

The third wave included only a subsample of respondents to the second wave. It excluded organizations outside of Cook County (which includes the city of Chicago) and those that concentrated their services in the areas of research, education, and arts or culture. Respondents to the first wave included 206 organizations that were candidates for the third wave of interviews on the basis of these criteria, of which 149 (or 72 percent) responded to the second survey in 1984. Interviews were completed in 1985 with executive directors of 130 organizations that had participated in the second wave (87 percent), but two of these organizations were dropped because they failed to meet initial sampling criteria. (For a description of the panel study and the sampling frame on which it is based, see Grønbjerg, 1989b, 1990b.)

Unless otherwise indicated, the analysis presented in this book focuses on only those organizations in the panel study that participated in the third wave of the panel study and were either social service organizations (42 agencies) or organizations primarily involved in community organizing or development (19 organizations). The remaining organizations in the full panel study include 23 single-purpose day-care centers and 44 organizations engaged in a variety of specialized services.

DCFS Provider Project. More recent data come from a mail survey conducted in the fall and winter of 1990–91 of the social service and day-care program units included in the list of providers maintained by the Illinois Department of Children and Family Services. The survey included a stratified sample of single-purpose day-care centers but included all other organizations that appeared to be involved in some form of direct client services.

A total of 465 organizations responded to the survey, about 63 percent of the valid sample, including about 50 to 53 percent of day-care agencies and 71 percent of all other organizations. More than two-thirds (70 percent) of these organizations operate under nonprofit auspices. The survey included detailed questions about the types of services provided, target populations, revenue sources, and extent of contractual relations with federal, state, local, and other nonprofit organizations. (For a description of the survey and findings, see Grønbjerg and Stagner, 1992; Grønbjerg, Chen, and Stagner, 1992.)

Illinois Facilities Project. Additional data come from a second statewide survey of nonprofit organizations conducted in Spring 1991 for the Illinois Facilities Fund. The 25 percent random sample was drawn mainly from a list provided by Independent Sector of Illinois-based nonprofit charitable organizations registered under section 501(c)(3) of the Internal Revenue Code. The sample list was restricted to broadly defined human service organizations, including residential services, advocacy organizations, community organizations, and health-related services. It excluded hospitals, educational institutions and schools, fund-raising and fund-distributing organizations, international charities, environmental organizations, fraternal organizations, and arts and cultural organizations. A second 25 percent random sample was drawn from similar types of nonprofit organizations listed in the United Way/Crusade of Mercy, *Human Care Service Directory of Metropolitan Chicago* (as of July 1990), but not included in the IRS listing.

The survey produced responses from 475 organizations, or 34 percent of the valid sample. They constitute about 10 percent of all nonprofit human service agencies in Illinois and represent a range of different service fields. Although the survey focused mainly on a broad range of facility-related issues, it also included basic organizational information about target populations, service fields, and revenue sources, as well as detailed information about lending relations and borrowing practices. (For a description of the survey and a summary of major findings, see Grønbjerg, Nagle, Garvin, and Wingate, 1992.)

The Case-Study Project

Identifying organizations appropriate for the Case-Study Project required me to specify in some detail the criteria to be used in defining the profiles. Because I relied mainly on the Chicago-area panel study for selecting the candidate organizations, we used criteria that were available from information in this data base. Making the actual selection of the organizations from among the possible candidates presented some problems.

Profile Criteria

To identify organizations with appropriate fields of activity to represent the two patterns of institutional relationships described in Chapter Two, I sought organizations that reported that direct social services or community organizing and development activities were their primary mission or constituted the service field that absorbed most of their operational expenditures. This information came from interview data collected in 1985, in which the organizations reported on their primary mission, and from survey data collected in 1982, where the agencies reported on the proportion of service expenditures in each of eight major categories. To supplement the list of community development organizations, we relied on published lists of organizations known to be active in the field.

To identify organizations with particular types of funding composition, we used data for the 1981–1985 period on total revenues and proportion from major funding sources as reported in 1982, 1984, 1985, and in some cases, 1986. We defined primary reliance on public funding as 70 percent or more in government grants or contracts and less than 10 percent in fee income; primary reliance on mixed funding as no more than 10 percent in fee income, with the remaining funding split about fifty-fifty between donations and government grants and contracts; and primary reliance on fee funding as 70 percent or more in fee income or similar commercial types of revenues.

We had initially sought to locate organizations that received at least 70 percent of their revenues from one of the three major funding sources: public, donations, commercial revenues. However, we were unable to find enough social service agencies with primary reliance on donations and relaxed the definition to the criteria specified above. We also could not find community organizations with primary reliance on fees and relaxed this definition to consider special event proceeds as a form of commercial revenues.

To locate organizations with particular types of funding stability, we defined those with an average annual change in funding that amounted to no more than 10 percent of prior year revenues over a four- to five-year period (all adjusted for inflation) as having stable funding. Those with average annual changes in funding that amounted to at least 25 percent of prior year revenues were categorized as having funding turbulence. It was difficult to locate community organizations with funding histories that fully met the criterion of stable funding. Some compromises were necessary, and we had to resort to the use of informants.

Finally, we limited the choice to medium-sized organizations—that is, organizations with total revenues in 1985 of at least $200,000 but no more than $1.5 million. At the time of the actual data collection for the case studies, two organizations had fallen below the $200,000 cut-off for their most recent fiscal year (see Table 2.2).

Candidate Organizations

For all profiles in the social service field and for two profiles in the community organizing and development field, the first choice among the possible candidates agreed to participate in the study. For the remaining four profiles in the community development field, we encountered difficulties in identifying appropriate candidates. The cells came up empty (primary reliance on public or commercial revenues), or potential candidates were reluctant to participate (one case) because of the time demands involved.

We therefore resorted to a second strategy: a combination of recommendations from experts in the field and analysis of available (but often incomplete) financial records on public file to locate organizations that appeared to meet our criteria. This seemed preferable to an alternative solution of relaxing the selection criteria further.

The supplementary strategy involved the use of a list of community organizations in Chicago published by the Institute of Urban Life (1988). We asked two key individuals with long-term experience in working with community organizations and a third person involved in administering the Community Development Block Grant program for the city of Chicago to review the lists. All three have long-standing expertise in the community organization and development field in Chicago. We asked them to identify organizations that in their judgment showed very stable or very turbulent funding and might meet our size requirement.[3]

We then examined available (but frequently incomplete) financial records on public file at the Charitable Trust Division of the Illinois Attorney General's Office to identify those among the possible candidates from this supplementary strategy that appeared to rely mainly on public funds or commercial revenues (including special events).

Readers should be aware of two other considerations as well. Prior to the Case-Study Project, I had a personal connection with one of the thirteen organizations that participated in the study. I knew some of the rest by name, but had no personal contact with them otherwise, although most of them participated in the several waves of surveys and personal interviews that I supervised for the Urban Institute panel study from 1982 to 1985.[4]

As a result of the Case-Study Project, however, I have come to know them all well. I maintain sporadic contact with some, have sustained relations with others, and have become closely associated with one.[5] As a member of the board of directors of the United Way of Chicago, I have additional opportunities to observe how several of them fare in this particular funding arena.

In order to help protect the identity of the participating organizations, I have changed their names and sought to eliminate very specific information about them. This is also the main reason why I have converted all financial data (except as noted) to constant 1981 dollars. This procedure makes it possible to compare organizations and financial information across time without the distortion of cost-of-living factors, but it obscures the current budget size of participating organizations by deflating its value. The use of 1981 is an arbitrary decision, although it coincides with the base year used for the Urban Institute Nonprofit Sector Project.

Data Sources

The Case-Study Project uses a wide variety of data sources: documents obtained directly from the organizations, interviews with staff and board members, and observations while completing the collection and analysis of other data. In addition, documents and information available from a variety of other sources were also examined.

Organizational Documents. For each organization included in the case studies, my students and I analyzed a wide range of documents. These include financial statements or audit reports, annual reports, board minutes, and documentation on fund-raising activities or plans over as many years as were feasible. We also reviewed publicity documents, brochures, flyers, and correspondence with donors.

The most intensive work involved detailed examination of all documentation related to all restricted grants and contracts that were active during the organization's most recent fiscal year. Appendix B shows the data collection instrument developed to ensure systematic and complete information on each grant and contract, the Grant-Contract Award Information Sheet. Because of the variety of information included and the systematic format by which data are recorded, the instrument represents a new tool in organizational analysis. It is the basis for the analysis presented in Chapter Nine. Appendix C summarizes the information generated from this instrument for the grants and contracts of Youth Outreach.

We examined RFPs or contract renewal letters issued by funders, grant and contract proposals submitted by the participating organizations, formal contracts or grant agreements, contract or grant amendments, client documentation, performance and financial reports, vouchers, payment schedules, licensing requirements, correspondence with funding sources, and site visit reports. Whenever possible, we also examined monthly cash-flow activities and accounts receivable for the same fiscal year.

Interviews and Observations. We conducted a minimum of two long interviews (one to three hours each) with the executive director, other key staff persons, and occasionally board members, in order to examine agency resource strategies. These interviews focused on the history of the organization and its basic definition of purpose. We also explored efforts to seek and secure different types of funding and assessments of these funding sources. We asked about the amount and type of efforts involved in working with other nonprofit organizations, keeping informed about trends and developments, finding and developing staff, and developing agency structure and culture (see General Agency Information in Appendix B).

The interviews also included questions about each restricted grant and contract from public or United Way sources (see Section IX of the Grants/Contract Award Information Sheet in Appendix B): Why this particular funding source? What was the history of the relationship with the granting agency? What problems were encountered? What was the relationship to other programs or awards? How is the impact on the organization and/or its clients assessed? What are your general impressions?

While conducting the interviews and reviewing document files (which in most cases took six to fifteen person-days of work), my students and I observed and recorded activities taking place in agency offices. We focused on our impression of events or encounters, staff-to-staff relations, and occasional client-staff interactions. We also observed and noted neighborhood characteristics, office site and condition, layout and decorations, and the nature and condition of filing systems.

Supplementary Data Sources. We obtained a variety of other data about the organizations and their communities from several other sources. We reviewed organizational documents on file with the Charitable Trust Division of the state's Attorney General's Office. These include mainly articles of incorporation, tax returns, and supplementary financial forms (most organizations involved in charitable trusts or solicitations are required to file such material on a regular basis). This allowed us to fill in gaps in financial data for some of the organizations (and aided in the selection of some of the organizations).

We also examined annual program reports for the Community Development Block Grant program from the city of Chicago for the 1979–1990 period, in order to make sure that we had a full count of CDBG grants to the organizations. In addition, I reviewed annual reports of the United Way of Chicago, to track any United Way funds to the organizations. For two of the organizations, I reviewed the annual financial and program reports submitted by them as members to the United Way when we could not locate complete information in their own files.

For the community development organizations, we reviewed newspaper cuttings on file in the Municipal Reference Library. Organized by name of the organization and of the community, the files appeared to be fairly complete for the 1980–1990 period and included cuttings from the two major daily newspapers (*Chicago Tribune* and *Chicago Sun-Times*) as well as eight to ten local community papers. For most of the community development organizations, we located twenty to thirty articles relevant to each.

Historical descriptions of the local communities and settlement patterns came from the Chicago Fact Book Consortium, *Local Community Fact Book: Chicago Metropolitan Area, 1980* (1984). This book also includes census data on population and housing characteristics for the community areas for the 1930–1980 period as well as data for census tracts for 1970 and 1980.

Financial Information

I sought to develop consistent, complete, and detailed financial data for as many years as possible for each organization. As noted, I made my selection of most of the participating organizations on the basis of available data that had been developed in three stages between 1982 and 1985 through two waves of mail questionnaires and one wave of personal interviews with executive directors. I used the original data base to identify social service and community development organizations and to single out those that matched particular funding profiles and patterns of funding dynamics for the 1981–1984 period. However, for reasons explained below, I based all my analysis of funding dynamics on information contained in tax returns or audit reports for the participating organizations. The resulting data base is neither consistent nor complete and varies considerably in level of detail.

Assessing the Data. The tax return that most tax-exempt organizations above a certain size must file (the 990 Form) employs standardized formats but lacks details. The form does not distinguish between program service revenues from private sources and from public fee-for-service or performance contracts. It does separate indirect public support (such as United Way allocations) from direct public support, but the latter category lumps together individual contributions, foundation grants, and corporate donations. Because I wanted to examine more detailed sources of revenues, the tax returns had low priority in the analysis.

Audit reports have greater levels of detail, but these may change over time and almost always differ from one organization to the next. For example, some audit reports include church contributions as a separate category; others do not. Some report all gross revenues and expenditure from special events; others include only net revenues, and others again exclude certain types of revenues and expenditures associated with events.

Accounting procedures vary as well. The organizations differ in whether they report their finances on a cash or accrual basis (as required by the United Way for its member agencies). Under the former procedure, revenues and expenditures are recorded when respective funds actually reach or leave the organization. Under the latter procedure, revenues and expenditures are recorded as they accrue to the organization (for example, when donation pledges or bills to be paid arrive in the mail and are recorded). Organizations differ also in whether they distinguish between capital and operating accounts. The latter difference complicates analysis of financial conditions for organizations that have sizable grants (and expenditures) for lengthy capital projects, as do several of the community organizations.

Completeness of Data. In four cases, we obtained data that extended back almost to the formal establishment of the organization. That was the case for Alcohol Treatment and Christian Therapists among the social service organizations and for Economic Development Commission and New Town Sponsors among the community development organizations. However, official reports or tax returns at times were not available in any accessible ·location or had been destroyed. That was the case for some of the older organizations. For example, Youth Outreach and Immigrant Welfare League were both established in the 1920s, and Preservation Council and Community Renewal date back to the early 1950s. The much younger Hispanic Youth Services operated out of extremely congested office space and could not easily locate the appropriate cardboard boxes that contained older records. Similarly, African-American Neighbors had stored its older records in a basement and discarded them when they became damaged by water and the organization had to vacate the building.

In other cases, data were missing for particular years because of an organizational crisis. For example, Immigrant Welfare League did not have final audit reports for the one year in which its executive director defrauded the organization and was fired. Nor did Christian Therapists for the year in which eleven of thirteen staff members, including the director, resigned.

Finally, one organization, Community Renewal, was reluctant to disclose any detailed information on its revenues and expenditures. As discussed in Chapter Seven, the organization maintains a very close relationship with a major community institution that helped establish it and that has provided it with the bulk of its funding since then. The organization's decision not to disclose detailed financial data about this relationship reflects its strategy to portray a separate identity for itself.

I examined several options for extending the time series for those organizations that had audit reports or tax returns available for only a limited number of years. In some cases, I located copies of audit reports, tax forms, or fiscal reports submitted by the organization to the United Way of Chicago as part of membership requirements or grant applications. In other cases, the Attorney General's Office had information in its files. I also explored whether responses from the survey and interview questions could fill in some of the existing data gaps. However, the standard categories included in the original data bases (see Table 3.1) did not match the great variety of reporting formats used in audit reports (nor did the original data bases include information on fund balances or types of expenditures).

Moreover, even when comparisons were possible for particular years, responses to the original survey and interview questions frequently deviated from the corresponding amounts listed in official audit reports or tax returns. That is because the surveys required respondents to make a best estimate of what their revenues would be for a given year. In many cases, their estimates were off—and frequently by more than trivial amounts. Because of these uncertainties, I do not use fiscal information from the original data base, but rely on official information collected directly from the case-study efforts. In some cases, this strategy eliminates data on earlier years, but it allows for more systematic and verifiable analysis of recent trends.

As a result of these efforts, I was able to obtain financial information on the thirteen organizations for periods of consecutive years that ranged between four years (Immigrant Welfare League) and thirteen years (Preservation Council, Alcohol Treatment), with a median of nine years. In one case (Hispanic Neighbors), data extend back to 1969 (twenty-one years) but include two gaps (a three-year gap and a one-year gap) during which the organization experienced major losses of funding.

Special Problems with Funding Sources. I encountered several problems associated with *fees* and *dues.* First, several community organizations appeared to use inconsistent definitions of donations and dues. Thus, support from local residents, businesses, or other organizations might be listed as dues or "assessments" in annual reports or newsletters. However, these same sources seemed to be recorded as donations in audit reports and tax returns, although it was difficult to estalish whether and how such a redefinition took place. I used the designation in official records as the criterion for deciding how to treat these revenue sources for this analysis.

The opposite problem surfaced with New Town Sponsors. The organization was initially selected to represent the fee/turbulent profile, based on its responses to the three waves of data collected for the panel study and confirmed from analysis of tax returns. However, discussions with the executive director revealed that the program receipts that accounted for all of the turbulence were not in fact program fees, but donations used to underwrite the major special event. I kept the organization in the Case-Study Project (the thirteenth organization) but replaced it with Hispanic Neighbors for the turbulent/events profile.

Although most of the *special events* analysis relies on revenues and expenditures as officially reported in audit reports, some analysis uses gross returns in order to document the amount of efforts involved and to facilitate comparison across the organizations. This adjustment is necessary because the organizations differ in how they report special event revenues in their audit reports. Thus, Hispanic Neighbors includes only special event revenues net of expenses in its audit reports, but provides supplementary information about gross revenues and expenditures associated with the event activities. New Town Sponsors provides fewer details in its audit reports but appears to include gross special event expenditures and revenues when reporting on total revenues and expenditures.

Until the early 1980s, Preservation Council reported on gross revenues, but it then shifted accounting procedures and now includes only net revenues in its official audit statement. In notes to the audit statement, the organization provides more details about revenues and expenditures from the event, but it includes only net revenues from food and beverage sales on the revenue side, and excludes the costs of these items from the expenditure side. In my analyses of the special event revenues and expenditures, I accepted the organization's definition of these categories, but I also developed a supplementary analysis in which I include gross revenues and expenditures from food and beverage sales along with all other items.

In addition to possible overlap between dues and donations, the analysis of *donations* is complicated by the diverse ways in which organizations separate or combine different types of donors in their audit reports. Some report all donations jointly, others provide detailed categories, most change over time. The number and types of categories appear to reflect efforts to maintain continuity with past practices, to document special fundraising initiatives, and to track salient types of donations. For example, Immigrant Welfare League lists donations separately for each of its four chapters and also singles out church contributions, United Way, and other types of donations, but not always. At times, Christian Therapists separated donations for each of six churches and also distinguished among church collections, board donations, and other support. However, for most years the organization reported only on aggregate donations.

To document the amount and structure of administrative tasks involved in managing *restricted grants and contracts*, we examined in detail all the documentation each organization had on its restricted grants and contracts from public or United Way sources that overlapped in part or in full the most recently completed fiscal year. Occasionally, full documentation was not readily available. In these cases, I relied on my own knowledge about specific programs but attempted to confirm the estimates by consulting with appropriate staff members.

At one point, I also sought to get executive directors or financial managers to estimate the amount of time they or their staff spent preparing proposals, contract amendments, vouchers, and the like. Staff time devoted to most of these efforts usually is not covered by the grant or contract. I had hoped to develop estimates of uncompensated management costs per funding source along the lines of Hartogs and Weber (1978).

However, it was difficult to get any clear documentation of these efforts, except for vague references to "days of work" or "hours and hours each time." Directors and staff members also found it difficult to distinguish among concurrent activities associated with different funding cycles of a given restricted funding source. Funding cycles involve work that extends considerably beyond the funding period itself. Not surprisingly, when pressed for estimates about a particular type of task for a specific funding source, staff members recounted efforts involved in the most recent set of tasks. But those tasks were associated with the current, ongoing funding cycle, and I was attempting to document the total amount of work associated with an already completed funding cycle.

Consequently, I simply counted the number of management tasks associated with public or United Way funding sources for which the organization had applied or for which it received funding that covered all or part of a fiscal year (see Tables 10.1 and 10.2). I excluded activities associated with the actual delivery of services, for which the organization presumably is compensated through the grant or contract.

Notes

1. Partial documentation for this observation comes from papers prepared for a special workshop on federal statistics and the nonprofit sector conducted by the Committee on National Statistics of the National Academy of Sciences (May 1992).
2. Thus, foundation assets are commingled with private household savings, making it impossible to track whether and how fiscal and monetary policies encourage individual savings or consumption.

3. The experts appeared to have broader familiarity with the overall level of funding (size and turbulence) than with patterns of funding reliance.
4. I was recovering from back surgery when the personal interviews took place in 1985 and could not complete my share of the interviews.
5. I have participated in several board retreats, prepared special summaries for their organizations, and provided informal advice and feedback on particular issues.

APPENDIX B
Grant-Contract Award Information Sheet

Date _____   Agency _____

Interviewer _____   Grant number _____

Agency contact person _____   Fiscal year _____

I. *Fact Sheet Information*

1. Grant/contract title _____
2. Source (name) _____
3. Source type (foundation/level of government, etc.) _____
4. Purpose _____
   _____
   _____

5. Official award starting date _____
6. Scheduled award termination date _____
7. Actual dates (if different) _____
8. Total award amount _____
9. Program name (if different) _____
   _____

10. Program purpose (if different) _____
    _____
    _____

11. Total program cost (if different) _____
12. Program starting date (if different) _____
13. Program termination date (if different) _____
14. Source and amount of remaining costs (if other grants/contracts, complete
    information sheet for each award) _____
    _____
    _____
    _____

15. Award program/client requirements (activities) _____
    _____
    _____
    _____
    _____

16. Award staff requirements _____
    _____
    _____
    _____

17. Award administrative/fiscal requirements _____
    _____
    _____
    _____

II. *Documentation of RFP, Proposal Contents, and Chronologies*

18. Date of RFP or notification _____ Check if new _____
19. Content of RFP or notification (list separately)

Preproposal

20. Date preproposal due _____   Check if no preproposal _____
21. Date preproposal submitted _____   Check if by messenger _____
22. Content and size of preproposal (list separately)
23. Amount requested in preproposal _____
24. Date preproposal accepted _____   Date notified _____
25. Amount approved in preproposal _____

Proposal

26. Date proposal due _____   Check if no proposal _____
27. Date proposal submitted _____   Check if by messenger _____
28. Content and size of proposal (list separately)
29. Amount requested in proposal _____
30. Date proposal accepted _____   Date notified _____
31. Amount approved in proposal _____

Contract

32. Date contract signed by funder _____
33. Date executed contract received _____
34. Content and size of contract (list separately)
35. Contract/grant type (performance, purchase of service, grant) _____
    _____
36. Program performance reporting requirements (obtain copies of forms if possible) ___
    _____
    _____
    _____
37. Frequency of performance reporting _____
38. Client data reporting requirements (obtain copies of forms if possible) _____
    _____
    _____
    _____
39. Frequency of client data reporting _____
40. Fiscal reporting requirements (obtain copies of forms if possible) _____
    _____
    _____
    _____
41. Frequency of fiscal reporting _____

III. *Contract Revisions* (repeat as necessary)

First Revision

42. Initiatied by funder or agency? _____
43. Date initiated _____
44. Content and size of proposed revisions (list separately) _____
45. Changes proposed _____
    _____
    _____
46. Reasons for changes _____
    _____

47. Date changes effective _____
48. Date revised contract executed _____
49. Content and size of revised contract (list separately)

Second Revision

42. Initiated by funder or agency? _____
43. Date initiated _____
44. Content and size of proposed revisions (list separately) _____
45. Changes proposed _____
_____
_____

46. Reasons for changes _____
_____

47. Date changes effective _____
48. Date revised contract executed _____
49. Content and size of revised contract (list separately)

Third Revision

42. Initiated by funder or agency? _____
43. Date initiated _____
44. Content and size of proposed revisions (list separately) _____
45. Changes proposed _____
_____
_____

46. Reasons for changes _____
_____

47. Date changes effective _____
48. Date revised contract executed _____
49. Content and size of revised contract (list separately)

IV. *Site Visits or Audits* (repeat as necessary)

First Review

50. Date of site visit or audits _____
51. Type of review _____
_____
_____

52. Results of review _____
_____
_____
_____

53. Date notified of results _____
54. Response to review _____
_____
_____
_____

Second Review

50. Date of site visit or audits _____

51. Type of review _____
_____
_____

52. Results of review _____
_____
_____
_____

53. Date notified of results _____

54. Response to review _____
_____
_____
_____

V. *Program and Client Reports* (list for each report)

55. Date due	Date submitted	Report size	Content included

VI. *Fiscal and Expenditure Reports* (list for each report, report vouchers separately)

56. Date due	Date submitted	Report size	Content included

VII. *Vouchers and Requests for Payments* (list for each voucher)

57. Voucher no.	Voucher date	Voucher amount	Voucher size	Voucher content	Date paid	Amount paid	Why difference?

VIII. *Chronology of All Other Events/Communications* (add additional sheets as necessary)

58. *Include* approximate date, nature of event (phone call, conversation, form letter, personal letter, report, documents), substance (include specifications of requirements, nature and amount of supporting documentation, name and position of correspondents)

Date	Event	Substance

IX. Grant/Contract Assessment

1. Why this grant? Where did idea come from? _____
_____
_____
_____

2. Previous relationship with grantor _____
_____
_____
_____

3. Problems encountered/how dealt with _____
_____
_____
_____

4. How relate to other programs/awards _____
_____
_____
_____

5. Impact on agency/clients/staff _____
_____
_____
_____

6. Other and general overall impression (report on separate sheets)

General Agency Information

Date _____   Agency _____

Interviewer _____   Agency contact _____

1. Fiscal year revenues and expenditures (only those confirmed)
   [*Note:* Use audit reports whenever possible]
   Comments:

2. Fiscal year dates _____

3. Annual reports obtained _____

4. What proposals are currently outstanding for next fiscal year? What are prospects for each?

5. What will you do if grants/contracts do not come through? How crippling will that be? Are you likely to find something else?

6. What does your agency do to obtain general operating/unrestricted funding? (Size and contents of mailing list? How often do you do mailings? Changes in these? Number of corporations/foundations contacted? How many successful this year? Last year?)

7. How did you use unrestricted funding in last fiscal year? This fiscal year? How important is unrestricted funding relative to restricted grants/contracts?

8. How well do grants/contracts match programs? Are they one-to-one matches, or are programs put together from different funding sources? What are the problems/strengths of this?

9. In retrospect, how well do grants/contracts actually match your agency's mission? Which are most closely related? Least?

10. How would you like to change current grant/contract specifications? Would that create problems for funders?

11. What would ideal funding conditions be? If so, what would your agency do?

12. How likely is it that you will be able to achieve some of these program goals in next five years even if you do not have ideal funding conditions? What would you need to do, and what is the likelihood of your being able to do these things?

13. How do you keep aware of changes in funding priorities/criteria? How early do you know about these? What is the best source of information (other nonprofits, funders, talk with board/staff, professional networks)?

14. What actions do you take to protect/secure funding? Which has been most effective (how to get access, develop influence)?

15. Any problem of having the right kind of staff for different programs? What has happened with program staff when programs changed? Was there staff turnover? Do you hire at low end, and then train and promote? Do you hire people with broad transferable skills? Do you only do programs that you have staff for?

16. During the last year or two, are there any major changes in agency operations, administrative procedures, record keeping as result of grants/contracts? Assessment of these changes?

17. In the last year, have you done any in-house informal data analysis or research (client records, surveys, environmental assessment)? What was done, why, and how useful was it? Did you end up making any changes as result of it?

18. How problematic is and how do you deal with:
    funding uncertainty?
    funding turbulence?
    program changes?

19. What is the best strategy to deal with these problems (funding diversification [what type?], program diversification, develop expertise in limited area, collaborate with other agencies, management changes)? Why this/these solution(s)?

20. Organizational structure: list job titles, brief description of responsibilities, program/administration/support category. Were there changes in the last year or two (types of job titles, incumbents)?

APPENDIX C
Detailed Tables for Youth Outreach

Table C.1. Fiscal Year 1988 Proposal Characteristics, Youth Outreach.

Grant/Contract	Formal RFP Issued	New/ Renewal	RFP/ Guide Size	Lead Time	Proposal Size	Items	Proposal Difficulty	Amount Requested
City Administered								
DHS/CD1	Yes	Renewal	13	4 wks[a]	25	5	High	150,000
DHS/CD2	Yes	Renewal	13	5 wks	47	7	High	192,000
MET/SYEP	Yes	Renewal	147	5 wks[a]	46	13	High	6,000
CBE	No	Renewal[b]	——	——	27	19	Medium	10,000
State Administered								
DMHDD	Yes	Renewal[b]	120	10 wks	10	9	Very high	142,381
DMHDD/								
Computer	No	New[b]	——	1 day	3	2	Very low	8,800
DPA/DMHDD/XX	Yes	Renewal[b]	111	3 wks	31	8	High	36,465
DCFS/SE	No	Renewal	24	4 wks[a]	108	20	High	111,931
DCFS/NNYO	No	Renewal	24	4 wks[a]	110	21	High	70,000
DCFS/LINK	Yes	New	?	6 wks	30	?	High	?
ISBE	?	Renewal	26	4 wks[a]	48	11	Medium	8,000
IAC	Yes	Renewal	32	6 wks[a]	14	6	Medium	20,800
Nonprofit Administered								
HHS/EF	No	Renewal[b]	——	——	——	——	Low	169,000
DCFS/CFC	No	Renewal[b]	——	2 wks[a]	——	——	Low	16,800
DPH/CDH/CNCE	Yes	Renewal	13	4 wks	19	9	High	63,903
UW	No	Renewal[b]	21	16 wks	18	6	High	271,700
UW/Special	Yes	New	?	16 wks	21	?	High	37,500

Note: (——) indicates none. (?) indicates information not available. Size reported in number of pages.

[a] Estimated.

[b] Continuation funding and/or proposal "preapproved."

Source: Case-Study Project.

Table C.2. Fiscal Year 1988 Grant/Contract Characteristics, Youth Outreach.

Grant/Contract	Proposal Approval Time	Proposal Approved Before/ After Start	Final Contract Before/ After Start	Contract Size	Items	Revised Contract Initiated by Rev I	Rev II	Final Dollars More/Less Than Request
City Administered								
DHS/CD1	3 + 1 wks[a]	+ 2 wks	− 4 wks	45	16	——		− 6,500
DHS/CD2	8 + 2 wks[a]	− 3 wks	− 5 wks	55	16	——		− 9,000
MET/SYEP	11 + 0 wks[a]	+ 2 wks	− 0 wks	64	15	——		0
CBE	0 wks	− 7 wks	− 14 wks	None		——		0
State Administered								
DMHDD	0 wks[b]	+ 1 wks	− 21 wks	8	5	Funder		− 5,476
DMHDD/ Computer	0 wks[b]	+ 0 wks	− 2 wks	7	4	——		0
DPA/DMHDD/XX	0 wks[b]	+ 5 wks	− 9 wks	29	8	Agency		0
DCFS/SE	11 wks	− 4 wks	− 21 wks	6	3	Funder		− 7,813
DCFS/NNYO	4 wks	− 1 wk	− 1 wk	5	3	Agency	Funder	0
DCFS/LINK	18 wks	+ 3 wks	+ 0 wks	Canceled				
ISBE	2 wks	− 0 wks	− 0 wks	48	12	——		0
IAC	8 wks	+ 26 wks	− 5 wks	1	1	Agency		− 10,400
Nonprofit Administered								
HHS/EF	0 wks[b]	− 4 wks	− 9 wks	——	——	——		0
DCFS/CFC	0 wks[b]	+ 6 wks	+ 5 wks	2	2	Funder	Funder	− 522
DPH/CDH/CNCE	2 wks	+ 4 wks	+ 0 wks	8	5	Funder		− 33,903
UW	0 wks[b]	+ 34 wks	+ 0 wks	1	1	——		− 5,755
UW/Special	5 wks	+ 1 wk	+ 1 wk	1	1	——		− 6,250

Note: Size reported in number of pages.
[a] Preproposal and proposal, respectively.
[b] Continuation funding and/or proposal "preapproved."
Source: Case-Study Project.

Table C.3. Fiscal Year 1988 Program Performance Requirements, Youth Outreach.

Grant/Contract	Frequency of Performance Report	Time Limit	Report Size	Level of Detail	Grant Performance Difficulty	Comments
City Administered						
DHS/CD1	Monthly	3 days	10	Very high	High	
DHS/CD2	Monthly	3 days	10	Very high	High	
MET/SYEP	Twice	4 wks	60	Very high	Medium	Combined with voucher
CBE	Quarterly	?	8	Medium	Medium	Combined with voucher
State Administered						
DMIIDD	Monthly	1 wk	110	Very high	Very high	Variance limit
DMHDD/						
Computer	——	——	——	——	Very low	Voucher only
DPA/DMHDD/XX	Monthly	1 wk[a]	?	High	Very high	Variance limit
DCFS/SE	Monthly	2 wks	10	High	High	Subcontracting
DCFS/NNYO	Monthly	2 wks	10	High	High	Subcontracting
DCFS/LINK	Canceled	——	——	——	——	——
ISBE	Year end	5 wks[a]	30[a]	High	Medium	
IAC	Year end	5 wks[a]	20[a]	Medium	Low	
Nonprofit Administered						
HHS/EF	Quarterly	8 wks[a]	22	Medium	Very high	
DCFS/CFC	——	——	——	——	Medium	Voucher only
DPH/CDH/CNCE	Monthly	3 days	36[b]	Very high	Very high	Combined with voucher
UW	Year end	14 wks	18	Very high	Low	
UW/Special	Year end	14 wks[a]	?	High	High	

Note: (——) indicates none. (?) indicates information not available. Size reported in number of pages.

[a] Estimated.

[b] Average of five pages for first seven months; average of seventy-eight pages for last five months.

Source: Case-Study Project.

Table C.4. Fiscal Year 1988 Fiscal Requirements and Payments, Youth Outreach.

Grant/Contract	Frequency of Fiscal Report	Time Limit	Report Size	Level Detail	Advance	Payment Form	Average Payment Time
City Administered							
DHS/CD1	—	—	—	—	Yes	Reimbursement	+ 9 wks
DHS/CD2	—	—	—	—	Yes	Reimbursement	+ 8 wks
MET/SYEP	—	—	—	—	No	Performance	+ 22 wks
CBE	—	—	—	—	No	Reimbursement	Delays
State Administered							
DMHDD	Monthly	3 wks	2	Medium	No	Flat monthly	2 wks[a]
DMHDD/							
Computer	Year end	8 wks[a]	3[a]	Low	No	Lump sum	?
DPA/DMHDD/XX	Monthly	3 wks[a]	2[a]	Medium	No	Flat monthly	2 wks[a]
DCFS/SE	Monthly	2 wks	1	Medium	Yes	Flat monthly	7 wks
DCFS/NNYO	Monthly	2 wks	1	Medium	Yes	Flat monthly	2 wks[a]
DCFS/LINK	Canceled						
ISBE	Quarterly	2 wks	5	Medium	No	Flat quarterly	Delays
IAC	Year end	6 wks[a]	3[a]	Medium	Yes	Lump sum	Prepaid
Nonprofit Administered							
HHS/EF	Quarterly	4 wks[a]	3	Medium	No	Flat quarterly	4 wks[a]
DCFS/CFC	—	—	—	—	No	Flat monthly	3 wks
DPH/CDH/CNCE	—	—	—	—	No	Reimbursement performance	+ 20 wks
UW	Year end	14 wks	18	Very high	No	Flat monthly	2 days
UW/Special	Year end	14 wks[a]	?	High	No	Quarterly	2 days

Note: (——) indicates none. (?) indicates information not available. Size reported in number of pages.

[a] Estimated.

Source: Case-Study Project.

Table C.5. Fiscal Year 1988 Voucher Requirements, Youth Outreach.

Grant/Contract	Frequency of Vouchers	Time Limit	Number of Vouchers	Level Detail	Voucher Size	Voucher Items
City Administered						
DHS/CD1	5 + /month	——	48	Very high	6	3
DHS/CD2	3 + /month	——	26	Very high	8	3
MET/SYEP	Twice	4 wks	2	Very high	66	6
CBE	Quarterly	——	3	Low	10	4
State Administered						
DMHDD	——	——	——	——	——	——
DMHDD/						
Computer	End	8 wks[a]	1	Low	2	3
DPA/DMHDD/XX	——	——	——	——	——	——
DCFS/SE	——	——	——	——	——	——
DCFS/NNYO	——	——	——	——	——	——
DCFS/LINK	——	——	——	——	——	——
ISBE	——	——	——	——	——	——
IAC	Beginning	——	1	Medium	2	4
Nonprofit Administered						
HHS/EF	Quarterly	——	4	Very low	1	1
DCFS/CFC	Monthly	3 wks[a]	12	Medium	4	2
DPH/CDH/CNCE	Monthly	3 days	12	Very high	36[b]	9
UW	——	——	——	——	——	——
UW/Special	——	——	——	——	——	——

Note: Size reported in number of pages.

[a] Estimated.

[b] Average of five pages for first seven months, average of seventy-eight pages for last five months.

Source: Case-Study Project.

References

Aiken, M., and others. *Coordinating Human Services: New Strategies for Building Service Delivery Systems*. San Francisco: Jossey-Bass, 1975.

Aldrich, H. (ed.) *Organizations and Environments*. Englewood Cliffs, N.J.: Prentice-Hall, 1979.

Alinsky, S. D. *Reveille for Radicals*. Chicago: University of Chicago Press, 1946.

Alinsky, S. D. *Rules for Radicals: A Practical Primer for Realistic Radicals*. New York: Vintage Books, 1971.

Andersen, R. (ed.) *Who Profits from the Non-Profit Hospital—Is the Tax Exempt Status Justified?* Thirty-First annual George Bugbee Symposium on Hospital Affairs, May 5, 1989. Chicago: Pluribus, 1989.

Arnold, D. O. "Dimensional Sampling: An Approach for Studying a Small Number of Cases." *American Sociologist*, 1970, *5*(May), 147–150.

Atkinson, R. C. "Supply and Demand for Scientists and Engineers: A National Crisis in the Making." *Science*, 1990, *248*, 425–432.

Bailey, A. L. "Salaries at New York Non-Profits Trail For-Profit World, but Pay Gap Narrows." *Chronicle of Philanthropy*, 1990, *2*(18), 19–20.

Bailey, R., Jr. *Radicals in Urban Politics: The Alinsky Approach*. Chicago: University of Chicago Press, 1974.

Barbeito, C. L. "The Non-Profit World Should Apply Its Values to the Salaries It Pays Its Workers." *Chronicle of Philanthropy*, 1990, *3*(5), 40–41.

Baum, J., and Oliver, C. "Institutional Linkages and Organizational Mortality." *Administrative Science Quarterly*, 1991, *36*, 187–218.

Ben-Ner, A., and Hoomissen, T. *A Portrait of the Nonprofit Sector in the Multisector Economy: New York, 1981–1987*. Durham, N.C.: Center for the Study of Philanthropy and Voluntarism, 1989.

Bennett, J. T., and DiLorenzo, T. J. *Unfair Competition: The Profits of Nonprofits*. Lanham, Md.: Hamilton Press, 1989.

Benton, B. F., and Millar, R. *Social Services: Federal Legislation Versus State Implementation*. Washington, D.C.: Urban Institute Press, 1978.

Bernstein, S. R. *Managing Contracted Services in the Nonprofit Agency: Administrative, Ethical, and Political Issues.* Philadelphia: Temple University Press, 1991.

Blau, P. M. *Bureaucracy in Modern Society.* New York: Random House, 1956.

Blau, P. M., and Scott, W. R. *Formal Organizations.* San Francisco: Chandler, 1962.

Brilliant, E. L. *The United Way: Dilemmas of Organized Charity.* New York: Columbia University Press, 1990.

Brown, J. *The History of Public Assistance in Chicago, 1833 to 1893.* Chicago: University of Chicago Press, 1941.

Bryson, J. M. *Strategic Planning for Public and Nonprofit Organizations: A Guide to Strengthening and Sustaining Organizational Achievement.* San Francisco: Jossey-Bass, 1988.

Buder, S. *Pullman: An Experiment in Industrial Order and Community Planning, 1880–1930.* New York: Oxford University Press, 1967.

Bush, M. *Families in Distress: Public, Private, and Civic Responses.* Berkeley: University of California Press, 1988.

Cameron, K. S. "Effectiveness as Paradox: Consensus and Conflict in Conceptions of Organizational Effectiveness." *Management Science,* 1986, *32*(5), 539–553.

Carver, J. *Boards That Make a Difference: A New Design for Leadership in Nonprofit and Public Organizations.* San Francisco: Jossey-Bass, 1990.

Chen, T. H., Grønbjerg, K. A., and Stagner, M. W. *An Analysis of Financial Payments to Service Providers of the Illinois Department of Children and Family Services.* Report prepared for the Children's Policy Project. Chicago: Chapin Hall Center for Children, 1992.

Chicago Fact Book Consortium. *Local Community Fact Book: Chicago Metropolitan Area, 1980.* Chicago: Chicago Review Press, 1984.

Cloward, R. A., and Epstein, I. "Private Social Welfare's Disengagement from the Poor: The Case of Family Adjustment Agencies." In *Proceedings of the Annual Social Work Day Institute.* Buffalo: School of Social Welfare, State University of New York at Buffalo, 1965.

Coleman, J. S. *The Asymmetric Society.* Syracuse, N.Y.: Syracuse University Press, 1982.

Coll, B. *Perspectives in Public Welfare: A History.* Washington, D.C.: U.S. Government Printing Office, 1969.

Commission on Private Philanthropy and Public Needs. *Giving in America.* Washington, D.C.: U.S. Department of the Treasury, 1975.

Committee on National Statistics. "Measurement of the Not-for-Profit Sector and Its Presentation in Federal Statistics." Workshop conducted by the National Academy of Sciences, National Research Council, Washington, D.C., May 1992.

Connolly, T., Conlon, E. M., and Deutch, S. J. "Organizational Effectiveness: A Multiple Constituency Approach." *Academy of Management Review,* 1980, *5,* 211–218.

Cooper, P. J. "Government Contracts in Public Administration: The Role and Environment of the Contracting Officer." *Public Administration Review*, 1980, *50*(September–October), 459–468.

Coser, L. A. *Greedy Institutions: Patterns of Undivided Commitment*. New York: Free Press, 1974.

Covelli, L. "Dominant Class Culture and Legitimation: Female Volunteer Directors." *Journal of Voluntary Action Research*, 1985, *14*(October–December), 24–35.

Daft, R. L. *Organization Theory and Design*. (3rd ed.) St. Paul, Minn.: West, 1989.

D'Aunno, T. "Effectiveness of Human Service Organizations: A Comparison of Models." In Y. Hasenfeld (ed.), *Human Services as Complex Organizations* (pp. 341–361). Newbury Park, Calif.: Sage, 1992.

Davidson, A. H. "Secrets of Success in Special Events." *Fund Raising Management*, 1987, *18*(April), 66, 68, 70, 73, 87.

DeHoog, R. H. *Contracting Out for Human Services: Economic, Political, and Organization Perspectives*. Albany: State University of New York Press, 1984.

Derrickson, M. C. *The Literature of the Nonprofit Sector: A Bibliography with Abstracts*. Vol. 1. New York: Foundation Center, 1989.

Derrickson, M. C., and Kurdylo, K. M. *The Literature of the Nonprofit Sector: A Bibliography with Abstracts*. Vol. 2. New York: Foundation Center, 1990.

Dess, G. G., and Beard, D. W. "Dimensions of Organizational Task Environments." *Administrative Science Quarterly*, 1984, *29*, 52–73.

Devney, D. C. *Organizing Special Events and Conferences: A Practical Guide for Busy Volunteers and Staff*. Sarasota, Fla.: Pineapple Press, 1990.

DiMaggio, P. J., and Powell, W. W. "The Iron Cage Revisited: Institutional Isomorphism and Collective Rationality in Organizational Fields." *American Sociological Review*, 1983, *48*, 147–160.

Douglas, J. *Why Charity: The Case for a Third Sector*. Newbury Park, Calif.: Sage, 1983.

Douglas, J. "Political Theories of Nonprofit Organizations." In W. W. Powell (ed.), *The Nonprofit Sector: A Research Handbook* (pp. 43–54). New Haven, Conn.: Yale University Press, 1987.

Dressel, P. *The Service Trap: From Altruism to Dirty Work*. Springfield, Ill.: Thomas, 1984.

Drucker, P. F. "What Business Can Learn from Nonprofits." *Harvard Business Review*, 1989, *67*(July–August), 88–93.

Drucker, P. F. *Managing the Nonprofit Organization: Practices and Principles*. New York: HarperCollins, 1990.

Duncan, R. B. "Characteristics of Organizational Environments and Perceived Environmental Uncertainty." *Administrative Science Quarterly*, 1972, *17*, 313–327.

Edsall, T. B. *The New Politics of Inequality*. New York: Norton, 1984.

Emery, F. E., and Trist, E. L. "The Causal Texture of Organizational Environments." *Human Relations*, 1965, *18*, 21–32.

Fuguit, G. V., and Kasarda, J. D. "Community Structure in Response to

Population Growth and Decline: A Study in Ecological Organization." *American Sociological Review*, 1981, *46*(October), 600–615.

Gagnard, A. "Community Study Suggests Segmentation Strategies." *Journal of Volunteer Administration*, 1989, 7(Summer), 14–18.

Galaskiewicz, J. *Social Organization of a Corporate Grants Economy: A Study of Business Philanthropy and Nonprofit Organizations*. Orlando, Fla.: Academic Press, 1985.

Galaskiewicz, J. *Gifts, Givers, and Getters: Business Philanthropy in an Urban Setting*. San Diego, Calif.: Academic Press, 1986.

Galaskiewicz, J., and Bielefeld, W. "Growth, Decline, and Organizational Strategies: A Panel Study of Nonprofit Organizations, 1980–1988." In *Spring Research Forum Working Papers, The Nonprofit Sector (NGO's) in the United States and Abroad: Cross-Cultural Perspectives* (pp. 167–179). Washington, D.C.: Independent Sector, 1990.

Galaskiewicz, J., and Bielefeld, W. "The Growth and Decline of Nonprofit Organizations: A Panel Study." Paper presented at the annual meetings of the American Sociological Association, Pittsburgh, August 1992.

Geiger, R. "Finance and Function: Voluntary Support and Diversity in American Private Higher Education." In D. C. Levy (ed.), *Private Education: Studies in Choice and Public Policy* (pp. 214–236). New York: Oxford University Press, 1986.

Gilbert, N. "Assessing Service Delivery Methods: Some Unsettled Questions." *Welfare in Review*, 1972, *10*(May–June), 25–33.

Gilbert, N., and Specht, H. *Coordinating Social Services*. New York: Praeger, 1977.

Glaser, B. G., and Strauss, A. L. *The Discovery of Grounded Theory*. Hawthorne, N.Y.: Aldine, 1967.

Greenwood, E. "Attributes of a Profession." In R. M. Pavalko (ed.), *Sociological Perspectives on Occupations* (pp. 3–16). Itasca, Ill.: Peacock, 1972.

Grønbjerg, K. A. "Private Welfare in the Welfare State: Recent U.S. Patterns." *Social Service Review*, 1981, *56*(March), 1–26.

Grønbjerg, K. A. "Private Welfare: Its Future in the Welfare State." *American Behavioral Scientist*, 1983a, *26*(July–August), 773–793.

Grønbjerg, K. A. "The Welfare State: Prospects for the 1980s." *American Behavioral Scientist*, 1983b, *26*(July–August), 685–697.

Grønbjerg, K. A. "Welfare Entitlements in the No-Growth Society." In G. D. Suttles and M. N. Zald (eds.), *Challenge for Social Control: Citizenship and Institution-Building in Modern Society: Essays in Honor of Morris Janowitz* (pp. 98–118). New York: Ablex, 1985.

Grønbjerg, K. A. *Responding to Community Needs: The Missions and Programs of Chicago Nonprofit Organizations*. Vol. 1: *Hardship and Support Systems in Chicago*. Chicago: Urban Institute Nonprofit Sector, 1986.

Grønbjerg, K. A. "Patterns of Institutional Relations in the Welfare State: Public Mandates and the Nonprofit Sector." *Journal of Voluntary Action Research*, 1987, *16*(January–June), 64–80.

Grønbjerg, K. A. "Trends in Public and Private Welfare, 1950–1985: A Research Note." Unpublished manuscript, Department of Sociology-Anthropology, Loyola University, Chicago, 1988.

Grønbjerg, K. A. "Communities and Nonprofit Organizations: Interlocking Ecological Systems." In D. A. Chekki (ed.), *Dimensions of Community: A Research Handbook* (pp. 35–69). New York: Garland, 1989a.

Grønbjerg, K. A. "Developing a Universe of Nonprofit Organizations: Methodological Considerations." *Nonprofit and Voluntary Sector Quarterly*, 1989b, *18*(1), 63–80.

Grønbjerg, K. A. *Managing Nonprofit Funding Relations: Case Studies of Six Human Service Organizations.* Working Paper no. 156, Program on Nonprofit Organizations. New Haven, Conn.: Institution for Social and Policy Studies, 1990a.

Grønbjerg, K. A. "Poverty and Nonprofit Organizational Behavior, Contingencies, and Linkages." *Social Service Review*, 1990b, *64*(June), 208–243.

Grønbjerg, K. A. "Managing Grants and Contracts: The Case of Four Nonprofit Social Service Organizations." *Nonprofit and Voluntary Sector Quarterly*, 1991a, *20*(1), 5–24.

Grønbjerg, K. A. "How Nonprofit Service Organizations Manage Their Funding Sources: Key Findings and Policy Implications." *Nonprofit Management and Leadership*, 1991b, *2*(2), 159–175.

Grønbjerg, K. A. "Nonprofit Human Service Organizations: Funding Strategies and Patterns of Adaptation." In Y. Hasenfeld (ed.), *Human Services as Complex Organizations*. Newbury Park, Calif.: Sage, 1992.

Grønbjerg, K. A., Chen, T. H., and Stagner, M. W. "The Service Provider System: Grants and Contracting Relations in the Youth Welfare System in Illinois." Paper presented at the annual meetings of the American Political Science Association, Chicago, September 1992.

Grønbjerg, K. A., and Harkins, J. A. "Managing Fee Income Among Nonprofit Organizations: Environmental Contingencies and Strategic Decisions." Paper presented at the annual meetings of the Midwest Sociological Society, Chicago, April 1990.

Grønbjerg, K. A., Kimmich, M. H., and Salamon, L. M. *The Chicago Nonprofit Sector in a Time of Government Retrenchment.* Washington, D.C.: Urban Institute Press, 1985.

Grønbjerg, K. A., Musselwhite, J., Jr., and Salamon, L. M. *Government Spending and the Nonprofit Sector in Cook County/Chicago.* Washington, D.C.: Urban Institute Press, 1984.

Grønbjerg, K. A., Nagle, A., Garvin, L., and Wingate, L. *Nonprofit Human Service Facilities in Illinois: Structure, Adequacy, and Management.* Unpublished report prepared for the Illinois Facilities Fund, Department of Sociology-Anthropology, Loyola University Chicago, 1992.

Grønbjerg, K. A., and Stagner, M. W. *Meeting the Needs of Children and Youth in Illinois: The Role of Direct Service Providers.* Report prepared for the Children's Policy Project. Chicago: Chapin Hall Center for Children, 1992.

Grønbjerg, K. A., Street, D. P., and Suttles, G. *Poverty and Social Change.* Chicago: University of Chicago Press, 1978.

Hall, H. "The Non-Profit Salary Gap." *Chronicle of Philanthropy,* 1990, *3,* 27–28.

Hall, P. D. "Abandoning the Rhetoric of Independence: Reflections on the Nonprofit Sector in the Post-Liberal Era." *Journal of Voluntary Action Research,* 1987, *16,* 11–28.

Hall, P. D. "Regulating Competition: A Reflection on History and Policy." Paper presented at Research Conference on the Commercial Activities of Nonprofits, Center for Entrepreneurial Studies, New York University, 1988.

Hall, R. H. *Occupations and the Social Structure.* Englewood Cliffs, N.J.: Prentice-Hall, 1969.

Hannan, M. T., and Freeman, J. "The Population Ecology of Organizations." *American Journal of Sociology,* 1977, *82,* 929–964.

Hannan, M. T., and Freeman, J. "Structural Inertia and Organizational Change." *American Sociological Review,* 1984, *49,* 149–164.

Hansmann, H. "The Role of Nonprofit Enterprise." *Yale Law Journal,* 1980, *89,* 835–901.

Hansmann, H. "Economic Theories of Nonprofit Organization." In W. W. Powell (ed.), *The Nonprofit Sector: A Research Handbook* (pp. 27–42). New Haven, Conn.: Yale University Press, 1987.

Harris, A. L. *Special Events: Planning for Success.* Washington, D.C.: Council for Advancement and Support of Education, 1988.

Hartogs, N., and Weber, J. *Impact of Government Funding on the Management of Voluntary Agencies.* New York: Greater New York Fund/United Way, 1978.

Hasenfeld, Y. "Client-Organization Relations: A System Perspective." In R. C. Sarri and Y. Hasenfeld (eds.), *The Management of Human Services* (pp. 184–206). New York: Columbia University Press, 1978.

Hasenfeld, Y., and Brock, T. "Implementation of Social Policy Revisited." *Administration and Society,* 1991, 22(4), 451–477.

Haveman, R. H. (ed.). *A Decade of Federal Antipoverty Programs: Achievements, Failures and Lessons.* San Diego, Calif.: Academic Press, 1977.

Hawley, A. H. *Human Ecology: A Theory of Community Structure.* New York: Ronald Press, 1950.

Hayghe, H. V. "Volunteers in the U.S.: Who Donates the Time?" *Monthly Labor Review,* 1991, *114*(2), 17–23.

Heath, R. L., and Associates. *Strategic Issues Management: How Organizations Influence and Respond to Public Interests and Policies.* San Francisco: Jossey-Bass, 1988.

Helyar, J., and Johnson, R. "Brawling City: Chicago Political Rift Deepens, Worsening City's Many Problems." *Wall Street Journal,* August 6, 1984, pp. 1, 13.

Herman, R. D., and Van Til, J. *Nonprofit Boards of Directors: Analyses and Applications.* New Brunswick, N.J.: Transaction Books, 1989.

Herzlinger, R. E., and Krasker, W. S. "Who Profits from Nonprofits?" *Harvard Business Review,* 1987, *65,* 93–107.

Hodgkinson, V. A., Lyman, R. W., and Associates. *The Future of the Nonprofit Sector: Challenges, Changes, and Policy Considerations.* San Francisco: Jossey-Bass, 1989.

Hodgkinson, V. A., and Weitzman, M. S. *Dimensions of the Independent Sector: A Statistical Profile.* (3rd ed.) Washington, D.C.: Independent Sector, 1989.

Hodgkinson, V. A., Weitzman, M. S., and the Gallup Organization. *Giving and Volunteering in the United States: 1988 Edition.* Washington, D.C.: Independent Sector, 1988.

Hodgkinson, V. A., Weitzman, M. S., and Kirsch, A. D. *From Belief to Commitment: The Activities and Finances of Religious Congregations in the U.S.* Washington, D.C.: Independent Sector, 1988.

Hodgkinson, V. A., Weitzman, M. S., and Kirsch, A. D. "From Commitment to Action: How Religious Involvement Affects Giving and Volunteering." In R. Wuthnow, V. A. Hodgkinson, and Associates. *Faith and Philanthropy in America: Exploring the Role of Religion in America's Voluntary Sector.* San Francisco: Jossey-Bass, 1990.

Hodgkinson, V. A., Weitzman, M. S., Toppe, C. M., and Noga, S. M. *Nonprofit Almanac, 1992–1993: Dimensions of the Independent Sector.* San Francisco: Jossey-Bass, 1992.

Hollingsworth, J. R., and Hollingsworth, E. J. "A Comparison of Non-Profit, For-Profit and Public Hospitals in the United States: 1935 to the Present." Working Paper no. 113, Program on Non-Profit Organizations. New Haven, Conn.: Institution for Social and Policy Studies, 1986.

Independent Sector. *Compendium of Resources for Teaching About the Nonprofit Sector, Voluntarism and Philanthropy.* Resource Packet Series no. 1. Washington, D.C.: Independent Sector, 1989.

Institute of Urban Life. *The Directory of Community Organizations in Chicago.* Chicago: Institute of Urban Life, 1988.

Jacobs, M. *Screwing the System and Making It Work: Juvenile Justice in the No-Fault Society.* Chicago: University of Chicago Press, 1990.

James, E. "How Nonprofits Grow: A Model." In S. Rose-Ackerman (ed.), *The Economics of Nonprofit Institutions: Studies in Structure and Policy* (pp. 185–195). New York: Oxford University Press, 1986.

James, E. *The Nonprofit Sector in an International Perspective: Studies in Comparative Culture and Policy.* New York: Oxford University Press, 1989.

Jenkins, J. C. "Nonprofit Organizations and Policy Advocacy." In W. W. Powell (ed.), *The Nonprofit Sector: A Research Handbook* (pp. 296–318). New Haven, Conn.: Yale University Press, 1987.

Johnson, A. *Public Policy and Private Charities: A Study of Legislation in the United States and of Administration in Illinois.* Chicago: University of Chicago Press, 1931.

Johnson, J. "Can a Black Be Quarterback?" *Nonprofit Times,* 1989, 2(January), 21–23.

Jurkovich, R. "A Core Typology of Organizational Environments." *Administrative Science Quarterly,* 1974, *19,* 380–394.

Kalberg, S. "Max Weber's Types of Rationality: Cornerstones for the Analysis of Rationalization Processes in History." *American Journal of Sociology*, 1980, *85*(March), 1145–1179.

Karwath, R. "New Foster-Care Crisis for DCFS: Private Providers Say They May Stop Accepting Agency's Kids." *Chicago Tribune*, Sep. 4, 1992, Sec. 1, p. 12.

Kettl, D. F. (ed.). *Third Party Government and the Public Manager: The Changing Forms of Government Action*. Washington, D.C.: National Academy of Public Administration, 1987.

Kimberly, J. R. "Environmental Constraints and Organizational Structure: A Comparative Analysis of Rehabilitation Organizations." *Administrative Science Quarterly*, 1975, *20*, 1–9.

Kimberly, J. R. "Issues in the Creation of Organizations: Initiation, Innovation, and Institutionalization." *Academy of Management Journal*, 1979, *22*(3), 437–457.

Knauft, E. B., Berger, R. A., and Gray, S. T. *Profiles in Excellence: Achieving Success in the Nonprofit Sector*. San Francisco: Jossey-Bass, 1991.

Koberg, C. S., and Ungson, G. R. "The Effects of Environmental Uncertainty and Dependence on Organizational Structure and Performance: A Comparative Study." *Journal of Management*, 1987, *13*, 725–737.

Koch, D., and Boehm, S. *The Nonprofit Policy Agenda: Recommendations for State and Local Action*. Washington, D.C.: Union Institute, 1992.

Kramer, R. *Voluntary Agencies in the Welfare State*. Berkeley: University of California Press, 1981.

Leibert, E. R., and Sheldon, B. E. *Handbook of Special Events for Nonprofit Organizations*. New York: Association Press, 1972.

Liner, F. "Selecting a Special Event." *Fundraising Management*, 1987, *18*(April), 56, 58–61, 62.

Lowi, T. J. *The End of Liberalism: Ideology, Policy, and the Crisis of Public Authority*. New York: Norton, 1969.

McCann, J. E., and Selsky, J. "Hyperturbulence and the Emergence of Type 5 Environments." *Academy of Management Review*, 1984, *9*, 460–470.

McCarthy, J., and Zald, M. "Resource Mobilization and Social Movements." *American Journal of Sociology*, 1977, *82*, 1212–1241.

McCarthy, K. D. *Noblesse Oblige: Charity and Cultural Philanthropy in Chicago, 1849–1929*. Chicago: University of Chicago Press, 1982.

MacGregor, D. *The Human Side of Enterprise*. New York: McGraw-Hill, 1960.

McGuire, S. "Party Time Can Be Best of Times, Worst of Times for Fund-Raisers." *Forum*, 1989, *6*(May–June), 1–3.

Majone, G. "Professionalism and Non-Profit Organizations." *Journal of Health Politics, Policy and Law*, 1984, *8*, 639–659.

Meyer, A. D. "Adapting to Environmental Jolts." *Administrative Science Quarterly*, 1982, *27*, 515–537.

Meyer, J. W., and Scott, W. R. (eds.). *Organizational Environments: Ritual and Rationality*. Newbury Park, Calif.: Sage, 1983.

Meyer, M. W., and Zucker, L. G. *Permanently Failing Organizations.* Newbury Park, Calif.: Sage, 1989.

Michel, R. C. "Economic Growth and Income Inequality Since the 1982 Recession." *Journal of Policy Analysis and Management,* 1991, *10*(Spring), 181–203.

Millikin, F. J. "Three Types of Perceived Uncertainty About the Environment: State, Effect, and Response Uncertainty." *Academy of Management Review,* 1987, *12*, 133–143.

Milofsky, C. "Neighborhood-Based Organizations: A Market Analogy." In W. W. Powell (ed.), *The Nonprofit Sector: A Research Handbook* (pp. 277–295). New Haven, Conn.: Yale University Press, 1987.

Milofsky, C. , and Romo, F. P. "The Structure of Funding Arenas for Neighborhood Based Organizations." In C. Milofsky (ed.), *Community Organizations: Studies in Resource Mobilization and Exchange* (pp. 214–242). New York: Oxford University Press, 1988.

Milward, H. B., Provan, K. G., and Else, B. A. "What Does the Hollow State Look Like?" In B. Bozeman (ed.), *Public Management: The State of the Art.* San Francisco: Jossey-Bass, forthcoming.

Mirvis, P. H., and Hackett, E. J. "Work and Work Force Characteristics in the Nonprofit Sector." *Monthly Labor Review,* 1983, *106*(April), 3–12.

Montague, W. "New Fund-Raising Sweepstakes Brings Legal Action by Several States Against Consultants and Clients." *Chronicle of Philanthropy,* 1988, *1*(5), 1, 18–19, 21.

Montague, W. "Connecticut Charities Found to Get Only Twenty-Five Percent of Nine Million Dollars Raised by Special Events." *Chronicle of Philanthropy,* 1989a, *1*(14), 25.

Montague, W. "Minnesota Charities Said to Get Thirty-Three Percent of Money Collected by Fund Raisers." *Chronicle of Philanthropy,* 1989b, *1*(18), 21–22.

Mulligan, T. J. "There's More to Special Events Than Raising Money." *Fund Raising Management,* 1987, *18*(April), 36, 38, 40, 43.

Nakamura, R. R., and Smallwood, F. *The Politics of Policy Implementation.* New York: St. Martin's Press, 1980.

National Center for Charitable Statistics. *Mapping the Nonprofit Sector: The National Taxonomy of Exempt Entities.* Washington, D.C.: Independent Sector, 1990.

Nemes, J. "Hospital Fundraising Faces IRS Scrutiny." *Modern Healthcare,* May 12, 1989, pp. 40–41.

Odendahl, T. "The Culture of Elite Philanthropy in the Reagan Years." *Nonprofit and Voluntary Sector Quarterly,* 1989, *18*(3), 237–248.

Odendahl, T. *Charity Begins at Home: Generosity and Self-Interest Among the Philanthropic Elite.* New York: Basic Books, 1990.

Olcott, W. "Helping Sick Kids." *Fund Raising Management,* 1988, *19*(December), 30–32, 80.

Olson, M. *The Logic of Collective Action: Public Goods and the Theory of Groups.* Cambridge, Mass.: Harvard University Press, 1971.

O'Neill, M. *The Third America: The Emergence of the Nonprofit Sector in the United States.* San Francisco: Jossey-Bass, 1989.

Orlans, H. (ed.). *Nonprofit Organizations: A Government Management Tool.* New York: Praeger, 1980.

Ostrander, S. A. *Women of the Upper Class.* Philadelphia: Temple University Press, 1984.

Ostrander, S. A., Langton, S., and Van Til, J. (eds.). *Shifting the Debate: Public/ Private Sector Relations in the Modern Welfare State.* New Brunswick, N.J.: Transaction Books, 1987.

Palmer, J. L., Smeeding, T., and Torrey, B. B. (eds.). *The Vulnerable.* Washington, D.C.: Urban Institute Press, 1988.

Pavalko, R. (ed.). *Sociological Perspectives on Occupations.* Itasca, Ill.: Peacock, 1972.

Perlmutter, F. D., and Adams, C. "The Voluntary Sector and For-Profit Ventures: The Transformation of American Social Welfare?" *Administration in Social Work,* 1990, *14,* 1–13.

Peterson, P. E., and Greenstone, J. D. "Racial Change and Citizen Participation: The Mobilization of Low-Income Communities Through Community Action." In R. H. Haveman (ed.), *A Decade of Federal Antipoverty Programs: Achievements, Failures, and Lessons* (pp. 241–278). San Diego, Calif.: Academic Press, 1977.

Pfeffer, J., and Leong, A. "Resource Allocation in United Funds: Examination of Power and Dependency." *Social Forces,* 1977, *55,* 775–790.

Pfeffer, J., and Salancik, G. *The External Control of Organizations: A Resource Dependence Perspective.* New York: Harper & Row, 1978.

Phillips, K. *The Politics of Rich and Poor: Wealth and the American Electorate in the Reagan Aftermath.* New York: Random House, 1990.

Piven, F. F., and Cloward, R. A. *Regulating the Poor: The Functions of Public Welfare.* New York: Pantheon Books, 1971.

Piven, F. F., and Cloward, R. A. *The New Class War: Reagan's Attack on the Welfare State and Its Consequences.* New York: Pantheon Books, 1982.

Preston, A. E. "Women in the White Collar Non-Profit Sector: The Best Option or the Only Option?" Program on Non-Profit Organizations, Working Paper no. 101. New Haven, Conn.: Institution for Social and Policy Studies, 1985.

Provan, K. G., Beyer, J. M., and Kruytbosch, C. "Environmental Linkages and Power in Resource-Dependence Relations Between Organizations." *Administrative Science Quarterly,* 1980, *25,* 200–225.

Rehfuss, J. *Contracting Out in Government: A Guide to Working with Outside Contractors to Supply Public Services.* San Francisco: Jossey-Bass, 1989.

Reiss, A. H. "At Your Place or Mine? Special Events Are the Sine Qua Non of Arts Funds." *Fundraising Management,* 1987, *18*(April), 26, 28, 30–32, 35.

Reynolds, M. O., and Smolensky, E. *Public Expenditures, Taxes, and the Distribution of Income: The U.S., 1950, 1960, and 1970.* San Diego, Calif.: Academic Press, 1977.

Roof, W. C., and McKinney, W. *American Mainline Religion: Its Changing Shape and Future.* New Brunswick, N.J.: Rutgers University Press, 1987.

Rose-Ackerman, S. "Social Services and the Market." *Columbia Law Review,* 1983, *83,* 1405–1438.

Rose-Ackerman, S. *The Economics of Nonprofit Institutions: Studies in Structure and Polity.* New York: Oxford University Press, 1986.

Rowan, B. "Organizational Structure and Institutional Environment: The Case of Public Schools." *Administrative Science Quarterly,* 1982, *27,* 259–279.

Rudney, G. "The Scope and Dimensions of Nonprofit Activity." In W. W. Powell (ed.), *The Nonprofit Sector: A Research Handbook* (pp. 55–64). New Haven, Conn.: Yale University Press, 1987.

Rushing, W. A. "Profit and Nonprofit Orientations and the Differentiation-Coordination Hypothesis for Organizations: A Study of Small General Hospitals." *American Sociological Review,* 1976, *41*(August), 676–691.

Saidel, J. "Resource Interdependence: The Relationship Between State Agencies and Nonprofit Organizations." *Public Administration Review,* 1991, *51*(November–December), 543–553.

Salamon, L. M. "Rethinking Public Management: Third-Party Government and the Changing Forms of Government Action." *Public Policy,* 1981, *29,* 255–275.

Salamon, L. M. "Partners in Public Service: The Scope and Theory of Government-Nonprofit Relations." In W. W. Powell (ed.), *The Nonprofit Sector: A Research Handbook* (pp. 99–117). New Haven, Conn.: Yale University Press, 1987.

Salamon, L. M. *Beyond Privatization: The Tools of Government Action.* Washington, D.C.: Urban Institute Press, 1989a.

Salamon, L. M. "The Changing Partnership Between the Voluntary Sector and the Welfare State." In V. Hodgkinson and R. Lyman (eds.), *The Future of the Nonprofit Sector: Challenges, Changes, and Policy Considerations* (pp. 41–60). San Francisco: Jossey-Bass, 1989b.

Salamon, L. M., Musselwhite, J. C., Jr., Holcomb, P. A., and Grønbjerg, K. A. *Human Services in Chicago: The Changing Roles of Government and Private Providers.* Washington, D.C.: Urban Institute Press, 1987.

Savas, E. S. *Privatizing the Public Service: How to Shrink Government.* Chatham, N.J.: Chatham House, 1982.

Schiller, H. I. *Culture, Inc.: The Corporate Takeover of Public Expression.* New York: Oxford University Press, 1989.

Scott, W. R. *Organizations: Rational, Natural, and Open Systems.* (3rd ed.) Englewood Cliffs, N.J.: Prentice-Hall, 1992.

Selznick, P. *TVA and the Grass Roots.* Berkeley: University of California Press, 1949.

Silvestri, G., and Lukasiewicz, J. "Projections of Occupational Employment, 1988–2000." *Monthly Labor Review*, 1989, *112*(11), 42–65.

Simon, J. G. "The Tax Treatment of Nonprofit Organizations: A Review of Federal and State Policies." In W. W. Powell (ed.), *The Nonprofit Sector: A Research Handbook* (pp. 67–98). New Haven, Conn.: Yale University Press, 1987.

Sommers, D. *Women in Organizations: An Analysis of the Role and Status of Women in American Voluntary Organizations.* Washington, D. C.: B'nai B'rith International, 1983.

Sosin, M. R. "Decentralizing the Social Service System: A Reassessment." *Social Service Review*, 1990, *64*(December), 617–636.

Steinberg, R. "Nonprofit Organizations and the Market." In W. W. Powell (ed.), *The Nonprofit Sector: A Research Handbook* (pp. 118–138). New Haven, Conn.: Yale University Press, 1987.

Straussman, J., and Fairie, J. "Contracting for Local Services at the Local Level." *The Urban Interest*, 1981, *2*, 43–50.

Suttles, G. D. *The Social Construction of Communities.* Chicago: University of Chicago Press, 1972.

Suttles, G. D. *The Man-Made City: The Land-Use Confidence Game in Chicago.* Chicago: University of Chicago Press, 1990.

Taub, R. P., Taylor, D. G., and Dunham, J. D. *Paths of Neighborhood Change: Race and Crime in Urban America.* Chicago: University of Chicago Press, 1984.

Taub, R. P., and others. "Urban Voluntary Associations, Locality Based and Externally Induced." *American Journal of Sociology*, 1977, *83*(September), 425–442.

Technical Assistance Center. *National Nonprofit Wage and Benefits Survey.* Denver: Technical Assistance Center, 1988.

Thompson, J. D. *Organizations in Action: Social Science Bases of Administrative Theory.* New York: McGraw-Hill, 1967.

Tocqueville, A. de. *Democracy in America.* New York: Harper & Row, 1966. (Originally published 1898.)

Tolbert, P. S. "Institutional Environments and Resource Dependence: Sources of Administrative Structure in Institutions of Higher Education." *Administrative Science Quarterly*, 1985, *30*, 1–13.

Trolander, J. A. *Professionalism and Social Change: From the Settlement House Movement to Neighborhood Centers, 1886 to the Present.* New York: Columbia University Press, 1987.

Tropman, J. E. *American Values and Social Welfare: Cultural Contradictions in the Welfare State.* Englewood Cliffs, N.J.: Prentice-Hall, 1989.

Tung, R. L. "Dimensions of Organizational Environments: An Exploratory Study of Their Impact on Organizational Structure." *Academy of Management Journal*, 1979, *22*(4), 672–693.

U.S. Bureau of the Census. *Statistical Abstract of the United States, 1990.* Washington, D.C.: U.S. Government Printing Office, 1990.

U.S. Bureau of the Census. *Statistical Abstract of the United States, 1991.* Washington, D.C.: U.S. Government Printing Office, 1991.

U.S. Small Business Administration. *Unfair Competition by Nonprofit Organizations with Small Business: An Issue for the 1980s.* Washington, D.C.: U.S. Small Business Administration, 1983.

United Way/Crusade of Mercy. *Human Care Service Directory of Metropolitan Chicago, 1991–92.* Chicago: United Way, 1992.

Useem, M. *The Inner Circle: Large Corporations and the Rise of Business Political Activity in the U.S. and U.K.* New York: Oxford University Press, 1984.

Vanecko, J. J. "Community Mobilization and Institutional Change: The Influence of the Community Action Program in Large Cities." *Social Science Quarterly,* 1969, *50*(December), 609–630.

Van Til, J. *Mapping the Third Sector: Voluntarism in a Changing Social Economy.* New York: Foundation Center, 1988.

Ware, A. *Between Profit and State: Intermediary Organizations in Britain and the United States.* Princeton, N.J.: Princeton University Press, 1989.

Weisbrod, B. "Toward a Theory of the Voluntary Non-Profit Sector in a Three-Sector Economy." In E. S. Phelps (ed.), *Altruism, Morality, and Economic Theory* (pp. 171–195). New York: Russell Sage Foundation, 1975.

Weisbrod, B. *The Voluntary Nonprofit Sector.* Lexington, Mass.: Lexington Books, 1977.

Weisbrod, B. *The Nonprofit Economy.* Cambridge, Mass.: Harvard University Press, 1988.

Weisbrod, B. "The Complexities of Income Generation for Nonprofits." In V. Hodgkinson and R. Lyman (eds.), *The Future of the Nonprofit Sector: Challenges, Changes, and Policy Considerations* (pp. 103–122). San Francisco: Jossey-Bass, 1989.

Weiss, J. A. "Substance Versus Symbol in Administrative Reform: The Case of Human Services Coordination." In C. Milofsky (ed.), *Community Organizations: Studies in Resource Mobilization and Exchange* (pp. 100–118). New York: Oxford University Press, 1988.

Werner, R. *Public Financing of Voluntary Agency Foster Care.* New York: Child Welfare League of America, 1961.

Wilensky, H. L., and Lebeaux, C. N. *Industrial Society and Social Welfare.* New York: Free Press, 1965.

Williams, W. *Government by Agency: Lessons from the Social Program Grants-in-Aid Experience.* San Diego, Calif.: Academic Press, 1980.

Williamson, O. E. "The Economics of Organization: The Transaction Cost Approach." *American Journal of Sociology,* 1981, *87,* 548–577.

Wolpert, J. "Key Indicators of Generosity in Communities." In V. Hodgkinson and R. Lyman (eds.), *The Future of the Nonprofit Sector: Challenges, Changes, and Policy Considerations.* San Francisco: Jossey-Bass, 1989.

Wood, J. R. *Leadership in Voluntary Organizations: The Controversy over Social*

Action in Protestant Churches. New Brunswick, N.J.: Rutgers University Press, 1981.

Wood, J. R. "Liberal Protestant Action in a Period of Decline." In R. Wuthnow, V. Hodgkinson, and Associates, *Faith and Philanthropy in America: Exploring the Role of Religion in America's Voluntary Sector* (pp. 165–186). San Francisco: Jossey-Bass, 1990.

Yancey, W. L., and Eriksen, E. P. "The Antecedents of Community: The Economic and Institutional Structure of Urban Neighborhoods." *American Sociological Review*, 1979, *44*(April), 253–262.

Ylvisaker, P. N. "Foundations and Nonprofit Organizations." In W. W. Powell (ed.), *The Nonprofit Sector: A Research Handbook* (pp. 360–379). New Haven, Conn.: Yale University Press, 1987.

Young, D. R. "The Nonprofit as the First Sector: Policy Implications." Discussion Paper Series, Mandel Center for Nonprofit Organizations, Case Western Reserve University, Cleveland, Ohio, 1988a.

Young, D. R. "Profitmaking by Nonprofits: Issues for Management." Paper presented at Research Conference on the Commercial Activities of Nonprofits, Center for Entrepreneurial Studies, New York University, 1988b.

Zammuto, R. F. "A Comparison of Multiple Constituency Models of Organizational Effectiveness." *Academy of Management Review*, 1982, *9*(4), 606–616.

Zammuto, R. F. *Assessing Organizational Effectiveness: Systems Change, Adaptation, and Strategy*. Albany, N.Y.: State University of New York Press, 1984.

Zucker, L. G. (ed.). *Institutional Patterns and Organizations: Culture and Environment*. Cambridge, Mass.: Ballinger, 1988.

Index